FRED DIBNAH'S
VICTORIAN HEROES

www.transworldbooks.co.uk

Fred Dibnah's Industrial Age
Fred Dibnah's Magnificent Monuments
Fred Dibnah's Age of Steam
Fred: The Definitive Biography of Fred Dibnah
Manchester's Finest
Fred Dibnah's Buildings of Britain
Fred Dibnah's Made in Britain

FRED DIBNAH'S VICTORIAN HEROES

DAVID HALL

BANTAM PRESS

LONDON · TORONTO · SYDNEY · AUCKLAND · JOHANNESBURG

TRANSWORLD PUBLISHERS
61–63 Uxbridge Road, London W5 5SA
A Random House Group Company
www.transworldbooks.co.uk

First published in Great Britain
in 2011 by Bantam Press
an imprint of Transworld Publishers

A CIP catalogue record for this book
is available from the British Library.

ISBN 9780593064900

Addresses for Random House Group Ltd companies outside the UK
can be found at: www.randomhouse.co.uk
The Random House Group Ltd Reg. No. 954009

The Random House Group Limited supports the Forest Stewardship Council (FSC®),
the leading international forest-certification organisation. Our books carrying the
FSC label are printed on FSC®-certified paper. FSC is the only forest-certification
scheme endorsed by the leading environmental organisations, including Greenpeace.
Our paper-procurement policy can be found at www.randomhouse.co.uk/environment.

To Suzannah

CONTENTS

Introduction

Fred and the Heroic Age of Engineering

Fred's view: The Victorian Age was an age when Britain led the world in the skills of making and inventing things: an age when the skills of mechanics and engineers were highly prized. Those men were the heroes of the day and their exploits captured the imagination of the Victorian public. They were treated like pop stars or footballers are today and for me the greatest one of the lot was Isambard Kingdom Brunel.

Fred Dibnah was, by his own admission, a man born out of his time. He should have lived and worked in the nineteenth century, the age he admired. His heroes were the great Victorian engineers like Brunel, Robert Stephenson, William Fairbairn and William Armstrong; uncompromising men who knew what they wanted and wouldn't let anything or anybody stand in their way. To Fred they were inspirational characters and he looked back enviously at the age that bred them. His house was full of the ornamentation, ironwork and bric-a-brac of the period, and in the workshop in his back garden he used many of the engineering techniques of his Victorian forebears, all driven by the force that powered the age – steam. With his gold watch chain and waistcoat Fred even looked like a Victorian gentleman. Above all, his opinions and attitudes were those of the Victorian Age: he believed in hard work, and that money should be acquired only through productivity and hard graft. If you went back to Victorian

1

times you would have found a lot of people like Fred. He would have fitted in very well.

Queen Victoria's reign lasted 64 years – the longest in British history – and spanned two-thirds of the nineteenth century. Her coronation in 1838 heralded the dawn of a golden age when her country emerged as a powerful and confident industrial nation at the heart of the greatest empire the world had seen for a thousand years. Between her coronation and her death in 1901, Queen Victoria saw Britain change beyond recognition. As well as witnessing the growth of the rail network across the country, she saw sail give way to steam at sea. She saw industry spread its smoky cities all over Britain. She saw electric trams and even the first motor cars. And one of the last great feats of nineteenth-century invention – the cinematograph – captured the Queen's Diamond Jubilee on film.

Victoria's reign saw the British Empire extend to the far corners of the globe and people felt that Britain led the world. The maintenance of political stability while governments and monarchies were crashing all over Europe brought a period of unparalleled commercial and industrial supremacy. Surging production levels, most notably in iron and steel, coal mining, textiles and engineering, were critical to British domination of the world economy as the nation became the 'workshop of the world'. The engineering industry in particular expanded and diversified, creating tens of thousands of jobs and earning millions of pounds in markets both at home and abroad. Shipbuilding, bridge-building and making all kinds of machinery including steam engines and everything associated with the railways were vital to the country's economic growth. Vast new fields of employment were opened up for mechanics and transport workers and the men who were for Fred the great unsung heroes of the age, the navvies – the men whose labours changed the whole landscape of Britain.

For the Victorians, the force that revolutionized industry was steam power. During much of the period, steam engines were built in modest workshops not much bigger than Fred's own steam-powered workshop, where he delighted in demonstrating the skills of the Victorian mechanics and engineers. 'It would have been nice to be around back in them days,' he used to say, 'in a little workshop just like mine. I'd have been a happy man then, putting all the poverty and awful things that there were in the Victorian period aside. I think if you were of a mechanical bent, you could survive then. I reckon I'd have been all right, I don't think I'd have been out of work.'

During the reign of Queen Victoria, there was a feeling of living at a time when the country was peopled with great men and that greatness was not confined to those who had achieved military victories. Engineers in particular occupied a special place in the Victorian mindset, as the peacetime equivalent of the soldier hero. The man in the street was deeply impressed by the exploits of the great engineers of the day and marvelled at the work of those who covered the land with canals and railway lines, built bridges, harbours and factories, launched ironclad steamships upon the oceans, constructed powerful steam locomotives to transport people and goods, and built huge engines to drive the wheels of industry. Talented and energetic engineers were able to make enormous personal contributions with works that were dramatic and visible, and their projects made an enormous impression on the Victorian imagination. So what was it about this period that made it possible for engineers like Robert Stephenson and Brunel to have such an impact?

In the later part of the eighteenth century, the process of industrialization had built a firm foundation for nineteenth-century growth and expansion. Central to this was a whole series of technological breakthroughs, especially in the field of metallurgy and in the use of steam power, resulting in the invention of machinery that revolutionized the various processes in the manufacture of textiles. Before 1800, brilliant engineers like James Watt and his entrepreneurial partner Matthew Boulton had made steam power a practical reality. By the nineteenth century new machines and production methods – not just in the textile industry but in iron and steel, coal mining and engineering – helped Britain dominate the global economy. To be able to take maximum advantage of these technological breakthroughs, however, there was another prerequisite – the availability of ample natural resources. Britain was blessed with vast quantities of coal and iron ore, plenty of fresh water to work machinery and a surplus of capital wealth available for investment.

At the beginning of the nineteenth century, steam power was adapted to provide revolutionary new means of transport. Thanks to railway pioneers such as Richard Trevithick, William Hedley, Timothy Hackworth and George Stephenson, Britain saw the development of the first steam locomotives and the world's first railways. With the opening of the line between Liverpool and Manchester in 1830, the railway age began in earnest, and by 1837, when Victoria came to the throne, armies of navvies were building railways that criss-crossed the land. The railways swiftly became the symbol of Victorian industrial and technical ingenuity, fundamental to the nation's prosperity. They produced massive changes in society and there was rapid economic growth as industrial cities and regions became connected to one another and to the ports. Fred's greatest hero, Isambard Kingdom Brunel, not only built the Great Western Railway to link London to the port of Bristol but also built the world's first steam-powered iron ship to connect the city to New York.

Engineers like Brunel were the architects of change and became the most important figures of the age, their projects attracting massive publicity and public interest. The Queen's husband, Prince Albert, took great interest in their achievements and worked with many of them to set up the Great Exhibition of 1851. It was the world's first trade fair, where the industries of all nations were on display, but more than any-thing it was an unashamed demonstration of British industrial and technical might. Overseas trade was one of the foundations of Victorian industrial and economic supremacy and great profits were made abroad by British railway engineers, technologists and industrialists. In the early years of Queen Victoria's reign, Britain's standing as a global industrial and trading power was unrivalled.

Colonial development was crucial in this regard and the expansion of the British Empire was inevitably tied up with the commercial exploitation of the colonies. In the 1860s 100,000 tons of British rolling stock and ironwork were exported to India to begin the construction of the sub-continent's railway network. India was also critical to the

Lancashire cotton industry, being far and away the largest single market. Profits were high and vast fortunes were made, but all this was cloaked in the pious conviction that Britain's wealth was God's doing and that the British had been chosen to do great work for mankind. Above all, though, the empire was a market. The explorer H. M. Stanley knew exactly how to combine commercial interests and piety when he addressed the Manchester Chamber of Commerce on 21 October 1884:

> There are forty millions of people beyond the gateway of the Congo and the cotton spinners of Manchester are waiting to clothe them. Birmingham foundries are gleaming with the red metal that will presently be made into ironwork for them and the trinkets that shall adorn those dusky bosoms and the ministers of Christ are zealous to bring them, the poor benighted heathen, into the Christian fold.

The British public loved it all. They liked the idea of a big, powerful Britain and for Fred, over a hundred years later, the fact that the Victorian Age was the time when Britain led the world was what made it great. He loved the jingoism of the age and was immensely proud to be British (although to Fred it was always England). He took pride in the achievements of an era when, in his words, 'we made the heavy stuff that we're not making now'. It was a time when Britain probably contributed more to progress than any other nation in the world. There's no reason to be ashamed of this, yet today, because of the exploitation of the working class and the evils of colonialism many people seem to be embarrassed to talk about those great days. So, it's good that Fred was able to say that, and say it with pride and enthusiasm. By drawing attention to the great achievements of our Victorian forebears, Fred made us realize that it wasn't all dark satanic mills.

Another element that characterized the Victorian Age was civic pride. The success and prosperity that the Industrial Revolution brought to towns like Fred's native Bolton left us with some magnificent buildings – town halls, libraries and swimming baths – and one of his favourites was Bolton Town Hall. The Victorians had a great respect for the past and wanted their buildings to reflect the values of an earlier age: they made their town halls look like Greek temples, and the new Houses of Parliament in London matched the medieval splendour of Westminster Abbey next door.

Fred had a great appreciation of the quality of Victorian workmanship, whether in buildings or engineering. 'The Victorians,' he said, 'went to great lengths to make things pleasing to the eye, whether it was a great civil engineering project or something as small as a window catch. In Victorian times the skills of making things were highly valued.' He would have liked to have lived then, 'when we made beautiful things like the whistles and the lamps on my engines. The modern equivalent wouldn't be anything like as beautiful.' Fred relished the fact that everything was made to a very high standard; that most things were made by hand and everything was built to last. He was very comfortable with the things the Victorians made, with their technology, and he was a great admirer of their craftsmanlike approach. He shared their values and their confidence and always wanted to draw attention to their achievements, their inventiveness, their workmanship and the sheer scale of their ambition. In this respect Prince Albert was a true representative of the age, a passionate believer in the moral and material rewards to be reaped from the advance of science, industry and technology. So the Great Exhibition wasn't just a celebration of British innovation but also a salute to the Victorian virtues of hard work and self-reliance. 'One of the virtues of the Victorian Age,' Fred said, 'were the business of self-help. If you worked down the pit or in the foundry, you could stay there for the whole of your life if you wanted to. There weren't much chance of them going out of business like they do now.' If a man wanted to get ahead, he could go to places such as the Mechanics' Institute and learn to read and write.

If you showed your mettle, what you were capable of doing, Victorian society admired them men and made them into heroes like Brunel. Weaknesses of any sort were frowned upon and you'd got to keep going at all costs. George Stephenson couldn't read or write but he became the father of the railways and one of the most famous men in the whole of England and his son became a national hero.

Self-Help, Samuel Smiles's book of 1859, encapsulated this Victorian philosophy of deserving men making good through hard work and application. In Smiles's own words, the purpose of *Self-Help* was 'to illustrate and enforce the power of George Stephenson's great word – perseverance'. Smiles advocated the cultivation of the intellectual and moral working-class self. Church and chapel, the mechanics' institutes and public libraries, he argued, all provided opportunities of self-improvement for the working man. The book reflected the spirit of its age and proved to be a bestseller.

Smiles came to regard the pioneering British engineers of the eighteenth and nineteenth centuries as archetypes of this ethos and he devoted himself to gathering biographical evidence to back this up. The result of his research was the three volumes of *The Lives of the Engineers*, which helped to turn these men into the heroes of the Victorian Age. Smiles's ideal was someone of humble origin, such as George Stephenson, who achieved great things through self-improvement. 'If we look carefully into the narratives of the lives of the most remarkable engineers,' he wrote,

we shall find that they owed very little to the seven years' rut in which they were trained. They owed everything to innate industry, energy, skill, and opportunity. Thus, Brindley advanced from the position of a millwright to that of a canal engineer; Smeaton and Watt, from being mathematical instrument makers, advanced to higher positions – the one to be the inventor of the modern lighthouse, the other to be the inventor of the condensing steam-engine. Some of the most celebrated mechanical and civil engineers – such as Rennie, Cubitt, and Fairbairn – were originally millwrights. All these men were many-handed. They had many sides to their intellect. They were resourceful men.

They were also, as Fred observed, a new breed of men. Their confidence and dynamism were unbounded, their energy immense.

Innovation was what they lived by and they felt they possessed the materials and techniques to build a new world. Fred admired them for their courage and their ingenuity, and because they were colourful, larger-than-life characters who had an unwavering confidence in their own ability to overcome any obstacle. They were men for whom no challenge was too great, whose 'tackle anything' approach was one that Fred shared. Many of them went on to make a fortune, especially if they belonged to the aristocracy of the profession, the civil engineers, and it was the building of the railways that gave them their greatest opportunities. What excited Fred was the way in which the British civil engineering industry rose to that challenge.

The inventiveness and the grand scale of many of the engineering projects captured the public imagination. Because of their heroic status, engineers were given special dispensation with regard to budgets and timescales. Brunel's Great Western went more than two and a half times over budget and he lost £400,000 on his unsuccessful attempt to build an atmospheric railway in Devon, but people felt that the scale of his achievements justified the cost. For a Victorian engineer the embarrassment of an overrun budget would soon be forgotten, but the glory of achievement would last for ever. Brunel's legacy, and that of contemporaries such as Robert Stephenson, James Nasmyth, Joseph Locke and William Fairbairn, was Britain's world leadership in industry, civil engineering and technology. Achieving this meant that risks were always being taken and not all experiments proved to be successful. It was the price that had to be paid for innovation. Backing big engineering projects in the nineteenth century could be a bit of a gamble. Brunel's SS *Great Britain* is now regarded as a landmark in ship design, but she was never really a commercial success and eventually bankrupted the company that built her.

For men like Brunel and Robert Stephenson, there was no problem in civil or mechanical engineering that an individual could not confront and conquer through his own inventiveness and application. But when these men died, their passing marked the beginning of the end of this can-do era for individuals. They and their generation bequeathed a sum of knowledge that had become too large and complicated to be mastered by a single mind. From then on, all scientific and technical development depended to an ever-increasing extent upon specialization. The great industrialists of the second half of the nineteenth century, like Armstrong and Whitworth, were businessmen first and foremost.

At the mid-point of Queen Victoria's reign, Britain was still reaping the benefits of industrialization. Record production levels in cotton textiles, iron and steel, coal mining and engineering were the linchpins of British domination of the global economy. The engineering sector in particular provided an ever-expanding range of products, creating thousands of jobs and earning millions of pounds in exports. The manufacture of machines, tools, steam engines and general products achieved unprecedented levels of technical precision and this, along with exports of heavy engineering, ships, locomotives, hydraulics and armaments, continued to secure Britain's position as world leader. But it couldn't last. Other countries, such as the United States, were quick to learn the lessons of industrialization and had much greater resources at their disposal than Britain.

The confidence of British engineers, industrialists and the governments of the day in the country's industrial lead was one of the factors that led to the loss of this advantage. The wholesale export of technology meant that other nations could use it to further their own industrial sectors and, in so doing, provide competition for Britain. Engineers continued to build larger and more impressive structures than ever before, and to adopt powerful new technologies in the shape of electricity and the internal combustion engine. After 1860, however, continental and American engineers came to take an increasingly prominent share of such innovations. Britain ceased to enjoy the unchallenged supremacy that had characterized the years around the Great Exhibition, and during the 1870s began to concede leadership in one area after another. As a result, the idea of empire began to hold even greater appeal. British people wanted something to feel proud of as well as having new markets for their goods. Empire meant not only an abundance of jobs for civilians but also regular military employment. British technology was used throughout the empire to build railways and assist the exploitation of natural resources to feed Britain's industries. Disraeli, as prime minister, spoke of the working classes as 'proud of belonging to a great country; proud of belonging to an Imperial country', and flattered the Queen's imperialist aspirations by bestowing on her the title of Empress of India in 1877.

But British industry had become very set in its ways. In textiles, for example, cotton-spinning mills still used the old system of mule spinning while foreign competitors had switched to the more advanced technology of ring spinning. British industry in general was slow to switch to any new technique such as electrical power in place of steam. The problem was that textiles, engineering and iron and steel continued to make profits. Many companies were still family firms and their owners were often reluctant to develop new products or invest in new machinery so long as the money kept coming in. Industrialists preferred the safety of tried and tested technology, even as it became increasingly outdated. Coming to the game later, Germany and America not only benefited from the export of British technological expertise but were willing to invest in the latest technology. The American steel magnate Andrew Carnegie pointed out that most British machinery was still in use twenty years after it should have been scrapped.

As he worked on his traction engine in his garden, Fred would talk of the gradual decline of British industry at this time, as complacency set in and people with the skills to do the sort of work he was doing on his engine virtually disappeared: 'By the end of the nineteenth century Germany and America were both benefiting from an emphasis on the practical and technical in their education systems – the very things that Brunel and Stephenson had had passed on to them by their fathers – while Britain failed to recognize the importance of science and technology in their education system.' For Fred, Brunel and Stephenson represented a lot of the values of an age when the skills of making things were highly regarded, when there was little sympathy for weakness and none at all for idleness. Above all, there had been an unbending faith in the ability to get things done, however great the challenge. 'They are all values which we've lost,' said Fred. 'If we still had them today Britain would still be a major industrial power.'

The decline of British industry certainly coincided with the loss of these values, but there were many other factors involved. Although the natural resources of coal and iron ore remained, the surplus capital and the willingness to take risks that had characterized the earlier part of Victoria's reign had gone. With growing competition, the markets of the past were no longer as secure. But perhaps, above all, the British were no longer prepared to accept the sort of jobs and working conditions that people had endured in earlier times. The dirty, dangerous, heavy manual work of the Victorian Age, when Britain was a developing country, became less acceptable as the twentieth century progressed and newly developing countries took it on instead. The heroic age of British engineering was drawing to a close.

PARSONS WATT

FAIRBAIRN WHITWORTH

GEORGE STEPHENSON

TREVITHICK MAUDSLAY PENN

FIRST PRESIDENT · 1847—1848

ROCKET

THE INSTITUTION OF MECHANICAL ENGINEERS

1

George Stephenson
1781–1848
The Father of the Railways

It was in the coalfields of the North East that railways as we know them really began to operate and it's the Northumbrian engineer George Stephenson who is credited as being the father of the railways. He came from a poor background and didn't get a proper education, but through his hard work, his passion for the locomotive and his technical genius, he became one of the world's most famous engineers. Stephenson wasn't the inventor of the locomotive but he played the leading part in turning the invention into a practical means of hauling coal and transporting passengers over long distances.

George Stephenson was the archetype for Samuel Smiles's philosophy of self-help. He came from an underprivileged background but through his own efforts he rose to become one of Britain's most famous engineers. In his day he was known for another quality that he shared with other engineers of his time: sheer physical toughness. But he was a stubborn, cantankerous character who didn't suffer fools gladly and was difficult to work with.

Everything Stephenson knew he learned on the job, not in a classroom or lecture theatre, and he always had a deep distrust of academics and engineering theorists. He was a man after Fred's heart but he was, and still is, a controversial figure. For some people, including Fred, he was the 'father of the railway' but many historians claim that all he did was copy the ideas of other men working in this field and exploit them and their skills. What is not in doubt, though, is that he was a man of great vision, determination and entrepreneurial spirit, backed up by sound and cautious judgement and an absolutely indomitable will, who demonstrated conclusively that steam railways were an efficient form of transport and pioneered the engineering techniques of railway construction that changed the landscape for ever.

The son of a colliery fireman, Stephenson was born on 9 June 1781, in the small colliery village of Wylam on the north bank of the River Tyne about eight miles west of Newcastle. In his *Lives of the Engineers* Samuel Smiles described it as a place where the traveller 'sees the usual signs of a colliery in the unsightly pumping-engines surrounded by heaps of ashes, coal-dust, and slag; whilst a neighbouring iron-furnace in full blast throws out dense smoke and loud jets of steam by day and lurid flames at night'. George was the second of six children and the family's poverty meant that they all had to live together in one room of a cottage. Three other families shared the other rooms.

The cottage was close to the horse-drawn tramway for Wylam Colliery, where Stephenson's father worked as a fireman, stoking the engine that pumped water from the mine. The wooden wagonway had been built in 1748 to take the coal from Wylam Colliery to the coal-loading jetties on the River Tyne. With six children to support on a wage of only 12 shillings (60p) a week his father was not able to send any of the family to school, but Stephenson grew up with a keen interest in machinery. As a child he was employed as a cowherd but would keep himself amused by making model engines in clay. He soon showed great mechanical talent and an unusual love of study.

Stephenson had a variety of other jobs as a young lad. One of the earliest was working down the pit as a trapper boy. For only tuppence a day, trapper boys would sit behind a trapdoor for twelve hours at a stretch, opening and closing it for the men who worked at getting the coal to the surface.* As a trapper boy, he couldn't leave the door when coal was being transported. If he did, not only would he be in trouble with the boss but he would also get a clip across the ear from the

14

miners. Working from such an early age meant that most of Stephenson's youth was spent in total darkness, either underground or on his late return home. At the age of eight, George got a job on the surface as a picker at the Dewley Burn Pit, cleaning the coal of stone, slate and other impurities on a starting wage of sixpence (2½p) a day.

As he grew older he never missed an opportunity to learn about the construction and management of machinery at the colliery, and at 15 he was promoted to the position of fireman where he would keep the steam-powered pumps at the mine running. He quickly established himself as a steady lad and his intelligence and attention to duty soon led to further promotion. At the age of 17, he was placed in charge of Water Row Colliery in Newburn, where his father was now working as fireman.

By the turn of the century, stationary steam engines were being introduced to many of the collieries in the North East and, with his mechanical aptitude, it was natural that Stephenson would find himself operating them. When a vacancy came up at Black Callerton Pit in 1801, he was given the job of brakesman on the steam winding engine, which hauled coal tubs from the coal faces to the shafts and from there to the surface. Although he'd received no formal education, Stephenson was ambitious, and while he was at Callerton he began a systematic course of self-improvement. After a day's work at the colliery, in the evening he taught himself to read and write. He then started to go to night-school classes in the nearby village of Walbottle and within a few years had achieved basic literacy skills. This wasn't something that came naturally to him and for the rest of his life he disliked these laboriously acquired skills so much that

---

* To keep mines clear of gas, a crude system of ventilation was used. Fresh air came in from the surface through ventilation shafts. Trapdoors shut off different areas of the mine to keep the fresh air in the sections where men were working and to stop pockets of poisonous gas getting in. Trapper boys (sometimes girls) would sit underground operating the trapdoors to let coal wagons through. Opening and shutting the doors also created a draught which would move fresh air through the mine and shift any build-ups of gas. If the doors were not operated properly the coal wagons wouldn't get through from the face to the pithead and there would also be a risk of explosion.

he never wrote a letter if he could avoid it and rarely read a book.

During his time at Black Callerton he met and fell in love with a woman 12 years older than him called Frances Henderson. Fanny, as she was known, worked as a servant at the farm close to the pit where George had lodgings. After working at Callerton for about two years, he received an offer to take charge of the engine used to haul coal wagons from Willington Quay Colliery near Wallsend. The money was better so he decided to accept it and, at the same time, to marry Fanny. He was only 21, but he had managed to save enough money to take a cottage at Willington Quay and furnish it in a humble but comfortable style. It was only one room but that was all a pit worker could expect. Here he set up home with his new bride. To earn extra money he repaired clocks and watches and mended shoes when he got home from work in the evening. He also started to build a reputation for fixing machinery and to be recognized as an inventor. His little cottage was always filled with models of engines and machines of various kinds, including a steam-engine brake mechanism and a model of a machine designed to create a means of perpetual motion.

While he was living at Willington Quay, on 16 October 1803 George Stephenson's only son, Robert, was born. The child was the apple of his father's eye and life in the Stephenson household was good. This happy existence was short-lived, however. Fanny suffered from poor health and died of consumption in 1806 shortly after giving birth to a daughter, who survived her mother by only a few months. George had been very close to his wife and felt her loss deeply. He thought about emigrating but his son's education was a priority and he decided to stay in Britain. Another factor was his fascination with the development of the earliest forms of railway locomotive, which was taking place locally. In 1804 the Cornish engineer Richard Trevithick was employed by the owner of Wylam Colliery, Christopher Blackett, to build a locomotive that would replace the horses used to draw the coal wagons. At five tons the Wylam locomotive proved too heavy for Blackett's wooden wagonway. The project was abandoned and the colliery reverted to the use of horses but Stephenson's interest in the potential of locomotives had been aroused.

In 1804, when Stephenson was 27, he got a job as an engineman at Killingworth Colliery. His sister Eleanor, known as Nelly, moved in to live with him at the West Moor cottage and look after young Robert. While he was at Killingworth he increased his reputation as a man who was good at mending machinery and engines and he struck up a friendship with a young trainee manager called Nicholas Wood, who shared his enthusiasm. He worked night shifts at the colliery, knowing that this would give him time for further study, particularly in mathematics and the principles of mechanics. He did his sums on a slate hung at the top of the shaft and got these corrected by a teacher during the day, who then gave him more to complete that night. For this he paid the teacher fourpence a week.

The engines at Killingworth included machines made by Thomas Newcomen and James Watt. Every Saturday Stephenson took these engines to pieces to help him understand how they were constructed. In doing this and being able to put them back together again, he showed so much mechanical aptitude that by 1812 he had been put in charge of the operation, maintenance and repair of all the engines and machinery in the collieries owned by the Grand Allies, a partnership of all the principal coal-mining families of the North East. This was a major step forward. His pay was increased to £100 a year and he was now recognized as a skilled worker. He constructed stationary engines for several collieries for underground haulage work and replaced the horse-drawn coal sleds with wagons rolling on rails. Colliery owners had been watching developments in the field of steam locomotion with interest and some were beginning to see the sort of steam-driven locomotive running on rails that Stephenson was experimenting with as an economically viable alternative to horsepower.

For a man who had received no formal education, Stephenson's achievements were remarkable and they provided an early example of the natural talent he had for anything to do with engineering. He knew that the wealthy colliery owners were relying more and more on men with engineering skills to help their businesses grow and that with education a young mechanic could gain increased recognition from them, so he was keen to learn more. In 1813, hearing of attempts by

William Hedley and Timothy Hackworth to develop a locomotive at Wylam Colliery, he went there to study their engine. He also visited Leeds to see an engine that John Blenkinsop had developed for the Middleton Colliery. At its trials Blenkinsop's locomotive had pulled a load of 70 tons at a speed of 3 mph, but when Stephenson saw it he was certain he could do better. He was determined to build his own locomotive and it wasn't long before he managed to convince one of the local mine owners, Lord Ravensworth, of the advantages of a travelling engine. Ravensworth advanced Stephenson the money that he needed and he started work on his first locomotive in the Killingworth Colliery workshops just behind his home at West Moor.

By 1814 he had constructed a locomotive that could pull 30 tons up a hill at 4 mph. Stephenson called his locomotive *Blucher* (after the general in the Prussian Army who would help Britain to defeat Napoleon at Waterloo). Like other machines made at this time, it had two vertical cylinders let into the boiler. These were attached to piston rods that drove the gears. There was nothing new in this design but there was one important difference in the way it worked. Where John Blenkinsop, William Hedley and Timothy Hackworth had built locomotives with gears that drove rack pinions, Stephenson's gears drove flanged wheels.

On 25 July 1814, *Blucher* was successfully put into operation on the Killingworth Waggonway. With it Stephenson became the first man to make and run a locomotive with flanged wheels on a track laid with cast-iron rails. *Blucher*, however, proved to be defective and the cost of running it was found to be about as great as that of using horsepower. One of the problems was that the engine could not travel round a curve, and those unwilling to believe that railways would ever succeed were amused to hear the story of the driver who had to shout out to his wife, 'Hey, Jean, come oot and gie us a shove round the turn!' People were not impressed and many said of Lord Ravensworth, 'A fool and his money are soon parted.' Like the other locomotives that had been developed, *Blucher* was rough, crude, slow and not very manoeuvrable – no more than a machine for moving coal around at a colliery. But Stephenson wasn't prepared to give up on the idea. He continued to try to improve his locomotive, and in 1815 he changed the design. The connecting rods now drove the wheels directly, and these wheels were coupled together by a chain. The new machine proved much more efficient than the original *Blucher*.

George Stephenson's name is always associated with railways but at this early stage of his career steam locomotives were not the only things he was working on. As a colliery man, he was well aware of the large number of accidents caused by explosive gases. One of the greatest perils facing miners working underground was methane gas (firedamp), which could cause fatal explosions if it came into contact with the naked flame of a candle or oil lamp. So, in his spare time, Stephenson began work on a safety lamp for miners. He tested it by taking it into a particularly volatile region of the mine and, although the experiment was risky, he emerged safely. By 1815 he had developed a lamp that did not cause explosions even in parts of the pit that were full of inflammable gases. Unknown to Stephenson, Humphry Davy was busy producing his own safety lamp. After some dispute as to whether the lamp was invented first by Stephenson or by Davy – who claimed the £3,000 reward that was on offer – a sum of £1,000 was raised and presented to Stephenson by north-eastern industrialists. For Stephenson, however, the lamp was to be a short-lived diversion, and with the success of his second locomotive he began to devote all his energies to making more efficient railway locomotives.

From 1815 onwards, he carried out key experiments at Killingworth Waggonway, and by 1818 the track had been entirely relaid with cast-iron edge-rails. This use of iron rails was an important advance as wooden ones were too weak to withstand the great weight of locomotives. By 1820 Stephenson had built sixteen engines at Killingworth. Most of these were used locally but some were produced for the Duke of Portland's wagonway from Kilmarnock to Troon. Haulage by horse virtually disappeared at Killingworth and the owners of the colliery were so impressed with Stephenson's achievements that in 1819 he was given the task of building an eight-mile railroad from Hetton Colliery to the River Wear at Sunderland.

While he was working on this, Stephenson became convinced that, to be successful, steam railways had to be made as level as possible, so he laid out the line in sections. The first part was worked by loco-motives and this was followed by fixed engines and cables. After the railway had reached a height of 250 feet the coal wagons travelled downhill over two miles of self-acting inclined plane. This was then followed by another two miles of locomotive haulage. When it was all finished, it was the first-ever railway that was completely independent of animal power. Stephenson's engines were remarkably well made and, in the words of one contemporary enthusiast, 'superior beyond all comparison to all other engines ever seen'. The Hetton Colliery line became a showpiece for Stephenson's railway-building and locomotive design skills.

While he was working on the Hetton Colliery Railway, Stephenson married again, 15 years after the death of his beloved Fanny. His bride was Elizabeth (Betty) Hindmarsh, a farmer's daughter from Black Callerton whom he'd courted in his teens, before he met Fanny Henderson. The couple had wanted to get married but Betty's father said no because of Stephenson's lowly status as a miner. Now that he was wealthier he was finally allowed to marry his first love.

Around this time he heard of a proposal to build a railway to trans-port coal from the collieries at Shildon in County Durham to a quayside on the River Tees at Stockton, with a branch line running to Darlington. The man behind the idea was Edward Pease, a Quaker wool merchant from Darlington. In 1821, with a group of business-men, Pease formed the Stockton & Darlington Railway Company. The initial idea was that horses would be the main motive power with possibly some stationary engines, and on 19 April that same year Parliament passed an Act that allowed the company to build such a railway. As soon as Stephenson heard about the project, he arranged a meeting with Pease and suggested he consider building a locomotive railway instead, informing him that the locomotives he had built at Killingworth were 'worth fifty horses'.

Pease took up Stephenson's invitation to visit Killingworth and, seeing *Blucher* at work, he realized immediately that Stephenson was right. He was also convinced that Stephenson was the man to take

charge of the construction of the line and the building of the locomotives, so he offered him the post of chief engineer of the Stockton &
Darlington Railway Company. A further Act of Parliament now had to
be applied for which would include a clause stating that Parliament
gave permission for the company 'to make and erect locomotive or
moveable engines'.

It was at this point that the width of the track that our trains still
run on to this day was fixed. Stephenson made up his mind about this
before the first passenger carriage was built and he never changed it.
Edward Pease suggested that he should make the width equal to that of
country carts and Stephenson, with characteristic thoroughness, had
measurements taken of around 100 carts used by farmers in the neighbourhood. The average width of these carts between their wheels was
4 feet 8½ inches and that, said Fred, 'was good enough for Stephenson
for the rest of his life and he went on to defend it against all comers'.

Stephenson now had to decide on the type of rail to use. William
Losh, who owned an ironworks in Newcastle, had developed, with
Stephenson's help, a new type of cast-iron rail and this was the first
choice. But another local ironmaster, John Birkinshaw from
Bedlington, was producing wrought-iron rails and when Stephenson
went to see them he could tell at once that they were superior, so he
decided to use these rather than the ones he was making with Losh.

With the help of his son, Stephenson began surveying the Stockton
& Darlington line in 1821. It was the start of the most famous and
successful partnership in railway history. Work on the track began in
1822 and it was kept on the flat as far as possible, in line with the thinking of the canal engineers. Where there were changes in level, wagons
would be hauled up the inclines by means of stationary engines at the
top. Stephenson oversaw the laying of the new malleable iron rails,
which were laid on wooden blocks for 12 miles between Stockton and
Darlington; then the 15-mile track from Darlington to the collieries at
Shildon was laid on stone blocks. The honour of laying the first few
lengths of rail in the presence of the mayor of Darlington and other
dignitaries fell to Mr Meynell, the chairman of the Stockton &
Darlington Railway Company.

Speaking to his men when the line was being built, Stephenson said:

> Now, lads, I venture to tell you that I think you will live to see the day when railways will take the place of almost any other method of conveyance in this country; when mail coaches will go by railway and railways will become the great highways for the King and all his subjects. The time is coming when it will be cheaper for a working man to travel on the railroad than to walk on foot. I know there are great and almost insurmountable difficulties to be encountered but what I have said will come to pass as sure as you live.

Many of those supplying the money for the line were still not keen on using the 'shrieking thing', as they called the steam locomotive, and would rather have had the carriages drawn by horses, but Pease continued to support Stephenson. He was so keen on getting steam locomotives to provide the power for the line that he not only backed Stephenson's design for the railway's first locomotive, *Locomotion*, but advanced £1,000 to help him begin the business of locomotive-engine construction at Newcastle.

By this time Robert was working with his father and in 1823 the world's first locomotive factory was set up at South Street, just off Forth Street in Newcastle upon Tyne. It became known as the Forth Street Works and the business formed to run it was Robert Stephenson & Company. Edward Pease was the principal shareholder and Stephenson recruited Timothy Hackworth, one of the engineers who had worked with William Hedley, to work for the company. Robert Stephenson, still only 20, became the managing partner in charge of running the works. But he had been in charge of the works for only a year when events took an unexpected turn. In 1824 he left his father and the business that bore his name to find his fortune as a mining engineer in South America. The company carried on without him and built four locomotives for service on the line.

Three-quarters of the finance for the railway had come from Darlington businessmen, so the line ran from Shildon in the heart of the Durham coalfield and went via Darlington to the coal port at Stockton. By the middle of 1825 all the track had been laid and work on *Locomotion* was completed in September of that year. Basically the engine was similar to those that Stephenson had built for the collieries at Killingworth and Heaton, with a single-fire-tube boiler that had two vertical cylinders let into the barrel. It also had four wheels coupled by rods rather than the chain he'd used on the colliery engines. 'Many people,' Fred said, 'think railway history started on 27 September 1825 when George Stephenson's *Locomotion Number 1* pulled a train of 34 wagons filled with passengers, flour and coal from Shildon to Darlington and then on to Stockton. The whole train weighed 90 tons and went at the unbelievable speed of 12 miles an hour.' Stephenson was the driver with his brother James beside him on the footplate. Timothy Hackworth was the guard.

That first journey was just under nine miles and it took two hours to complete. During the final descent into the Stockton terminus, however, staggering speeds of 15 mph were reached. The speed startled one man so much that he fell from one of the wagons and was badly injured. *Locomotion* ran on four wheels, with a four-wheel tender to carry the coal and water. The boiler was a single flue and it had two vertical cylinders that drove crossbeams and connecting rods. The driver had to balance precariously on a platform on the left-hand side of the engine, where he could let the steam into the cylinders and work all the levers of the primitive valve gear. The fireman rode on the front of the tender, although when he was not stoking the fire he could ride on the platform on the opposite side of the engine to the driver. 'It must've been quite exciting really,' Fred once said, 'like being an airline pilot in 1825. Incredible! It had no brakes, like, and to stop the thing the fireman had actually to jump off and pin down the brakes on the coal wagon. Quite a hairy occupation.'

Tickets had been issued for 300 passengers but the organizers couldn't control the numbers and anybody who could scramble on to the train was on board for that historic first journey. On the way from Shildon to Darlington people on horseback and on foot tried to race the train as it passed along triumphantly. Spectators came out in their thousands to line the track, waving and cheering as this strange contraption went past. When they got to Darlington it seemed that the whole town had turned out to see the train arrive, and then steam off towards Stockton.

After the events of the opening day the railway had to settle down to earning money and doing what it had been planned to do. Traffic soon built up and in the first three months 10,000 tons of coal were transported on the new line. A second locomotive, *Hope*, built by Robert Stephenson & Co., was delivered on 1 November 1825, and two more, *Black Diamond* and *Diligence*, followed in 1826.

In spite of the initial success of the Stockton & Darlington, George Stephenson was still involved in the construction of other types of railway. The Bowes Railway, developed to carry coal from local collieries to Jarrow on the River Tyne for shipment, was one of the last places to use a rope haulage system. The line originally used three rope-haulage inclines for the first 2¼ miles and two locomotives for the final four miles to Jarrow. In 1826 an extension to Mount Moor Colliery at Black Fell used two rope-worked inclines originally powered by a stationary steam engine at Blackham's Hill.

The scheme at Bowes was old technology and its future was limited, but the Stockton & Darlington Railway didn't bring a revolution overnight. There were teething troubles, particularly with steaming. Timothy Hackworth, who was put in charge of mechanical engineering, went back to an idea that had been used by Trevithick, of diverting exhaust steam up the chimney. This was fine in that it improved the steaming, but it meant that the extra blast this created tore at the fire and hurled hot ash and burning coal up the chimney. It was so bad that firebeaters had to be employed to patrol the track and put out the flames. There were also boiler explosions on *Locomotion* and on *Hope* that killed members of the crew. These early locomotives didn't have any effective gauges so crews had no way of telling when the boiler needed to be filled.

All this meant that horses still did a great deal of the work on the line, as did the stationary engines on the inclines. Basically it was still a colliery line that employed a mixture of new and old technology. For the passengers it carried it was still very much old technology. They travelled for most of the way in a conventional stagecoach with flanged iron wheels that was drawn along the track by horses.

In spite of the problems, the momentum for the steam locomotive did begin to gather pace. It was clear that the Stockton & Darlington line had successfully reduced the cost of transporting coal and this made the merchants of other towns turn to the idea of railways to speed up transportation of their own goods and reduce expenses. Building railways, they realized, brought great benefits and one railway that was set to change the course of transport history was a proposed line to link two of the most important cities of the industrial age, Liverpool and Manchester.

The existing links between the manufacturing heart of the cotton industry in Manchester and the port of Liverpool depended on canals, but the canal network was slow. A group of businessmen led by Joseph Sandars got together to build a railway between the towns, with the principal objective of reducing the costs of transporting raw materials and finished goods between the port and the factories. The group agreed to finance a survey for their proposed railway and recruited George Stephenson to do the job.

Railway location was just as controversial in the 1820s as it is in the twenty-first century, and the landed gentry in particular didn't want a dirty, noisy railway anywhere near them. The Duke of Wellington was certainly opposed to the idea of railways and he is reported to have said, 'It will only encourage the lower classes to move about.' Local landowner Robert Bradshaw, who managed the Duke of Bridgewater's estates and controlled the Bridgewater Canal, was one of the fiercest opponents of the scheme; hardly surprising because the canal was very profitable.

In planning the route, the self-taught man from Tyneside was faced with some immense engineering challenges. Chat Moss, a vast peat bog lying right across the route, was the most serious natural obstacle, but Stephenson argued that it was possible to cross it. Thomas Harrison, an opponent of the railway, criticized Stephenson's plan: 'It is ignorance almost inconceivable. It is perfect madness. Every part of this scheme shows that this man has applied himself to a subject of which he has no knowledge and to which he has no science to apply.' Other major feats of civil engineering he was faced with along the 30-mile route included building a tunnel at Edge Hill, a two-mile cutting to get into the centre of Liverpool and a nine-arched viaduct over the Sankey Valley.

The strength of the opposition meant adequate surveying could not be carried out. The landowners hated the very name of the steam engine and whenever a surveyor appeared they would turn him off their land. One of them, Lord Sefton, threatened to have 100 men standing by to stop the surveyors going about their work. Stones were thrown and even guns fired at the workers. One railway surveyor had to pay a prizefighter to carry his surveying instruments to protect them from the angry crowds who gathered to obstruct his work. In his *Life of George Stephenson*, published in 1857, Samuel Smiles wrote:

> Pamphlets were written and newspapers were hired to revile the railway. It was declared that its formation would prevent cows grazing and hens laying. The poisoned air from locomotives would kill birds as they flew over them and make the preservation of foxes and pheasants no longer possible. People were told that their houses would be burnt up by the fire thrown from the engine chimneys, while the air around would be darkened by clouds of smoke. There would no longer be any use for horses. Boilers would burst and blow passengers to atom.

Someone asked Stephenson, 'Suppose one of these engines to be going along a railroad at the rate of nine or ten miles an hour and that a cow was to stray on the line and get in the way of the engine. Would not that be a very awkward circumstance?'

'Yes,' Stephenson replied with a smile, and, in his rough Northumbrian accent, he added, 'very awkward indeed – for the coo!'

At the time of the survey, Stephenson was still fully occupied with the Stockton & Darlington Railway so most of the work had to be done by his assistants, who were easily intimidated by the opposition they were meeting. The result was that the survey was rushed, inaccurate and didn't stand up to scrutiny when Stephenson and the promoters had to go to Parliament for cross-questioning by a select committee looking into the proposal. Things might have gone better if Stephenson had taken more time to familiarize himself with the survey his assistants had conducted, but when he gave evidence it was clear he was ignorant of a lot of the details. Edward Alderson, the counsel employed by those who were opposed to the railway, soon exposed Stephenson's ignorance: 'His is a mind perpetually fluctuating between opposite difficulties; he neither knows whether he is to make bridges over roads or rivers, or of one size or another; or to make embankments or cuttings or inclined planes or in what way the thing is to be carried into effect.' Alderson questioned whether the committee could pass a Bill 'involving property to the extent of £400,000 to £500,000 when [Stephenson] is so ignorant of his profession as to propose to build a bridge not sufficient to carry off the flood water of the river or to permit any of the vessels to pass which of necessity must pass under it.'

After the inadequacy of the proposals had been exposed, it was no surprise that Parliament rejected the Liverpool & Manchester Company's plans in 1825. Stephenson had been humiliated. The men in London had laughed at his accent and suggested that he was mad, and the company called in George and John Rennie to take his place. It was the lowest point of his career, but Stephenson was a fighter who had great confidence in his own abilities. He felt sure they couldn't manage the project without him on board. The Rennies were experienced engineers and also well versed in dealing with parliamentary committees. They employed an up-and-coming young engineer called Charles Vignoles to do most of the work on the survey and their experience helped to ensure that the Bill for the railway passed smoothly through Parliament in 1826. Work on the Liverpool & Manchester Railway could begin.

The Rennies were invited to take on the work of supervising engineers and two names were put forward for the job of operative engineer – George Stephenson and John Rastrick – both of whom they turned down. After several months of wrangling the Rennies pulled out, leaving the inexperienced Vignoles to carry on. Josias Jessop, the son of an experienced canal engineer, was brought in to supervise the project and Stephenson was brought back to work alongside Vignoles as working engineer. But Stephenson, an obstreperous character, was difficult to work with and first Jessop and then Vignoles left, putting Stephenson back where he wanted to be, in sole charge of the construction of the 31-mile railway. It was typical of the way Stephenson operated. Somehow or other he always seemed to get the better of his opponents in the end. This was in 1826. In the same year he was appointed engineer and provider of locomotives for the Bolton & Leigh Railway.

Stephenson didn't have the engineering experience for such a major project as the Liverpool & Manchester, but one of the things he had realized when he was supervising the construction of the Stockton & Darlington was that a railway had to be specially designed to avoid changes in gradient. This meant that considerable time and money would have to be spent on digging cuttings, tunnels and embankments. What Stephenson lacked in engineering experience he made up for with his dogged determination and, undeterred by criticism, he went ahead with his plans for a level, straight route whatever obstacles lay in his way.

At the Liverpool end of the line the Edge Hill Tunnel was the first obstacle he had to overcome. The techniques for boring a straight tunnel had been worked out by the canal engineers in the eighteenth century, so Stephenson wasn't venturing into the unknown. The job involved sinking shafts down to the level the line would run at and working outwards from the bottom of them on set headings. If the surveys for the tunnel were accurate and the work was done properly, the different sections would all meet and run in a straight line. But, possibly because of Stephenson's inexperience, this didn't happen at Edge Hill. The alignment of the shafts was so far out that when they started to dig the tunnels from the bottom of each of the shafts it became clear that they were not going to meet each other as they should have done, and a lot of time and effort had to be spent correcting this. The work was difficult and dangerous, and the workers' only light came from candles. Excavating the tunnel cost many lives including the first recorded death of a navvy, reported in the *Liverpool Mercury* in August 1827. Water, seeping in through the rock and earth that surrounded the workings, was a constant threat and on several occasions the men were driven from their work by floods.

For Fred, the navvies who built the railways were the great unsung heroes of Victorian engineering. The name originated from the time the British canal network was being laid out, in the eighteenth and early nineteenth centuries. It was known as the Inland Navigation System and the men who dug the canals, officially called 'excavators', became known colloquially as 'navigators', which was later abbreviated to 'navvies'. 'Most of these early navvies who did the tunnelling had been miners,' Fred explained, 'and it weren't that important down below in the pit keeping everything perfectly straight and I think this rather accounted for the amount of "funny twists and turns" to be found in a lot of canal tunnels, where they'd not quite got it in line because the art of surveying then weren't as good as what it is now. All the digging was done with pick and shovel and "spoil" (soil) was moved by hand in small barrows. They lived in squalid hutment townships and the locals viewed them as lawless gypsies. They were frequently undisciplined and spread terror to the villages, especially on pay nights. They lived on steak and gin and were described as being drunk most of the time.' Nevertheless, 'It was incredible how many yards of earth a man could move with a wheelbarrow and a shovel.'

When the railways started to appear a lot of the canal network was abandoned, but there remained a ready source of labour and engineering expertise. It was by appreciating and overcoming the engineering difficulties involved in canal building that the civil engineering profession came into being. The construction methods pioneered by the canal builders were adapted by the railway engineers and the labour force on these projects continued to be known as navvies. They would all have been out of work if it hadn't been for the railways. They constructed some unbelievable cuttings and embankments to try to get the lines level. The tunnelling was exceptional. A lot of people died in the process and the work took many years to

Navvy with the tools of his trade

complete. As Fred acknowledged, 'the business of health and safety didn't come into it much.'

At the peak of 'railway mania' in 1847 there were 250,000 navvies at work all over the country. But back in the 1820s the first work for the navvies was on the Liverpool & Manchester. Using little more than pick-axes, shovels and wheelbarrows they excavated the Edge Hill Tunnel. Just beyond it a great cutting had to be dug out at Olive Mount by drilling the rock with hand drills, shattering it with gunpowder and then carting out all the debris. As it was two miles long and more than 100 feet deep in places, it involved the removal of nearly half a million cubic feet of stone. But the biggest challenge Stephenson had to face was getting the line across the bog at Chat Moss.

The first step was to dig drainage ditches and over 200 men were employed to lay drains on each side of the track area. Although this worked in the shallower parts it made no impact on the deeper areas of the bog, so Stephenson was forced to change his plan. The drainage ditches were replaced with barrels and casks joined together and coated with clay to create a form of pipe. This was an improvement, but at an area known as the Blackpool Hole the barrels continued to rise to the surface. The work was difficult and the men had to tie planks to their feet to stop themselves from sinking. At first it was all trial and error. Building a railway line across a bog was taking a step into the unknown, and in the early days Stephenson himself was full of uncertainties. 'After working for weeks and weeks, we went on filling in without the slightest apparent effect,' he would recall later in life. 'Even my assistants began to feel uneasy and to doubt the success of the scheme. The directors too spoke of it as a hopeless task and at length they became seriously alarmed, so much so, indeed, that a board meeting was held on Chat Moss to decide whether I should proceed any further.' Other engineers reported unfavourably on the scheme's prospects. But, Stephenson said, 'We had to go on. An immense outlay had been incurred and a great loss would have been occasioned had the scheme been then abandoned.'

Stephenson believed that it would be possible to use a floating raft to support the four-mile trackbed across the bog. Samuel Smiles explained Stephenson's thinking in his biography:

As a ship or raft, capable of sustaining heavy loads, floated in water, so in his opinion, might a light road be floated upon a bog. The first thing done was to form a footpath of heather along the proposed road, on which a man might walk without risk of sinking. A single line of temporary railway was then laid down, formed of ordinary cross-bars about 3 feet long and an inch square, with holes punched through them at the ends and nailed down to temporary sleepers. Along this way ran the wagons in which were conveyed the materials requisite to form the permanent road. These wagons carried about a ton each, and were propelled by boys running behind them along the narrow iron rails. The boys became so expert that they could run the 4 miles at the rate of 7 or 8 miles an hour without missing a step.

Much to Stephenson's satisfaction, his idea of a 'floating' railway was an unqualified success. The self-taught engineer had triumphed and crossed the treacherous bog where better-educated critics and rivals had feared to tread.

As the line neared completion the company had to settle the question of what sort of motive power was to be used. Some of the directors and their advisers were still keen to use horses; some thought stationary hauling-engines were preferable; and the remainder were undecided. Most were worried that the only locomotives available at the time were too slow and inefficient. Stephenson was almost alone in backing the locomotive and after long debates he persuaded the board to give the travelling engine a chance. A competition was set up with a prize of £500 for the best locomotive engine – and if the locomotive was good enough, it would be used on the new railway.

The reward was printed, published and circulated throughout the land, and a number of engines were constructed to compete at the trial. Eight conditions were laid down, including the stipulations that the maximum weight of the engine was to be six tons, that all wheels had to be sprung and that the cost of the locomotive had to be less than £550. They named the competition the Rainhill Trials and it was scheduled to take place near Liverpool on a stretch of line about 1¾ miles long. Each locomotive had to pull three times its own weight along the track 20 times, to equal the distance from Liverpool to Manchester. Then it had to fill up with coke – the engine fuel of the day – and water, and make another 20 runs along the track. The average speed with a load behind the engine had to be not less than 10 mph.

By this time Robert Stephenson had returned from South America and was back at the Forth Street Works. His main task was to produce an engine that would win the Rainhill Trials. The engine that took shape was called *Rocket* and Robert had it ready for the competition that began on 6 October 1829 in front of over 10,000 spectators. Ten locomotives were originally entered for the competition but only five turned up. Of these only three, *Rocket*, *Sans Pareil* and *Novelty*, actually took part in the trials. When the trials began, *Novelty* was the popular favourite. It was the work of two engineers, John Braithwaite and John Ericsson, neither of whom had ever designed a railway locomotive before. In spite of or perhaps because of this, they came up with a revolutionary new design consisting of a lightweight body with a water tank underneath. It had a vertical boiler surrounding the firebox; fuel was fed in from the top and steam went into two cylinders that drove a cranked axle. In the trials, however, the engine didn't perform well and it soon became clear that the competition was between *Rocket* and Timothy Hackworth's *Sans Pareil*. *Rocket* won the day, and Fred gave his view on what made the Stephensons' engine superior and why it was such a major breakthrough in locomotive design: 'Stephenson had wandered way off track with his design and came up with a brand new, revolutionary idea that incorporated the fire tube boiler. This really is the prototype for all modern locomotive boilers that we know today.' In relation to its weight and power, it went much faster than any locomotive that had been built before. As Fred explained:

Stephenson's main innovations were tubes, connecting rods and a blast pipe. He did away with the business of a beam engine on top of the boiler and the complicated gears and levers of previous locomotives. In the boiler the hot gases from the burning coal went through 25 tubes, which were surrounded by water. This helped to boil the water faster,

Fred's own drawing of Stephenson's *Rocket*

which in turn made faster running possible. The blast pipe was used to send exhaust steam up the chimney, which Stephenson knew would improve the air draught through the firebox. It's this powerful draught that creates the familiar 'chuff, chuff' of the steam locomotive.

His biggest innovation, though, was direct drive from the cylinders and pistons to the wheels, which eliminated the need for complicated gears and levers. The connecting rods linked the piston directly to the crank pin on the hub of the front wheels and this in turn led to nice smooth running. The crank pins were like two tennis balls. The brasses on the ends of the connecting rods were hollowed out like spheres inside, so when the front axle moved on the springs it wouldn't bind up and the crank pins wouldn't get hot. The locomotive went at about 30 miles an hour, an unbelievable speed for 1829. Using many tubes in the boiler, instead of one or two big ones, were the brilliant idea of a man called Henry Booth. Booth did a bit of a drawing on the back of a fag packet . . . and of course Mr Stephenson were very good at weighing up what were the best on the market and if it hadn't been patented using it himself. And of course it turned out really successful.

Timothy Hackworth's *Sans Pareil*, or Sarsaparilla as I call it, was the only really serious competition that Stephenson faced. Hackworth had just built the most powerful locomotive ever constructed for the Stockton & Darlington and *Sans Pareil* was based on this design. Hackworth must have fancied his chances but his engine wasn't a patch on *Rocket*. The driver and fireman were at opposite ends of the locomotive, heat from the fire passed through the length of the boiler in one direction and back again, using old technology which wasn't as efficient as Stephenson's multi-tube boiler. After a promising start, disaster struck. One of the cylinders split from top to bottom and the water pump failed and they nearly ran out of water, which might have caused an explosion. It must have been difficult for Hackworth to build a locomotive because he didn't have a workshop. Instead he had to get all the parts manufactured outside by independent contractors and the main parts, the cylinders, were actually made by his rival George Stephenson. When the cylinder split, Hackworth were rather bitter because the word sabotage came into it. In any event, it ruined his chance of winning the Rainhill Trials.

Sadly, *Rocket*'s prize turned out to be just a few years' service on the Liverpool & Manchester Railway before it was sold to work as a freight engine. It was, after all, only a prototype and was soon replaced by more refined production models. The problem was that the cylinders were too high up so the whole thing were too top heavy and used to rock about when it was opened up. The young man who had the job of driving the *Rocket* – everybody started early because life expectancy wasn't that long – actually asked the management if he could go back on one of the beam engine type jobs that crawled along at unbelievable speed of four or five miles an hour. The 30-mph *Rocket* was a bit nerve-racking for him.

Reporting on the Rainhill Trials, the *Scotsman* said, 'The experiments at Liverpool have established principles which will give a greater impulse to civilization than it has ever received from any single cause since the press first opened the gates of knowledge to the human species at large.' *Rocket* marked one of the key advances in railway technology. The new features that Stephenson had put into his engine were to become standard for all steam locomotives. 'Until Stephenson came along with *Rocket*,' Fred said, 'everything else had been a beam engine on wheels. *Rocket* was the future – the first steam locomotive as we know them – the granddaddy of them all.' Stephenson had built a prototype that was capable of development. It paved the way for every other steam locomotive right up to the 1960s. It also confirmed him as one of the leading engineers of his age and a major engineering contractor for the emerging railway network.

The Liverpool & Manchester Railway was the biggest railway engineering project ever undertaken up to this point. It was opened on 15 September 1830 in the presence of the Duke of Wellington. George Stephenson was the driver for the first journey on an engine called *Northumbrian* but the day was marred by tragedy, as Fred recounted:

On the opening day they had a disaster along the route – the very first railway disaster on record. The locomotives were pulling carriages with passengers and halfway along they alighted to stretch their legs. The signal was given to get back on and continue on the journey towards Manchester and a local MP called William Huskisson managed to get in front of *Rocket* and it ran over his leg. They unhooked *Rocket*, put him on the tender and sped off to Manchester, but I'm afraid it was too late and poor Mr Huskisson died. At the side of the track there is a monument in memory of him.

The Liverpool & Manchester Railway was the first genuine modern railway; not just a freight line on to which passengers were admitted like the Stockton & Darlington. The new line was an immediate success and was soon followed by other railway schemes that were to see the major British towns and cities linked by rail by the middle of the century. George Stephenson, self-educated, barely literate and cantankerous, had made his mark on history. He now devoted his whole time to building railways, assisted by his son, Robert, who eventually took over the business from him. For the next 15 years, George was involved in most of the railway schemes of the time and he continued to work on improving the quality of the locomotives used on the railway lines he constructed. Manchester became the first great railway centre and lines were built in all directions. An important consequence of Stephenson's involvement and his vision of a national, unified rail network was the adoption of his 4-foot 8½-inch gauge as standard.

Stephenson's involvement in other projects had begun while work was still in progress on the Liverpool & Manchester Railway. In addition to the Bolton & Leigh Railway he was also invited to survey the line for a proposed railway between Leicester and Swannington. When he'd completed the survey, the men behind the scheme told him they were having difficulty raising the finance for the line. 'Don't worry,' Stephenson said, 'I will raise the money for you in Liverpool.' He knew that if he said he supported the scheme, the merchants who had backed the Liverpool & Manchester would invest in this one. The result was that in a short time he returned with the backing.

Of the numerous projects that followed upon the completion of the Liverpool & Manchester line, the one for a railway between London and Birmingham was the most important. At a meeting of the promoters to decide on the appointment of the engineer for the railway there was strong backing for George Stephenson, but, in spite of the reputation he brought with him, some were not convinced that he had the management skills for such a major project and they wanted to bring in another engineer to work with him. When the offer was made to him that he should be joint engineer he asked for time to consider the proposal and discuss it with his son. George was in favour of accepting, but Robert could see there would be problems, particularly because he knew how difficult it was for his father to make the compromises that would be needed when working with somebody else, so he advised him to turn down the offer. When George returned to the committee to announce his decision, however, they decided to appoint him the engineer of the undertaking in partnership with his son. George and Robert Stephenson readily accepted an offer that put them in charge of the biggest and most prestigious railway project so far undertaken. Work on the line was carried out by Robert while his father kept a watching brief and got involved with other railway projects. These included the Grand Junction between Warrington and Birmingham, and a line between Manchester and Leeds.

Stephenson also superintended the Manchester & Leeds project with Thomas Gooch, the brother of Daniel (see Chapter 6), as engineer. Predictions were made that the line through the Pennines could never succeed. There was a general feeling that not even the greatest engineering skills would be sufficient to construct a railway through such a difficult terrain of hills and hard rocks. People said that, even if it could be done, the cost would be ruinous. The project was dogged by problems and, as a result, went over budget. The most daunting job was the construction of the 2,869-yard Summit Tunnel, near Littleborough. The tunnel had to be dug out of solid rock and over 1,000 navvies were employed on its construction for nearly four years. They used 23 million bricks to line it and 8,000 tons of cement. Thirteen stationary engines and about 100 horses were also employed in drawing the earth and stone out of the shafts. When it was nearing completion, there was a rumour that it had fallen in and buried a number of workmen. Stephenson went to investigate. He went into the tunnel with over 50 navvies, each bearing a torch. After walking about half a mile, they arrived at the scene of the 'frightful accident', about which so much alarm had been spread, but all that was visible was a certain unevenness of the ground. The walls and the roof were still as perfect as in any other part of the tunnel.

Throughout the 1830s Stephenson was involved with other projected railways all over Britain. He surveyed several lines in the neighbourhood of Glasgow, and routes along the east coast from Newcastle to Edinburgh with a view to completing the link with London. By this time Isambard Kingdom Brunel had appeared on the scene and was advocating a novel system, the atmospheric railway, which dispensed with the locomotive altogether. The promoters of the railway in the North East heard about the system and expressed an interest in it, but Stephenson dismissed it as humbug. He was proved right when Brunel went ahead with it in Devon and it proved to be a disaster.

Among the other projects George was involved with was a projected line between Chester and Holyhead, and plans for the west coast line to Scotland between Lancaster and Carlisle. Because of the amount of parliamentary business involved with proposals for new lines, the Stephensons also found it necessary to set up an office in London in 1836. Between 1834 and 1837 Stephenson travelled more than 20,000 miles by post chaise and spent six months out of the three years in London. Many nights he had to snatch his sleep while travelling in his chaise; and at break of day he would be at work, surveying until dark. His correspondence increased so much that he found it necessary to engage a private secretary, who accompanied him on all his journeys. To compensate for his dislike of writing letters, he developed great skill in dictating them. On one occasion his secretary said he dictated reports and letters for 12 continuous hours. In addition to running his own railway and colliery businesses he was also frequently called upon to inspect and report upon colliery works, salt works and engineering works.

As well as his journeys around Britain, on more than one occasion Stephenson was called abroad on railway business. As the world's leading railway engineers, George Stephenson and his son were consulted by King Leopold of Belgium on the best plans for the country's rail network. This led to several visits to assist Belgian engineers and the first line in Belgium opened in July 1835 with two Newcastle-built locomotives, one named *Stephenson*, providing the motive power. Father and son were invited to the opening and the King said he was honoured to meet such a famous engineer. He then appointed George Stephenson a Knight of the Order of Leopold and Robert was given a similar honour. By this time Stephenson had moved from the North East and was living at Alton Grange, near Leicester, with his second wife, Betty. But he spent so much time travelling about from one committee of directors to another, inspecting work in progress on the various lines and visiting the locomotive works in Newcastle, that he often did not see his home for weeks on end.

With the opening of the London & Birmingham Railway in 1838, the main system of railway communication between London, Liverpool and Manchester was open to the public. Many other openings of railways constructed or supervised by George Stephenson took place about the same time. The Birmingham & Derby line was opened for traffic in August 1839; the Sheffield & Rotherham in November 1839; and in the course of the following year, the Midland, the York & North Midland, the Chester & Crewe, the Chester & Birkenhead, the Manchester & Birmingham, the Manchester & Leeds and the Maryport & Carlisle railways were all opened to the public in whole or in part. The ceremonies that accompanied the opening of these lines usually concluded with a public dinner; and in the course of the speeches that followed, Stephenson would revert to his favourite topic – the difficulties he had encountered in the promotion of the railway system and the establishment of the superiority of the locomotive in the early days.

One of Stephenson's favourite projects was the Midland Railway, which he was involved with in the late 1830s. It formed part of the great main line that was being built in stages between London and

Edinburgh and it passed through several rich mining districts. In 1837, when the mile-long tunnel was being bored under Clay Cross in Derbyshire, coal was discovered in commercial quantities. Stephenson was well aware of the potential of this find and with his eye for a business opportunity he decided that, if mines were opened there, the railway would provide the means of transporting the coal to the Midlands and London. In order to exploit the opportunity he set up a new business, George Stephenson & Company, and it didn't take much persuasion to get some of his Liverpool friends to join him in a coal-mining venture. A lease was taken on the Clay Cross estate and mining operations were begun there.

Stephenson was now a wealthy man and in 1838 he purchased Tapton House, a Georgian mansion near Chesterfield. At the same time he went into partnership with George Hudson and Joseph Sanders and together they opened coal mines, ironworks and lime-stone quarries in the area. Their great limeworks, close to Ambergate station on the Midland Railway, produced more than 200 tons a day when it was in full operation. The limestone was brought on a tramway from the village of Crich two or three miles away and the coal was sup-plied from his adjoining Clay Cross Colliery. It was a busy time for Stephenson. Besides directing the mining operations at Clay Cross, the establishment of the lime kilns at Ambergate and the construction of the extensive railways still in progress, he occasionally paid visits to Newcastle, where his locomotive works was in full production. At the same time, his services were very much in demand at meetings of mechanics' institutes held throughout the North. From his earliest days he had taken an active interest in these institutions and it was now felt to be an honour to secure Mr Stephenson's presence at any public meetings held for the promotion of popular education. He hadn't learned to read until he was 23, so now in his later years he always encouraged young men to attend night classes.

Throughout this time he continued to make improvements in locomotive design. In the next generation of locomotives after *Rocket*, the angle of the cylinders was lowered so that it was closer to the horizontal and the weight of the engines was increased. As railway mania took a grip on the country many wild ideas were expressed about railway speed, with some people claiming that a speed of 100 mph was practicable. Not many years earlier Stephenson had been pronounced insane for stating his conviction that an engine could run at 12 mph. But now that he had greatly exceeded that speed, he was thought behind the times because he recommended the rate be restricted to 40 mph. There were, he felt, limits to the strength of iron, whether it was manufactured into rails or locomotives, and he believed there was a point at which both rails and wheels would break.

The end of George Stephenson's active career as an engineer coincided with Queen Victoria's accession to the throne, but it continued to give him great pleasure to follow his son's progress. Robert was now one of the world's leading railway engineers in his own right and George took great interest in his designs, paying frequent visits to Conwy and to Menai to see the development of his bridges there. Towards the end of his life, he withdrew from the active pursuit of his profession almost entirely, devoting himself chiefly to his extensive collieries and limeworks. In 1847 he became the first president of the Institution of Mechanical Engineers. His support for this fledgling institution in the last year of his life was a final and lasting legacy to his chosen profession. At home he lived the life of a country gentleman, enjoying his garden and grounds, and indulging his love of nature, which through all his busy life had never left him. He also owned a small farm where he experimented with stock breeding and with new types of manure and animal food. In this field he was very much a man of his time, doing things that would have earned him a bad press today, including his development of a method of fattening chickens in half the usual time by shutting them in dark boxes after a heavy feed.

Stephenson's second wife, Elizabeth, died in 1845. It had been a long and happy marriage but he was to marry for a third time. Ellen Gregory had been his housekeeper at Tapton. They were wed in February 1848 but later in that year, while returning from a visit to Spain, he contracted pleurisy and never completely recovered. Nevertheless, as late as 26 July he felt sufficiently well to attend a meeting of the Institution of Mechanical Engineers at Birmingham and to read the members his paper 'On the Fallacies of the Rotatory Engine'. It was to be his last appearance before them. Shortly after his return to Tapton, he had an attack of fever. He seemed to recover but then suffered a sudden effusion of blood from the lungs and died on 12 August 1848 at the age of 67.

George Stephenson is known as 'the father of the railways' for building the first lines from Stockton to Darlington and Liverpool to Manchester and for designing the first truly successful steam locomotive. He was a man of vision who took the lead in turning the steam locomotive into a practical means of hauling coal and passengers over long distances. But it was his son, Robert, who would go on to make even greater advances, refining the primitive, spindly-looking engines that he had built for his father and turning them into big, powerful engines capable of transporting hundreds of people the length and breadth of the country at high speeds.

2

Robert Stephenson
1803–1859
The First Engineering Millionaire

In the early years of Queen Victoria's reign, Robert Stephenson was in the forefront of creating a railway network that was to transform the lives of millions. By the 1840s the small workshops that had been set up by men like the Stephensons were getting bigger and more industrialized. Their Forth Street Locomotive Works at Newcastle where Rocket *had been built was expanding rapidly and was the leading place when it came to the development of the steam locomotive. Robert Stephenson soon turned it into the biggest locomotive manufacturer in the world. Customers from far and wide would come here to discuss their requirements with him. Rapid advances were made in a very short time and not just in locomotive-building. Robert Stephenson and his company also built the lines and the bridges, and all the engineering works involved in the construction of a full-size railway. He built several famous bridges including the Victoria Bridge in Berwick-on-Tweed; the Britannia and Conwy bridges, tubular girder structures in North Wales; two bridges across the Nile in Egypt; and the Victoria Bridge, which spans the St Lawrence in Montreal. Newcastle High Level Bridge stands to this day, carrying road and rail traffic on its two decks. It's the last and greatest monument of cast-iron bridge construction; a symbol of the highest engineering skill of the time. Really it's a credit to him.*

Robert Stephenson was the only son of George Stephenson and many of the achievements credited to his father, such as the building of *Rocket*, were, in reality, the joint effort of father and son. Like his father he was an engineering genius, but unlike George he had the benefit of a full education.

He was born on 16 October 1803 close to the colliery at Willington Quay where his father, George, worked. The following year the family moved to Killingworth when George became an enginewright at the local colliery. Robert's mother died of consumption at Killingworth in 1806 and from then on he was looked after by his father, whose main concern was his son's education. While working on the pithead at Killingworth, George often thought about times he had been held back in life because of his own lack of schooling; and he decided that nothing should be spared to give his son the best education possible. As soon as he was old enough, Robert was sent to the school at Long Benton, which was run by a man called Rutter, the parish clerk, but the boy was soon helping his father at the colliery and could be seen most mornings laden down with picks to be sharpened at the local black-smith's shop before he went to school.

George might not have been educated himself but he knew exactly what he wanted for his son. He was aware that in a rapidly changing world, for a man to be able to make the most of the opportunities on offer he would have to be well educated. The education Rutter could give, however, was very limited and George wanted better for his son. George Stephenson's growing success as a locomotive engineer meant that he could afford to pay for Robert to have a private education, so when he was 12 he was sent to Mr Bruce's school in Percy Street, Newcastle. Robert's classmates were all the sons of well-to-do families. He had to walk ten miles each day and eventually his father felt it was too much for the young boy, so he bought him a donkey. He rode into Newcastle on it every day with his bag of books slung over his shoulder. Robert was a shy, unsophisticated country lad who spoke with a broad accent, and the other boys at the school teased him. But as a scholar he was steady and diligent, and his master would often hold him up to the time-wasters of the school as an example of good behaviour and hard work. At home in the evening he gave his father lessons, helping him to achieve the education he had never had the opportunity to acquire in childhood. The boy made particularly good progress in mathematics, and many years later he said, 'It was to Mr Bruce's tuition and methods of modelling the mind that I attribute much of my success as an engineer.'

While he was at the Bruce Academy, Robert became a member of the Newcastle Literary and Philosophical Institute, and any spare time he had during his days in the town he would spend there. When he went home in the evening, he would tell his father all about the things he had read. They built a sundial together, which they placed above the front door of the cottage. Throughout this time George would give his son practice in reading plans and drawings without reference to the written descriptions. He used to say, 'A good plan should always explain itself.' Placing a drawing of an engine or machine in front of his son he would say, 'Describe that to me; the arrangement and the action.' Soon Robert was able to read a drawing as easily as he could read a page of a book. Father and son both profited from this practice in later life, and both were able to understand the details of even the most complicated mechanical drawing.

Robert left the academy in the summer of 1819, and was apprenticed to Nicholas Wood, the manager of Killingworth Colliery. The aim of this apprenticeship was to learn the business and workings of the colliery. He served for three years and during this time he became familiar with all aspects of underground work. The practice he had begun with his father when he was at school continued and most evenings were devoted to reading and study. Friends who used to drop in at the cottage remembered the animated discussions they had, especially about the developments that were being made on the steam locomotive. If anything, the son was even more enthusiastic than the father on this subject. Robert would suggest numerous alterations and improvements in details, while his father would offer every possible objection to them. But George was proud of the progress his son had made and was excited that he was showing so much enthusiasm for the locomotive and the development of railways. The result was that in 1821, at the age of 18, Robert left the colliery to join his father and help him survey the proposed Stockton & Darlington line. He was still officially an apprentice at the colliery, working under Nicholas Wood, but his health was poor and Wood released him from the heat and dust of the colliery to work outdoors on what was to prove one of the most important projects of the age.

Remembering the disadvantages he'd experienced in his work through his ignorance of practical chemistry, George wanted to make sure that his son had as complete a scientific education as his own means could afford. He believed that a proper training in technical science was indispensable to success in the higher walks of the engineer's profession; so in October 1822 he sent him to Edinburgh University to study science. Robert took careful notes of all the lectures and, when he returned to Killingworth, read them to his father. He took a special interest in geology, but generally he wasn't very impressed by university. For him university was all about acquiring knowledge that didn't have any practical application. Fred was always dismissive of this sort of knowledge too. He was a firm believer in the principle that knowledge of mechanics and engineering should be learned on the shop floor and out on site, and this is exactly what Robert Stephenson wanted. Towards the end of the summer of 1823, therefore, the young student returned to Killingworth. The six months' study had cost his father £80; but George felt this was amply repaid by the greater scientific knowledge Robert had gained and it was now time for him to get some more hands-on experience.

In the same year that George Stephenson was made engineer of the Stockton & Darlington Railway, 1823, Robert joined with his father and Edward Pease to form a company to make locomotives. He was still only 19 years of age when the Robert Stephenson & Company works was founded on South Street, within the new industrial area around Forth Street in Newcastle upon Tyne. The name of the company says a lot about the faith George had in his son's abilities. The building of the workshop, which went on to become one of the most famous establishments in the history of railways, was begun in 1824 and Robert became the managing partner. However, Robert left the works when the Colombian Mining Association offered him a job in Mariquita, where he was to take charge of engineering operations at their silver mine. It seems a strange decision and the precise reasons for his departure are not known. Whether he'd fallen out with his father or whether he just wanted to gain further experience elsewhere is not clear. George Stephenson was certainly strongly opposed to the venture. His son had shown strength of character as manager of the works and he felt his presence was essential there. But travel fascinated Robert and he insisted on taking the job. George even questioned the move on medical grounds, because of Robert's constitution, but his physician said he would thrive, especially with the change of climate.

Robert Stephenson left England for Colombia in June after finishing the designs for the Brusselton stationary engines for the Stockton & Darlington Railway. He landed at La Guaira, on the north coast of Venezuela, and from there had to travel by mule over 1,200 miles to his destination on the eastern slopes of the Andes. When his party of miners arrived from England, they were a rough, drunken crowd from Cornwall. He set them to work at the Santa Anna mine but the captain of the miners was hostile and insubordinate. He quarrelled and fought with the men, who were also insolent to Stephenson himself. The captain told Stephenson that because he was a north-country man and not born in Cornwall, he couldn't possibly know anything about mining.

The working atmosphere was not pleasant and Stephenson became ill, but he stuck to his post. The yield of silver was not as good as had been expected and Stephenson calculated that it would take three years of costly operations before the mines would be productive. He decided to leave at the end of his three-year engagement, and communicated his decision to the directors in London. They tried to persuade him to stay on but his father said that he needed his son's assistance, and that he must return. At the same time, Edward Pease also wrote to Robert urging him to come home.

On his way back to England Stephenson had to wait at the port of Cartagena for a ship. While he was there he saw two strangers, both of whom were English. One was a tall, gaunt man, who was shabbily dressed and looked poverty-stricken. When Stephenson enquired who the man was he found out it was none other than Richard Trevithick, who had played such an important part in the early development of the steam engine. Trevithick was returning home penniless from the silver mines of Peru and Stephenson lent him £50 to enable him to reach England. Stephenson left Cartagena on a brig bound for New York but suffered near-disaster when it was wrecked. Fortunately it was within sight of land and he, along with all the other passengers, was rescued. He then took a trip to Niagara Falls and arrived back in Liverpool in November 1827.

When he got back to Newcastle he found the finances of the factory were not in a healthy state. During the time he had been in South America it had operated at a loss. Edward Pease was disheartened by the whole business and wanted to retire, but George Stephenson was unable to buy him out. The company carried on in the hope that the locomotive might yet be established as a practical and economical means of transport, but this was far from certain. Robert Stephenson immediately conducted an inquiry into the workings of the company. He unravelled the accounts, which had fallen into confusion during his father's absence while he was directing the building of the Liverpool & Manchester line, and he soon succeeded in getting the affairs of the factory on to a more healthy footing. Before leaving for Colombia, he had met Fanny Sanderson, the daughter of Mr John Sanderson of Broad Street, London. In 1828, he proposed to her and they married on 17 June 1829 in London. They set up home together in Newcastle but Fanny died in 1842. The couple had no children and Stephenson never remarried.

With Robert Stephenson back in charge at the Forth Street Works the main task was to design and build an engine that would win the Rainhill Trials. Robert began work on the *Rocket* locomotive. Throughout all the discussions that were taking place about the kind of power to be used on the Liverpool & Manchester Railway, George Stephenson was in constant communication with his son, who made frequent visits to Liverpool to assist his father in the preparation of his reports to the board on the subject. They also had many conversations as to the best way to increase the power and perfect the mechanism of the locomotive. Henry Booth, the treasurer of the Liverpool & Manchester Railway, contributed to these discussions and he came up with an idea for a multi-tubed boiler. Copper tubes running the whole length of the boiler would, he suggested, greatly increase the efficiency and power of the engine. At the works Robert supervised every detail of the building of the engine and when it was completed he tested it on the Killingworth Waggonway. Here it achieved a top speed of 12 mph while pulling a tender and 5 wagons carrying 40 men. It was a very satisfactory performance and after the test run he took it back to Forth Street. Here it was dismantled, loaded on to horse-drawn wagons and taken by road to Carlisle, where it was loaded on to a steamship bound for Liverpool.

Robert's abilities as an engineer were clearly demonstrated by the success of *Rocket* at the Rainhill Trials in October 1829, where she outperformed all the competition. Her basic design principles had been ground-breaking, particularly the multi-tube boiler that greatly reduced the chances of the engine running out of steam, and were included in all the steam locomotive designs that followed. Orders for more locomotives from the innovative engineer soon came in and Stephenson went on to build for the Bolton & Leigh Railway, the Liverpool & Manchester and the Canterbury & Whitstable Railway. For this last he built *Invicta*, a locomotive of the *Rocket* type, with tubes in the boiler surrounded by water, a blast pipe to send exhaust steam up the chimney and connecting rods that created a direct drive from the cylinders to the front wheels.

By 1830, around 100 locomotives had been built in Britain and most of these were of the type used in the Rainhill Trials, but Robert Stephenson was taking a major step forward in locomotive design, as Fred explains:

Robert Stephenson introduced the 2-2-0 Planet class of locomotive. The first one, *Planet*, was delivered to the Liverpool & Manchester in 1830. The main problem of the period was that they couldn't make really big castings. So, they tended to make frames for steam engines of one sort or another out of two big plates of iron sandwiched with oak or some form of hardwood in between, and lots of nuts and bolts through to make it strong as well as slightly flexible. The Planet class of engine had the cylinders on the inside, underneath the smoke box, and the wheels and connecting rods were laid horizontal along the bottom. This meant that the cylinders, connecting rods and valve gear were all inside the frames, giving the whole thing a much neater and more compact layout.

Another new feature was that the boiler was carried on a wooden platform outside the engine. This enabled the first Planet, which was a passenger engine, to be easily converted to a heavy goods locomotive by changing from 5-foot driving and 3-foot carrying wheels to 2 pairs of coupled 4-foot 6-inch wheels. The coming of the Planet class meant the emergence of the steam engine as it was to develop over the next 100 years.

Robert Stephenson & Co. in Newcastle upon Tyne provided engines for countries all around the globe, including some of the first locomotives for railways in Germany, Russia and the United States. Before long, other people jumped on the bandwagon. In Bolton, Hick Hargreaves & Co. made locomotives under licence from Stephenson for the American railway builders. The small workshops Stephenson had set up around Forth Street were getting bigger and more industrialized and the Robert Stephenson & Co. Engine Works was expanding all the way up the street. Customers from far and wide came here to discuss their requirements with Mr Stephenson.

Progress demanded more powerful locomotives and, for the comfort of the travelling public, more stability. To meet this need, in 1841 Robert Stephenson developed a locomotive with longer framing and a longer firebox. These 'long-boilered' locomotives had all the axles in front of the firebox. They also had inside frames of iron plate and the inside cylinders shared a common steam chest between them, which had the effect of making it a better steamer. Stephenson added another set of wheels, so the engines now had six wheels and went quite fast. The resulting locomotive, the Patentee 2-2-2 Type, was standard for the next

40 years and used extensively in Europe. The North Eastern Railway, which had succeeded the Stockton & Darlington, had 125 long-boilers in use. The design was suitable for carrying passengers or goods, but the short wheelbase, dictated by the turntables then in use, increasingly made it unsafe for the travelling public.

In spite of this, up until the 1950s there were engines still running which had been made in the 1890s and were basically the same design. Visitors can see the sort of long-boiler locomotive that would have been built at the Forth Street Works at the National Railway Museum in York. The long-boiler main-line tender engine on display there was built to a design that had been patented by Robert Stephenson. A replica of *Rocket* stands close by and it's amazing to see the massive advances that were made in locomotive design in little more than ten years.

In 1842, two of Stephenson's employees, William Williams and William Howe, designed a simplified version of the complex valve gear that had been first used on the Patentee class. It became known as Stephenson's link motion and the importance of its invention has been compared to that of Watt's parallel motion. It was a simple arrangement of rods and links that enabled the driver to reverse the locomotive by moving a single lever and, by adjusting the same lever, to vary the moment when the steam supply to the cylinder was cut off. This brought about great economies in steam consumption and consequently in fuel. Stephenson was delighted with the invention, saying that 'the contriver of it should be rewarded'. In spite of this the patent was taken out in the name of Robert Stephenson & Co., not Williams and Howe. The mechanism proved so effective that it was soon adopted on all locomotives and was still the most popular type of valve gear at the end of the century.

By the early years of Queen Victoria's reign the steam locomotive had become a highly refined machine, fast, reliable and powerful, with most of the features that were destined to remain until the end of the age of steam on the railways. They were everything that the visionary George Stephenson and his talented son had believed they would be and the railways they ran on had rapidly gained acceptance as a

An early trade card advertising Robert Stephenson & Co. (top) – the first locomotive works in the world – based at Forth Street, Newcastle (above)

swift and efficient mode of transport. The railways had come to stay.

The Liverpool & Manchester Railway had been an impressive engineering achievement but its real significance lay in the economic effect of the transport revolution that followed. While work on the line was still in progress George Stephenson had been consulted about a proposal for a short railway between Leicester and the coalfields in the western part of the county, at Swannington. In 1830 he was invited to take on the post of engineer for the line, but as he already had 30 miles of railway in hand he recommended Robert for the job. So Robert Stephenson, at 27 years of age, was installed as engineer for the line and began the construction of the railway, which was about 16 miles in length.

The works were comparatively easy, except at the Leicester end, where the young engineer encountered his first difficult bit of tunnelling. The line passed underground for 1¾ miles, and 500 yards of its course lay in loose dry sand. To overcome the problem he constructed a wooden tunnel to support the soil while the brickwork was built. While work was in progress, Robert kept up a regular correspondence with his father in Liverpool, consulting him on all points on which his greater experience would be valuable. Until this time he had always been in the shadow of his illustrious father but he was about to come into his own. His big breakthrough came later that year when a group of Birmingham businessmen approached George Stephenson about the possibility of building a railway to link Birmingham with London. Stephenson advised them on the route that the railway should take and gave the job of surveying it to Robert. But the line, like the Liverpool & Manchester, was very strongly opposed, especially by landowners. Public meetings were held in all the counties the line would pass through. At all of these the project was denounced, and strong resolutions were passed against it. The opposition was so powerful that it was only with the greatest difficulty that an accurate survey of the line could be made. Much of the work had to be done at night. One clergyman made such confrontational demonstrations of his opposition that it was only possible to survey his property when he was otherwise engaged in the pulpit.

Robert Stephenson was not deterred by this level of opposition and his application to the job was so great that he is said to have walked the whole distance between London and Birmingham more than 20 times during the course of the survey. When the Bill for the railway went before the committee of the House of Commons in 1832, the need for improved communications between London and Birmingham was clearly demonstrated and the Bill was passed. It was then sent to the House of Lords, and the promoters had cause for concern when they found that many of the lords who were to decide on the Bill's fate were the very landowners who were so opposed to the line. However, the supporters of the railway circumvented this obstacle by paying their lordships off. It meant that the landowners were paid three times the original estimate, some £750,000 in total. A lot of the funding came from Lancashire, where great profits were being made from the cotton industry.

With the Bill safely through both houses, contractors were brought in and construction work started in 1833. Stephenson, who was still only 30 years of age, was given the post of chief engineer and moved to London with his wife, Fanny. He concerned himself with every aspect of the work except the actual organization of the labour force, which he left to contractors. This was the way of working favoured by other railway engineers throughout the land. But, even with this level of delegation, Stephenson was still very hands-on. F. R. Condor, an engineer who worked on the project, said, 'Robert Stephenson almost lived on the line. In the earlier days he charmed all those who came into contact with him. Kind and considerate to his subordinates, he was not without occasional outbursts of fierce northern passion.'

Stephenson faced many seemingly insurmountable problems in building the 112½-mile line, mainly because his route crossed a series of valleys separated from each other by ridges. His principal objective was to make the line as flat as possible, crossing the valleys as high up and the hills as low down as possible. This meant that the high ground had to be cut into and the earth that was taken out was used to build embankments. In some places, open cuttings were made through the high ground; in others, it was necessary to bore tunnels with deep cuttings at each end. The tunnels presented particular problems as they had to be driven through unknown strata, and miles of underground excavation had to be carried out in order to form a level road from valley to valley. The survey that Stephenson had done had given him a good idea of the problems he would have to face but even this, combined with all the practical knowledge of tunnelling he had gained from his early work in the collieries of the North East, could scarcely have prepared him for some of the obstacles he would come across when it came to actually excavating the ground.

The most off-putting excavations Stephenson encountered were those at Tring, Denbigh Hall and Blisworth. At Tring he had to cut an immense 2½-mile chasm across the great chalk ridge of Ivinghoe, with one quarter-mile stretch 57 feet deep. A million and a half cubic yards of chalk and earth were taken out of this cutting by horse-runs and deposited in spoil banks. The Blisworth cutting is 1½ miles long and 65 feet deep in some places. More than a million cubic yards of earth, heavy clay and hard rock had to be dug, quarried and blasted out of it. One-third of the cutting was stone, and beneath the stone lay a thick bed of clay, under which were found beds of loose shale. These were so full of water that constant pumping was required at many points to enable the works to proceed. For a year and a half the contractor who had been brought in for the job contended with these difficulties before he was forced to abandon the venture. Stephenson stepped in and took on the works himself as contractor. Steam engines were set to work to pump out the water and two locomotives were brought in, one at each end of the cutting, to drag away the excavated rock and clay. Some 800 men and boys were employed digging, wheeling and blasting, as well as a large number of horses. The extent of the blasting operations can be gauged from the fact that 25 barrels of gunpowder were used each week and the total quantity needed to form this one cutting was about 3,000 barrels.

At Watford the chalk ridge was penetrated by a tunnel about 1,800 yards long; and at Northchurch, Linslade and Stowe Hill there were other smaller tunnels. But the most difficult undertaking on the whole route was the digging of the 2,400-yard tunnel under the Kilsby Ridge in Northamptonshire. Trial shafts were sunk and at the bottom of them the excavation of the tunnel commenced, but the excavators soon hit a layer of quicksand under a bed of clay 40 feet thick. As fast as the quicksand could be dug out, more flowed in to fill the space, and worse was to follow when the roof suddenly gave way. A torrent of spring water burst into the workings and a party of workmen were lucky to escape on a raft towed by one of the engineers, who managed to swim with a rope in his mouth to the lower end of the shaft. Work was stopped and the contractor was released from his engagement. In spite of this he was so distressed by the disaster that he fell ill and died soon after.

The question now was whether, in the face of such fearsome difficulties, work on the tunnel should proceed or be abandoned. Stephenson sought the advice of his father, who was in favour of pumping out the water from the top with powerful engines erected over each shaft. Robert agreed with his father's recommendation, and although other engineers came out strongly against the scheme the directors authorized him to proceed. Powerful steam engines were ordered to operate the pumps and, protected by them, the workmen went back to building the tunnel. They walled in the most dangerous sections as quickly as possible, and the excavators and bricklayers laboured night and day until this part of the job was finished. The work was difficult and dangerous, and on numerous occasions the bricks were scarcely covered with cement before they were washed clean by streams of water pouring in from overhead. As the work dragged on, Kilsby was renamed Quicksand Hill and seven pumps were at work there night and day. The quantity of water pumped out of the sand bed during eight months of constant pumping averaged 2,000 gallons per minute and this was raised from an average depth of 120 feet. Progress was slow and it took 18 months to complete less than 600 yards of tunnel, but the rest of it, away from the quicksand, was completed in another six.

The difficulties encountered at Kilsby meant that the cost of the line was greatly increased. The original estimate for the tunnel was only £99,000; but before it was finished it had cost nearly £300,000.

The cost of other parts of the line also exceeded the original estimate and before the works were finished the total cost of construction had more than doubled. Very few of the contractors were able to complete their sections without the assistance of the railway company and many became bankrupt. Work on the Kilsby tunnel was not completed until September 1838 so the railway was opened in stages. The first part, between Euston and Hemel Hempstead, opened on 27 July 1837, but because of the delays at Kilsby the full line could not be finished in time for the coronation of Queen Victoria on 28 June 1838. Well aware of the lucrative traffic this event would generate, the company opened the north end of the line between Birmingham and Rugby and the south end from London to Bletchley with a stagecoach shuttle service to link the two sections, which allowed through journeys to be made to London. Complaints from travellers were reported about the slowness of the stagecoaches on this part of the journey compared with the railway.

After battling with engineering, political and commercial problems, Stephenson finally completed the construction of the railway on 17 September 1838. As the Grand Junction Railway had been finished in July 1837, the four major cities in England – London, Birmingham, Manchester and Liverpool – were now linked together. In the end the 112½-mile line had taken 20,000 men nearly five years to build at a total cost of £5,500,000, which works out at a staggering £50,000 a mile. Starting at Birmingham's Curzon Street Station and finishing at Euston Station in London, it was a massive engineering achievement.

The career of George Stephenson was drawing to a close, but as Robert was now firmly established as a leading railway engineer in his own right his father was happy to hand over to him, with the blessing of the companies concerned, nearly all the railway appointments he held. Robert was appointed engineer for the Eastern Counties, the Northern & Eastern and the Blackwall railways, besides many other lines in the Midlands and the South. At one time he was engaged as engineer on no fewer than 33 new schemes. The promoters of these railways thought themselves fortunate if they could secure his services and as a result he was able to name his own terms. His workload was enormous but his income was far greater than anything any previous engineer had earned.

At the time Queen Victoria came to the throne the rapidity of the construction of the railway network was staggering, and a new generation of railway engineers rose to meet the challenge. Joseph Locke, John Rastrick and John Rennie were all engineers whose daring made almost any obstacle seem inconsequential. Stephenson was regarded as the foremost and his achievements were making him one of the great heroes of the Victorian Age. But that was not all; they were also making him wealthy. The man from the poor pitman's cottage in the North East and his wife Fanny were now living comfortably in London, enjoying the lifestyle of rich Victorians. The one thing that marred their happiness was the fact that they had no children. Then, in 1842, Fanny died of cancer. It was a massive blow to Stephenson and he never remarried. But he still had his father, from whom he continued to take much of his inspiration.

All of the leading engineers of the day had dealings with the Stephensons and they provided Robert with competition. But there was one engineer, above all others, who became his greatest rival as well as one of his best friends: Isambard Kingdom Brunel. One of the earliest battles fought between the Stephensons and Brunel was for the railway between Newcastle and Berwick, forming part of the great east coast route to Scotland. As early as 1836, George Stephenson had surveyed two lines to connect Edinburgh with Newcastle, but both projects lay dormant for several years until the completion of the Midland and other main lines as far north as Newcastle.

On 18 June 1844, the Newcastle & Darlington line – an important link in the great railway to the North – was opened. On that day the Stephensons, with a distinguished party of railwaymen, travelled by express train from London to Newcastle in about nine hours. After the opening, the east coast project from Newcastle to Berwick was revived and George Stephenson was called in again to advise the promoters. He once more recommended the route he had previously surveyed and when this was adopted the necessary steps were taken to bring the scheme before Parliament. However, there was another proposal that had Isambard Kingdom Brunel behind it and the Bill for the line was not to be allowed to go through without a fight. Brunel was enthusiastically promoting his idea for atmospheric railways, a completely new system which dispensed with the locomotive altogether. Instead, a tube with a slot in the top ran the length of the track. Each carriage had a piston underneath which went into the tube. Air was sucked out of the tube by stationary steam engines situated beside the rails and this pulled the piston and the train along the track. George Stephenson dismissed the idea as humbug and when Robert looked into the system he said it was no different in principle from the old idea of haulage by cable between stationary engines, except that the rope in this case was made out of thin air. He was sceptical about the system's prospects, but even if it did work, he pointed out that it would have one major disadvantage: any fault anywhere in the system would bring the whole line to a standstill.

Despite these drawbacks the scheme had its supporters. Lord Howick, one of the MPs for Northumberland, believed this was the way forward not just for the Newcastle & Berwick but for railways everywhere. A man of great local influence, he succeeded in forming a powerful confederation of Northumberland's landed gentry to back Brunel's proposals for an atmospheric railway to run through the county. The rival projects went before Parliament in 1845 and the issue was closely contested, but the locomotive triumphed. The Stephensons had argued their case persuasively and their proposals secured the approval of Parliament. When the news reached Newcastle, the workmen from Robert Stephenson & Co., now more than 800 in number, celebrated by walking in procession through the main streets of the city, accompanied by music and banners.

There are no fewer than 110 bridges on the east coast line between Newcastle and Berwick, including Stephenson's Royal Border Bridge at Berwick where the railway crosses the River Tweed into Scotland. The great viaduct is 2,160 feet long and at its highest point it rises 126 feet above the bed of the river. It is a magnificent example of railway engineering, consisting of a series of 28 semicircular arches, each

61 feet 6 inches in span. However, in Fred's view, this wasn't Stephenson's greatest bridge.

Fred believed Stephenson's greatest was the one needed to complete the east coast route from London to Edinburgh: the High Level Bridge at Newcastle upon Tyne. 'Really,' he said, 'it's a monument of the highest engineering skill of the time, the last and greatest example of cast-iron bridge construction and it's still going strong to this day.' A prospectus for the bridge was issued in 1843 with Robert Stephenson named as the consulting engineer, and the project was taken up by the Newcastle & Darlington Railway Company. The major challenge Stephenson faced was to throw a railway bridge across the deep ravine that lies between the towns of Newcastle and Gateshead, at the bottom of which flows the navigable River Tyne. For about 30 years Newcastle Corporation had discussed various methods of improving communications between the towns, so, when the railway company got the go-ahead for their bridge, the local authorities on either side of the river took advantage of the opportunity and insisted on the provision of a road for ordinary vehicles and foot passengers in addition to the railway. It was agreed, therefore, that the bridge would have two decks: the upper one would carry three lines of rails while the lower would carry a roadway. The breadth of the river at the point of crossing is 515 feet, but the length of the bridge and viaduct between the Gateshead station and the terminus on the Newcastle side is about 4,000 feet.

Work began on the bridge in 1845 and the first difficulty Stephenson met was securing a solid foundation for the piers. The dimensions of the piles to be driven were so great that he had to bring in James Nasmyth's new Titanic steam hammer to do the job. Temporary staging was erected for the steam engine and hammer apparatus and Stephenson was present to see the first pile driven on 6 October 1846, to a depth of 32 feet in four minutes flat. When all the piles had been driven and the coffer dams were formed, the water was pumped out with powerful steam engines. However, getting the foundations in for the middle pier proved to be particularly difficult because of quicksand underneath, which meant the water forced itself through as fast as it was removed. This went on for months until

Stephenson came up with a solution, putting large quantities of concrete into the bottom of the coffer dam.

Queen Victoria opened the bridge on 15 August 1849, and a few days later the royal train passed over it, halting for a few minutes to enable Her Majesty to survey the scene below. 'Newcastle on Tyne's High Level Bridge is quite an unusual structure,' Fred said:

It's a two-tier job: the locomotives are on the top and the road traffic is underneath. The most novel feature of the double bridge structure is the way it combines the two principles of the arch and suspension. The railway is carried over the back of six ribbed arches with a span of 125 feet each, while the road is suspended from these arches by wrought-iron vertical rods. Basically it's a collection of cast-iron arches held together by wrought-iron tie rods supported by five sandstone pillars.

As a material for railway engineering on a grand scale like this, cast iron wasn't ideal. A cast-iron beam has great strength in compression but is weak in tension, so Stephenson designed bow and string girders resting on five stone piers 146 feet above the river. This design is calculated to avoid excessive tension, but even so Stephenson was taking no chances. The spans are short and particular care was taken over the casting and testing of all the ironwork. Really it's a great credit to him and his engineering skills.

Stephenson built the Royal Border Bridge over the River Tweed at Berwick, a stone viaduct of 28 spans, for the same line, the viaduct over the estuary of the River Kent at Arnside in Cumbria and another joint road and rail bridge over the River Nene at Sutton Bridge in Lincolnshire. With the advances he had made in locomotive design and his great engineering triumphs such as the High Level Bridge Robert Stephenson had amply repaid his father's investment in his education and the knowledge he had passed on to him. He was a quieter, more thoughtful, less argumentative character than George, who was well liked by most of those who knew him. But it was his father's example of application, industry and thoroughness in all that he undertook that made him the man he was. 'I am fully conscious in my own mind,' Robert said at a meeting of the Institution of Mechanical Engineers at Newcastle in 1858, 'how greatly my civil engineering has been regulated and influenced by the mechanical knowledge which I derived directly from my father; and the more my experience has advanced, the more convinced I have become that it is necessary to educate an engineer in the workshop. That is, emphatically, the education which will render the engineer most intelligent, most useful, and the fullest of resources in times of difficulty.'

One of the characteristics Robert inherited from his father was his dogged determination. It was a quality that Fred greatly admired:

> Robert Stephenson wouldn't let anything stand in his way. In the 1840s he was building the railway from London to Holyhead. When he reached Conwy he not only had a river to cross, which he did with his tubular bridge, but he also had to bypass a castle and get under the medieval town walls. The basic design of his tubular bridge consisted of two rectangular tubes made of wrought-iron rolled plates, which were hand-riveted together. These carried each of the tracks between the masonry abutments. The tubes, which weighed 1,300 tons each, were prefabricated on the shore and floated into position by means of pontoons. When they were under the abutments, the tubes were raised into position by hydraulic presses. The whole thing must have been a heck of a job.

At one point Stephenson said: 'The difficulty we are contending with is much greater than I anticipated but I will never give up.'

George Stephenson had surveyed a line from Chester to Holyhead as early as 1838, but it wasn't until 1844 that the Act was passed to authorize its construction. Robert Stephenson was once again appointed as engineer. The greatest difficulty he faced in building the railway was carrying it across the Menai Strait, which separated the Isle of Anglesey from the North Wales mainland, and across the estuary of the River Conwy. Thomas Telford had already crossed both with suspension bridges, but they were ruled out because a degree of rigidity and strength greater than that of a suspension bridge was considered indispensable for a railway bridge.

Robert had time to consider his options because the Chester end of the railway was completed first. This included a bridge over the River Dee, just outside the city. His first plan was for a five-span brick bridge, but he reduced this to three because of doubts he had about the stability of the river bed to carry the foundations. The river was spanned with cast-iron girders, each 98 feet long. There were four girders to each span, making twelve in all. The Dee Bridge was completed in September 1846 and on 20 October it was inspected and passed for traffic. Passenger trains began using the bridge immediately, until 24 May 1847 when a passenger train bound from Chester to Shrewsbury met with disaster. The train had reached the last of the three spans when the outermost of the girders broke into three pieces. The locomotive driver, sensing trouble, accelerated, but the engine coupling parted and the rest of the train plunged into the river, killing a guard, two coachmen and one passenger, and injuring 16 others.

An inquest was held at Chester and many respected engineers, including Brunel and Joseph Locke, came to give evidence on Stephenson's behalf. But the engineer of the Shrewsbury & Chester Railway said Stephenson's design was at fault and that he should be charged with manslaughter. For an engineer of Stephenson's standing it was a major embarrassment, but what was worse was that he knew it could destroy his career. He was persuaded by the solicitor for the Chester & Holyhead Railway to defend the action on the grounds that the girder had fractured after receiving a heavy blow. It was argued that the fracture had been caused when one of the wheels broke and caused the train to derail. This defence was given added weight by the fact that there had never been any problems with a similar Stephenson-designed bridge spanning the River Tees at Stockton. The jury returned a verdict of accidental death but added that they considered the bridge unsafe and recommended a government inquiry into the safety of similar bridges. Other bridges with cast-iron girders were immediately strengthened and cast iron was soon superseded by the use of wrought iron.

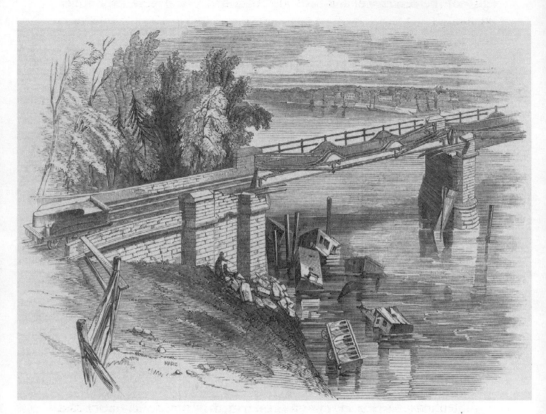

Accident on the Dee Viaduct, Chester

Stephenson's name was cleared, but giving evidence at the trial had proved a harrowing experience. The incident did in fact cast a shadow over his career for a short period, but Robert had inherited his father's gift of perseverance and was determined to put this right. The Britannia Bridge over the Menai Strait and the Conwy Bridge over the River Conwy would give him the chance to do so. They presented him with a formidable engineering challenge.

Stephenson decided early on that the best place for the bridge over the Menai Strait was where the Britannia Rock stood in the middle of the channel. The width of the channel here at high water was about 1,100 feet and the rock provided a convenient base for a central pier. His first idea was to construct the bridge of two cast-iron arches, each spanning 350 feet, but this plan was rejected by the Admiralty, who insisted on limiting the size of the central pier because of shipping passing through the strait. They also specified that there had to be a uniform headway of 105 feet between pier and abutment to allow tall-masted ships to pass underneath, and this ruled out an arched construction. With so many restrictions, Stephenson was faced with the problem of devising some sort of flat girder bridge. It was an issue that would take some time to solve. When the Act authorizing the railway was officially passed in 1845 there was still a gap of five miles in the plans because the question of the Menai crossing remained unanswered.

Stephenson's next idea was for some form of box girder, supported by chains like a suspension bridge. He envisaged that rather than running on top of it, the trains would run inside a huge hollow wrought-iron girder about 25 feet in diameter, making it a tubular bridge. There was, however, a clear problem with the idea. In a proper suspension bridge, deck and chains are both flexible, and the deck rises and falls as the chains expand or contract. There were serious objections to the combination of flexible chains and rigid beams because the beams meant the deck would not be flexible, so he began to consider some form of girder construction that would not need chains. Stephenson, though, was by nature a cautious man and he was worried about the practicality of the scheme. Although there was some understanding of the use of wrought iron in shipbuilding and boiler-making, there was no knowledge of its properties when used as a beam. He therefore brought in two distinguished engineers to act as consultants.

The first, William Fairbairn, was an old friend of his father. An experienced builder of iron ships, he was able to show Stephenson a 220-foot ship propped up at bow and stern but unsupported in the middle. The second, Eaton Hodgkinson, was the foremost authority of the day on the theory of iron beams. He believed that it wouldn't be possible to make the tubes stiff enough to carry the weight of a steam train, so he advised that they should be suspended from chains. Fairbairn, however, expressed the confident view that a tube of wrought iron would possess sufficient strength and rigidity to support a railway train running inside it without the help of chains. Providing the parts were well proportioned and the plates properly riveted, he said, chains would not be needed. Many engineers of the day agreed with Hodgkinson, but Fairbairn argued with great conviction that a tubular wrought-iron beam was the only structure which combined the necessary strength and stability for a railway with the conditions that had been laid down as essential for the protection of the shipping that would pass under the bridge. He needed to get the right cross-section for the tubes, so he set up a series of experiments at his Millwall shipyard. Using models, circular, oval and rectangular wrought-iron beams were loaded at their midpoint until failure occurred.

Stephenson had initially asked for the tubes to be elliptical in section. He believed that this shape would give them the required strength, but when tested the upper surface of the tubes buckled under compression when weight was put on them. After the tests had been carried out, therefore, Fairbairn's preference for a rectangular section large enough for a train to pass through was adopted. In the final experiment, a one-sixth scale model of a tube like this withstood a weight of 86 tons before failing, so the idea that the bridge would need chains was dismissed. Stephenson announced his conclusion to the directors of the railway: in his opinion the most feasible method of bridging the strait at Menai and the river at Conwy was by means of a hollow beam of wrought iron. He then gave instructions to two of his assistants to prepare drawings of such a structure.

While discussions about the tubes were in progress, work began on the masonry of the bridges at Conwy and Menai. The foundation stone of the Britannia Bridge was laid on 10 April 1846, and on 12 May that of the Conwy Bridge was laid. It was decided to build the main tube sections for both bridges on stages along the shore, float them out to the site and then lift them into position on the tall stone towers by hydraulic means. Suitable platforms and workshops were erected at both sites for the punching, fitting and riveting of the tubes. About 1,500 men were employed on the Britannia Bridge alone, and they mostly lived on site in specially erected wooden cottages. In fitting the Britannia tubes together, no fewer than 2 million bolts, weighing around 900 tons in total, were riveted. The iron plates were brought in shiploads from Liverpool, Anglesey marble was shipped in from Penmon and red sandstone from Runcorn, in Cheshire.

The Britannia Bridge consists of two independent, continuous tubular beams, each 1,511 feet in length, and each weighing 4,680 tons. These immense beams are supported on the abutments and on three towers. The central tower, known as the Great Britannia Tower, is 230 feet high and is built on the Britannia Rock in the middle of the strait. The bridge has four spans, two of 460 feet over the water and two of 230 feet over the land. The tubes sit solidly on the central tower, but on the land towers and abutments they lie on roller-beds to allow for expansion and contraction. As the bridge was for a double line of railway track there were four main tube sections and Stephenson decided to join each of these main tube sections not only to each other but also to the two half-sections of tubes built out from the abutments to the land towers. This meant the bridge would have two continuous tubes, each 1,511 feet long, anchored on the central Britannia tower and extending from abutment to abutment and beyond, which contributed greatly to the strength of the structure. To roll large plates or girders was beyond the capacity of the iron industry of the day so the tubes were made entirely from small plates and angle sections riveted together with Fairbairn's recently invented steam-powered riveting machine.

The Conwy Bridge is, in most respects, similar to the Britannia, consisting of two 400-foot tubes, each weighing 1,180 tons, placed side by side. The principle adopted in the construction of the tubes, and the mode of floating and raising them, were nearly the same as at the Britannia Bridge. When it came to getting the tubes into place Stephenson decided to start with the shorter Conwy Bridge. With their movement controlled by cables and manually operated capstans, the great tubes were floated into position from their construction points on the shore by means of pontoons. Hoisting them into place in the recesses in the masonry of the towers was an anxious operation. Stephenson himself directed proceedings, assisted by Brunel and other engineering friends, including the steamship owner Captain Claxton, who had worked with Brunel. George Stephenson was there to view the operations as well. On 16 April 1847 the first tube was raised and lowered successfully on to its permanent bed. The rails were laid along it and, on the 18th, Robert passed through on board the first loco-motive. Work on the second tube was started straight away and it was completed and floated at the end of that same year.

The much more formidable enterprise of floating and fixing the great Britannia tubes was made easier by the experience gained at Conwy. At Menai it had been decided to construct the shorter outer tubes of the bridge on scaffolding in the positions in which they were to remain, and to erect the larger tubes on wooden platforms at high-water mark on the Caernarfon shore. From here they were to be floated out on pontoons. Stephenson superintended the floating of the first of the tubes in person, giving pre-arranged signals from the top of the tube he was standing on. Thousands of spectators lined the shores of the strait as the actual work of hoisting the tube was carried out by a team of sailors under the direction of Captain Claxton. When they got it into place the achievement was greeted by a cannon salute and the cheers of the spectators. This first main tube was floated and raised in June 1849 and the bridge was ready for single-line traffic the following January. The other tubes were then floated and raised, and on 5 March 1850 Stephenson himself put the last rivet in the last tube.

His success here and at Conwy meant much to him after the terrible disaster of the Dee Bridge. He travelled through the completed bridge on 18 March, accompanied by about 1,000 people drawn by three locomotives. The bridge was opened for public traffic that same day. On completion the cost of the whole work was £234,450. In his *Lives of the Engineers* Smiles described the Britannia Bridge:

> One of the most remarkable monuments of the enterprise and skill of the present century ... the result of a vast combination of skill and industry. But for the perfection of our tools and the ability of our mechanics to use them to the greatest advantage; but for the matured powers of the steam-engine; but for the improvements in the iron manufacture, which enabled blooms to be puddled* of sizes before deemed impracticable, and plates and bars of immense size to be rolled and forged; but for these, the Britannia Bridge would have been designed in vain. Thus, it was not the product of the genius of the railway engineer alone, but of the collective mechanical genius of the English nation.

With the exception of the two great bridges, the construction of the Chester to Holyhead line presented no great difficulties other than the terrace that had to be cut under the steep slope of Penmaen Mawr. About midway between Conwy and Bangor, the mountain comes down to the sea in a steep headland. There was not enough space for the line between the mountain and the shore so the rock had to be blasted to form a terrace, and at its steepest point a tunnel had to be cut through the headland itself. These operations proceeded successfully. At the celebration of the opening of the North Wales Railway at Bangor, almost within sight of his iron bridge across the Menai Strait, Robert Stephenson referred to the great advances that had been brought about by the use of iron: 'We are daily producing from the bowels of the earth a raw material, in its crude state apparently of no

* Puddled iron is wrought iron that has been refined with coal as a fuel. It is worked from a bloom, which is a porous mass of iron mixed with slag and other impurities.

Box sections for the Britannia Bridge were first assembled onshore,
before being floated out into position and lifted into place

worth, but which, when converted into a locomotive engine, flies over bridges of the same material, with a speed exceeding that of the bird, advancing wealth and comfort throughout the country. Such are the powers of that all-civilizing instrument, iron.'

When George Stephenson died in 1848, he bequeathed to his son his valuable collieries, his share in the engine manufactory at Newcastle and his large accumulation of savings, which, together with the fortune he had himself amassed by his work for the railway, made Robert an engineering millionaire. In spite of these riches, he continued to live in a quiet and unostentatious way and, although he bought occasional paintings and statues and indulged in the luxury of a yacht, he continued to accumulate wealth rapidly until his death. Robert Stephenson worshipped his father's memory, and was always ready to recognize the major influence he had had on his own achievements as an engineer. 'It was his thorough training,' he said, 'his example and his character, which made me the man I am. It is my great pride to remember that whatever may have been done, and however extensive may have been my own connection with railway development, all I know and all I have done is primarily due to the parent whose memory I cherish and revere.'

With his beloved wife and father both dead, Stephenson was on his own and he concentrated on work as opportunities opened up around the world. In 1851 he was appointed chief engineer for a railway from Alexandria to Cairo. The tubular system he had used for his bridges in North Wales was now applied here when he had to build two bridges across the Nile. One of these, near Benha, consists of eight spans or openings of 80 feet each, with two central spans that form one of the largest swing bridges ever constructed. The total length of the swing-beam is 157 feet and there is a clear waterway of 60 feet on either side of the centre pier. The difference between these bridges and his other tubular bridges consisted in the railway track being carried on top of the tubes instead of inside them. For their construction, workmen, materials and plant were sent out from England. A ferry service was introduced while the bridges were being constructed and it was adapted to take locomotives by having rails laid on the deck. This was the world's first genuine rail ferry.

Stephenson's services were now so much in demand that he was able to be selective and decline some of the new contracts on offer. Of the projects that he did get involved in, one of the most notable was the Victoria Bridge he built over the St Lawrence Seaway in Canada. For many years this was the longest bridge in the world. Another tubular bridge, it was regarded as the greatest work of its kind. The entire bridge, with its approaches, is about 60 yards short of two miles, making it five times longer than the Britannia Bridge. It has 24 spans of 242 feet each, one great central span – an immense bridge in itself – of 330 feet and the railway is carried within iron tubes 60 feet above the level of the St Lawrence.

When Stephenson surveyed the site and began work on it in July 1854, the river was shallow and running over a rock bed, which meant the piers could be constructed without too many problems. However, Stephenson hadn't allowed for the extremes of the Canadian weather. In winter everything froze but in spring, as the snows of winter melted, the swollen river flowed at high speed, bringing chunks of ice with it that crashed into the piers. It meant that Stephenson had to build cutwaters at the foot of each pier to withstand the hammering they were taking from the ice. The weather also led to terrible working conditions. Men suffered from frostbite in the winter and in summer cholera became a scourge of the navvy camps. The work was finally completed way behind schedule, and rising prices resulted in heavy losses for Stephenson. On 17 December 1859 the bridge was taken off the contractor's hands. It was formally opened for traffic early in 1860, though Robert Stephenson would not live to see its completion.

Stephenson's fame had spread far and wide and his services were sought by governments and railway companies all over the world. He was consulted by the King of Belgium on plans for his country's railways and made Knight of the Order of Leopold, just as his father had been. He was also consulted by the King of Sweden about a railway between Christiana and Lake Miösen, and for his services there he was decorated with the Grand Cross of the Order of St Olaf. He also visited Switzerland, Piedmont in Italy and Denmark to advise on their railway systems, and at the Paris Exhibition of 1855 the Emperor of France decorated him with the Legion of Honour in recognition of his public services. At home the University of Oxford made him a Doctor of Civil Laws and in 1855 he was elected president of the Institution of Civil Engineers, an office he held for two years. Stephenson now had success and fame. He'd achieved things and had honours bestowed on him that neither he nor his father could have dreamed possible as they sat together in their pitman's cottage reviewing what Robert had learned at school.

During those later years, Stephenson began to take considerable interest in public affairs and in scientific investigations. In the 1847 General Election he was elected Conservative MP for Whitby. He was on the right wing of the party, which was hostile to free trade, and generally he was opposed to change of any kind. But he didn't take a very active role in the House of Commons and usually contributed only to debates on engineering issues. Like his father before him he was offered a knighthood, and like him he declined it. Father and son were not keen on titles. Both seem to have respected the ordinary working man more than those with wealth and power. Great value was given to his opinion on all engineering matters because of his experience, sound judgement and upright character. As a result he was frequently called upon to act as an arbitrator between contractors and railway companies, or between one company and another. He was always ready to lend a helping hand to a friend or fellow engineer and never allowed petty jealousies to stand between him and his rivals in the engineering world.

Smiles recalled being with Stephenson one evening at his house in Gloucester Square when a note was put into his hands from his friend Brunel, who was engaged in efforts to launch the *Great Eastern*. In the note Brunel asked Stephenson to go down to Blackwall early the next morning to give him the benefit of his judgement. Stephenson was happy to oblige and shortly after six the following morning he was down at the shipyard, where he remained until dusk. About midday, Smiles reported, while Stephenson was superintending the launch operations, the length of timber he was standing on tipped up, and he fell waist deep into the Thames mud. He was dressed as usual without an overcoat, even though it was a bitterly cold day, and had only thin boots on his feet. He was urged to leave the yard and change his clothes or at least to dry himself; but with his usual disregard for his health, he replied, 'Never mind me, I'm quite used to this sort of thing,' and went paddling about in the mud, smoking his cigar, until almost dark, when the day's work was brought to an end. The result of this exposure was an inflammation of the lungs, which kept him in bed for a fortnight.

His attitude to his health may have been cavalier but that was far from the case in his business affairs. Throughout his later years, with characteristic caution, he avoided holding unguaranteed railway shares; and though he built magnificent structures like the Victoria Bridge in Canada he was careful not to invest any part of his own fortune in the ordinary capital of these ventures. In 1845, for example, he had shrewdly foreseen the inevitable crash that would follow the railway mania of that year; and while shares were still at a premium he took the opportunity of selling all that he had. His father was still alive at the time and he urged him to do the same thing, but George's reply was characteristic. 'No,' he said. 'I took my shares for an investment, and not to speculate with, and I am not going to sell them now because folks have gone mad about railways.' In consequence George continued to hold the £60,000 that he had invested in the shares of various railways until his death, when Robert sold them immediately for much less than their original value.

Robert Stephenson had never enjoyed good health and early in 1859 he was advised to retire from business and politics. He set out on a yachting cruise to Norway but on arrival his health had deteriorated so much that he was rushed back to England. By the time he returned, a fatal illness had seized him. He was attacked by congestion of the liver, which manifested itself first as jaundice and then developed into dropsy. Ultimately this condition led to his premature death on 12 October 1859. He was just 56 years old. When he died he was hailed as a national hero and the whole nation mourned him. His funeral cortège passed through Hyde Park on its way to Westminster Abbey, where he was buried by the side of one of the other great engineering heroes of the age, Thomas Telford. The whole route of his funeral procession was lined by silent mourners and in his home country of the North East all shipping lay silent on the Tyne, the Wear and the Tees, work ceased in all the region's towns and flags flew at half-mast. In Newcastle, the 1,500 employees of Robert Stephenson & Co. walked in procession through silent streets to a memorial service.

The Institution of Civil Engineers regarded him as a 'genius' and his achievements were immense. The Forth Street Works was the site of a revolution for its time. Previously engines were constructed by common mechanics in collieries and engine workshops but Robert Stephenson's factory was at the forefront of railway development, creating and requiring specialist mechanics and technical advances. Under his management the factory was a driving force in locomotive construction but as well as building the machines that changed the world, Robert Stephenson left us with engineering wonders that transformed the landscape for ever. To do this, however, he needed to work with other great engineers of the Victorian era like William Fairbairn, the 'man of iron', whose specialist knowledge of iron working and the design of girders capable of bearing great weights were vital in the construction of Stephenson's bridges.

3

William Fairbairn
1789–1874
The Iron Man

William Fairbairn was a Scottish engineer who set himself up as a mill-wright in Manchester. With a partner called James Lillie, he made great improvements to the system of driving textile mills when he invented a system of high-speed transmission. This made use of lightweight line shafting running in self-aligning bearings to replace the old slow-speed power transmissions that had been in place until then. His line shafting was widely copied in other industries, including engineering. He also opened a shipbuilding yard in London where he pioneered the use of wrought iron for hulls. For Stephenson's bridges over the Menai Strait and at Conwy, he designed the rectangular tubes and the hydraulic riveting machines that were partly used for their construction. But for me his greatest claim to fame is that he was the gentleman who invented the Lancashire boiler.

William Fairbairn, an eminent structural engineer, was one of the primary forces in the development and introduction of mechanized manufacturing processes. His high-speed transmission system using light line shafting became widely copied in many industries and the tests he carried out on the strength of wrought-iron structures laid the foundations for much of modern structural engineering theory.

He was born at Kelso in the Scottish Borders on 9 February 1789. His father, Andrew, had been brought up as a farm worker and was an expert ploughman with a lot of practical agricultural knowledge. Fairbairn's first schoolmaster was an old man who went by the name of Bowed Johnnie Kerr, but after a short time he was transferred to the Kelso parish school run by a Mr White, a severe disciplinarian, who administered punishment by cracking his pupils on the head with his knuckles. While at this school the young Fairbairn gained some knowledge of arithmetic and out of school hours he spent his time climbing on the ruined walls of the town's old abbey.

In 1799, when William was ten years old, his father took a job running a farm at Moy in Ross-shire. Belonging to Lord Seaforth of Brahan Castle, it was about 300 acres and situated on the banks of the River Conan, about five miles from Dingwall. The journey to the family's new home was around 200 miles and they travelled there in a covered cart through wild and hilly country. His mother never enjoyed good health and on the journey she was so ill that she had to be lifted in and out of the cart every morning and night. When they reached their destination in October they found the land overgrown and covered with great stones and rocks. The house that was being built for them was not finished and Andrew Fairbairn, with his wife and five children, had to take temporary refuge in a miserable hovel. Their hearts must have sunk when they saw how different the place was to the comfortable house they had left at Kelso. Fortunately they only had to put up with it for around six months until their new house was completed the following spring and Andrew Fairbairn set to work on reclaiming the land. After around two years' labour he had completely changed the face of the farm and in place of stones and brambles there were crops of barley and turnips.

While the family were first living at Moy, none of the boys went to school as they couldn't be spared from all the work that needed to be done on the farm. Those who were too young to work on the land were given jobs around the house, and one of William's duties was to nurse his younger brother Peter, a delicate child who wasn't yet two years old. To relieve himself of the trouble of carrying Peter on his back, William built a little four-wheeled wagon and by attaching a piece of rope to it, he could drag his little brother around. Building the wagon was a difficult task as the only tools he had were a knife and an old saw, but with these and a thin piece of board and a few nails he succeeded in building a serviceable wagon body. His main difficulty was making the wheels, but he overcame this by cutting sections from a small alder tree and boring holes in their centre for the axle with a red-hot poker. His father encouraged him in his endeavours and he soon progressed to building miniature boats, windmills and watermills.

The boys were eventually sent to school at Munlachy, about a mile and a half from the farm. About 40 barefoot boys in tartan kilts and about 20 girls, all from poor backgrounds, attended the school. The schoolmaster, Donald Frazer, was a good teacher but another strict disciplinarian. Under him, however, William made good progress in reading, writing and arithmetic. But his father was not finding his work satisfactory and crop failure in 1801 was a major setback, so after two more years on the farm Andrew Fairbairn decided to move back south with his family. They set sail from Cromarty for Leith in June 1803. They settled back in Kelso and William was placed in the charge of his uncle William, the parish schoolmaster of Galashiels, to receive instruction in book-keeping and land-surveying.

When he was 14 William started his first job on the new bridge that was being built at Kelso by the distinguished engineer John Rennie. One day, however, a barrowload of stone tipped over and fell on William. His leg was severely injured and the accident left him a cripple for several months. At about this time his father took the job of manager of the Percy Main Colliery Company's farm near North Shields and, as soon as William had recovered from his injury, he went to work at the colliery. His first job was to deliver coal to the pitmen's houses, but his Scottish accent and his awkwardness brought a lot of teasing from the pit lads. They were a rough lot and, as boxing was a favourite pastime, the young Fairbairn had to use his fists to earn their respect. Life was tough and he was on the point of leaving the job rather than put up with the constant insults and fights, when he came out on top in an epic bout with one of the colliery's most noted fighters, which brought an end to the persecution.

The following year, at the age of 15, Fairbairn was articled as an engineer for seven years to the owners of Percy Main and placed in the charge of Mr Robinson, the enginewright of the colliery. His starting wage as an apprentice was five shillings (25p) a week, but by working overtime, putting his skills to good use making wooden pit-props and cutting out oak panels for walling the sides of the mine, he was able to increase his earnings greatly, sometimes doubling his wage. This enabled him to make a sizeable contribution to the family income. When he was not working overtime in the evenings, the industrious young Fairbairn spent his time improving his education. He drew up a scheme of daily study: Monday evenings were devoted to mensuration and arithmetic; Tuesdays to history and poetry; Wednesdays to recreation, novels and romances; Thursdays to algebra and mathematics; Fridays to Euclid and trigonometry; Saturdays to recreation; and Sundays to church, Milton and recreation. His father enrolled him in the North Shields Subscription Library, which enabled him to extend the range of his reading, and he devoured anything he could find on scientific matters. He went to the library every other night and soon became a favourite with the librarian's daughter, who let him see all the new publications before they went into general circulation.

Young Fairbairn also devoted some of his spare time to making things, and he developed the art of handling tools. One of the first things he made was a fiddle, and he had ambitions to become a performer. It must have been a reasonable instrument because a professional player offered him twenty shillings (£1) for it. But, although he persevered for some time in trying to play his fiddle, he never succeeded in producing any sort of melody from it, and at length gave up the attempt, convinced that nature had not intended him to be a musician. Long after, when he was married and settled in Manchester, the fiddle, which had been carefully preserved, was taken down from the shelf for the amusement of the children. They were always pleased to see their father's creation, but the instrument was never brought from its place without creating alarm in the mind of their mother lest anybody should hear it. At length a dancing master who was giving lessons in the neighbourhood borrowed the fiddle, and, to the great relief of the family, it was never returned.

Back at the colliery Fairbairn was put in charge of the pumps and the steam engine that provided the power for them. The work was hard, especially in the winter, and the engineer was likely to be drenched with water every time he went down the shaft to regulate the pumps. 'The depth was 150 fathoms,' he recalled, 'with four sets of pumps; and what with broken pump rods and other casualties, I have frequently been suspended by a rope during the winter months, with water pouring on me for seven or eight hours at a stretch, until every limb was numbed with cold.' It was all very tiring but there was no rest on his days off, for Fairbairn continued to apply himself diligently to his reading and study.

While he was working at Percy Main he got to know George Stephenson, who was at that time employed on working the ballast engine at Willington Quay. The two young men, who were nearly the same age, shared a passion for mechanics and they formed a friendship that was to last for the rest of their lives. Stephenson had recently married Fanny Henderson and Fairbairn became a frequent visitor to the comfortable home they had set up at Willington Quay. On summer evenings he would often go over to the quay and take charge of Stephenson's engine to enable him to earn a few extra shillings heaving ballast out of the collier vessels. Fairbairn developed a great admiration for the other man's qualities as a workman and Stephenson's zeal in the pursuit of mechanical knowledge had a lasting influence, encouraging Fairbairn in his efforts to improve himself.

When the young Fairbairn had completed his seven years' apprenticeship at Percy Main, he put his natural flair for engineering to good use and took on small commissions, which helped to broaden his knowledge of all things mechanical. By this time he had decided to leave the colliery and go out into the wider world. He found employment as a millwright in Newcastle and worked on the erection of a sawmill, but he had been there only a few weeks when he was offered more money to work at a sawmill in Bedlington, where he spent the rest of the summer. During his time there he met Dorothy Mar, the youngest daughter of John Mar, a farmer from Morpeth. Miss Mar lived in Bedlington with an elderly lady called Mrs

Barker and William started to visit her at the house.

Work was scarce in the North East, however, and when the job in Bedlington came to an end he set out with a friend to try his fortune in London, where he thought his chances of advancement were greater. He took his leave of Dorothy after 'an interchange of promises of unalterable affection' and with four pounds in his pocket he set off. His companion was David Hogg from Tweedmouth, whom he'd worked with at Bedlington. The cheapest way to get to the capital was to take a passage on a Shields collier and the two young men sailed for the Thames on 11 December 1811. The vessel was very short-handed – its crew consisting of three old men and three boys, with the skipper and mate – so Fairbairn and Hogg had to lend a hand in working her. The weather was stormy and off the Norfolk coast they narrowly escaped shipwreck, but eventually, after 14 days, they reached the Thames and went into the city in search of work. They had only about eight pounds between them, so they needed to find employment quickly and were delighted when they got the promise of a job from John Rennie, the celebrated engineer, whose works were at the south end of Blackfriars Bridge.

Rennie sent the two young men to his foreman, Mr Walker, with a request that he should set them to work, but the foreman referred them to the secretary of the Millwrights' Society. Rennie's workshop was filled with union men and Fairbairn found that it was a closed shop. The workers would not allow anybody, however skilled, to have a job there if they could not produce evidence that they had complied with all the rules of the trade. Describing his first experience of London unionists nearly half a century later, before an assembly of working men at Derby, Fairbairn said:

> When I first entered London, a young man from the country had no chance whatever of success, in consequence of the trade guilds and unions. I had no difficulty in finding employment, but before I could begin work I had to run the gauntlet of the trade societies; and after dancing attendance for nearly six weeks, with very little money in my pocket, and having to 'box Harry' all the time, I was ultimately declared

illegitimate, and sent adrift to seek my fortune elsewhere. There were then three millwright societies in London: one called the Old Society, another the New Society, and a third the Independent Society. These societies were not founded for the protection of the trade, but for the maintenance of high wages, and for the exclusion of all those who could not assert their claims to work in London and other corporate towns. Laws of a most arbitrary character were enforced, and they were governed by cliques of self-appointed officers, who never failed to take care of their own interests.

With very little chance of work in their chosen trade in the capital the two frustrated youths decided to try their fortune in the country, and headed north before daylight the next morning. After nearly eight hours' walking through slush and snow they reached Hertford. They were soaked to the skin and the only sustenance they'd had was a penny bread roll and a pint of ale between them. They immediately sought out a master millwright and applied for work with him, but he had no vacancies. Taking pity on them, the millwright offered them half a crown (12½p) to get themselves some food and lodging, but Fairbairn had an independent spirit and didn't want to take charity, so he turned the offer down. Weary, wet and disheartened, the two turned into Hertford churchyard and rested for a while on a tombstone. Fairbairn's dispirited companion wanted to go back to London but Fairbairn himself remonstrated, saying, 'It's no use lamenting; we must try what we can here. Then if the worst comes to the worst, we can enlist; you are a strong chap – they'll soon take you; and as for me, I'll join too; I think I could fight a bit.' With this the pair decided to find lodgings in the town for the night, and begin their search for work afresh the following morning.

Next day, when they were passing along one of the back streets of Hertford, they came across a wheelwright's shop and enquired within for work. The wheelwright told them he didn't think there were any jobs in the town, but if they went on to Cheshunt they might find work at a windmill. The millwright there was under contract to get the mill finished in three weeks and was desperate for extra hands. They set out immediately, walking the seven miles to Cheshunt, and succeeded in getting jobs. The work there lasted for a fortnight, after which, with nearly three pounds in their pockets, Fairbairn and Hogg went back to London, where they both eventually managed to find regular employment.

Fairbairn's first job in London was at Grundy's Patent Ropery in Shadwell. While he was there he continued to study in his leisure hours. Among the acquaintances he made was an enthusiastic inventor by the name of Hall, who had taken out a patent for making hemp from beanstalks, and was thinking about taking out another for a system for spade tillage by steam. The young engineer was invited to make a model of the steam tillage engine, which he did, and it was agreed that Hall would share the cost of this with him. Hall was also going to write a paper in their joint names for the Society of Arts and, if their presentation proved to be successful, they would take out a patent and make their fortunes. Constructing the model cost Fairbairn a lot both in time and money, which the penniless inventor was unable to repay; and all that came of the project was the exhibition of the model at the Society of Arts, where it met with considerable opposition, and before the Board of Agriculture.

Another, more successful machine constructed by Fairbairn about the same time was a sausage-chopping machine, which he designed and built for a pork butcher for £33. It was the first order he had ever had on his own account and, as the machine did its job efficiently, he was naturally very proud of it. It had a flywheel and double crank, with connecting rods that worked a cross-head, and it contained a dozen knives crossing each other at right angles in such a way as to enable them to mince or divide the meat on a revolving block. Another part of the machine filled the sausage skins. With this invention, Fairbairn had embarked on a path that was to make him one of the most celebrated machine builders of his age.

However, these early years were not easy. Work was just as scarce in London as it had been in the North East and contracts like the one he'd just completed for the butcher were difficult to come by. Fairbairn was keen to gather more experience in his trade so he decided to make a tour round the South of England and South Wales looking for work. He set off from London in April 1813 with £7 in his pocket and, after visiting Bath and Frome, he settled to work for six weeks at Bathgate. From here he travelled through South Wales, spending a few days each at Newport, Llandaff and Cardiff. Then he took ship to Dublin. By the time he reached Ireland his money had run out, but he found a job straight away at the Phoenix Foundry, where he was put to work on a set of patterns for some nail machinery. The construction of the nail-making machinery occupied him for the entire summer and on its completion he set sail in October for Liverpool. He arrived there after a voyage of two days and went straight on by coach to Manchester, which had already become the principal manufacturing centre in the North of England.

Manchester offered great opportunities for skilled mechanics and Fairbairn settled down there in 1814. He brought no capital with him, but at 25 he had an abundance of energy, skill and practical experience in his trade. He succeeded in finding employment with a local mill owner, Adam Parkinson, and remained with him for two years, working as a millwright. Later in his career, Fairbairn said of his profession:

> In those days a good millwright was a man of large resources; he was generally well educated, and could draw out his own designs and work at the lathe; he had a knowledge of mill machinery, pumps and cranes, and could turn his hand to the bench or the forge with equal adroitness and facility. If hard pressed, as was frequently the case in country places far from towns, he could devise for himself expedients which enabled him to meet special requirements, and to complete his work without assistance. This was the class of men with whom I associated in early life – proud of their calling, fertile in resources, and aware of their value in a country where the industrial arts were rapidly developing.

During his two years with Parkinson, Fairbairn kept up his correspondence with Dorothy Mar and began to entertain thoughts of marrying her. Arrangements were made for the wedding as soon as he could save enough money to furnish a small house. With this in view he determined to work hard and spend little. His wages were good and out of them he saved enough to furnish a two-roomed cottage. On 16 June 1816 he married Dorothy at Bedlington. It was a marriage that was to last for 58 years and produce nine children. After a few days in Morpeth and Newcastle the newly-weds took the coach to Manchester where they set up home together.

The year after they got married he and Dorothy had their first child, a daughter. His domestic life now established, Fairbairn intended to improve himself further and entertained ambitions of setting up his own business.

One of his first efforts in this direction was the design of a cast-iron bridge to cross the River Irwell at Blackfriars. A prize was offered for this and, although a stone bridge was eventually decided on, his effort was creditable and proved to be the beginning of many designs for bridges. In 1817 the 28-year-old Fairbairn went into partnership with another mechanic, James Lillie, to establish the mill-machinery business Fairbairn and Lillie Engine Makers. It proved to be the start of a 15-year partnership, one whose reputation for millwork and the construction of iron machinery generally became known all over the world. It provided the foundation for what would eventually become a massive engineering concern employing hundreds of men at the firm's Canal Street Works in the Ancoats area of Manchester.

The new firm's first contract didn't take long to come in, but it wasn't for a mill machine. It was for the erection of an iron conservatory and hothouse for the home of Mr J. Hulme of Clayton, near Manchester, but there was an early setback for the young entrepreneurs. The patterns for the conservatory were all made and the castings were begun but they couldn't proceed with the work because of a notice from a firm in Birmingham that the design was an infringement of their patent. The young firm had to get in other work quickly and in preparation for turning out orders they hired a small shed at a rent of twelve shillings (60p) a week. They made their own lathe, capable of turning shafts of from three to six inches in diameter, set it up in the shed and hired a strong Irishman to drive the wheel and assist with the heavy work.

George Stephenson and his son Robert (*seated*) made many remarkable contributions to railway developments during the early 1800s. Here they are discussing plans for the Britannia Bridge.

Below: There was much scaremongering in the earlier days of the railways by those opposed to them. One of the perceived threats was that boilers were capable of frequently exploding and killing passengers.

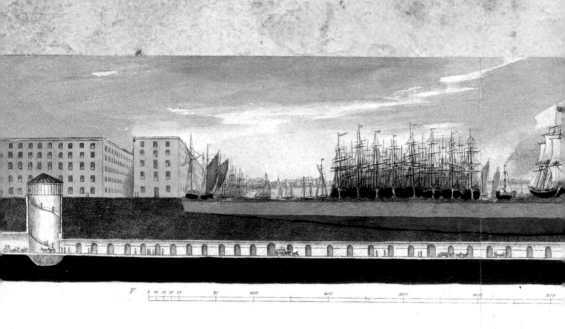

The Thames Tunnel from Rotherhithe to Wapping was the first underground crossing of the Thames. Work began in 1825 using Marc Brunel's tunnelling shield – a large iron box divided into thirty-six separate cells, each containing a single worker who dug at the face in front of him – but was only completed in 1843 because of persistent flooding problems.

When visiting the National Railway Museum, Fred always enjoyed a ride on the footplate of this replica of Stephenson's *Rocket*.

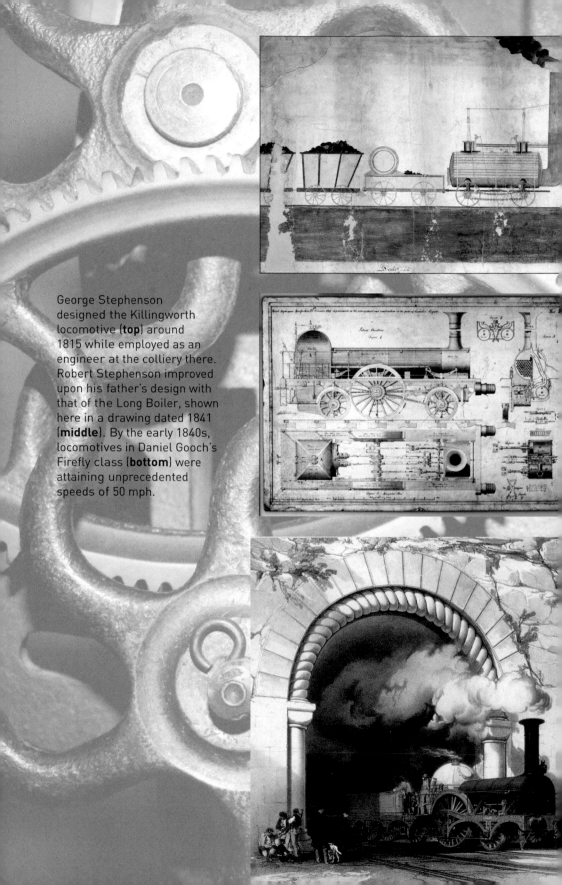

George Stephenson designed the Killingworth locomotive (**top**) around 1815 while employed as an engineer at the colliery there. Robert Stephenson improved upon his father's design with that of the Long Boiler, shown here in a drawing dated 1841 (**middle**). By the early 1840s, locomotives in Daniel Gooch's Firefly class (**bottom**) were attaining unprecedented speeds of 50 mph.

UNDULATION OF CLAY AT THE POINT OF IRRUPTION OF WATER MAY 18TH 1827.
and also shewing by the light Blue the height which the Water gained in the Vertical Shaft
& by the Darker Blue the level of the Water when pumped out to the base of the same.

4

Above: Large crowds gathered all along the route to watch the opening of the Stockton & Darlington Railway on 27 September 1825. It actually ran from the collieries at Shildon and was built to transport coal to the docks on the river Tees at Stockton.

View of the Railway across Chat Moss.

The English landscape presented railway engineers with numerous challenges:
Brunel's 2-mile tunnel through Box Hill (**left**), Robert Stephenson's immense
2½-mile cutting at Tring (**top**) and George Stephenson's unqualified success –
a floating raft to support the 4-mile trackbed across the bog at Chat Moss (**above**).

Cragside (**top**), the house built for William Armstrong at Rothbury in Northumberland, was the first house in the world to be lit using hydroelectric power. His hydro-electric machine (**above**) was capable of powering, amongst other things, domestic light fittings (**right**).

Their next order was for the construction of a calico-polishing machine, but subsequent orders came in slowly and James Lillie began to despair of success. His more hopeful partner urged him to persevere and he decided to go on a little longer. They issued business cards and distributed them to Manchester's manufacturers, and made a tour of all the principal firms, offering their services and looking for orders. Among those that Fairbairn called upon, taking with him his designs for his iron bridge, was the large cotton-spinning firm of Messrs Adam and George Murray. Adam Murray received him kindly, heard what he had to say and invited him to call on the following day with his partner. The manufacturer must have been favourably impressed by this interview, for next day, when Fairbairn came back with Lillie, he took them around his mill and asked whether they felt they were competent enough to renew all of the horizontal cross-shafts that turned the mule-spinning machinery.

It was a massive job for a young firm without capital and almost without plant to take on but they had every confidence in themselves and replied boldly that they were willing and able to do the work. When he heard this, Murray said he would call and see them at their own workshop to satisfy himself that they had the means of undertaking such an order. This was not good news and the partners feared that once Murray saw how modest their operation was, he would withdraw his order. But they needn't have worried. He paid his visit and confirmed the order. It's clear that he was much more impressed by the personal qualities he saw in the partners than by the size of their premises or the excellence of their machine tools – of which they had only one: the lathe they had made and set up themselves.

Murray's confidence in the partners was fully justified. One of the conditions he laid down was that Fairbairn and Lillie had to carry out the alterations without stopping the machinery. This they managed to do and, by working from five in the morning until nine at night for several months, they succeeded in finishing the alterations to Murray's complete satisfaction within the time specified. He was so pleased with their work that he began to recommend them to his friends in the cotton trade, among whom was John Kennedy, of McConnel and

Kennedy, the largest cotton spinners in Britain. The cotton trade had by this time become a major industry and was expanding with extraordinary rapidity. Population and wealth were pouring into South Lancashire, and supporting industries and enterprises were springing up all over the region. The foundations were being laid for a system of manufacturing in iron, machinery and textile fabrics, the like of which had never been seen before. For the most part, the early Lancashire manufacturers started out on very nearly equal footing. Most were men originally of limited means – ordinary working men, weavers, mechanics and labourers – coming to the fore and over the course of time building up huge manufacturing concerns by sheer force of industry, energy and personal ability. The description given by one of Lancashire's largest late-nineteenth-century employers might have applied to any of them: 'When I married,' he said, 'my wife had a spinning-wheel, and I had a loom – that was the beginning of our fortune.'

When Fairbairn and Lillie undertook the extensive alterations in Murray's factory, both were largely unacquainted with the working of cotton mills. Until that time they had been occupied principally with corn mills, and with printing and bleaching works. Now an entirely new field was opened up to them and the young partners made sure that they applied themselves to mastering the practical details of cotton-mill work. They soon saw that the gearing of even the best mills was clumsy and imperfect, so they set out on a series of improvements that were of major importance for the cotton industry. The machinery was currently driven by large, square cast-iron shafts, on which huge wooden drums, some of them as much as four feet in diameter, revolved at the rate of about 40 revolutions a minute. The couplings were so badly fitted that they could be heard creaking and groaning a long way off. Straps and counter drums that transmitted power to the line shafting were so big that they crowded the rooms and seriously obstructed the light where it was most required, for carrying out the delicate operations on the different machines. Another serious defect lay in the construction of the shafts themselves, and in the mode of fixing the couplings, which were constantly breaking.

It occurred to Fairbairn that these problems could be remedied by the introduction of lighter shafts driven at double or treble the velocity, smaller drums to drive the machinery, and the use of wrought iron wherever practicable because of its lightness and strength compared to wood. He also introduced new designs that simplified the hangers and fixings which supported the shafting. The opportunity to introduce these improvements soon came up in a large new McConnel and Kennedy mill erected in 1818. Fairbairn drew up the plans for all the machinery in the mill, calculated the sizes and strength of the parts and fixed the different machines' position and arrangement.

The machinery that Fairbairn and Lillie installed proved to be a major improvement on anything that had gone before, and when John Kennedy added an original invention of his own in a system of double speeds, designed to give an increased amount of twist in the yarn, the work put the firm at the cutting edge of engineering millwrights. Kennedy's praise for Fairbairn and Lillie's work was in itself a passport to fame and to new business, and as he was more than satisfied with the manner in which his mill machinery had been designed and installed he sounded their praises in all quarters. Orders poured in so quickly that Fairbairn and Lillie had difficulty in keeping pace with the demands. They moved from their original shed to larger premises in Mather Street, where they erected additional lathes and other machine tools, and eventually a steam engine. Later on they added a large cellar under an adjoining factory to their premises, before erecting a factory of their own, fitted with the most improved machinery for turning out millwork.

The firm was innovative and forward-looking and soon gained a reputation for the manufacture of advanced mill machinery. One of the defects they had observed in existing machinery was in the construction of the shafts and in the method of fixing the couplings, which were constantly giving way. This meant that a week seldom passed without a breakdown. For the first six years of the company's operations the partners could never count on Sunday as a day of rest as they were constantly employed in doing repairs. Fairbairn was designer, draughtsman and book-keeper while Lillie took charge of the workshop. Fairbairn often rode 15 or 16 miles a day to consult with mill owners, take dimensions and work out the plans for different jobs.

In the course of a few years they brought about a revolution in the gearing of mill machinery. Ponderous masses of timber and cast iron, with their enormous bearings and couplings, gave way to slender rods of wrought iron and light frames or hooks by which they were suspended. Lighter but stronger wheels and pulleys were introduced, and because the workmanship was much more accurate, friction was avoided, while the speed was increased from about 40 to upwards of 300 revolutions a minute. These improvements represented a major step forward in the history of mill machinery and had a very significant influence on the development of cotton, wool, flax and silk manufacture. Although he was initially met by resistance from some engineers who were not convinced, the improvements introduced by Fairbairn came to be adopted wherever steam or water was employed as motive power in mills.

Fairbairn and Lillie had a difficult uphill battle to fight while these improvements were being introduced but their hard work and perseverance, guided by sound judgement, brought its reward and it wasn't long before the firm became known as one of the most enterprising in Manchester. The vertical engine that Fairbairn developed took up very little space in workshops where its crankshaft could be coupled directly to the line shafting. It proved very popular in small machine shops and was also used for colliery winding. The improved efficiency that such machinery brought to the manufacturing process was a key feature of the industrial economy, helping British manufacturers to out-perform their rivals and turn Britain into the 'workshop of the world'.

Steam may have been the driving force of British industry but it didn't take over in factories overnight. In many textile mills, the power to drive the machines was still provided by water so Fairbairn now turned his attention to improving waterwheels. He devised a new bucket design that helped the air to escape as the water entered the bucket above, and to be re-admitted as the water emptied itself out below. This arrangement ensured that the water had the maximum effect on the wheel and it soon became adopted in most watermills at home and abroad. Between 1826 and 1827, Fairbairn and Lillie supplied the waterwheels for the extensive cotton mills belonging to Kirkman Finlay and Company, at Catrine Bank in Ayrshire. These wheels were regarded as among the most perfect hydraulic machines in Europe.

The company's reputation was spreading far and wide, and at about the same time they supplied the mill gearing and water machinery for Messrs Escher and Company's works in Zurich, which was one of the largest cotton factories on the continent. Another contract was for the supply of the millwork and waterwheel for a cotton mill at Wesserling in Alsace belonging to Messrs Gos, Deval and Co. The wheel was the first one in France erected on the suspension principle. Fairbairn himself attended the opening of the mill, which was followed by dinner and entertainment. M. Gos spoke some English and during dinner Fairbairn explained to him the nature of home-brewed beer. Gos was a great admirer of this, having tasted it when he had been in England. The dinner was followed by music, and as part of the performance M. Gos played the violin. When Fairbairn complimented his host on his playing, M. Gos asked him if he played. 'A little,' was the almost unconscious reply. 'Then you must have the goodness to play some,' Gos said and placed the instrument in his hands, amid urgent requests from all present that he should play for them. There was no alternative, so Fairbairn self-consciously proceeded to perform one of his best tunes, 'The Keel Row'. The company listened with amazement, until the performer's career was suddenly cut short by the host exclaiming at the top of his voice, 'Stop, stop, Monsieur, by gad that be home-brewed music!'

Fairbairn's machinery was helping to transform the face of industry but it wasn't his only enthusiasm. In the 1820s his interest in iron structures led him to design a bridge over Water Street for the Liverpool & Manchester Railway. Further diversification came with the manufacture of boilers for locomotives and a move into shipbuilding. Several of his inventions from this time were patented, including a riveting machine. This sort of diversification would become important for the company as the cotton industry went into recession in the 1830s.

Fairbairn was a lifelong learner and he joined the Institution of Civil Engineers in 1830. Like all the great Victorian engineers so admired by Fred, he was forever pushing the boundaries and he was one of the first to turn his attention to the use of iron for building ships. His first sign of interest in shipbuilding came in 1829 when Mr Houston of Johnstown, near Paisley, launched a light boat on the Ardrossan Canal to work out the speed at which it could be towed by horses with two or three persons on board. To his surprise, it was found that the labour the horses had to perform in towing the boat was much greater at six or seven miles an hour than it was at nine miles an hour. This anomaly puzzled the experimenters, and at the request of the Council of the Forth and Clyde Canal, Fairbairn, who had already established his reputation as a scientific mechanic, visited Scotland to institute a series of experiments with light boats to determine the law of traction and clear up, if possible, the apparent anomalies in Houston's experiments. This he did, and the results of his research were published as 'Remarks on Canal Navigation'. In this he illustrated the advantages of the use of steam as a means of moving vessels on canals.

His work in this field led to further experiments. Perceiving a ship as a floating tubular beam, Fairbairn criticized existing design standards dictated by Lloyd's of London. His first experiments were made with wooden vessels, but this eventually led to the construction of iron vessels based on an entirely new principle of construction, with angle-iron ribs and wrought-iron sheathing plates. His first iron ship was the little paddle steamer *Lord Dundas*, built at his works in Manchester in 1831. 'This little vessel was constructed exclusively for lightness,' Fairbairn said, 'and in order to give her bows and sides the required tenacity and stiffness, light angle-irons were introduced as ribs, and the whole firmly riveted together. When the boat was finished, I was forcibly struck with her lightness, solidity and strength.' *Lord Dundas* went to sea the same year and was such a success that Fairbairn was encouraged to begin iron shipbuilding on a large scale.

But before he could do this troubles began to arise, which resulted in a major change for the business.

The problems arose because of a scheme that Fairbairn and Lillie had got themselves involved in a few years earlier, to convert buildings intended for a dye-works at Egerton near Bolton into a cotton mill. It was a tempting venture because they were able to get the land and the property for a knock-down price, but the drain on the firm's capital for all the work involved was so great that it began to cripple their primary business as millwrights. In 15 months the buildings were converted, the weir and overflows were completed, a waterwheel was erected and machinery was installed, all at considerable expense. Then, after the mill was set to work, all the money that was made was used for enlargements and other capital investments, leaving no return for the proprietors. Several years went by in this way, all outlay and no income, and it became a source of friction between Fairbairn and his partner. Fairbairn's solution is recorded in his diary: 'All these circumstances convinced me of the necessity of a speedy dissolution of the partnership, and from 1830 to 1832 I urged upon Mr Lillie the necessity of change.'

At first Lillie refused to listen to the proposal. He felt Fairbairn was being unreasonable in wishing to break up a partnership that had been successful for so many years. But Fairbairn was convinced they could no longer go on together in their present circumstances. He offered to take the concern entirely into his own hands or for Lillie himself to take it. Eventually it was arranged that Fairbairn would take the works on payment of a sum of money equivalent to Lillie's share as it stood in the books. This was accomplished in 1832 by Fairbairn handing over his share in the Egerton Cotton Mills. Fairbairn was now on his own and he turned his attention to shipbuilding. Following his work in Scotland he saw an opportunity to open a steamboat connection between Glasgow and the towns on the eastern coast by way of the Forth and Clyde Canal. For this he built an iron steamer called *Manchester* on the same principle as the *Lord Dundas*, with the paddle at the stern for negotiating the canal. She was launched on the River Irwell and fitted with high-pressure 40-horsepower engines. After trials at Liverpool she made the passage to Glasgow and on to the canal, where she went into service between Port Dundas, the towns along the Firth of Forth and Dundee.

The success of *Manchester*, her great strength, buoyancy and lightness, and her overall qualities for sea travel convinced Fairbairn of the advantages to be gained from the use of iron and led him to build other iron vessels. Over the next two years eight more iron ships were built in sections in Manchester, taken to pieces and rebuilt at the ports. Four of them were for Scottish canals; there were two passenger boats with 40-horsepower engines for the Humber and two for the lakes of Zurich and Walenstadt in Switzerland. The Swiss boats were sent in pieces to Hull, where they were put together to make the voyage to Rotterdam. After completing this they then steamed up the Rhine as far as the Rhine Falls, where they were again dismantled and carried overland to Lake Zurich.

The trouble was that Manchester, 35 miles from the sea, was hardly the ideal place for shipbuilding, so this branch of the business was moved to Millwall on the River Thames in 1835. Here Fairbairn laid out a yard for building iron ships and, as these were going to be steamers, he erected workshops to manufacture their engines and machinery. The following year he had orders for 12 iron vessels from the East India Company for navigating the Ganges, and four others for different parts of Europe. He went on to build more than 80 vessels of various sizes including some for the Royal Navy. At the same time the Canal Street Works in Manchester were enlarged and improved, and here Fairbairn branched out into the manufacture of steam engines. There were no striking innovations in design, but he paid great attention to the quality of workmanship and the engines he built became noted for their efficiency and for economy of fuel.

The next 15 years saw Fairbairn devoting much of his energy to shipbuilding, and during this period he oversaw the building of 80 iron ships and developed new forms of design and construction. At first it was difficult, as Fairbairn himself recorded: 'We made many blunders as to prices &c in a business which we had yet to learn, and the rapid increase in demand for iron vessels and the consequent necessary outlay and extension of the works in buildings, tools &c trenched so hard upon our limited capital as to hamper us for a long time.' Fairbairn couldn't neglect his Manchester establishment. The shops for general engineering work in Manchester were the source of finance for his expansion into shipbuilding and marine engineering at Millwall, so for more than five years he hurried backwards and forwards between them. His Millwall yard became the first great iron shipbuilding yard in Britain and by the mid-1830s his two works were employing over 2,000 men.

Fairbairn was a great experimenter in iron and for his shipbuilding enterprise he investigated in great detail its strength, the value of different kinds of riveted joints compared with solid plate, and the distribution of the material throughout the structure, as well as the shape of the vessel itself. In 1839, in order to speed up the construction of his iron-sided ships, Fairbairn invented a machine for riveting boiler plates by steam power. Until this time this job had been done by hand-hammers, worked by men on each side of the plate to be riveted. But this process was slow and laborious, and didn't produce the best results. Some other more rapid and precise method of fixing the plates firmly together was urgently needed and Fairbairn's machine provided the answer. With it the rivet was driven into its place and firmly fastened there by a couple of strokes of a hammer powered by steam. It heralded a revolution in shipbuilding and boiler-making. It fixed, with two men and a boy, as many rivets in one hour as could be done by three men and a boy working a 12-hour day, and the superior quality of the work produced ensured that the machine went into general usage in less than 12 months.

Shipbuilding, boiler-making, iron bridges and buildings, mill machinery and waterwheels – Fairbairn had his finger in a lot of pies and it's no surprise that with railway mania at its height he began building railway locomotives at Millwall. The first designs were the four-wheeled Bury type, built for the Manchester & Leeds Railway. As with his mill engines, there were no great innovations in this branch of the business and generally the company built to the design specified by the customer or something similar to those produced by Edward Bury and Company, and Sharp, Roberts and Company. In all they produced over 69 locomotives for the Manchester & Leeds Railway, their main customer, but they also built for the North Western Railway, for lines in Ireland and for the first railway company in Brazil. Their production was mainly lightweight 0-4-0, then 2-2-2, 2-4-0 and 0-4-2 engines typical of the day, but in 1851–5 they built 40 larger engines to the design of James McConnell for the Southern Division of the London & North Western Railway. Around 1840, no doubt as a result of taking on so much work, Fairbairn began to get into difficulties managing the Millwall establishment and this led to the introduction into the business of his son Thomas, who joined him as a partner in 1841. A few years later, in 1846, another son, William Andrew, joined and the business became known as William Fairbairn & Sons. This led to further expansion of the Manchester factory, which became highly profitable.

Throughout the 1840s Fairbairn was very active, chiefly directing operations at his Manchester and London establishments. He also wrote several important papers for learned societies and he was frequently called on to provide his expertise on government inquiries. One of the first of these was in 1841, when he was asked to give advice as to the best means of preventing accidents in which factory workers got entangled in machinery.

In September of that same year Fairbairn's daughter Anne was married to a young engineer, Mr J. F. Bateman. It was an alliance that gave him great pleasure, not least because Bateman's engineering experience enabled him to be of considerable service to Fairbairn. Indeed, for many years there was scarcely any engineering scheme or scientific investigation in which his assistance was not called upon.

The revival of the cotton trade from 1843 led Fairbairn back to the requirements of Lancashire's textile mills. Their development and the power demands for driving the machinery had been made possible by the rotative beam engine and by boilers that were capable of generating and withstanding steam at high pressure. The first boilers were the Cornish type invented by Richard Trevithick in 1812. Built from wrought-iron plates riveted together, the Cornish boiler was cylindrical in shape with a large central flue running through it. In the 1840s the Lancashire mill owners were rapidly expanding older mills or building big new mills as the demand for cotton production gathered momentum. As the mills became larger, the demand for bigger, more powerful steam engines grew apace. This meant that longer large-diameter boilers were needed to generate higher volumes of steam at ever-increasing pressures. The Cornish boiler was still the one in general use, but Fairbairn believed he could improve on this and generate more steam, which would provide more power for the machinery in the mills. Until this time boiler-making had been con-sidered a separate trade and most manufacturers of steam engines ordered their boilers from boiler makers. But Fairbairn had strong views about the importance of this fundamental part of the steam engine and didn't want its design or manufacture to be out of his hands.

In 1844 Fairbairn took the Cornish boiler and made it much bigger in diameter and, instead of having one fire tube through it, he put in two fire tubes, one beside the other. Each fire tube had its own large furnace, and the two furnaces were set side by side in a robustly constructed cylindrical shell. This was made up of around ten sheets of wrought-iron plate, bent to shape and riveted together. The design was stronger by far and considerably more efficient than its predecessor. Lancashire boilers also burned coal extremely efficiently, as the furnaces could be alternately stoked. The coal was shovelled into underfeed stokers up to the furnace beds. Draught from the fans and the chimney supplied the air and the resulting hot gases passed through the furnace tubes to the back of the boiler. They were then drawn underneath the boiler and to the front, where they divided and passed along both sides of the boiler, into the main flue and out of the chimney. One of Fairbairn's objectives in introducing this boiler was to produce less smoke by using two furnaces, each fired alternately, but the additional heating provided by the two flues would also generate much more steam than the Cornish boiler. If correctly fired by an experienced firebeater using good-quality coal, Lancashire boilers could maintain the boiler's maximum working pressure for a whole

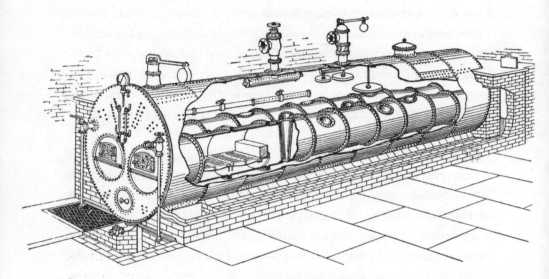

The stronger and more efficient Lancashire boiler,
complete with twin fire tubes

shift with the minimum of smoke. Fairbairn's Lancashire boiler proved so successful that it was quickly and widely adopted, not just in the textile mills but throughout the growing number of industries that were driven by steam power. It soon established itself as the most successful boiler of all time. Fred always found it fascinating:

> I know that when I was little there were two Lancashire boilers at Marsden's bleach works, where my mum worked. They had them in all the mills around Bolton and the beauty of them was that you could burn anything on them. All of the soot fell to the bottom, and you could go for twelve months without cleaning them. Then you'd have to sweep out the flues. For this the Black Gang would come in and they'd have to clean all the soot out. They only got a meagre pittance for this work, and when they'd got the job done they'd go to the pub and get inebriated.

It was not just the machinery in the mills that Fairbairn improved. As an expert in the use of iron he was one of the first engineers to conduct systematic investigations into the failure of structures, including the collapse of mills. His report on the collapse of a mill at Oldham showed that the poor design methods used by the architects when specifying cast-iron girders for supporting heavily loaded floors were one of the principal causes. He had himself pioneered the use of iron structures in many buildings for which he had been responsible. Fairbairn started to use iron as a building material in 1839 when, at his Millwall shipyard, he built the first of a series of small prefabricated buildings that were later dismantled and exported. Recalling these early experiments in a lecture on the progress of engineering, he said:

> It is now twenty years since I constructed an iron house, with the machinery of a corn-mill, for Halil Pasha, then Seraskier of the Turkish army at Constantinople. I believe it was the first iron house built in this country; and it was constructed at the works at Millwall, London, in 1839. Since then iron structures of all kinds have been erected: iron lighthouses, iron-and-crystal palaces, iron churches, and iron bridges. Iron roads have long been worked by iron locomotives; and before

many years have passed a telegraph of iron wire will probably be found circling the globe. We now use iron roofs, iron bedsteads, iron ropes, and iron pavement; and even the famous wooden walls of England are rapidly becoming reconstructed of iron. In short, we are in the midst of what has been characterized as the Age of Iron.

In all matters connected with the qualities and strength of iron, Fairbairn came to be regarded as a leading authority, and his advice was often sought and highly valued. The knowledge he had gained from the experiments he had conducted at his Millwall shipyard into the strength of wrought iron in the form of the hollow beam, which is what a wrought-iron ship really is, led to him being consulted by Robert Stephenson about the bridges he was building for the Chester to Holyhead Railway. As we have seen, Stephenson was considering some form of girder construction but the bridge over the Menai Strait would require two spans of 460 feet each. As the largest girder bridge built up to this time had a span of only 60 feet he knew that it would be pushing the boundaries of civil engineering design and technology. Fairbairn had by this time gained a lot of practical experience in the use of wrought iron in boiler-making and shipbuilding but there was no theoretical knowledge of its properties when used for a load-carrying beam of this length. Reporting on his involvement in the project, Fairbairn said:

Mr Stephenson asked whether such a design was practicable, and whether I could accomplish it: and it was ultimately arranged that the subject should be investigated experimentally, to determine not only the value of Mr Stephenson's original conception [of a circular or egg-shaped wrought-iron tube, supported by chains], but that of any other tubular form of bridge which might present itself in the prosecution of my researches. The matter was placed unreservedly in my hands; the entire conduct of the investigation was entrusted to me; and, as an experimenter, I was to be left free to exercise my own discretion in the investigation of whatever forms or conditions of the structure might appear to me best calculated to secure a safe passage across the Straits.

Although the Menai Strait and River Conwy bridges are always attributed to Stephenson, there is no doubt that a large share of the credit for working out the practical details of the structures belongs to Fairbairn. But the tubular bridge ultimately proved far too expensive a concept for widespread use, owing to the sheer mass and cost of the wrought iron needed. Fairbairn's work, however, established him as the expert on the design and building of iron bridges, and with new railway lines requiring bridges in large numbers he was inundated with orders. For some of them he developed wrought-iron trough bridges that used some of the ideas he had explored in the tubular bridge. Bridge-building became an important part of the business and by 1851 he had erected more than 100, ranging in length from 40 to 180 feet.

In 1852 the government contracted Fairbairn to work on the establishment of a small-arms factory at Enfield. Working with officials from the Ordnance Department he laid out the works and constructed most of the machinery and ironwork. At the same time he finished the largest work he had undertaken in mill construction – the great woollen mill of Titus Salt at Saltaire, near Bradford. This was still very much his core business, but other parts of his empire were not faring as well, and in 1847 his Thames Shipbuilding had collapsed. Locomotive-building continued on the Millwall site and by 1862 William Fairbairn & Sons had constructed more than 400, including locomotives for the Great Western and the London & North Western railways. Throughout this period Fairbairn secured big contracts not just for locomotive manufacture but also for bridge-building. His reputation was now so great that he was consulted by factory owners and railway builders from all over the world and these consultations nearly always led to large orders. The firm undertook all sorts of engineering work and in the manufacture of bridges, girders, cranes and anything else that involved the application of wrought iron for structural and mechanical purposes they became world leaders. A full order book meant that between 1848 and 1860 the large losses that had been incurred by Thames Shipbuilding were made good by the Manchester works.

But Fairbairn wanted to move on. His own role began to change as he took on more and more consultancy work. To accommodate this the company was slimmed down and the locomotive-building part of the business was sold to Sharp, Stewart and Company in 1863. Fairbairn had long been a pioneer in the study of metal fatigue and this was a subject on which he was increasingly being called upon to give his expert opinion. In one of his early reports he had condemned the use of trussed cast-iron girders, and advised Stephenson not to use them in the bridge he was building over the River Dee at Chester in 1846. Stephenson chose to ignore his advice and when the bridge collapsed in May 1847, concerns were raised about the integrity of many other railway bridges already built or under construction. It was an era when many engineering ventures ended in disaster, and failures of bridges and other structures as well as boiler explosions were relatively common. Tunnelling, bridge-building, mining, driving steam locomotives and factory and foundry work were all dangerous occupations and the Victorians lived much closer to death and disaster than we do. Popular newspapers of the day were full of gruesome stories. Every issue of the *Household Narrative* contained the goriest details under the heading 'Accidents and Disasters'. The *Illustrated London News* went one better. It commissioned artists to portray the plight of trapped miners or passengers on a sinking ship, or the agonizing fate of foundry workers blown to bits in an explosion.

Steam-boiler explosions were a cause of particular concern and there was increasing public anxiety about the number and frequency of them all over the country. The results were often devastating as boilers exploded like bombs. Pieces of iron were blasted over considerable distances resulting in many deaths and injuries. One of the main problems was that there were many types of boilers, some of which were poorly designed and badly constructed. When they were installed into mills and factories they were often overworked; very little servicing was done on them and the boiler stokers, or firebeaters as they were known, were generally untrained. There was no regulation of the use of boilers and when explosions killed people there would be a simple investigation conducted by a coroner. An independent engineer would

Popular newspapers of the day, such as the *Illustrated London News*, fuelled the Victorian appetite for the macabre with their detailed depictions of railway disasters

generally be invited to advise the court and Fairbairn's reputation was so highly valued that he was frequently called upon to lend his expertise.

It soon became evident to Fairbairn that the majority of the explosions he was called in to investigate arose from mechanical causes resulting from bad workmanship, poorly carried out repairs and, above all, the general ignorance of factory owners and operators. Fairbairn knew that many of these problems could be avoided and he concluded that boilers should undergo detailed periodic inspections. He got his chance to do something about this when, in 1854, he was invited to attend a meeting of engineers and cotton-mill owners in Manchester that had been called to establish an official body to regulate the use of boilers and reduce the number of explosions. The meeting resulted in the formation of the Manchester Steam Users Association, which became the pioneer organization in the field of boiler inspection. Fairbairn was elected president of it in 1858. Two hundred and seventy-one owners of steam boilers became members of the association, whose main role was to carry out periodic inspections of boilers, safety valves, mountings and feedwater systems.

In all matters connected with the qualities and strength of iron, Fairbairn came to be regarded as a first-rate authority. In 1861, at the request of Parliament, he conducted early research into metal fatigue, raising and lowering a 3-ton mass on to a wrought-iron cylinder 3 million times before it fractured, and showing that it would need a load of 12 tons to cause any damage. He built large-scale testing apparatus for these studies, and was partly funded by the Board of Trade. He showed that fracture could occur by crack growth from incipient defects, a problem now known as fatigue. The elaborate experiments instituted by him as to the strength of iron of all kinds formed the subject of various papers he presented to the British Association, the Royal Society and the Literary and Philosophical Society of Manchester. His practical enquiries as to the strength of boilers and the study of this subject led him to define the law according to which the density of steam varies throughout an extensive range of pressures and atmospheres. His discovery of a reliable method of preventing the tendency of tubes to collapse, by dividing the flues of long boilers into short lengths by means of stiffening rings, which arose out of the same investigation, was one of the many valuable results of his studies. It proved to be of essential value in industrial areas around the world because it lessened the chances of boiler explosions, and avoided the loss of life caused by badly constructed boilers.

Fairbairn himself died of a severe bronchial cold on 18 August 1874 at the house of his son-in-law, Mr Bateman of Moor Park, near Farnham in Surrey. Although he was a Scot, he had lived in Manchester for most of his life and built up his engineering works in the town, so his body was taken there to be buried at Prestwich parish church. Along the route of his funeral procession large crowds gathered to pay their last respects to one of their most eminent citizens. The number of people present at the funeral was estimated to be between 50,000 and 70,000. He is remembered as one of Britain's greatest nineteenth-century engineers and, in his lifetime, in recognition of his work he had been elected a Fellow of the Royal Society in 1850 and made 1st Baronet of Ardwick in Manchester in 1869. But it is his invention of the Lancashire boiler and the experiments he carried out with it that made him such a hero for Fred:

> I've got a wonderful book in the house called *Red Hot Furnace Crown Experiments*. During the 1870s a gent called William Fairbairn in Manchester tried to prove once and for all that squirting cold water into a red-hot boiler didn't make it blow up. He actually got a full-size Lancashire boiler 30 feet long and 8 feet in diameter with two 3-foot fire tubes and they dug a big trench in a field nearby and built a bunker round and a blockhouse. There were no fancy electronics then but they had it all controlled with pulley wheels and wires and everything. They made it so they could lower the water in the boiler below the top of the fire tubes and let them become red hot. They had wires through stuffing boxes on top of the boiler braced to hooks on top of the fire tubes. So when it got red hot and the steam pressure began to shove down the crown of the firebox, they knew, from graphs and rulers in this bunker,

exactly where the crown of the fire tube was in relation to the rest of the boiler. Because there was no welding then it used to wrench the plates where the rivets were and of course the boiler would leak profusely. They did this so many times to prove that you could not blow a boiler up by putting freezing cold water on to a red-hot plate.

Some of the eminent engineers of the time believed that it flashed it into steam too quickly for the safety valves. But they proved that this was not the case. The pressure does go up just a few pounds but the cooling effect of the cold water on the plates puts it all to nothing again. It just stays pretty well the same. It is rather frightening when you get a boiler with a lot of pressure on and you don't know where the water level is and you're tempted to put more water in it, because you often think about the disaster that could ensue if you did this. But it is proved with theory and with practice that it does not blow up and William Fairbairn was the first man to do this.

Fairbairn's various enterprises were at the very heart of the development of a truly industrial economy in Britain. The widespread adoption of the sort of machinery that Fairbairn introduced to mills and factories helped to create large-scale industrial enterprises and usher in an engineering industry that, in the course of a few decades, made Britain the envy of the world. With developments in the use of iron and knowledge of its strengths and properties, transport and heavy industries prospered. The output of British iron doubled between 1835 and 1845 and a vast new field of employment was opened up for engineers and transport workers, and for the huge force of navvies needed for the heavy construction work involved in building the railways. Many thousands of wrought-iron rails were laid and thousands of wrought-iron plates were used for building bridges and making locomotive boilers as the continued expansion of British industry and the potential for transporting passengers stimulated the rapid growth of the railway network. Railways very quickly established a reputation as a great improvement on canal transport, especially in terms of speed and, above all, cost. On average the early railways undercut canals by 30 per cent on freight charges and their efficiency and competitiveness, along with rapid technological progress, ensured that British business rapidly transferred its allegiance. It was a time of great opportunity for talented, inventive, hard-working engineers and Joseph Locke was one of the men who seized his chance.

4

Joseph Locke
1805–1860
A Great Railway Engineer

Joseph Locke was one of our greatest railway engineers. He's not as well known as Brunel and Robert Stephenson but like them he dominated the world of engineering at the start of the Victorian Age, when railways were being built all over the country. He didn't leave us with anything quite as spectacular as their Royal Albert or Britannia bridges, but some people think he had a bigger influence on railway engineering and civil engineering generally than either of them. His father was an experienced mining engineer who was able to do surveys, sink shafts and construct railways, tunnels and stationary engines, so he had the right background for railway-building. He got the right start as well because when he was 18 he was apprenticed to George Stephenson and he became a great friend of Robert Stephenson, who was about the same age as him. But he fell out with both the Stephensons after he'd worked with them on a study of the merits of locomotives and standing engines that pulled trains along the track with cables and George claimed all the credit for the published report. Because of this Stephenson didn't appoint Locke as chief engineer for his Liverpool to Birmingham line but he was overruled by the directors and Locke got the job. Locke built a lot more important lines and fell out with Stephenson again over the west coast route from Lancaster up into Scotland. Locke was in favour of a direct route over Shap Fell but Stephenson wanted to take the line through flatter country, even though it meant increasing its length. In the end a royal commission chose Locke's proposal and the west coast main

111

line became his greatest work. All of his lines were noted for their economy of construction and avoidance of tunnels. He kept tight control over contractors and expenditure and, unlike a lot of his contemporaries, he completed his lines on time and on budget.

Joseph Locke was the youngest of the four sons and sixth of the seven children of William Locke, a colliery manager who had moved down to Yorkshire from the North East. Joseph was born in Attercliffe, Sheffield, in 1805 and moved to nearby Barnsley when he was five years old. He received his early education from his father but after a couple of years he went to Barnsley Grammar School, where he was educated from 1810 to 1820. When he was 15 he was placed under William Stobart at Pelaw, on the south bank of the Tyne, as an engineering apprentice. He was with him for two years before he went back home to Barnsley.

As a colliery manager William Locke was glad of any assistance he could get, so he took his son on to work at the pit. Joseph was mostly employed in the office, where he showed an aptitude for figures and calculations that would stand him in good stead later in his career. He liked the work and it was very much in keeping with his talents, but his time wasn't fully occupied. His father gave him the job of delivering coal in a cart to houses in and around Barnsley. Unfortunately Joseph felt degraded by this treatment and became so disgruntled that whenever he saw anyone coming whom he recognized, he would lie down in the cart to avoid being seen. And, although he didn't have much money, he used to pay a man threepence to do the end bit of the round for him.

He was now nearly 18 years old and was finding the modest amount of office work he was doing far too easy. Salvation was close at hand from an unexpected quarter. Before moving to Yorkshire William Locke had been a manager at Walbottle Colliery on Tyneside when George Stephenson was a fireman there and he now received a letter from his old friend. In it Stephenson informed him that he had moved on from the colliery and was now working as a civil engineer in different parts of the country. He proposed to pay Locke a visit when he was next passing through the area.

When he came, Stephenson was impressed with Joseph, who had

listened intently to much of Stephenson's conversation with his father. Hearing of the young man's dissatisfaction with his work, Stephenson suggested that he could be employed to better purpose with him. William Locke readily agreed and towards the end of 1823, when Joseph was 18 years old, he was articled to George Stephenson at Newcastle and went to work at his Forth Street Works, which had just been set up to manufacture locomotives for the new Stockton & Darlington Railway. His father was to pay no premium but the son was to receive no salary for three years; he was to learn the business and make himself useful.

Stephenson's workshops were establishing themselves as the leading locomotive manufactory in the world and working there gave Joseph Locke a wonderful opportunity to get on in the engineering profession. Earnestness and concentration were the characteristics of his youth; qualities that were to lead him on to fame and fortune. Throughout his time in Newcastle he worked steadily at self-improvement. During the day he received practical education in the workshop; at night he went back to his lodgings to study the theory, applying himself to the study of mathematics in particular with great diligence. As a result of his efforts, Locke soon established a position of authority and he and Robert Stephenson became close friends. A year before the end of Locke's three-year apprenticeship, George Stephenson proposed a fresh arrangement. He wanted to secure Locke's services for another three years and offered him a salary of £100 per annum. Locke accepted the offer gladly and became one of Stephenson's assistants on the surveying and building of the Liverpool & Manchester Railway.

Stephenson was not an experienced civil engineer and the Edge Hill Tunnel at the Liverpool end of the railway was causing him great problems. Locke was called in by the directors of the railway after a section of the tunnel collapsed because of faulty surveying work. He was asked to carry out another survey and produce a report. The fears of the board were justified when Locke found that errors in the original survey were so serious that, had they not been discovered in time, the different sections of the tunnel would never have formed a

The entrance to the Edge Hill Tunnel under construction

straight line; in one instance, two parts of the tunnel, instead of meeting, would have completely passed by each other. The report he produced was highly critical of the work already done, which reflected badly on Stephenson. This was embarrassing for Locke as he was employed by Stephenson, but he did his job honestly. Stephenson was furious and from this time on relations between the engineer and his young protégé were strained.

However, Stephenson recognized Locke's abilities, so in spite of their disagreement he continued to employ the young engineer. On the Liverpool & Manchester, Locke worked as his assistant alongside Charles Vignoles, until a clash of personalities between Stephenson and Vignoles led to the latter's resignation. Locke then took over responsibility for the western half of the line. One of the major obstacles was the boggy expanse of Chat Moss and, although Stephenson usually gets the credit for building a railway line across it, it is believed to have been Locke who suggested the correct method for crossing it.

During the construction of the Liverpool & Manchester, Locke was also sent by Stephenson to survey other railways he was involved in. One of the most important was the Manchester & Stockport. The directors of the Liverpool & Manchester objected to this, considering themselves entitled to Locke's undivided services. His absence, they maintained, would be detrimental to their interests. Stephenson replied that Locke was his assistant, that his presence on the Stockport line was absolutely necessary, and pledged his word that the interests of their line would suffer no injury. But the directors wouldn't yield. Their line had to come first; it was due to open soon so it required the full attention of the man who'd had so much to do with both its survey and its construction. So the directors got their way.

As the line neared completion, the directors were still trying to decide whether to use standing engines or locomotives to propel the trains. Robert Stephenson and Locke were both convinced that locomotives were vastly superior and in March 1829 the two men wrote a report demonstrating that cable haulage was more expensive, unable to cope with heavy loads and much slower. Locomotives, they concluded, were the better choice for use on a busy railway that was to carry freight and passengers.

When their report was going to press George Stephenson insisted that the title page should bear his name and his name alone. Locke objected, but ultimately agreed to the addition of the words 'Compiled from the Reports of George Stephenson' to his own and Robert Stephenson's names. The concession was made, but, on Locke's part, it was done with great reluctance and he continued to assert that the experiments on which the pamphlet was based were carried out personally by Robert Stephenson and himself during a period of several weeks that they'd spent around Newcastle. The report turned out to have great significance, and led to the directors holding an open trial to find the best locomotive. This was the Rainhill Trials, won by *Rocket* with George Stephenson at the controls and Locke on board as fireman. When the line was finally opened in 1830, George Stephenson drove the leading train, *Northumbrian*, and Joseph Locke drove *Rocket*. Sadly, Locke had the misfortune of being the driver of *Rocket* when it was involved in the first recorded fatal railway accident, striking and killing Liverpool MP William Huskisson.

Despite the strains that had been put on their relationship during the surveying and building of the Liverpool & Manchester Railway, Locke continued to work for Stephenson, but a bigger rift was to come about on their next major project. In 1829 Locke was given the job of surveying the route for the Grand Junction Railway. This new line was to join Newton-le-Willows on the Liverpool & Manchester Railway with Warrington and then go on to Birmingham via Crewe, Stafford and Wolverhampton, a total of 80 miles. Other lines were being considered at the same time, which were laid out by Locke, but it was the Grand Junction that provided the turning point for his career.

After the passing of the Grand Junction Bill in 1833, when the appointments on the line came to be made Locke expected to get the job of resident engineer. From 1830 he had devoted his services to the Grand Junction and was regarded by everybody concerned as George Stephenson's special representative. He was also held in high esteem by the Liverpool directors because of his work on the Liverpool

& Manchester, particularly for the way he had sorted out the problems with the Edge Hill Tunnel. George Stephenson might have been the chief engineer for the Grand Junction, but during the construction of the Liverpool & Manchester it was felt that he had shown a lack of ability to organize major civil engineering projects. On the other hand, Locke's ability to manage complex projects had become very clear. Aware of the directors' preference, Locke thought that the position of resident engineer should be his. But Stephenson proposed that there should be three resident engineers, Locke being one of them. The Grand Junction directors objected to this and on the very day that Locke offered to withdraw, they took the initiative and appointed him resident engineer for the northern half of the line while Stephenson was given responsibility for the southern half. Stephenson cannot have been very happy that the man he had employed as his assistant was now being treated as his equal.

Locke was only 28 years old but his earnestness, concentration and hard work had brought him to the pinnacle of his profession. It was only now that he felt he could turn his thoughts to marriage. He was not the sort of man who would have considered marriage if he did not have the wherewithal to support a wife and family, but with a salary of £800 a year plus £3,200 for expenses, which he said was beyond his expectations, he decided that now was the time to tie the knot. So in 1834, while he was working on the Grand Junction, he married Phoebe McCreery, the daughter of John McCreery, a poet and printer. Her father described her qualities in verse:

> With gentle soul and heart sincere
> And only to herself severe.

Locke, it would appear, had made a good choice. According to his biographer Joseph Devey, 'he had fortunately become united with one who was as prompt in spurring his ambitions as in solacing his fatigue.'

This was just the sort of support he needed because the works to be carried out on the Grand Junction were unprecedented in their size and complexity and the outlay was to be enormous. It was not only necessary that the engineer should have an exact idea of the materials required for every yard of the line, and the proper price of those materials, but also that he should be able to anticipate the requirements of construction before they actually arose. It wasn't enough for him to know these things himself; he also had to be able to communicate them to the contractors who would tender for these works. To do this, it was essential that he should prepare detailed specifications. The idea of drawing up specifications for railway-building soon became the norm, but it was not such common practice at first. Locke, however, not only urged that all contracts should be tendered for after distinct specifications, he also laid down that the contracts should be awarded for lengths of the line not exceeding ten miles.

Locke estimated the costs for his section of the line so quickly and meticulously that he had all of the contracts signed before a single one had been signed for Stephenson's section. With Stephenson's administrative inefficiency becoming so apparent, the railway company lost patience with him. They tried to compromise by making the men joint engineers, but Stephenson's pride wouldn't let him accept this so he resigned from the project. By the autumn of 1835, therefore, Locke had become chief engineer for the whole of the line. This deepened the rift between the two men, and strained relations between Locke and his old friend Robert Stephenson. Up to this point Locke had always been in George Stephenson's shadow but from this time on he would be his own man, and stand or fall by his own achievements.

Locke's route for the Grand Junction avoided as far as possible major civil engineering works. Even so, it required the construction of four major viaducts, an aqueduct and a two-mile cutting at Preston Brook. The most impressive engineering feats were the Dutton Viaduct over the River Weaver and the Weaver Navigation between the villages of Dutton and Acton Bridge in Cheshire. The viaduct, which took 700 men two years to build, is nearly 500 yards long and consists of 20 red sandstone arches with spans of 20 feet that stand 65 feet above the river.

When the line was opened on 4 July 1837 an important feature of the new railway was the use of double-headed wrought-iron rail supported on timber sleepers at 2-foot 6-inch intervals. It was intended that when the rails became worn they could be turned over to use the other surface, but in practice it was found that the chairs into which the rails were keyed caused wear to the bottom surface so that it became uneven. Nevertheless, this was an improvement on the fish-bellied wrought-iron rails still being used by Robert Stephenson on the London & Birmingham Railway, which was under construction at the same time.

Robert Stephenson, along with most of Locke's contemporaries, massively underestimated not only the cost but also the time needed to build a new railway line. For the London & Birmingham he estimated a cost of £21,736 per mile but the actual cost turned out to be nearer £50,000 per mile. Brunel estimated £2.5 million for his Great Western line from London to Bristol, whereas the actual cost was £6.5 million. One of the reasons seems to have been the fact that, in the early days of railway construction, most engineers appear to have thought that building a sufficient sum for contingencies into the estimates would deter the promoters and the lines would never have been built. Locke, on the other hand, never hesitated to put contingencies into the budget, aiming to give the promoters of a railway a realistic forecast of probable costs no matter how unpalatable they might be.

Another reason why costs were so inflated was that the actual building of the lines was carried out by a large number of small contractors. Many of them were inexperienced and soon fell into financial difficulties. The engineers were partly responsible for this state of affairs because they usually failed to provide the contractors with sufficiently detailed and accurate specifications for the work they were taking on. Joseph Locke was the exception and he set new standards of accuracy in estimating by supplying contractors with minutely detailed specifications. He also kept tight control over expenditure on every one of his projects and had a hands-on management approach to the work of his contractors.

Locke first applied these methods on the Grand Junction. The sheer scale of the railway had put paid to George Stephenson's way of doing things, where he would organize and oversee all the work himself without bringing in other contractors. On the Grand Junction, the projects for different sections of the line and for all major structures on it were undertaken separately by different contractors. More than any other engineer, Locke was responsible for the rise to power of a new profession – the railway contractor. The method he had devised of costing jobs based on detailed specifications could be applied much more easily if he had a few large contractors working for him who understood what he needed. Several of these men emerged above the rest. They were individuals who were capable of organizing large numbers of rough navvies and winning their respect; the sort of men whose abilities gave an engineer the confidence to hand over responsibility to them entirely for the construction of a length of railway. One of these contractors, a Cheshire surveyor called Thomas Brassey, became the greatest, richest and most efficient of them all and went on to work with Locke on many railway projects.

Brassey, the son of a landowner, was well connected within both the railway and the financial worlds. He had been a minor land and property developer and assisted in doing the surveys for turnpike roads in Cheshire and North Wales before Locke and Stephenson encouraged him to make the move to civil engineering contracting. He soon developed a reputation for efficiency, organization and ingenuity in a remarkable career that saw his firm construct 1,900 miles of railway in Britain, 3,000 miles in the rest of Europe and 1,550 miles further afield. On the Grand Junction, he completed the Penkridge Viaduct in Staffordshire on time and on budget. It was a project that perfectly illustrated Locke's management skills, especially when he spotted that the viaduct had been greatly overpriced in comparison with others on the line and secured Brassey's agreement to reduce his price. The partnership of engineer and contractor developed into the most successful in the history of the railways and they got it off on a very sound footing. Assistant engineers and contractors would complain that Locke used to walk them off their legs. He thought nothing of walking along the line from Warrington Junction to Birmingham in three days. But Brassey never flinched; Locke had met his match in his contractor's willingness to put in the work.

The construction of the Grand Junction was a great engineering success, but even more importantly it provided proof of Locke's ability to estimate costs accurately and manage projects economically. The line cost £18,846 per mile as against Locke's estimate of £17,000. No other engineer of the day got anywhere near as close as this with their estimates. On completion of the line Locke stayed on as chief engineer of the Grand Junction Railway until 1846, and, though he was concerned mainly with civil engineering, he was the man who suggested Crewe as the site for the locomotive and rolling-stock works, who drew up the first plans and estimates, and supervised the organization of the factory. So, as well as building the lines, he had a big influence on locomotive development.

During this time he and his wife adopted a child and he was elected to the Royal Society in 1838. In his private life and in the management of his personal affairs he did everything in exactly the same careful and meticulous manner that he applied to the control of major contracts. He gave away hundreds of pounds every year to charity but only after making detailed enquiries about the organization he was supporting and the way they used their funds. Locke was still only in his thirties but he was now spreading his energies far and wide. The first Scottish railway he laid down was a 22-mile line connecting Greenock, Paisley and Glasgow. Locke brought the line into Greenock close to the harbour and, to provide for the increase in traffic this brought, he widened the harbour and built new quays. The railway itself involved a lot of heavy work, particularly on one section where a six-mile route had to be hewn out of the solid rock of a ridge that stood in the way. In the centre of the ridge he had to bore a tunnel. From the end of the tunnel, Paisley lay in a straight line ahead and here Locke had to build a viaduct to carry the railway right over the centre of the town.

Another project Locke got involved in was a railway from London to Southampton. A line had been projected as early as 1834 and the promoters appointed Frank Giles as the engineer. Giles was an experienced engineer but a poor organizer and he couldn't keep control of his contractors. Matters became so unsatisfactory that Giles was forced to resign and Locke was appointed to succeed him. Locke went back to the drawing board and designed a fine railway that was straight and had only minor gradients. This approach was still considered essential at the time because of concerns about the inability of locomotives to handle inclines. But progress on the line was slow, much slower than far more ambitious projects in the North. The main labouring work on the line involved digging deep cuttings and building high embankments, and more than 16 million cubic yards of earth had to be removed. By 1839, five years after work had started, only the first 47 miles from London to Basingstoke had been opened and the line was not completed to Southampton until a year and a half later. While working on it Locke built up a productive relationship with Thomas Brassey, awarding him contracts covering 118 miles of the line worth £4.3 million.

When the London to Southampton line was about half completed, Locke was appointed to replace Charles Vignoles as engineer on a 42-mile line across the Pennines between Manchester and Sheffield after Vignoles had run into financial difficulties. The line had been projected some years earlier, but, owing to the difficulty of the work, construction had been suspended. The major obstacle was the three-mile-long summit tunnel that had to be dug at Woodhead, some 1,000 feet above the Manchester level. The maximum depth below the bleak Pennine moorland was 600 feet, with an average depth of 450 feet. It was such a huge and difficult undertaking that George Stephenson claimed it could not be done, declaring that he would eat the first locomotive that got through the tunnel. Vignoles had estimated £98,467 for the job on the assumption that it would not need to be lined, but when Locke took on the project his first action was to double this estimate because he knew that the lining of the tunnel would be essential for its long-term durability. His reputation was riding so high, however, that the directors immediately accepted this revised figure. Vignoles had contracted out the work in sections to several different small contractors, but as soon as Locke got the go-ahead to take over, the whole project was placed in the hands of Nicholas Wood, the Killingworth Colliery manager who had worked closely with George Stephenson on the development of some of his earliest locomotives and had moved on to become a well-regarded railway contractor.

Lord Wharncliffe, a prominent politician, turned over the first spadeful of earth for the Woodhead Tunnel on 1 October 1838, but, even though the work continued unremittingly night and day, it was not completed for more than six years. Sunday, instead of being a day of rest for the workmen, generally turned out to be the busiest of the week. A force of over 1,000 navvies, some with their women and children in tow, worked on the line, living on the bleak and desolate moorland in a shanty town of dry-stone-walled huts, sometimes as many as 20 to a hut. If living conditions were appalling, working conditions were even worse, especially in the tunnel. The rock strata were insecure and variable, making the work treacherous, and streams cascaded down from the roof so that the men were always soaked to the skin and had to work knee-deep in mud and water.

One thousand feet above sea level and nine miles from the nearest town, the site was extremely difficult to provision. The contractors had to open their own shops and pay their men partly in food. The men and their families were visited by dissenting ministers, who preached to them in rainy weather under tarpaulins. The men organized sick clubs and had a surgeon to attend them. His services were requested far more than those of his clerical colleagues because, in addition to the disease that plagued the camps, the number of casualties was so high that it led to a parliamentary inquiry. Twenty-eight men were killed; there were 200 severe accidents that crippled their victims for life, and 450 recorded minor accidents. When this, the longest tunnel so far driven in England, was completed in 1845, after six years' work, the proportion of the workforce killed or maimed for life by blasts, rock falls and other accidents was greater than the rate of casualties sustained in any of the major battles of the century, including Waterloo. It was estimated that the mortality rate among the navvies at the Woodhead Tunnel was just over 3 per cent, whereas that among soldiers at the Battle of Waterloo was only 2.1 per cent.

The tunnel was a single bore and in 1847 work on driving a second bore to run alongside it commenced. This proved to be an easier technical task, mainly because they'd learned from the experience of the first one, but it was made just as grim by an outbreak of cholera among the navvies. As well as the tunnel there were several other major works on the line, including a viaduct of five arches across the River Tame and another at Gorley consisting of nine arches. But the most beautiful and lofty structure on the line was the 500-foot Eterow Viaduct, which crosses the River Mersey at a height of 136 feet. Some 186,000 cubic feet of stone and 41,000 cubic feet of timber were used in its construction. Despite the expense of these works, Locke tendered to bring the cost of construction under £25,000 per mile, and got contractors to undertake the work on that basis.

The great railway boom was now at its peak. Within 20 years of the Rainhill Trials of 1829, around 5,000 miles of track criss-crossed the country and the nineteenth-century railway pioneers had brought the British nation to the forefront in the field of civil engineering. It seems incredible today that great feats of engineering were achieved in the days when precision tools and mechanical aids to labour were unknown. Whatever the terrain, engineers like Locke overcame every obstacle that got in their way, building their lines across hills and valleys, rivers, mountains and marshland. Their legacy is the great embankments, viaducts, tunnels and bridges that cover Britain, in many cases still visible long after the trains they served have disappeared. The cost of all this was enormous and was met mainly through the issue of shares in the railway companies. Shares were available to the general public and the newly emerging middle class were particularly prominent in railway investment. Some lost their money in highly speculative schemes but the major trunk routes like the west coast main line proved lucrative for shareholders. The joint stock banks also invested large sums, but, more than anything else, it was the middle class's surplus capital that made railway-building on a vast scale possible.

For the speculator the railway boom seemed to offer the prospect of earning unimaginable riches almost overnight and the passion to get rich quick gripped the nation. Between 1825 and 1875, £630 million was invested in British railways, a figure far in excess of investment

Angry railway shareholders at a meeting to announce a dividend of just 2d ½

in any other industry. But this wasn't the only cost. During this period the railways were built at a terrible price in human lives. The race to complete new lines and hasten the day when they would bring in revenue put heavy pressure on everybody involved in their construction. From chief engineer to navvy, the men were forced to take huge risks.

As the railway was, in essence, a British creation, British-made locomotives, rolling stock and railway equipment were readily exported to many parts of the world. Great profits were made overseas by British railway engineers and construction teams as British capital built railways throughout the empire, in the Americas and in many parts of Europe. In 1841 Thomas Brassey took an army of navvies with him to embark upon the construction of the French railway system and he went on to build railways in Italy, Belgium, Spain, Russia, India, Argentina and Australia. Imperial railway-building projects were often inspired by military as well as industrial and commercial motives, but such projects, notably in India and Africa, also opened up huge and long-lasting markets to British manufacturers.

His position as a leading railway engineer now firmly established, Locke was well set to take advantage of railway expansion. He was the favourite engineer of merchants and shareholders, the practical engineer who offered to make investments remunerative to everybody, and projects came flooding in. While work continued on the Manchester & Sheffield Railway, a line was proposed between Preston and Lancaster, a distance of 21 miles, and Locke was appointed engineer. But a government requirement to raise the height and widen the bases of the bridges and the exorbitant price the railway company was forced to pay for the land interfered with his estimate. Nevertheless the project went ahead, and while the Preston & Lancaster was being built Locke proposed the continuation of the line from Lancaster through Penrith to Carlisle, as part of a Grand Trunk railway that would link up with the Caledonian Railway and unite the capitals of England and Scotland.

In the South, Locke continued to work on the London & Southampton Railway, later called the London & South Western Railway, designing, among other structures, Richmond Railway Bridge and Barnes Bridge, both across the River Thames, a tunnel at

Micheldever, and the 12-arch Quay Street Viaduct and 16-arch Cams Hill Viaduct, both in Fareham. The line is one of Locke's greatest monuments, crossing the great chalk ridges of the South Downs virtually without tunnels, but with massive cuttings and embankments. It is, and always has been, a route designed for high speeds.

In the planning and execution of large-scale works Locke set new standards of efficiency for his profession. One drawback to his way of operating, though, was that his desire to save money for promoters and shareholders of new lines led him to choose routes that kept capital costs down but landed the companies who operated the lines with higher expenses. This was largely due to the maintenance costs involved on all the extra bridges, viaducts and cuttings, and because climbing up hills rather than going round them made heavy demands on fuel. Because George Stephenson had started his career at a time when locomotives had little power to overcome excessive gradients, he had always maintained that railway routes should be planned and surveyed in the same way as canals, with the longest possible stretches of level line. Both he and Robert Stephenson were prepared to go to great lengths to avoid steep gradients that would tax the locomotives. George felt that the power of the steam locomotive could be used most economically in hauling maximum loads at a good average speed and shouldn't be wasted on climbing hills. The theory was good, but in practice the nature of Britain's landscape meant that a level route would be either very circuitous or would involve costly engineering work. Locke had more confidence in the ability of the latest locomotives to climb gradients. He believed that the Stephensons underestimated their power and that the shortest practicable route should be chosen, even if it involved steep climbs. His reasoning was that by avoiding long routes and tunnelling, the line could be finished more quickly, with lower capital costs, and would bring in revenue earlier.

The route of the west coast line between Lancaster and Carlisle, which had to cope with the barrier of the Cumbrian fells, became the subject of the first major clash between these two schools of thought. Locke's proposal was for a direct line over Shap Fell, but Stephenson favoured a route that went round the Cumbrian coast because it was flat and could be built at a comparatively low cost. It would also, he argued, open up a valuable iron-mining district, from which a large traffic in ironstone could be expected. Another advantage, in Stephenson's view, was that by building the railway directly across Morecambe Bay a large tract of valuable land could be reclaimed from the sea, and the sale of this would considerably reduce the cost of constructing the line. He estimated that by building a ten-mile embankment across the bay between Poulton and Humphrey Head on the opposite shore, 40,000 acres of rich agricultural land would be gained. His plan was to drive in piles across the entire length and form a robust embankment of stone blocks on the landward side. This would retain the sand and silt brought down by the rivers that flowed into the bay. Arches would be built in the embankment to allow for the flow of the river waters into the bay.

The advocates of the coastal route maintained that no standard locomotive could climb the Shap Fell summit and that trains on that part of the line would be continually bedded down in snow during the winter. Locke's route was thirty miles shorter and its advocates countered the arguments of Stephenson's supporters by saying that the extra cost of the motive power required would be less than the interest on the additional capital needed to build Stephenson's more circuitous line. They also argued that no embankment across Morecambe Bay could be built to withstand the battering of winter seas. The debate went on. The advocates of the coastal route said that the expense of cuttings and embankments on the Shap line would bankrupt the Treasury, while the value of the land which the coast line could reclaim from the sea would liquidate the greater part of its expenses.

In the end Stephenson's coastal route was rejected on the grounds that it would take more years to build the line than its promoters were prepared to wait, and Locke's plan for a shorter line over Shap Fell was adopted. It was also felt that even if 90 miles could be built for as little cost as 60, which was doubtful, no one could keep 90 miles in repair for the same cost as 60; nor could anyone expect to travel over that increased distance without a proportionate loss of both time and money. Work started on the railway in July 1844 and, with as many as 10,000 navvies employed, the line was opened as far as Carlisle in December 1846. Trains could now run from London to within a few miles of the Scottish border, but only after negotiating a gruelling gradient culminating in a four-mile 1-in-75 stretch from Tebay to Shap summit.

Britain now had the basis of a railway network and most of the main lines that are still in use today had been or were being built, giving people the opportunity to move around the country in a way that had never previously been possible. Journeys were slow by modern standards, with express trains timed to run at between 20 and 30 mph, but this was unbelievably fast in comparison with contemporary alternatives. More lines were proposed but there were some doubts about whether the country needed them. An article in the *Athenaeum* made the case that millions of pounds were being wasted on building railways that ran parallel to each other, linking the same parts of the country. It questioned whether the Manchester & Leeds and the Manchester & Sheffield should have been built as separate railways, and gave support to a popular view that the government should have laid out a plan for a national railway network as had been done in Belgium.

Even though railways covered most of the country there were still some large gaps in the network and Locke was now focusing on one of these. At this time the railways in England and Scotland were not connected and the best mode of linking up the whole of Scotland with the whole of England had still not been determined. Large trunk lines now existed, connecting the North and South of England, and the Caledonian Railway operated lines around Glasgow and Edinburgh. An extension north of the border into Scotland linking the English lines with the Caledonian's was the logical next step. The problem was how to connect Carlisle with Glasgow and Edinburgh. The obvious route was to follow Thomas Telford's coach road through Annandale and Clydesdale but the central part of southern Scotland was mountainous and, in spite of the fact that he had proposed a direct line over Shap Fell, Locke didn't believe a locomotive would be able to climb the hills at Beattock and Moffat. So again it became a question of winding round hills and thereby increasing the length of the line, or confronting steep gradients and heavy cuttings to obtain a shorter route.

In 1836, breaking from his usual approach, Locke had proposed a route to Glasgow via Dumfries and Kilmarnock. This was 17 miles longer than the more direct route, which would have to cross the 1,000-foot Beattock summit in the Southern Uplands before dropping down into the Clyde Valley and following it into Glasgow. However, Locke's route had the advantage of passing through the main towns of Dumfriesshire and Ayrshire. But no railway company was prepared to pursue this idea and the plan was shelved, perhaps because the route was strongly opposed by local landowners and the cost of buying them off would have made it commercially unviable. The situation was also complicated by the fact that there was a rival scheme for a route into Scotland up the east coast from Newcastle to Edinburgh, with which George and Robert Stephenson were involved. Locke himself felt that the Scottish market would not be able to sustain both lines and recommended that a commission be set up to establish the best single route.

When it reported in May 1841 the commission backed Locke's view that the Scottish economy could support only one line and recommended the western route running from Carlisle to Glasgow. Following this report, the Caledonian Railway revived plans for the west coast line, but they preferred the Clyde Valley route to Glasgow with its climb over Beattock. Locke was the ideal man for the job and he was asked to survey the route. By this time he had become the foremost of a group of engineers and surveyors generally referred to as the 'up and over' school, and he was prepared to take on the challenge of crossing Beattock. Although this route was technically more difficult, its shorter length at an average construction cost of £16,000 per mile meant a saving of £272,000 over his earlier route. Moorland would be much cheaper and easier to purchase than land in the low-lying and prosperous agricultural areas, and the line could split at Carstairs with a branch to Edinburgh. Locke designed the line with John Errington, whom he'd taken into partnership in 1840, and brought in Thomas

Brassey as the contractor. Brassey had by this time built up a formidable reputation for his efficiency, organizational skills and integrity. With Locke and Brassey in partnership, the Caledonian started out with as good an engineer and contractor as it was possible to find.

Work started in February 1845 but did not begin well. Just north of Carlisle lay the Solway marshes and flooding there made the terrain challenging for the railway builders. In spite of this, by August Brassey's men were ready to begin the most difficult part of the line, over Beattock summit. Many of the Lancaster & Carlisle navvies had now joined the workforce and the 10,500 workers completed five miles of track in six months. The Beattock section was pegged out and workmen's huts were erected on the desolate moorland. As soon as the Lancaster & Carlisle Railway was complete, more materials and gangs of well-trained men moved to these new construction sites. Locke was confident that the line would open on schedule in March 1848, but the engineering difficulties that Brassey had to face were so great that they threatened to bring down his entire business. Locke stepped in and persuaded the Caledonian board to cover some of Brassey's additional costs, and thus the contractor was able to stay on schedule.

The line from Carlisle to Beattock opened in 1847 and from Beattock to Glasgow and Edinburgh in 1848. It was now possible to travel between London and Glasgow, by express train, without needing to change. The total journey time was 12½ hours. The most distinctive features of Locke's railway works were economy, the use of masonry bridges wherever possible and the absence of tunnels. Despite the hilly terrain the line traverses, there is not one tunnel between Birmingham and Glasgow.

While Brassey's navvies were fighting floods on the Solway and cutting into the hard rock of the Beattock summit, Locke had moved on to yet another project, to lay down a 48-mile line between Castlecary and Perth called the Scottish Central. The line opened in two years. This was remarkably quick in view of his continued involvement with the Caledonian line and another from Perth to Forfar.

Locke certainly never had cause to complain about lack of work. His reputation was spreading far and wide and not all of his projects were in Britain. His work on the London & Southampton Railway had brought him into contact with the promoters of a plan to build a railway from Paris to Le Havre, from where it would be linked by ferry to the line he was working on and open up a direct route between London and Paris. The line would also bring the sea within a few hours' ride of the French capital. It was first surveyed by Charles Vignoles in 1833, but initially the French were reluctant to invest. It was not until 1839 that agreement was reached with the help of finance from the French government. Locke was brought in as chief engineer for the first part of the project, from Paris to Rouen, which was about three-quarters of the complete route and by far the easiest portion to build. His efforts were greatly helped by the keenness of the French government to remove all obstacles from his path and make everything as smooth as possible.

When he was awarded the contract Locke's initial thought was to use local labour, but he soon found that the French contractors demanded prices nearly double those of the English, who had so much more experience of the work. He also found out quickly that when the work was done by the French, it couldn't be relied on for safety and durability, so once more he turned to Brassey. Brassey went into partnership with another big contractor, William Mackenzie. They took an army of 5,000 experienced English navvies to France to work alongside local labourers. At the start of the project the English navvies earned twice as much as the French, but that was because, thanks to their experience, they were able to do twice as much work. The French workers were happy with this because, even though they were getting less than their English counterparts, they were still making twice as much as they had before the railway came. They were also aware that there were jobs the English navvy would do that they themselves wouldn't take on. With tunnelling or other dangerous work, the French labourer could not be induced to join in, unless an Englishman was at the head of operations.

When it came to building locomotives for the line, the same superiority Locke had found in the English labourer he also found in the English mechanic. France had only one or two steam-engine manufactories and these could supply only a few locomotives of a very inferior sort. The bulk had to be obtained from England, so Locke decided to establish English workshops at Rouen modelled on Robert Stephenson's, and he brought over a team of English mechanics to teach the French to construct and repair their own engines.

Locke had undertaken to construct the line in five years, but progress was so rapid that the opening was announced for 3 May 1843. As the line to Rouen was nearing completion, preliminary steps were taken to continue it to Le Havre and it was here that the real difficulties began. The terrain was chalky and the route was intersected by deep and abrupt valleys. Though the distance was less than half that of the section from Paris, Locke's estimate for the work was greater as five tunnels were needed, as well as a succession of embankments and an immense viaduct to take the line across one of the valleys. The viaduct, at Barentin, near Rouen, was built of stone and brick and it was the longest and highest on the line. At 108 feet high, it consisted of 27 arches, each 50 feet wide, with a total length of over 1,600 feet.

Brassey and Mackenzie won the contract for the viaduct, under-bidding their French competitors by 10 per cent. But securing the work had meant that potentially dangerous savings were made to keep costs down. Mackenzie wrote to Locke to inform him that the mortar they were using wasn't good enough and he was prepared to use a better quality mortar if the company would pay half the extra cost. Locke refused and the work went ahead, but it proved to be a false economy. Early one morning in 1846 a boy hauling ballast for the line up an adjoining hillside saw the fifth arch on the Rouen side collapse, and the rest followed suit like a pack of cards. Fortunately, no one was killed, but several workmen were injured in a mill below the structure.

Locke was quick to attribute the catastrophic failure to frost action on the mortar and premature off-centre loading of the viaduct with ballast, but it is more likely the cause was the suspicious quality of the mortar. Whatever the reason, Brassey and Mackenzie shouldered the entire blame and announced that they would rebuild the viaduct at their own expense. They were as good as their word and the entire structure was completed in only six months, but the episode served as

Opening ceremony and benediction of the
Rouen to Le Havre Railway in 1847

a warning about the dangers of cutting costs in order to secure contracts.

Locke went back to France some years later to build the Paris, Nantes & Cherbourg Railway. While he was inspecting a tunnel on the line he had a serious accident, when scaffolding he was standing on gave way. He landed on his feet but a beam struck him below the knee and he sustained a double fracture. He was taken to Rouen and then on to Paris, where surgeons advised amputation. But Locke, with characteristic firmness, rejected their advice and insisted on an English surgeon being sent for. Under his treatment the fracture was healed and he was back on his feet again in time for the opening of the railway.

As a result of the experience he gained building railways in France, Locke became an early advocate of direct government control of Britain's rapidly expanding rail network. In 1845, he and his old friend Robert Stephenson were called to give evidence before a House of Commons Select Committee investigating the atmospheric railway system proposed by Brunel, and to assist the Gauge Commissioners to arrive at a standard gauge for the whole country. Locke and Robert Stephenson had been good friends at the beginning of their careers, but their friendship had been marred by Locke's falling out with Robert's father. It seems that, for Robert, loyalty to his father required that he should take his side. But giving evidence at these committees brought Locke back into contact with Robert Stephenson and it is significant that after the death of George Stephenson in August 1848 the two men's friendship was revived. When Robert Stephenson died in October 1859, Locke was a pallbearer at his funeral. He is reported to have referred to Stephenson as 'the friend of my youth, the companion of my ripening years, and a competitor in the race of life'.

The impact of the railways created by engineers like Stephenson and Locke and their great contemporary Brunel was changing the face of Britain, but their impact on the lives of millions of ordinary people was even greater, especially after third-class fares were fixed at one penny a mile in 1844. In the days of the stagecoach the return fare from Manchester to London was £3 10s. In 1851 the railway offered a special cheap ticket for five shillings (25p). Excursion trains were packed with holidaymakers, which made them inexpensive to run and provided a means of cheap travel for the masses. In one week in August 1850 more than 200,000 people left Manchester by excursion train, enjoying a welcome release from the toil and grime of the factories and, for many of them, a first-ever glimpse of the sea.

Locke himself was now a rich man, living in comfort with his wife at Oatlands Park, his house on the banks of the Thames at Weybridge. One of his last ambitions was to continue the South Western Railway from Salisbury to the junction with the Great Western at Honiton, Devon, and in 1847 he bought the manor of Honiton. Like Robert Stephenson, in his later years Locke went into politics. In 1847 he was elected Liberal MP for Honiton and sat on the Liberal benches, where he supported the causes of religious and civil liberty, extension of the franchise and reform of obsolete institutions. He was very popular with his constituents but his parliamentary life was generally a quiet one. With Robert Stephenson's death and Brunel's soon following, Locke was without rival in his profession, but he sought no new engagements and turned down many. His partner, John Errington, was younger than him and still an active worker, and many of his own pupils were now well established in their own right. It seems that it was enough for him to know that the work was being done by capable hands. He acted as an adviser to a number of companies, and was occasionally called in to get others out of trouble. He was forever being summoned back to his native Barnsley. Whether it was a station that had to be opened or a school foundation stone to be laid, Barnsley would send for its distinguished townsman. But the most important job he did in his closing years was between December 1857 and December 1859, when he served as president of the Institution of Civil Engineers.

He no longer walked from Warrington to Birmingham in three days, as he had done as a young man when building the Grand Junction, but he was still active in the pursuit of his great love of shooting. He had made several attempts to purchase an estate in Scotland, but had never found one that was quite right. Instead he would rent a place near Moffat, in the Borders. Here he surrounded himself and his guests with the comforts of home during the shooting season, and with the Caledonian line running along their base he was content with the thousands of acres of the Beattock Hills to shoot over. He crossed the line he had built every morning on his way from Moffat to the moors, and every evening on his return. On 12 August 1860 he was joined as usual by friends whose shared enjoyment of the moorland sport made it all the more pleasurable for him. In their company he was readier than ever, of an evening, to sing his favourite songs with them. His only regret was that for the last few years his wife had been forbidden by her doctors to risk the fatigues of so long a journey.

On Sunday, 16 September, he was in excellent health and enjoyed the day's sport. In the evening he was even more talkative than usual, but his conversation was all retrospective. The following morning he did not come down for breakfast, and sent word that he would not go out shooting that day. He was visited by the local doctor, but at dinner-time he was still in bed suffering from acute pain in his bowels. He died the next morning. He was just 55 years old, and the cause of his death was given as appendicitis. His professional friends talked of Westminster Abbey for his burial place but his widow silenced all such suggestions. He should, she said, be quietly laid where she might one day join him. She was quite sure that such would be his wish. He must be buried in Kensal Green Cemetery.

Along with Robert Stephenson, Joseph Locke was one of our greatest railway builders and railways had become the symbol of Victorian industrial might. His greatest legacy, without a doubt, is the modern-day west coast main line. Around three-quarters of its route was planned and engineered by him. But there was another man who had an even greater impact on the Victorian Age. Isambard Kingdom Brunel ranked alongside Locke and Robert Stephenson as one of the major pioneers of railway development. On Locke's death *The Times* referred to them as the 'triumvirate of the railway world'. But Brunel was outstanding not only as a railway builder but in every branch of engineering to which he turned his hand.

5

Isambard Kingdom Brunel
1806–1859
The Little Giant

As well as having one of the most unusual middle names of all time, Isambard Kingdom Brunel is famous for his technological achievements as an engineer. He was a man who had very wide interests, but what made him outstanding was his all-round ability at everything he turned his hand to. He dominated every field of engineering – railway builder, civil engineer, shipbuilder, the lot. No branch of his profession seemed to be beyond his capacity. For me he was the greatest of the Victorian heroes; a larger-than-life character who would rise to any challenge – throwing dramatic bridges across great rivers and gorges; building an iron steamship that would have to carry tons of coal across the Atlantic; digging a tunnel under the River Thames. He was known by the navvies, the shipwrights and the other engineers who worked for him as the Little Giant because he was only little, you see, and because he was never afraid to roll up his sleeves and get his hands dirty as he worked alongside them. He became a very recognizable figure as he went round supervising all his engineering projects, always wearing a tall hat and smoking a cigar. I think he kept himself going chain-smoking cigars and working 20 hours a day.

Isambard Kingdom Brunel was a man of great vision, energy and enterprise – a genius who made a major and lasting contribution to our railway system, to bridge-building and to ship design and construction. Nothing appeared to be impossible for him. He defied conventional wisdom and was a pioneer in many engineering skills we take for granted today, such as the use of the screw propeller in ships. The lines of his design for the Clifton Suspension Bridge can still be seen in the great suspension bridges of today like the ones over the Humber, the Severn and the Forth. Brunel had an unshakeable confidence in himself and his abilities that was amazing even by the standards of his day. 'He were so confident,' Fred said, 'that he actually invested his own money in most of the projects that he undertook. His energy was immense and there was no detail of any project he were involved in that he didn't want to know everything about. For the Great Western Railway he designed the track layout, the track itself, the rolling stock, the tunnels, the bridge. He even designed the lamp-posts for the stations, was a director of the station hotel at Paddington, and, when the going got tough, was not above doing some actual digging on the line.' Then he built the ship, the *Great Western*, to take passengers to the United States from Bristol at the end of the railway line.

It took confidence on a massive scale, in the days of wooden-hulled ships, to build an ocean liner of metal, which was powered by steam, but that's what he did. He was a truly great all-round engineer and he clearly had such a strong sense of his destiny that when he was only 21 years old he wrote in his diary: 'I am afraid that I shall be unhappy if I do not reach the rank of hero.'

Brunel may have been the greatest of Fred's heroes but he was very different from most of the others. For a start, he didn't come from the North and he certainly wasn't a man from a poor working-class background who pulled himself up by his bootstraps. This no doubt explains his exclusion from Samuel Smiles's *Lives of the Engineers*. With his dark hair and olive complexion Isambard Kingdom Brunel looked what he was – the son of a Frenchman, Sir Marc Brunel, and his English wife, Sophia.

Marc, an eminent engineer in his own right, had a remarkable story. He was born near Rouen, the son of a wealthy farmer who insisted that his son should have a career in the church. But Marc had other ideas and went to sea, serving as a cadet on a naval frigate for six years. Returning home at the height of the French Revolution, he met and fell in love with Sophia. She was the youngest of the 16 children of a Portsmouth naval contractor, William Kingdom, who had come to live in France after his father's death. When his support for the monarchy led to fears for his safety, Marc was forced to flee to America, leaving Sophia behind. In his new life he established himself as a surveyor, architect and civil engineer, took US citizenship and became chief engineer to the city of New York. But Britain had declared war on France and while Marc prospered, Sophia was imprisoned along with all British nationals.

On her release she returned to her family's London home. But Marc hadn't forgotten Sophia and in February 1799 he decided to leave America to be reunited with her. They were married in November of that same year and set up home in London. Marc Brunel had brought back from America plans he had drawn up for mechanizing the manufacture of pulley blocks for ships and when he secured a government contract to build a block-making factory at Portsmouth he and Sophia moved to a small terraced house at Portsea with their newborn daughter, also called Sophia. It was here that Isambard Kingdom Brunel was born on 9 April 1806.

Young Isambard began to show a talent for drawing when he was only four years old. His father encouraged this, giving him more formal instruction and teaching him geometry before sending him off to boarding school in Hove. While he was there he carried out a survey of the town and made drawings of many of the buildings. His father always insisted that the ability to draw was as important to an engineer as the ability to read and write.

When his son was 14 Marc sent him to France to be educated at the College of Caen in Normandy and the Lycée Henri-Quatre in Paris, which was famous for its maths teachers. His education in France was completed with a short apprenticeship under Louis Breguet, a renowned maker of watches, chronometers and scientific instruments.

He returned to England in August 1822 when he was 16 years old and began work in his father's office. It was the start of one of the greatest careers in engineering, much greater in its range than anything before or since, as Fred explained:

His projects were astonishing for their scale, their versatility and their daring. And it's no wonder he thought he could do anything when you look at that first project, which was almost his last because he nearly got killed in trying to do it. The tunnel under the River Thames between Wapping and Rotherhithe was a project that was handed on to him by his father, who had been engaged to construct it by means of a new tunnelling shield that he had invented. The tunnel is over 400 yards long and it was the first tunnel under a river of any great size. In spite of all the great engineering wonders he went on to, I think this tunnel was one of Brunel's greatest achievements.

Two hundred years ago, the only means of crossing the River Thames as it flowed through London was over the medieval London Bridge or by using a ferry. The sheer volume of river traffic this generated caused a lot of congestion as bigger ships made their way to and from the docks. It was clear that a new crossing would have to be built. A bridge was not feasible because it would have to be high enough to clear the masts of tall ships, so a tunnel was the obvious answer. Several unsuccessful attempts were made, including one by Richard Trevithick, before Marc Brunel patented a tunnelling shield that he believed would make it possible to bore safely through water-bearing strata.

Work began on the tunnel in March 1825 with Marc in charge. His plan was to sink two great shafts, one on each side of the river, with spiral ramps in them to take traffic into the tunnel. The first shaft was sunk at Rotherhithe on the south bank and by July it had reached a depth of 55 feet. The tunnelling shield was assembled at the bottom and by November tunnelling under the Thames had begun. Marc was optimistic that the project would be finished in three years but it was beset by problems. The tunnel was only about eight feet below the bed of the river and they were working in silt a lot of the time. On two occasions the workings flooded, and in January 1827 Marc Brunel was forced to retire after being injured by falling timber and then catching pleurisy. Isambard was appointed resident engineer at the tender age of 20.

Setting the pattern for his career, Isambard worked tirelessly for nearly two years, driving the tunnel from one side of the Thames to the other, under the most difficult and dangerous conditions. The Thames river bed at Rotherhithe was often little more than waterlogged sediment and loose gravel. It was particularly unpleasant because the Thames at that time was still little better than an open sewer, so the tunnel was usually awash with foul-smelling, contaminated water, bringing an ever-present threat of cholera and a fever that caused blindness. Breaches of the tunnel roof and the resulting emergency evacuations were made doubly risky because the Irish navvies, who were doing the digging, used to extinguish all the lights if ever a leak developed, believing, it was said, that this would save them from drowning because the water would not find them in the dark. The massive task was complicated by many other factors, including a decision by the tunnel management, in the face of strong opposition from Brunel, to allow spectators to be lowered down to observe the diggings at one shilling (5p) a time.

On 18 May 1827 the tunnel flooded and washed all the workers out into the great chamber at the bottom of one of the shafts. One hundred and fifty men were working down there and, as the dirty Thames water rushed in, the lights went out. Brunel was also in the tunnel at the time and twice risked his own life to save workers. Amazingly, no one was seriously injured and everybody managed to escape, but the pumps couldn't work fast enough to get rid of the river water. To solve the problem Brunel borrowed a diving bell from the West India Dock Company to go down to the river bed and inspect the damage himself. There he found that a great depression had been caused by gravel dredging and the brickwork of the tunnel was exposed at the bottom of it. He ordered a huge canvas sheet to be placed over the breach and weighed down with chains around its edges. Bags of clay held together

Brunel's diving bell

with hazel rods to form a bond were laid on the sheet to fill the depression and then the water was pumped out of the tunnel. When the water was out, the hole in the tunnel roof was plugged from the inside with clay and puddling.* 'You have to hand it to him,' Fred said:

> When you think the guy was only 21 years old and he was doing a thing like this that nobody else had ever attempted before. In November 1828 a celebratory dinner was held in the tunnel for the directors of the Tunnel Company. A couple of years ago somebody from the Brunel Society rang me up one evening and said they were going to put a great big table down into the tunnel with all the candelabra on and have a dinner down there to re-enact the event. Can you imagine all the modern Brunel fanatics all down there dressed up with all the gear and big tall hats? But somebody in authority said they couldn't do it because it was too dangerous so it never come off.

With his Thames Tunnel Brunel was pushing the boundaries of engineering expertise and in early 1829 disaster struck again. On 12 January the tunnel flooded for a second time; all the lights were blown out but on this occasion not all the workmen were so lucky. Six men drowned including the two most senior miners, Collins and Ball, and Brunel himself narrowly escaped death. The great rush of water hurled him from the tunnelling platform and he was soon in it up to his waist. Then his leg got trapped under a timber beam and it was only after a great struggle that he managed to free it, injuring his knee. As he made for the safety of the shaft another huge wave swept through the tunnel and swamped him. He was washed up to the other end of the tunnel and, as the water rose, he was carried up a service stairway, from which, luckily, he was plucked unconscious from almost certain death by an assistant moments before the surge receded.

Although it was obvious that he was seriously hurt and his leg was giving him acute pain, he refused to leave the works until he had learned the full extent of the damage. He went to Brighton to recuperate,

---

* Clay that was used to line the bottom of a canal to stop the water running out.

and there it was discovered that his injuries were far worse than he had first thought. In addition to his damaged knee he had serious internal injuries and he suffered the first of a series of haemorrhages. The disaster ended work on the tunnel for several years. It was eventually completed 'but it were never open to traffic,' Fred said.

> It were a foot walk and a home for waifs and strays and for ladies of the night. In spite of the problems though it was the first major sub-river tunnel ever built and it succeeded where other attempts had failed, thanks to Marc Brunel's ingenious tunnelling shield – the human-powered forerunner of today's mighty tunnelling machines – which protected workers from cave-in by placing them within a protective casing. The tunnel is still in use today on the London Underground between Rotherhithe and Wapping.

Brunel may have nearly lost his life, but he'd started to build his reputation. He moved on to Bristol to continue his convalescence, and while he was there, he became acquainted with an enterprising group of Bristol merchants and industrialists. Through them he became associated with a scheme to bridge the 200-foot-deep Avon Gorge to the west of the city. On 1 October 1829 a competition to design the Clifton bridge was announced, with a prize of 100 guineas (£105) offered for the winner. The design was for the longest suspension bridge yet attempted and Brunel was so keen to get the job that he submitted not just one but four designs. Each of them involved some form of suspension bridge construction, but the plans went way beyond mere technicalities to include arguments based on, among other things, the grace of his tower design. Brunel wasn't just a great engineer, he was also very good at persuading committees to accept his plans and award contracts to him. This was the case here, as Fred explained:

> Brunel had an ability to sort out committees and boards of directors, and convince them about the practical side of his ideas and his big projects. At Clifton when they had the competition to build the bridge

he put in his designs and they had no less a man than Thomas Telford to be the judge. The first designs that he submitted were turned down with Telford saying that Isambard's proposed span was too long. The bridge committee asked Telford to draw up a scheme of his own and he produced plans for a suspension bridge supported by two towers set into the bed of the gorge. But Brunel was very critical of Telford's plans and he didn't give in. Eventually he managed to overturn the committee's decision and have his own designs for a suspension bridge accepted.

While he was working on those designs, Brunel also became involved in a scheme for improvements to the Floating Harbour at Bristol. The Floating Harbour was an enclosed dock which allowed ships to stay afloat regardless of whether the tide was in or out, and it had brought great prosperity to the city. In 1831, when Brunel was appointed chief engineer at the Bristol Docks, it came under his management and he proposed improvements that included widening the entrances and installing sluices and a dam for regulating water inflow and scouring silt. Brunel went on to design and build docks at Monkwearmouth, Plymouth, Cardiff, Brentford and Milford Haven, but the Clifton Suspension Bridge was the project that had really captured his imagination.

His work in Bristol had greatly raised his standing in the port and when more funds were raised for the bridge project Brunel was given the go-ahead. The span of his bridge was over 700 feet, longer than any that had previously been built, and the height above the river was 245 feet. The technical challenges of the project were immense, but Brunel dealt with them with his usual thoroughness and ingenuity. Fred told us how he went about it:

At Clifton one of the first things they did was to blacksmith an iron rod two inches in diameter and they stretched it from one embankment to the other to allow men and materials to be moved across. I should imagine they first started off with a piece of string and then a bit of decent rope and then a carrier on that with a wheel running on the rope and they would keep pulling each rod as it were hammer welded on across the valley to the other side. The first time it was being manoeuvred into position there was a bit of a mishap and the bar plunged into the river below. The wrought-iron bar was suspended across the gorge with a basket hanging from it which was used to transport those who were brave or foolhardy enough to risk the journey across. Isambard insisted that he should be the first to ride across in the basket and when it got stuck in the middle of the bar he swung himself up from the basket to the bar and freed it.

The construction of the bridge was dogged by problems and it took 33 years from its commission in 1831 to its completion in 1864. The main difficulty was that the directors didn't raise enough revenue to complete construction of the bridge, so work on it had to be stopped. It was only completed five years after Brunel's death. But it was through that same group of Bristol merchants connected with the bridge project that Brunel became associated with the project that was to bring him lasting fame – an ambitious scheme for a railway between Bristol and London.

Most of the early development of the railways had been done in the North of England but down in the South they were catching up, and it was the merchants of Bristol who took the lead. They decided that they wanted a railway that would run from Bristol all the way to the capital, and in 1833 the Bristol Chamber of Commerce sanctioned the building of a quadruple line of railway between the two cities. Along with several rivals Brunel was invited to survey a route. The winner, they were told, would be the one whose route was the cheapest, but Brunel wouldn't listen to this. He told the railway committee that he would only survey the best route, not the cheapest. He presented his plans for the line very skilfully and somebody who observed his performance in hearings in the House of Lords described him as 'rapid in thought, clear in his language and he never said too much or lost his presence of mind'.

It was the turning point of Brunel's career when, in 1833, at the age of just 27, he was appointed engineer to the new railway and commissioned to plan the line. Six months after his appointment the name Great Western Railway was adopted, and it has remained ever since. The route was to run via Reading and Bath, a course selected because it had easy gradients and opened up possibilities for extensions to be added. 'He surveyed most of it himself from the back of a horse,' Fred said, 'and stopped in some pretty ropy inns and digs on his way.' It was a magnificent feat of engineering. Among the great railway engineers, Brunel was the only one who insisted on retaining personal responsibility for architectural design. Where others were prepared to delegate, Brunel had to be involved in everything. His vision was one of a complete railway system, which would include innovations in architecture, track work, locomotives and above all track gauge. Brunel was something of a wayward genius and he was also a perfectionist, with little concern for the pockets of shareholders.

When he designed his railway he felt that the railways being built by the Stephensons were too narrow, so he decided to make his wider. He said that their 4-foot 8½-inch gauge had been arrived at quite arbitrarily because it happened to be the width of the early coal wagons on Tyneside, and he contemptuously called it 'the coal wagon gauge'. Brunel felt that his broader gauge was the optimum width to provide stability and a comfortable ride for passengers. It also meant that the railway could have bigger carriages, which would allow for more passengers and greater freight capacity. When Brunel was asked about it later, he said he couldn't remember when it was he decided to opt for a 7-foot gauge instead of the 4-foot 8½-inch gauge. 'I think the impression grew on me gradually,' he said.

Whenever it was he made the decision, he was careful to keep it to himself initially. The first Great Western Railway Bill, thrown out by the House of Lords in 1834, included a clause stipulating that the new railway should be built to the narrower gauge. When the second Bill came up early in 1835 Brunel managed to persuade Lord Shaftesbury, the chairman of committees in the House of Lords, to drop the clause and leave no mention of the gauge. It was only after the Bill was passed and had received royal assent that Brunel sprang his scheme on the directors of the Great Western in a letter dated 15 September 1835.

In this he said that 'with regard to gauge there should be a deviation from the dimensions adopted in the railways hitherto constructed.' He quoted friction, resistance and wheel size to support a wider gauge. 'Although it used more land,' Fred said, 'track laid at this broad gauge, and the trains designed to run on it, gave a faster, smoother and more fuel-efficient ride. He just wanted to be the best and only his gauge was good enough. If they had kept that width, the size of trains today and the speeds that they would have been able to go at would really have been something.'

The stealthy, almost underhand way he got the idea accepted would indicate that he was well aware of the concerns others had about adopting the system, but he didn't seem to see it as a problem that the rest of the railways in Britain were being built to a different gauge. At the time he couldn't foresee that there would be many people travelling the length of the country by train and for those who did, he didn't think it would be a problem for them to change trains when they went from the lines of one railway company on to his. But every other railway in the country adopted the 4-foot 8½-inch gauge, so it was inevitable that Brunel would eventually lose the battle. The tracks we now travel on are Stephenson's narrower gauge. The London terminus of the Great Western was originally going to be Euston. The plan was to share it with the London & Birmingham Railway, but the company decided to have their own termini in the suburb of Paddington and at Temple Meads in Bristol.

With Brunel established as the chief engineer of one of Britain's biggest railway-building projects and prospects looking good, he decided at the age of 30 that it was time to marry. Mary Horsley was the eldest child of William Horsley, an organist, music teacher and composer, and she was regarded as the family beauty. Brunel had first met her in 1832 when she was 19 and had been dazzled by her charms. The attraction, it would seem, was mutual and Brunel became a frequent visitor to her parents' house. In 1836 he decided that the moment had come and proposed marriage to Mary, who accepted. Once he'd taken the plunge Brunel saw no reason for delay, particularly as he suspected the longer he waited, the more deeply he would

The inconvenient transferral of goods from Brunel's broad
gauge to the narrower gauge railway at Gloucester

become involved in railway affairs. The wedding took place on 5 July 1836 and, after a fortnight's honeymoon, the couple returned to London and moved into 18 Duke Street in Westminster, which was to be their home for the rest of their married life. It proved to be a happy relationship, but Brunel didn't involve his wife in his work and didn't let his marriage have any influence on the course of his career.

By the time of his marriage the construction of the Great Western Railway was under way and in 1838 the line was opened from Paddington to Maidenhead, where the railway crossed the River Thames over the longest and flattest brick arches ever built – a record that still stands today. The Maidenhead bridge has two main spans, each 128 feet long and semi-elliptical in form, with a rise of only 24 feet. The Brent Valley just west of London was spanned by a viaduct 960 feet long. At Sonning, east of Reading, a cutting had to be excavated to take the line through a small hill. Nearly two miles long and up to 60 feet deep in places, it was one of the biggest excavations of the early railway age, taking a team of 1,200 navvies and 200 horses to dig it out.

From London to Chippenham the line was so flat that it soon became known as Brunel's billiard table, but between Chippenham and Bath it had to penetrate the massive barrier of the 400-foot-high Box Hill. This involved a lot of deep cutting and a tunnel at Box, which, at nearly two miles in length, was by far the longest railway tunnel that had ever been attempted at this time. Many people said the tunnel would be impossible to build. It has a gradient of 1 in 100, which led one MP to warn that the slope was so great that if the brakes failed, a train could run out of control in the blackness and accelerate up to speeds of 120 mph, suffocating all those on board. Another MP argued during a debate in the House of Commons that if the tunnel were built, no one would be brave enough to enter it. Undeterred, Brunel and his resident engineer, William Glennie, began to dig the tunnel in September 1836. Some 1,200 navvies were engaged on the project, backed up by 100 horses to carry out the spoil, which eventually totalled 247,000 cubic yards. Work went on around the clock. 'It was a huge undertaking,' said Fred, 'especially when we remember that apart from the steam pumps which kept the workings clear of water and the power of gunpowder that was used to blast away the rock, it was all done entirely by the strength of men and horses and the whole proceedings were lit by candle power. I mean, when you think about it: what an achievement!' But it came at a price. Accidents caused while working in the primitive conditions claimed the lives of nearly 100 navvies and many more were maimed for life. The tunnel was completed on 30 June 1841. Brunel had driven it through at a cost of £100 per yard and for two and a half years its construction had consumed a ton of gunpowder a week. It was completely straight and, in a final touch of virtuosity, it had been designed so that the sun shone through it from end to end at dawn on Brunel's birthday, 9 April.

As the line had by then also been built from Bristol eastwards to Box, the end of work on the tunnel marked the completion of the route from London to Bristol. With the whole line open, Brunel began to plan numerous branches to towns and cities near its route, such as Oxford and Cheltenham. Swindon, about halfway between London and Bristol, was chosen as the junction for the line to Gloucester and as the site of the Great Western Locomotive Works. Daniel Gooch, who had worked with Robert Stephenson in Newcastle upon Tyne, was put in charge of locomotive production. An extension to Exeter was also in hand. The first passengers on the Bristol & Exeter Railway were 400 invited guests. They were taken on a special train from Bristol to Bridgewater in 1 hour 45 minutes behind Firefly class 2-2-2 *Fireball* on 1 June 1841. The full 76-mile line through to Exeter was opened on 1 May 1844 when Daniel Gooch drove Firefly class locomotive *Actaeon* the 388 miles from Paddington to Exeter and back. Five-hour Exeter expresses were soon running and tourism to Exeter became big business.

If it had anything to do with engineering Brunel would have a go at it, and his versatile genius allied to his capacity for work was so great that in the middle of his hectic career as a railway engineer he also designed three steamships. Each of them at the time of its launch was the largest ever built, and each was a milestone in shipbuilding. While Brunel was building the Great Western Railway he began to develop the idea of linking it with a series of ships in a combined land-and-sea transport system. The railway was already about 100 miles long but when the directors complained that this was too long Brunel suggested that he would like to make it much longer. His dream, he told them, was to link a steamship service to New York with the Great Western Railway at Bristol, so that you could buy a through ticket from Paddington to New York. The directors thought he was joking. 'He'll have us going to the moon yet,' one of them is reported to have said. But Brunel was serious.

In the 1830s, the paddle steamer had proved its viability on shorter coastal routes, but the lucrative transatlantic trade was still dominated by American sailing packets. Brunel had decided right from the outset that his ships were going to be powered by steam. At first, most people thought he was mad. Until that time it was believed that steamships were not practical for ocean crossings because so much fuel would be required there would be no room left on board for any passengers or cargo. But Brunel was a mathematician and he worked out that while a ship's carrying capacity increases by the cube of its dimensions, its resistance to motion through the water, and hence the force needed to propel it, increases by the square of its dimensions. As a result, he calculated that ships would need less energy per ton to propel them, the larger they were. He argued that to design a steamship of any given length was simply a question of determining the correct proportions. Although the board of the Great Western Railway were not convinced by the idea, a group of Bristol merchants became persuaded that it was sound and together with Brunel they formed the Great Western Steamship Company.

The keel of Brunel's first ship was laid at the yard of Bristol ship-builder William Patterson in the Floating Harbour in June 1836, the year before Queen Victoria came to the throne. Built of oak, using traditional methods, the 236-foot-long, 3,200-ton *Great Western* was launched in 1838. She was powered by sail and paddle wheels, and immense strength was built into her to withstand the storms of the North Atlantic. Lambeth manufacturer Maudslay, Son and Field, the leading builders of marine engines, were selected to supply engines for the ship. The *Great Western* sailed round the south coast and up the Thames to London to have them fitted. The work was done by Maudslay in the East India Dock at Blackwall over a six-month period, and by March 1838 she was ready for preliminary trials. The engines had massive cylinders with a stroke of seven feet to drive twin paddle wheels, each 28 feet in diameter. The *Great Western*, with Brunel on board, sailed from the Thames on 31 March 1838, bound for Bristol. But fire broke out because the boiler lagging was too close to the base of the funnel. The fire was put out, but in fighting the flames Brunel was injured and had to be put ashore at Canvey Island.

The *Great Western* arrived in Bristol on 2 April, but many of the passengers who had booked for the first transatlantic crossing had cancelled because of rumours about the ship's failings. The first trip to New York took just 15 days and 5 hours, establishing the start of the modern steamship era and the famous Blue Riband contest for the fastest transatlantic passage by passenger ships. Sailing clippers of the era took 35 days to travel to New York and 25 days for the return with a favourable wind, so for speed, reliability and comfort the *Great Western* was a big improvement on the packets. She proved beyond doubt that a steamship could cross the Atlantic without running out of coal – when she first arrived in New York, she still had 200 tons of coal in her bunkers – and she cut travel times dramatically. But she had some serious weaknesses. Her sails had to be used in conjunction with the engines and paddles did not perform well under ocean conditions. But the biggest drawback was the fact that the ship was built out of wood, and it was costly to build wooden ships that were strong enough to withstand the stress from the engines.

The *Great Western* was the first steamship to be used for a regular transatlantic service and made 74 crossings to New York, but competition was intensified when Samuel Cunard set up a new shipping line. In July 1840 his first ship, *Britannia*, crossed the Atlantic in 11 days and 4 hours. Brunel needed to move on to a bigger and better vessel. His next ship, SS *Great Britain*, was one of the outstanding engineering achievements of the Victorian Age and it revolutionized ocean travel. Brunel knew that the *Great Western* represented the limit of what was possible with wood, which was why he decided the SS *Great Britain* would have to be built of iron. One of the factors which persuaded him was the great advances that had been made in the development of iron angles and plates.

The size of iron ships up to this time had been restricted by problems in using magnetic compasses, but fortunately the Astronomer Royal, Professor Airey, had devised a system of correcting magnets. The new system was installed on *Rainbow*, an iron paddle steamer that visited Bristol in 1838, and two of Brunel's colleagues, Captain Christopher Claxton and William Patterson, reported favourably on the system after joining *Rainbow* on a voyage to Antwerp. This convinced Brunel and he decided he would be able to build his new ship of iron. To build the ship the Great Western Dock at Bristol was extended, warehouses and workshops were erected and construction machinery was installed.

The hull of the *Great Britain* is clinker-built, constructed of wrought-iron plates, which were shaped and riveted in the dock where she was built. They each measure about 6 feet by 2½ feet, overlap horizontally and are connected by two rows of rivets. This overlap gave 15 per cent more strength than if they had been laid edge to edge, and the hull has always been remarkably watertight. Wrought iron is a malleable, workable metal that is strong under tension, highly rust-resistant and is made from cast iron in a process called puddling, which includes two further stages of reheating and re-rolling before the finished iron bar is ready. It is the oldest commercial form of iron and was used extensively in the nineteenth century. In mid-nineteenth-century Britain about three million tons were produced every year. As well as for the SS *Great Britain*, it was used for Robert Stephenson's Conwy and Britannia tubular bridges, for anchors and for anything requiring its high tensile strength.

The initial plan for the new ship had been to incorporate into the design the largest paddle wheels that had ever been built, but Brunel knew that paddles weren't really the best form of propulsion for crossing the ocean. They are large and complicated compared to the modern propeller, and their depth in the water can affect their performance. When a paddle steamer is heavily loaded the wheels sink further below the surface and in rough seas, when a paddle steamer rolls, one wheel may come out of the water while the other is completely submerged.

Far-sighted people in the shipping business could see what needed to be done to make a steamship that would be commercially profitable in competition with sailing ships. Marine engines before the 1860s consumed so much fuel that by the time a vessel was loaded with cargo there was only enough space left for coal for a few days' steaming. First and foremost, a much more efficient and economical engine than anything that had been developed up to this time was needed. Next, metal construction was essential to take the stresses and strains of power propulsion. And finally, ships would have to be bigger in order to be more economical to run per ton-mile and therefore more profitable. To make any of these changes, something better than the paddle was needed as a means of propulsion, and by the 1840s a new propeller, attached to the stern of the ship below the waterline, was being perfected.

The development of the screw propeller was one of the most important events in the history of seafaring and one that Brunel watched with great interest. In Britain it had begun in 1836 when Francis Pettit Smith, a farmer by profession, took out a patent placing the screw between the sternpost and the rudder. He set up a company called the Screw Propeller Company and built a ship called *Archimedes*, which was launched in 1838. Ten months after the keel of Brunel's new ship was laid on 1 July 1839, *Archimedes* arrived in Bristol and demonstrated her revolutionary propeller. Brunel chartered the ship for six months and was convinced that a fully immersed propeller represented a huge advance on the paddle wheel. In December 1840 he declared that his new ship should be driven by one. However, the adoption of the screw propeller presented Brunel with fresh problems. The engine that had been planned for the *Great Britain* couldn't be adapted, and so an entirely new configuration was required. The project was delayed for two years while Brunel carried out more research into propellers and the engines they required with Pettit Smith. Eventually they came up with a design based on the Triangle engine patented by Brunel's father, which involved using a chain drive for the propeller.

Brunel was now pressing ahead on all fronts. By 1844 the Great Western line from Bristol to Exeter was fully open as was the Bristol to Gloucester branch, where it met the standard gauge of the Birmingham & Gloucester line. As the Great Western Railway expanded its network further, Brunel continued to take charge of each line, always laying broad gauge. The South Devon line presented particular problems: it had to run between the sea and the cliffs at Dawlish so a sea wall needed to be built to protect it. The line then extended into Cornwall with many timber viaducts built over deep valleys. Pleasing as they were to the eye, they were later replaced by more durable structures. In the other direction, the railway was also stretching towards the Midlands with a new line from Swindon to Gloucester and Cheltenham.

Brunel was rapidly establishing himself as one of the most famous men of the age and his projects were attracting massive publicity and public interest. The Thames Tunnel had been finally opened at the end of March 1843, just over four months before the launch of the *Great Britain* on 19 July, and the *Illustrated London News* had special coverage of both events. The launch of SS *Great Britain* was a landmark in the progress of steamship development. It was a monster – 322 feet long with 3,675 tons displacement – the like of which had never been seen before. She was the world's first fully powered big steamship and, although she carried masts, spars and sails to back up the engines, the aim was that her engines would drive her all the time. The launch took place in the presence of Prince Albert, who travelled down from London on Brunel's new Great Western Railway on a special train driven by Daniel Gooch.

The Queen's husband was the driving force behind the Great Exhibition, held in 1851 to demonstrate the industrial supremacy and prosperity of Britain. Needless to say, Brunel was involved with the exhibition in a whole variety of ways. It wasn't just a celebration of British innovation and manufacturing invention, but also of the Victorian virtues of hard work and self-reliance.

This was the spirit of the age – epitomized for many by Brunel.

After her launch, the *Great Britain* was moved back into the dry dock for fitting out. The work was completed in March 1844, but then it was discovered that she was too big to get through the locks that linked the Floating Harbour to the River Avon. Brunel released the ship from the Floating Harbour by partially dismantling the locks at night. This difficulty in getting the ship out of the port signalled the decline of Bristol as a great maritime centre and the end of Brunel's dream of the direct Paddington–New York link. The *Great Western* had already been transferred to the more convenient port of Liverpool in 1843 and it was decided to move the *Great Britain* there as well.

Designed for speed and comfort, she was the most revolutionary steamship of the early Victorian period. Equipped with cabins and state rooms for 360 passengers and the biggest and most lavish dining room afloat, she set the standard for large liners for many decades to come. But the ship still had to overcome fears about her safety and so, on 26 July, she sailed for New York with just 50 passengers and 600 tons of cargo. '*Great Britain*,' said Fred, 'crossed the Atlantic in 14 days 21 hours in grand style. They didn't have to resort to burning any doors or furniture. In fact, I think they had a bit of coal left when it got there, which was all to the credit of Mr Brunel. Of course the ship received a tremendous welcome as she steamed up the Hudson and into the port of New York.'

Considering the ship was not just the largest that had ever been built but combined two innovations of iron hull and screw propeller, she had surprisingly few teething troubles and made four round trips to New York before disaster struck in September 1846, when she ran aground off the coast of Ireland. The large amount of iron in the hull had affected the ship's compass. This was just the sort of unforeseen peril that affected great engineering innovations, but much was learned from this early mishap. As she ran aground, the *Great Britain* had scraped across rocks hidden under the sand. No other vessel in the world could have withstood this without breaking up, but the ten iron girders that ran the length of the ship gave the *Great Britain* immense strength. The ship was floated off the following spring and towed back to Liverpool, where she was repaired and recommissioned. By 1853 SS *Great Britain*, refitted to accommodate up to 630 passengers, was operating an efficient London-to-Australia service and continued to do so for nearly 20 years. Her importance lay in the prestige she conferred on Brunel, who was retained as the consultant engineer for the navy's pioneer screw-driven steam warship.

Brunel was rapidly emerging as one of the key characters of his century, the archetype of the heroic age of the engineer. Although he made it a principle throughout his career to invest in his own schemes and thus to share their financial risks, his money-making instinct was not a guiding force. His pride, his ambition to distinguish himself in the eyes of the public and his self-admitted love of glory were much more of a spur. When he was at the height of his fame he undoubtedly earned a lot from his endeavours but to him this wealth was incidental and much of it was used for keeping up appearances, especially those of his wife. Brunel wanted a wife of whom he could be proud; she needed to be a walking manifestation of his success. Mary's beauty and the quality that had won her the nickname 'Duchess of Kensington' when she was a girl enabled her to play her role to perfection. Brunel took great delight in his ability to enhance his wife's charms and he spared no expense on luxurious clothes and jewels to enhance her loveliness.

But none of this tells us the whole story. To find out more about Brunel the man, Fred went to Bristol University to view a collection of his letters and diaries. Recalling that time, he said:

> It was one of the most exciting things we did in all of our filming; to be able to read the actual letters and papers of my greatest hero . . . There's a lovely letter in the library to his wife Mary. In it he says, 'I have walked today 18 miles from Bathford bridge and I am not really tired.' In fact he goes a bit further on and says that if he'd got there a bit earlier he would have caught the train down to London and come back on the goods train early in the morning. What a fella; it's harder than climbing chimneys, that! He says, 'The hotel, which is the best of a deplorable set of public houses, is full', and he was staying at the Cow and Candle

Snuffers. He goes on to describe his room: 'There are four doors and two windows. What's the use of the doors I can't conceive for you might crawl under them the gap's that big.' He ends his letter, 'Goodbye my dearest love, yours I. K Brunel.'

Many of the entries in his diary show that, although he was outwardly confident, bordering on arrogant, he was also deeply insecure. One of them says, 'Everything's prospered, everything at the moment is sunshine. I don't like it; it can't last. Bad weather must surely come. Let me see the storm in time to gather in the sails.' When recession forced him to dismiss a number of his young assistant engineers he wrote, 'I have general anxieties and vexations of my own, and at present they are certainly not below the average, but they are completely absorbed and overpowered by the pain I have to undergo for others.'

In spite of this insecurity, the inventiveness and the grand scale of the projects he took on captured the public imagination. However, because of the sheer number of chances and risks he took, it was inevitable that not everything he attempted was successful. In the library at Bristol University Fred discovered something about one of his failures, the South Devon Atmospheric Railway:

It were an absolute disaster, but he had great faith at the beginning that he could make it work, but he were also warned by Stephenson and Daniel Gooch that the thing were a bit iffy. But Brunel's ready acceptance of new ideas overpowered good engineering judgement when he advocated the installation of an 'atmospheric railway'. It had the great attraction of doing away with the locomotive, and potentially could deal with steeper gradients.

The basic idea for the atmospheric railway, which had been patented by William Clegg and the brothers Joseph and Jacob Samuda, was to propel trains by compressed air acting on a piston travelling in a tube. The system involved a series of stationary engines in pumping stations built along the length of the line. Laid between the railway lines, there was a 15-inch-diameter pipe with a slit cut along the top.

Into this pipe a piston was fitted and this was connected to the railcar above by an arm. As the train moved along the track, a series of pumps stationed about two miles apart emptied the pipe of air ahead of the piston, thus creating a vacuum. The atmospheric pressure in the pipe then drove the train. Fred explained how the system worked in his own inimitable style:

> When the brakes were released the train would be drawn swiftly and smoothly along the line. Really, a good explanation of it for anybody who's over middle aged is if you remember going to the co-op for the groceries with your mam when you were little. There were this strange collection of pipes that almost looked like large bore central heating pipes. When you gave the man behind the counter your money, he would go to this strange-looking cupboard door and open it. There were a hissing noise and he put all the money in a thing that were a bit bigger than a bean tin with two rubber rings round each end and when he bobbed it in it just shot away up the pipe and it were magic for a small child. Within a second or two of your money shooting off it sort of reappeared with what they used to call the divi and your change. It were quite magic. I'd never ever heard of the atmospheric railway then, but this thing at the co-op always fascinated me as a kid and it worked on the same principle.

Despite not being the inventor of the atmospheric railway, Brunel enthusiastically proposed its development for the South Devon Railway from Exeter to Plymouth and he was appointed consulting engineer for the whole project. Because there were some steep hills along the route, Brunel doubted the capacity of steam locomotives of the day to work the railway and strongly favoured the possibility of using some other form of motive power.

Brunel's enthusiasm was shared by the Prime Minister, Sir Robert Peel, who wanted to see all railways converted to the atmospheric system. Its appeal was obvious: one of the biggest complaints about steam trains, in those days of open carriages, was that they frequently showered passengers with boiling water and hot cinders. In contrast, here was a system that promised to be clean, silent and fast. Trains would, it was claimed, be lighter and more efficient because there was no engine, and hilly terrain could be tackled easily because all that was needed was a pumping station nearby. Daniel Gooch was not convinced and he joined forces with Robert Stephenson to argue the case against the system. But, persuaded by Brunel's argument that huge savings could be achieved, the South Devon directors unanimously approved his plans to use atmospheric propulsion over the whole length of the 52-mile route from Exeter to Plymouth.

Brunel built grandiose Italianate engine houses at two-mile intervals along the route and the first section of the atmospheric railway from Exeter to Newton Abbot was completed. High speeds were achieved just as Brunel had predicted: 68 mph with a 28-ton load and 35 mph with 100 tons. This was a phenomenal speed for the day, but sadly the system could never be relied on to work properly on a regular basis. Because the connecting arm that the piston was attached to had to run along the slit, it had to be opened through a flap as the train progressed and closed airtight behind it. However, materials available at the time were not up to it and this arrangement was troublesome and expensive to keep in repair. Leather flaps were used to seal the vacuum pipes and the leather had to be kept supple by the use of tallow, which was attractive to rats. With the rats feeding off this key component, the air-powered vacuum system lasted less than a year.

The whole project was hopelessly uneconomic and Brunel had no option but to recommend to the directors of the railway that the atmospheric workings be pursued no further. The South Devon shareholders had lost nearly £500,000 on the scheme and were faced with an additional bill of £25,000 to turn the line over to locomotive haulage. In a rare admission of failure, Brunel faced angry shareholders at a meeting in Plymouth and admitted that he had been wrong about atmospheric propulsion. 'If the materials had been a bit better,' Fred said, 'and the rats hadn't eaten the zip fastener . . . it could possibly have been a success and the development of the railways would have been very different.' As it was, he put a lot of money, time, energy and thought into the atmospheric railway and in the end it came to nothing.

Even a man as great as Brunel was hoodwinked with it a bit. Brunel admitted his failure and took responsibility. He took no fee for his work, setting a good professional example. It were the most costly disaster in the history of engineering up to that time . . . From looking at his papers at Bristol University it's clear that commercial failures like the SS *Great Britain* and the South Devon Railway meant that Brunel wasn't always popular with shareholders. And he wasn't liked any better by a lot of the contractors who worked for him.

As a perfectionist who liked to check on every detail of his projects and change the specification if he thought of a better way of doing things, Brunel was very difficult to work with. This can be seen clearly in his final great project, the *Great Eastern*, and his partnership with the eminent shipbuilder John Scott-Russell. In 1851 Brunel started work on designs for a vessel four times the size of the *Great Britain*. The SS *Great Eastern* would be the queen of ships, capable of taking a year's exports to India in one trip and returning without refuelling. Brunel designed it with a double iron hull split into 22 compartments and this great monster of the oceans, originally called *Leviathan*, was to have three sources of propulsion: two paddle wheels each 58 feet across and a single screw propeller 24 feet across to be driven by a separate engine. To save fuel when possible, the ship was built with six masts, giving it 58,500 square feet of sail. It was built in London on the Isle of Dogs and there was little doubt that a ship of such size would push the boundaries of existing technology. Its construction was one of the most remarkable single feats in the whole field of Victorian engineering, but its story cast a shadow over Brunel's last years.

To get backing for the project, Brunel had gone into partnership with John Scott-Russell, one of the leading marine architects of the day, who was commissioned to build the actual hull. Scott-Russell drew up detailed plans for the project, including a new design for a hull that featured girders running between the inner and outer skin, and came up with a tender to build and fit out the *Great Eastern* as well as provide the paddle engines and boilers for £275,200. This was accepted, but his price was hopelessly over-optimistic. Brunel had originally estimated £500,000 and it's hard to understand how such an experienced shipbuilder thought it could be done so cheaply. As it turned out, it couldn't and Brunel soon fell out with Scott-Russell.

Construction of the hull was begun early in 1854, but the work was dogged by minor setbacks. It took a lot longer to build it than had been anticipated. One of the main problems was that they were always running out of money and Scott-Russell was permanently at logger-heads with Brunel. The contractual arrangements were unsatisfactory. Brunel maintained overall control of the project, despite the fact that Scott-Russell was ultimately responsible for building the vessel. Brunel's attention to detail and his insistence on making alterations to plans slowed everything down, the costs escalated and things became impossible for Scott-Russell.

Brunel's relationships with contractors, shareholders and business partners weren't helped by the fact that he always had so many things on the go at the same time. While the *Great Eastern* was being built, Brunel was also busy extending his broad-gauge empire from Devon into Cornwall. This included building the Royal Albert Bridge to carry the line over the River Tamar at Saltash. It was to be the last of his great railway engineering projects.

Built between 1853 and 1859, the Royal Albert Bridge is the only railway-carrying suspension bridge in Britain. It is a magnificent engineering achievement, over 700 yards long, with two great spans joined by a single deep-water pier in the middle of the river. The rock foundation for this pier lay beneath 80 feet of mud and water, so a wrought-iron tube 35 feet in diameter and 85 feet in length was con-structed on the shore, towed out to mid-stream, upended and sunk down to the bedrock. Within this caisson, the largest that had been employed in civil engineering up to that time, the water was removed using compressed air. This difficult and dangerous operation was carried out successfully and the pier for the bridge was built inside the caisson, which was designed in two halves so that when the masonry pier had been built it could be removed.

The bridge at Saltash is one of Brunel's masterpieces and contains a number of engineering innovations. The suspension chains are not anchored into the ground on either side of the bridge as is normal for a suspension bridge. Instead Brunel braced them against two wrought-iron cylinders that arch upwards in a curve in the opposite direction to the chains. The bridge took seven years to build and cost £225,000. It still stands today with the simple inscription 'I. K. Brunel. Engineer. 1859' high over the tower arches. His confidence in taking on projects like this was amazing. The soundness of his engineering means that even today, although the broad gauge has long disappeared, trains speed over a virtually unchanged railway. Fred remembered a couple of stories he'd heard about the building of the bridge:

> They were lifting great iron girders up when something went wrong with a winch. It ripped one of the operatives in half and a great block of stone came down which hit the plinth round the bottom of one of the pillars. The article said even though the man died, which was bad news, the base of the pillar wasn't damaged! It didn't knock the moulding off the bottom – incredible! Another story was about a guy who got his arm blown off when they were blasting their way through a tunnel. They didn't sack him or throw him out but found him a soft job. He ended up driving a winding engine at the top of one of the airshafts, which were needed for driving the tunnel down below.

While all this was going on, work continued on the *Great Eastern* on the Isle of Dogs. The job bankrupted Scott-Russell with only half the hull built and Brunel took over the construction himself. The ship was built in cradles and it was intended to push these down a slipway and into the Thames so that she could be floated off on the high tide. But the dead weight of the hull was over 12,000 tons, a greater weight than anybody had ever attempted to move on land, so the operation proved very difficult. Chains and hawsers parted, the cylinders of hydraulic presses cracked and it was not until the end of January 1858 that she was successfully floated off and moored at Deptford to complete her fitting out. 'It took six months before he could get it into the water,' Fred said, and all the difficulties he'd had with her construction, added to the problems of trying to get the ship launched, exhausted even the prodigious energies of Brunel. The huge and costly effort of launching the *Great Eastern* sideways into the Thames in January 1858 and preparing it for its first sea trials the following September proved to be too much for him ... He was too ill to attend the opening of his Royal Albert Bridge by Prince Albert and had to be carried over the bridge lying on a wagon a few days later.

The press coverage of the launch was hostile and, despite the public acclaim he had received for a lot of his work, Brunel came in for a lot of criticism. The press accused Brunel of megalomania. 'I've read the whole saga of the building of the *Great Eastern* and the problems it caused him,' Fred said,

in some old copies of the magazine *The Engineer* that I've got upstairs. I used to lie in bed with my lamp on and a pint of Guinness, and I used to read them until I fell unconscious ... They didn't half slag him off when he was building the *Great Eastern* ... The last known picture of Isambard himself is on the deck of the enormous ship. You've only got to look at it to see he looks very disappointed. It's a very sad picture, he's not even got his tall shiner on and his cigar's not going. He looks about 70 and yet he was only 52 years old at the time.

Soon after the picture was taken, Brunel was seized by a stroke on the deck of his great ship and was carried home to Duke Street. The day before the sea trials, there was an explosion on its trial run that would have destroyed a lesser ship. Somebody had forgotten to undo a stopcock on a feed water heater and the pressure built up and blew the back funnel off. While this drama was taking place, Brunel waited at home for news. When it arrived it was the final blow for the great engineer. He suffered a further stroke, from which he died on 15 September 1859. 'That ship killed Brunel,' said Fred. His great friend Robert Stephenson, who remained a staunch supporter throughout all his troubles with the *Great Eastern*, died within a few weeks of him.

Stephenson and Brunel had often clashed in the course of their professional life and the seven-foot gauge was a particular cause of contention. But Brunel was his own man and the very fact that another engineer had fixed the gauge of a railway, or built a bridge, or designed an engine, was in itself a good enough reason for him to follow a completely different course. Robert Stephenson, though less bold, was more practical, preferring to follow tried and tested ways and tread in the safe steps of his father. But, while their professional rivalry was intense and their engineering and commercial policies were worlds apart, they maintained a close personal friendship throughout their careers. 'It is very delightful,' Brunel wrote, 'in the midst of our incessant personal professional contests, carried to the extreme limit of fair opposition, to meet him on a perfectly friendly footing and discuss engineering points.' So, when Stephenson was floating the first tube of his Britannia Bridge, Brunel dropped all his own engagements and hurried to North Wales to give his friend his support.

Brunel's technical achievements astounded his contemporaries and set new standards in civil engineering, but to do this he had to take chances. The atmospheric railway was a disaster and his broad gauge was abolished by the Gauge Commission. But he was regarded with great respect by fellow engineers and Clifton Suspension Bridge was completed after his death as a memorial to him. And over 150 years later, much of what he designed is still being used for its original purpose, including most of the Great Western line.

The deaths of Brunel and Stephenson in 1859 heralded the end of an era. In many ways it was the end of that heroic age when there was no problem in civil or mechanical engineering that individuals like them were not eager to confront and conquer. They and their generation bequeathed a sum of knowledge that had become too large and complicated to be mastered any longer by one mind, and all scientific and technical development from then on depended to an ever-increasing extent upon specialization. Brunel had been able to move easily between the marine, civil, railway and mechanical engineering fields, which later engineers were not able to do as projects got bigger and the profession began to divide into more specialist fields. Brunel

The ghost of Brunel laments the eventual
abolition of his broad-gauge railway

was a great individualist – a quality that was greatly admired by the Victorians. He had tremendous vision and energy, but he liked to be able to do everything himself. He wasn't really a good team player. From the 1860s onwards the big engineering projects became much more of a team effort.

Brunel's unremitting search for new techniques and his willingness to experiment made him always a controversial figure. The idea of a steam-powered iron ship that had to carry a huge weight of coal in order to raise the steam was greeted with incredulity and Brunel was seen by some as a madman. SS *Great Britain* bankrupted the company that built it, but is now regarded as a major landmark in ship design. We see now, particularly in the criticisms of his design for the *Great Eastern* and his attempts to launch it, that his genius wasn't always recognized in its time. Yet today the ship is regarded as the prototype of modern luxury liners. Brunel's engineering innovations made the building of large-scale, screw-driven, iron steamships a practical reality, but the prevailing economic and industrial conditions meant that it would be several decades before trans-oceanic steamship travel emerged as a viable industry. The records of scale set by *Great Eastern* were finally broken only by the super-liners of the Edwardian era, *Lusitania* of 1907, *Titanic* of 1912 and *Imperator* of 1913. The ship has been portrayed as a white elephant, but like all of Brunel's ships and much of his other work it was simply years ahead of its time. He was a visionary who recognized that technology had the power to change the world and he took the technology of his day to the limits. A man of extravagantly imaginative ambition and sometimes wild ideas, he didn't always get things right and sometimes he got them catastrophically wrong. Although the Great Western Railway is seen as his greatest monument, there was one important aspect of that where even Fred, his great admirer, felt he'd got it wrong:

There is an intriguing story about Brunel's broad-gauge railway. When the railway was first planned it was Brunel's intention to have loco-motives for his new line built by manufacturers to specifications he had produced himself. But Brunel's weak point was the fact that he wasn't good at designing locomotives. Although he was a brilliant civil engineer, his attempts at locomotive design were not quite as successful. In fact his early attempts became known as freaks and it was reported that they could hardly pull themselves along, let alone a train, so they were quietly forgotten about. If you look at his drawings and at one example that was actually manufactured, they weren't very good, which is a bit unusual for Brunel because he had a wonderful eye for beautiful things. So, to look after the locomotive-building side of the business, he enlisted the services of a gentleman called Daniel Gooch as his locomotive superintendent and Gooch became another of the great engineering heroes of the Victorian Age.

6

Daniel Gooch
1816–1889
The Battle of the Gauges

Daniel Gooch was the first locomotive superintendent of the Great Western Railway. His first job was in an ironworks, but he soon got into the railway business when he went to work for Robert Stephenson, who was a friend of the family. But he wasn't there for long and when he moved on to the Great Western he developed the basic Stephenson locomotive into a broad-gauge machine which, for the 1840s, reached some amazing speeds. His Great Britain 8-foot single-driver hauled a 100-ton train at an average speed of over 50 mph for 77 miles and his famous 8-foot singles were the most powerful express passenger engines in the country, putting the Great Western ahead of any other company in Britain in locomotive power. Like Brunel, he wanted a railway with broad-gauge locomotives because he said they were 'safer, swifter, cheaper to run, more comfortable for passengers and more commodious for goods'. Unfortunately, the narrow gauge was taken up everywhere else and Brunel and Gooch were defeated. But there can be no dispute that Gooch's designs were at the leading edge of locomotive design. They were eventually improved on and the broad gauge passed away, but it was Gooch more than anybody else who laid the foundations for the Great Western to grow into one of the big four railway companies in Britain and one of the most widely respected in the world.

Daniel Gooch was born at Bedlington in Northumberland on 24 August 1816, the son of John Gooch, an iron founder, and his wife Anna, who also came from a famous North East family of iron founders. Her father, Thomas Longridge, was a partner in the Bedlington Ironworks where the rails for the Stockton & Darlington Railway were made and her cousin, Michael Longridge, was one of the founding partners of Robert Stephenson & Company.

When he was four Daniel was sent to his first school. His teachers were the two daughters of a local gentleman called Gilbert Robson, who had a schoolroom by the cross in the centre of Bedlington. He stayed there for three or four years and was then sent to join his brother Tom at the best school in the neighbourhood, Mr Thompson's at Cow Hall.

John Gooch was a friend of George Stephenson, and the 'father of the railways' was a frequent visitor to the Gooch household. Whenever he came he would sit the young Daniel on his knee and tell him all about steam engines and coal mines. John Gooch gave his son a lathe and a box of tools, and sent him for lessons in turning.* The boy soon became highly skilled and developed a great interest in mechanics as well as ironworks. In February 1831 his father fell on hard times and left Bedlington for the Tredegar ironworks in Monmouthshire, taking his family with him. 'I remember well what a pleasant journey it was,' Gooch recalled. 'We had a kind of omnibus built, with curtains round it, in which we all travelled. I do not know how many days it took us to make the journey, but I well remember it, and the beautiful view as we crossed the Malvern Hills on a bright moonlit evening.'

When the family were settled at Tredegar, Daniel Gooch began his working life in the ironworks. His first job was in the moulding department, where he started work at six o'clock in the morning. During the first few months he was employed mainly in making cores. These are placed within the moulding box to produce cavities within a casting.

* The removal of metal from the outer diameter of a rotating cylindrical piece of work. Turning is used to reduce the diameter of the piece to a specified dimension and to produce a smooth finish to the metal.

In doing this he learned how to handle sand, the moulder's basic material, and he was soon given the more responsible task of moulding tram wheels. This was a very heavy job as the wheel pattern alone weighed 50 or 60 lb. He had to set a heavy moulding box around it, shovel in sand and ram it to firmness. Then the pattern had to be rapped to loosen it and drawn out, leaving the shape of the casting behind. Gooch had nine boxes to mould twice a day, the first lot before nine o'clock in the morning, when the furnace was run off and they were cast. While they were being cast he had a couple of hours off for his breakfast and when he returned he moulded a second set.

During the course of his work there he survived several accidents, all of which could have been fatal. The most serious was when he was caught inside the blowing engine when lime was being applied to keep the leather bellows airtight, and the engine was started. He managed to get out, but if he had been trapped inside it would have been fatal. A more stupid and pointless mishap came when he challenged himself to be lowered into a 30-yard-deep pit while holding on to the end of a chain. He reached the bottom but as he was being lifted out he began to lose his grip and only just managed to hold on to the chain. The experience he gained of working with iron at Tredegar was to stand him in good stead, but the hard work and the atmosphere in the hot and dusty furnace house began to affect his health. Hoping that sea air would do him good, he took a ship to Liverpool and from there he went to Warrington to spend a few days with his brother John before sailing home.

On his return he moved to the carpenters' shop at the ironworks, a much cleaner and healthier place than the foundry. In August 1833 his father died and soon after that the family moved from Tredegar to Coventry where his older brother Tom was resident engineer on the northern stretch of Robert Stephenson's London & Birmingham Railway. Tom helped his younger brother to get a job at the Vulcan Foundry at Newton-le-Willows in Lancashire. It was an excellent opportunity as Robert Stephenson and his partner, Charles Tayleur, had set it up to build locomotives.

By the beginning of 1834, when Gooch joined the factory, it had about 100 employees. Gooch worked in the fitting shop, helping to put the locomotives together. He was again learning on the job. At the same time he became friendly with the locomotive foremen on the Liverpool & Manchester Railway and they allowed him to go out with them on the footplate. Gooch enjoyed a good social life and was happy during his time at Vulcan, but in the summer, after he had been there for about six months, he became ill again and had to return home. Under his mother's care he soon recovered but he didn't go back to Vulcan. Instead he asked Robert Stephenson to allow him to go to the Dundee Foundry to learn about steamboat engines.

Work on the factory floor was now regarded as too much for his limited strength so he was given a job as a draughtsman. He was 18 years old and his wages were £1 a week, but he didn't like it there. In Dundee families were crammed into tenements of one or two rooms and Gooch found the whole way of life unpleasant. 'The habits of the people,' he said, 'were somewhat different from what I·had been accustomed to and I cannot say I liked them.' To make matters worse, he didn't get on with his manager, who saw him as a potential rival and, as it had never been his intention to stay for more than a year, he moved on to Robert Stephenson & Co. in Newcastle, continuing work as a draughtsman.

Gooch was now 19, and from Monday to Saturday he was expected to be at his drawing board by 7 a.m. He was one of only five or six draughtsmen at Stephenson's works and he was fortunate to be there when important technical changes were being introduced. At a time of rapid innovation like this, Gooch was able to show what he had to offer and soon his wage was increased to 30 shillings (£1.50) a week. Among his first projects was the design of a 6-foot-gauge locomotive for a railway from Moscow to St Petersburg and another for two 5-foot 6-inch gauge locomotives for the New Orleans Railway. While working on these he first became aware of the advantages of a wider gauge than the one that had been adopted by the Stephensons. 'I was much delighted,' he wrote later, 'in having so much room to arrange the engine. I was very much impressed in making these drawings with the importance of a wider gauge, and no doubt thus early became an advocate for the broad gauge system, altho' at the time Mr Brunel had not propounded his views and I did not foresee how important a matter it was to be in my future life.'

While he was working at Robert Stephenson's another event occurred that was to have great significance for him, when he met a young lady called Margaret Tanner at a party in Sunderland. He recorded in his journal that he didn't have 'any particular fancy for her' but he was well aware that she was a person of some importance. Her father, Henry Tanner, was a shipowner and one of the wealthiest men in Sunderland. At the time, marriage was out of the question for a hard-up young draughtsman, particularly marriage to a young lady from such a wealthy background. Nevertheless, after the party Gooch continued to see Margaret.

By 1836 locomotive-building had become a rapidly expanding industry and Sir Robert Shafto Hawks, a North East dignitary distantly related to Gooch, decided to set up as a locomotive manufacturer in Gateshead. He asked Gooch to join the firm as manager on a salary of £150 a year, twice what he was getting with Stephenson. Gooch gave his notice at Forth Street immediately, leaving Robert Stephenson furious that his young protégé was taking the experience he had gained with him to yet another competitor. The new company received an order for two locomotives for the Newcastle & Carlisle Railway, and Gooch's first job was to look after these and draw up plans for additional facilities. However, there were no further orders and the company was wound up after less than six months. Though the scheme never got off the ground properly, it indicates how well thought of Gooch was at such a young age. He left Hawks on 15 March 1837 and four weeks later Margaret Tanner came to Gateshead to stay with her aunt. Gooch saw her nearly every day and before the end of April they were engaged. It was just nine months after their first meeting at the party. They didn't have her father's permission so the penniless draughtsman and the wealthy shipowner's daughter decided to keep their engagement secret. But Tanner found out and, much to the couple's surprise, he agreed to the match. The depths of his daughter's feelings for Gooch had clearly been sufficient to persuade him. After the engagement Margaret returned to the family home in Sunderland and Gooch made frequent visits. Before they could marry, though, Gooch needed to better himself.

Gooch went to work with his brother Tom, who was engineer to the Manchester & Leeds Railway. But Daniel had become a broad-gauge enthusiast, so in July 1837, when he found out that the Great Western were looking for somebody to look after their engines, he wrote to Brunel applying for the job. Although he'd not had any dealings with him, the Gooch name must have been familiar to Brunel. The two men met for the first time three weeks later in Manchester and Brunel was so impressed that he immediately offered Gooch a post on the Great Western Railway as 'Superintendent of Locomotive Engines'. His starting salary was to be £300 a year, increasing to £550 when the line opened. 'I was very glad of this appointment,' Gooch said, 'as I felt it was a permanent thing in which, by dint of attention and perseverance, I might hope to get on. I was also very glad to manage the broad gauge, which filled my mind as the great advance of the age, and in the soundness of which I was a great believer.' It was typical of Brunel that, in appointing the man who was to be responsible for designing and building the right locomotives for the broad gauge, he ignored the experienced engine-builders and went for an engineer who was to celebrate his twenty-first birthday six days after taking on the job. Gooch, though, was a confident young man and the post didn't intimidate him. 'I was very young to be entrusted with the management of the locomotive department of so large a railway,' he said in later years, 'but I felt no fear.' And events were to prove that Brunel couldn't have made a wiser choice. Gooch would prove to be a great engineer, a tireless champion of the broad gauge and a firm friend. Their partnership would greatly advance transport and technology within a very short space of time.

Gooch gave up his job on the Manchester & Leeds and within five days of his interview with Brunel he was hard at work in London, striving to get the first section of the Great Western open by the end of the year. Brunel might well have devised a railway system that to him and his supporters was superior to any other, but it was Gooch who provided him with the means to run it. When he started work on the railway Gooch was thrown in at the deep end.

From 1836, Brunel had been buying a curious assortment of locomotives from various different makers: in all he had ordered 19 locomotives but few of them were satisfactory. As Fred explained:

The first locomotive that Brunel was responsible for were the greatest and most inexplicable blunder in his whole working career. The problem was that when he placed orders for the first engines he imposed impossible conditions on the builders, especially by limiting piston speed to 280 feet per minute, which was little more than half the speed to be found on some other locomotives. This meant that the engines had to have huge driving wheels to compensate. Other conditions imposed by Brunel meant they were grossly under-boilered. The first locomotives to arrive were *Premier* and *Vulcan* from the Vulcan Foundry and *Thunderer* and *Hurricane* built by Hawthorns of Newcastle. In order to keep the axle load down to a figure that had been specified by Brunel, the boiler was mounted on a separate six-wheeled carriage and connected to the motive unit by flexible steam and exhaust pipes. These first locomotives delivered to the railway to meet Brunel's specifications were such a collection of oddities and freaks that the motive power department was a mess.

With their huge driving wheels, these first engines may have looked impressive to the untrained observer but Gooch was horrified by what he saw. He knew they wouldn't do the job. In the case of *Thunderer* and *Hurricane*, he wrote that when he first saw them he came to the conclusion that they would have enough to do just to pull themselves, let alone a train.

Brunel was building a railway line with no locomotives to run on it, so Gooch had to get hold of some sound locomotives as quickly as possible. Fortunately, owing to some financial difficulty, the two locomotives he had designed for the New Orleans Railway while he had been at Stephenson's hadn't been exported to America and were still sitting in the Newcastle works, too wide to be adapted to

Stephenson's 4-foot 8½-inch gauge. Stephenson must have breathed a sigh of relief when Gooch persuaded Brunel that the Great Western should buy these two engines and get Stephenson to alter the gauge to seven feet. One of them, the *North Star*, was fitted with 7-foot single driving wheels. To accommodate them, the frames were replaced by an arrangement with an arched top that was to become a feature of Gooch's designs. While he was having his meetings with Stephenson Gooch began buying other equipment, including machine tools, mill-work and taps and dies from Joseph Whitworth, who had started his own firm in Manchester just three years earlier. Gooch became one of the first engineers to adopt Whitworth's standardized screw threads and it was the start of a lifelong friendship.

The first stretch of the Great Western ran from London to Maidenhead and Gooch set up his base at West Drayton, halfway between the two. He built an office, repair shops and a shed for the first engines. Now that he had a good job Gooch felt confident enough to marry Margaret Tanner and Tuesday 20 March was the date set for the wedding. In the meantime *North Star* was completed and delivered to the Great Western. She arrived at Maidenhead by barge at the end of November 1837 and waited until the track was laid. Until the arrival of her sister, *Morning Star*, *North Star* was the only reliable locomotive the company possessed, mainly because, unlike the others, Brunel had not been able to influence her design. She was also the predecessor of a long line of broad-gauge flyers designed by Gooch for the Great Western. She was heavy on fuel but her reliability meant that she was chosen to haul the directors' special at the opening of the first section of the line, from London to the village of Taplow, a mile short of Maidenhead, in May 1838. She drew out of the partially completed Paddington terminus with 200 passengers at eleven o'clock and made good speed to Maidenhead, averaging nearly 28 mph.

Normal passenger services commenced on 4 June 1838 and every bridge along the line was crowded with spectators who marvelled at the speed of the trains. All was not well, however. With only two good, reliable locomotives, Gooch spent his earliest days on the railway in a constant struggle to keep the rest of the miscellaneous collection of locomotives working. Reports began to spread doubt about the viability of the railway and, although 30,000 passengers were carried during June, the Great Western's share price fell. Because the engines were so unreliable, timetable running was stopped and Gooch had to spend most nights at Paddington, grabbing some sleep in a carriage, so that he could be on hand to supervise overnight repairs. He knew the only option was to rebuild or replace most of the locomotive stock.

Gooch proved to be a first-class locomotive engineer and it was largely through his efforts that the best of Brunel's 'freaks' were kept in good enough working order to run trains during the railway's difficult first year. While his days and nights were spent in the engine house, the Great Western directors blamed him quite unjustly for the repeated engine failures. In December 1838, George Henry Gibbs, one of the directors, wrote: 'Our engines are in very bad order, and Gooch seems very unfit for the superintendence of that department.' Gooch was in a difficult position. He knew very well the cause of the trouble was Brunel's initial designs but out of loyalty to his boss he couldn't openly say this. Eventually a direct request from the board for information forced him to tell the truth. He had no option but to point out all the faults in the design of the locomotives. As a result he was asked to submit a report directly to the board, and, although he did not mention Brunel specifically, there can have been little doubt in the directors' minds where the fault lay. Brunel was not pleased and sent Gooch a sharp note, but deep down Brunel had great respect for Gooch's abilities and knew that he was right. Any breach between them was soon healed.

The business association between Brunel and Gooch soon developed into a close friendship. What was remarkable about this was that the two men were very different in character and in way of life. Both men had a vast capacity for hard work, but for Brunel his career was a great adventure and when he allowed himself to take time off he was eager to go out and enjoy himself. Gooch on the other hand was a quieter, more reserved individual. Only a few months after his appointment, Gooch was invited by Brunel to a party at his London home, but the younger man wasn't impressed. 'Went to my first London party,' he wrote in his diary, 'and left it disgusted with London parties, making a note in my memo book never to go to another.' Gooch's comments led some people to regard him as a prime example of the dour North Country puritan for whom pleasure appeared to be a sinful waste of God's time. But this wasn't really the case. He enjoyed good company just as much as the next man, but it was then the height of fashion for a London party to be crammed to the doors and this was what he disliked.

While the Great Western line was still under construction, Gooch set up a small locomotive-building workshop at West Drayton and began to produce serviceable designs for the future. He shared Brunel's deep conviction that the 7-foot gauge was the real way forward for railways, but the pair had their opponents. The early problems with locomotives and track had resulted in the directors of the Great Western bringing in the independent engineers Nicholas Wood and John Hawkshaw to report on the deficiencies not only in the broad gauge itself but also in the locomotives. The professional discord created during this period had Brunel threatening to resign. Nevertheless he knew that new locomotives needed to be designed and built to replace his 'freaks'. Gooch rose to the challenge, and, when the passenger service was extended over Maidenhead Bridge to Twyford, the board ordered him to design and buy locomotives capable of handling this longer run.

Taking the Star class as a model Gooch went to the drawing board. Working closely with Brunel, he did a lot to improve the steaming and reduce the coke consumption of *North Star* when it became evident that she was not as efficient as she might be. *North Star* had shown that she was incapable of drawing more than 16 tons at 40 mph but, following modifications by Gooch and Brunel, which included increasing the size of the blast pipe and altering its position in the smoke box to ensure that the exhaust steam was discharged up the middle of the chimney, she proved capable of pulling 40 tons at 40 mph while using less than a third of the quantity of coke. The decisive way in which Brunel and Gooch dealt with the shortcomings of the *North Star*, combined with the inconclusive reports from Wood and Hawkshaw on the deficiencies of the broad gauge, won the day as far as the gauge was concerned, at least for the time being.

Despite the success of the revamped Stars, Gooch believed he could do better and Brunel agreed that he should draw up new designs and specifications. The result was a 7-foot single which was a further development of the Stars. On this Gooch introduced a large haystack-style firebox, which became typical on broad-gauge engines, outside frames and inside cylinders, and a domeless boiler that provided ample steam space. It was *Firefly*, and it quickly relegated Brunel's early 'freaks' to the scrapyard as it became the prototype for a successful new class.

Next off the Gooch drawing board was the Sun class. Like the Fireflies they were 2-2-2, but they were smaller with 6-foot driving wheels. The Great Western Railway still didn't have the manufacturing capacity to build the quantities of locomotives that were needed, so, when his design work was complete, Gooch had comprehensive drawings and specifications printed out. When the orders were placed, iron templates were sent to the manufacturers for all the parts because he wanted them to be identical in every engine. This standardization of his engines set him well ahead of any of his contemporaries.

On 1 June 1839, Anna, the first of Gooch's six children, was born. By this time he had moved from West Drayton to Paddington. Gooch had his office at the terminus, a few hundred yards from his home. He was still only in his early twenties and his job and financial future were secure. In addition to his salary there was £100 a year coming into the household from Margaret's father. Gooch was prudent and cautious, living well within his means, and he invested as much as he could. He involved his father-in-law in his ventures and in 1839 Tanner sent him £350 to invest in railway shares. On the Great Western the first Firefly was delivered on 12 March 1840 and it hauled a directors' special made up of two carriages, carrying 40 passengers, to Reading and back just five days after delivery. On the return journey the new locomotive covered 31 miles in 37 minutes at an average speed of 50 mph. Sustained high-speed running such as this was unprecedented in 1840 and was a great tribute to Gooch and the improvements he had effected.

The company needed to start earning money without delay so the first public services began soon after, on 30 March. Within a few weeks the traffic began to build up and by July there were 17 Fireflies and 7 Suns in service. They didn't disappoint. 'They all gave everyone general satisfaction,' Gooch wrote. 'We could now calculate with some certainty not only upon the speed they could run, but upon their not breaking down upon the journey. We had no difficulty in running at 60 miles per hour with good loads.' In June 1842 Gooch had the honour of driving the first Royal Train, when Queen Victoria travelled on a special from Slough to Paddington behind his Firefly-class locomotive *Phlegethon*. The Queen wrote that her journey had been free from dust, crowds and heat, and that she had been quite charmed with it. The fact that Gooch drove this and the directors' special highlights the fact that he was not just a brilliant engineer but a hands-on engineman as well.

With the Firefly design the Great Western had a reliable locomotive fleet of their own and they were soon proving their superiority over their narrower gauge rivals, mainly because of their performance. However, although the broad gauge created a great stir, with people flocking to see its locomotives, it certainly had its critics. The difference between the Great Western and other railways made it necessary for goods and passengers to change trains when going out of the Great Western area. Standardization was called for and so in 1841 the Gauge Commissioners organized high-speed trial runs. In comparative trials Gooch's Firefly-class locomotive *Ixion* proved capable of speeds greater than its standard-gauge challenger. In mid-December 1841, the locomotive made three round trips between Paddington and Didcot with loads of 80, 70 and 60 tons. Pulling the 80-ton train she averaged 52.8 mph on the fastest section of the track and with the wind behind her attained a maximum speed of 59 mph, while with the 60-ton load she averaged just over 56 mph. They were amazing figures but it was all to no avail. Despite the broad gauge being considered far superior, it was the standard gauge that was selected, due almost entirely to the fact that by this time there was far more of the narrower gauge track. An Act of Parliament in 1848 enforced this so the Great Western had to lay a third line throughout their system to enable standard-gauge and broad-gauge trains to run on the same track.

The Firefly class eventually totalled 62 engines. Built by seven different outside manufacturers in just two years, they had a wheel arrangement of 2-2-2, the middle 2 referring to the driving wheel, which was 7 foot in diameter. The Fireflies, along with the eventual total of 12 Stars, were to prove the backbone of the early Great Western passenger service. The excellence of Gooch's designs soon became apparent and even Stephenson's Stars, designed and built by the most experienced locomotive firm in the world, couldn't match the Fireflies. Once Gooch had produced a successful locomotive design, his policy was to develop it to its limits rather than innovate. This may have seemed conservative, but it generated results that astounded the railway world and engines that remained in service for nearly 30 years. Twelve were ferried across the Bristol Channel for use on the South Wales Railway in 1850 and they were also used for the postal service between London and Bristol, introduced in 1855. As locomotive design evolved and newer engines with greater capacity were needed to replace them, some of the Fireflies were rebuilt to stay in service as saddle tanks.* Each of them gave an average of around half a million miles in service and they were so successful that the last one wasn't withdrawn until as late as 1879. Twenty-one Sun class engines were built by outside manufacturers, but their performance didn't match that of the Fireflies and all of them were rebuilt as saddle tanks before the end of the decade.

With all of his engines Gooch took particular care when it came to boiler design, rightly considering it to be the heart of the locomotive upon which all else depended. By 1842 the Great Western had 136 Gooch-designed locomotives from 11 different manufacturers. However, as well as maintaining them, Gooch knew that the company had to start building its own. He was a stickler for high standards of

---

* Locomotives on which the water tank sits on top of the boiler like a saddle.

workmanship and it was his disappointment with the workmanship of some of the leading manufacturers of the day, coupled with his desire for standardization within locomotive classes, that spurred him to press the directors to construct one of the first railway-owned locomotive works in the country at Swindon, where it would be able to build its own. It was also clear to him and to Brunel that the railway would need a central repair depot for carriage and wagon maintenance.

As early as 1839 the two men had discussed the question of where to establish the railway's chief locomotive depot and repair shop. Reading was the first place to be suggested and then Didcot, the junction for a branch to Oxford. But it was Gooch who identified a site in the fields below the little market town of Swindon, where the Cheltenham branch joined the main line. Gooch had noted that the nearby Wilts & Berks Canal gave Swindon a direct connection with the Somerset coalfield. He also realized that engines needed to be changed at Swindon or close by, as the gradient of the hills from Swindon to Bristol was much steeper than that between London and Swindon. Gooch proposed that they should build locomotives with smaller driving wheels to haul the trains between Bristol and Swindon and then use his fast 7-foot singles on the long level line between Swindon and Paddington. Although Swindon was closer to Bristol than to London, Gooch pointed out that if the distance was measured in engine revolutions instead of miles, Swindon would become the halfway point if locomotives with smaller driving wheels were used on the Swindon–Bristol section. On 13 September 1840 Gooch wrote to Brunel putting forward his proposal for the building of the much-needed engine works.

Gooch recorded at the time: 'I reported in favour of Swindon, it being the junction with the Cheltenham branch and also a convenient division of the Great Western Line for the engine working. Mr Brunel and I went to look at the ground, then only green fields, and he agreed with me as to its being the best place.' The two men met at Swindon to consider their options and, according to one account, one of them threw a rock to decide where the foundation stones should be laid.

With Brunel's backing, Gooch made his proposal to the Great Western directors and on 25 February 1841 they authorized the establishment of the Swindon locomotive works.

Work started immediately, with many of the buildings constructed using stone obtained from the excavation of Box Tunnel. The first building, the Locomotive Repair Shed, was completed in 1841 and all the machinery was installed by 1842. When it opened 200 men were employed, but by January 1843 this had risen to 400 men, including 72 enginemen and 73 firemen. Gooch himself didn't move to Swindon. He and his wife were settled in London, he wanted to stay close to the directors of the railway at Paddington and it was easy enough for him to travel down to the works. If he needed to stay there overnight he had a bedroom next to his office. Repairs began in 1843, but as soon as Swindon Works was able to provide the infrastructure for the manufacture of engines, in 1846, Gooch started his locomotive-building operation. An 0-6-0 goods engine, *Premier*, was the first to emerge from Swindon Works in February of that year, but because the boiler had been supplied by outside contract she was not classed as entirely 'home produced'. The first to be wholly produced there was called *Great Western*. She was to set new standards of power and speed and be produced in record time to meet the biggest challenge the railway was facing – the 'battle of the gauges'.

With another round of the gauge war imminent in the parliamentary session of 1846, Brunel had decided he would have to give a convincing demonstration of broad-gauge superiority, so he asked Gooch to design and build a new and more powerful express locomotive. Speed, not just in performance but in getting the engine built, was vital. Gooch worked night and day at his drawing board and at the workbench alongside his works manager, Archibald Sturrock, and the men in the workshops. There wasn't enough time to do detailed drawings so *Great Western* was built from simple drawings and sketches. Just 13 weeks from the date of Brunel's request, *Great Western* steamed out of the workshops. It was a remarkable achievement in such a short period of time. By the standards of the day, the locomotive was colossal. Her single driving wheels were eight feet in diameter and she had the biggest boiler yet seen on a locomotive, with a huge haystack firebox made of wrought iron. As in all of Gooch's designs ample boiler power was the secret and this boiler was not just large; it also had steam pressure of 100 lb to the square inch, an unusually high pressure at that time.

On 1 June 1846, only a month after leaving the workshops, *Great Western* was given her first run with the Paddington to Exeter express. Her running time for the 194 miles was 208 minutes down and 211 minutes up – an average speed of over 55 mph. It was an astonishing achievement for the 1840s, turning a journey that took several days by stagecoach into one that could be done in a morning or afternoon. The general public had by this time become besotted with the sensation of speed and the *Great Western* was setting new standards, taking the steam engineering work of the Stephensons to a completely new level. She was to be the forerunner of a line of express passenger engines built for the broad gauge. They were all designed for speed. In 1848, less than 20 years after the Rainhill Trials, a Gooch express made the journey from London to Didcot in 47½ minutes at an average speed of 60 mph. He'd achieved much of his success through the standardization of his locomotive fleet but Gooch was not afraid to modify and experiment. The initial drawback of the *Great Western* was the excess weight over the front carrying wheels, which eventually broke its leading axle, so Gooch modified his design by extending the frame and converting it into an even more successful 4-2-2. The extra axle gave more support to the massive engine and she remained in service for 24 years – long after Gooch himself had passed on his responsibilities for the GWR's locomotives.

The first complete class of engines Gooch built entirely at Swindon were the Princes, six 2-2-2s, all with 7-foot driving wheels. They were highly successful, averaging around 2,000 miles a month for the next 25 years, and they were used at first on the Paddington–Exeter run. But they'd really been designed for shorter distances than this. What Gooch needed was a new class of engine to haul the company's crack long-distance expresses and to this end he designed a new locomotive that was to become the broad-gauge flagship – the Iron Duke class of express locomotive, 29 2-2-2s with 8-foot driving wheels. Built at Gooch's Swindon Works from 1851 onwards, they are seen as the high point of the broad-gauge era. The GWR broad-gauge classes usually took their name from the first to be built. *Iron Duke*, completed at Swindon in April 1847, was so called because its trial run took place on 29 April, the Duke of Wellington's birthday. Swindon built 22 Iron Dukes between then and 1851, while Rothwell and Co. at Bolton made another 7 between 1854 and 1855.

These powerful engines were the mainstay of the company's express passenger services and included the most famous engine of this class, the *Lord of the Isles*, considered the fastest broad-gauge engine of its day. The locomotive, which clocked up nearly 80,000 miles in 30 years with its original boiler, was one of the stars of the Great Exhibition of 1851. Raised up on a plinth, it dominated the machinery hall. The Iron Dukes were the ultimate land transport of the day and the pride of Gooch's enginemen. In 1848, one of them, *Great Britain*, maintained average speeds of 67 mph on its runs from London to Didcot and regular timetabled trains were doing 60 mph. *Iron Duke* ran up 607,412 miles before she was withdrawn from service in 1873, while the highest mileage by a locomotive in that class was that of *Lightning*, which reached 816,601 miles in 31 years of service. The Iron Dukes were Gooch's most successful locomotives but the largest class in terms of numbers was his Standard Goods or Ariadne class. One hundred and two were built at Swindon in a period of 11 years from 1852 and they were so successful that they survived right up to the end of the broad gauge in 1892.

Gooch was proud to be called 'the father of Swindon Works'. He appointed works managers to oversee day-to-day operations, but retained overall control himself. He was a hard-working man who expected the same of the men he appointed. He was also aware that a company had obligations to its workforce that went beyond the workbench, and with this in mind he took a personal interest in the social life of the town. It was a town that he had put on the map and, although he lived in London himself, when complaints of drunkenness, boredom and social deprivation reached him he did something about it. He organized the formation of a Mechanics' Institute. An office was turned into a reading room, and dances and theatrical performances started as soon as a workshop could be spared. Within four years there were 250 members and a library of 1,200 books.

Gooch also persuaded the directors of the Great Western to appoint a doctor and he secured free lodgings for him. A Medical Fund Society was established, the first of its kind in the world, which would, a century later, become the model for the National Health Service. Gooch wrote: 'While I strove to do my duty I remembered that the moral welfare of those under me was a thing for which I would have to answer at a higher tribunal. The happiness of my men and their families depended much upon the influence I exerted over them, and I have striven to make the influence beneficial.' In return, Gooch expected the same dedication as he put into his own work. In one incident, a driver leapt from his engine just before it crashed. The man was concussed but there was no sympathy from Gooch, who dismissed him for deserting his post.

By 1851 the Swindon Works was employing over 2,000 men and turning out one locomotive a week. Like most early railways, the Great Western was built with gentle gradients and the minimum of curves. This enabled it to operate fast lightweight 'single-wheelers', but from 1849 Gooch also built 4-4-0 saddle tank locomotives for the hillier routes in Devon. New lines, mostly worked by Gooch's engines, were opened, and between 1852 and 1857 the mileage covered increased by 60 per cent. Many new locomotives were needed and almost a third of all those he designed were built during this period. A lot of them were goods engines for freight traffic in the Midlands and Wales. The first of these were the Caesar class, then the Banking class. More than 100 of these were needed and 31 had to be put out to tender as the works was so busy. In 1853 the board voted £25,000 for extensions to the workshops.

Gooch expected the running costs of his locomotives to be low, because the width of the gauge and their low centre of gravity made them steadier. 'It requires very little consideration,' he said, 'to arrive at the conclusion that the less a piece of machinery is shaken about, the less must be the destruction of the parts.' He also set up a system of recording each engineman's use of fuel and oil, which enabled him to detect any waste. In a further move to ensure the railway ran economically, he persuaded the board to buy their own colliery near Pontypridd because the railway had found its coke supply vulnerable to strikes and price rises. It became part of his division, giving him direct control over the quality and stock levels of his coal supplies.

Gooch's only new broad-gauge design during the 1850s was the Waverley class. These were 4-4-0 tender engines designed for the heavier gradients in Wales and Gloucestershire, and each of them went on to complete half a million miles during their 20 years of service. Although they were very different in layout to any of their predecessors, many of their parts were from earlier locomotives. Their boilers had been designed for the Standard Goods class, their cylinders and crankshafts for the Caesars and most of the other parts for the Iron Dukes. No longer did a new class take him beyond the limits of his experience and he had carried his ideas on standardization to such a level that only a bare minimum of expenditure on drawings, patterns and spares was needed for the new engines to go into service. Though his locomotives were principally for the broad gauge, Gooch eventually and very reluctantly had to accept that the 'superior' 7-foot gauge's days were numbered, and he turned his skills to designing standard-gauge locomotives as well. In 1854 the Shrewsbury & Birmingham and Shrewsbury & Chester Railways amalgamated with the Great Western and Gooch took over responsibility for their stock. Between 1854 and 1864 he designed and built a number of standard-gauge classes for this new Northern Division.

A total of 407 broad-gauge and 98 narrow-gauge locomotives were built to Daniel Gooch's designs. These included locomotives for the Bristol & Exeter Railway, the Vale of Neath Railway and the South Devon & Cornwall Railway as well as the Great Western. To tackle the steep inclines on the South Devon line between Exeter and Plymouth, he designed the Corsair class of 4-4-0 saddle tanks with a leading bogie axle, which was then a major innovation. When the first two went into service the railway's directors were delighted with their performance.

They wanted more like them but they were in no position to buy them as they had lost over £350,000 on Brunel's atmospheric venture. They approached the Great Western for help but money was tight and they were turned down. It was an ideal opportunity for Gooch, who offered to find partners and raise capital in return for a ten-year contract to work the line. The offer was accepted and Brunel was instructed to negotiate an agreement with his locomotive engineer.

Since the problems he'd had as a young man Gooch's health had given him no cause for concern, but in September 1857 he had to have an operation. It is not known what it was for but his condition must have been threatening because no one took the risks of surgery at that time without a very good reason. He recovered fully, well in time for the marriage of his younger daughter, Emily, the following year. Her sister Anna married ten months later. Gooch was sorry to lose both his daughters so early, saying, 'I had little opportunity to have them with me at home. I hope it is for the future happiness of both.' A week after Emily's wedding his father-in-law, Henry Tanner, died at the age of 74 leaving about £7,000 to each of his daughters. This provided Gooch's wife, Margaret, with her own independent income. Gooch himself was now a wealthy man, whose fortune had grown to at least £100,000. Throughout the 1850s profits poured in from the South Devon contract and investments he'd made in other railway schemes had been successful. The Gooch family were now spending their summers in lodgings at Windsor, away from the dust and heat of the capital. Just beyond the town were the beauties of the River Thames and the Berkshire countryside and this was the Windsor that Gooch loved. In March 1859 Clewer Park, a large house standing in 30 acres of parkland, came on to the market and Gooch bought it. He made it his country house and became a deputy lieutenant for Berkshire.

Gooch produced his last locomotive design in 1861, when the Metropolitan Railway Company was building the first underground line from Paddington to Farringdon Street. The Great Western had a big stake in the venture and Gooch got the job of designing some sort of motive power that would not fill the tunnels with smoke and steam. He carried out tests to discover how far an engine could travel with the blast off, coasting along on the steam that was stored in the boiler. The results were encouraging and so he built the world's first condensing locomotives for the railway. The 2-4-0 Metropolitan Tanks differed from normal engines in that they had two large water tanks under their boilers. In the open they were worked normally, but as they entered the tunnels a changeover valve was operated so that the engine could work without choking the passengers. Twenty-two of them were built between 1862 and 1864 and they were the only Great Western broad-gauge engines to have outside cylinders.

Locomotive design was not the only area of innovation for Gooch's inventive mind. His dynamometer car for measuring locomotive performance is believed to have been the world's first and was built in cooperation with the mathematician and pioneer of computing, Charles Babbage. A rolling mill was installed in 1861 for manufacturing rails and in 1867 the Swindon Works was extended and made the central workshop for the construction of carriages and wagons. With its broad gauge the Great Western could take heavier loads than the narrower gauge, so a six-wheeled truck was introduced. This could carry nine tons compared to the six tons of the four-wheelers. Gooch described the type as 'probably the most economical we have for carrying loads'.

After Brunel's death in 1859, Gooch inherited the *Great Eastern* project when he was brought in by the board of the Great Western Steamship Company as engineer. A sum of £100,000 was raised to make the ship ready for sea and Gooch went down to Southampton to superintend the work. On 17 June 1860 the ship sailed for New York with Gooch and his family on board. But Brunel's great ship was dogged by misfortune, the company made huge losses and, in a shrewd move, Gooch joined a consortium that purchased her at a bankruptcy sale. The *Great Eastern* had cost £900,000 to build and was worth at least £100,000 for the materials in her alone, but Gooch and his partners got her for the knock-down price of £25,000. Brunel would have been devastated, but he would have got some consolation from the fact that she was to come into her own as the layer of the first transatlantic cable.

Gooch remained in the background while the sale was being completed but he was busy making plans for the laying of the cable. It was technology he was well aware of because Brunel had recommended to the board of the Great Western Railway as early as 1839 that cable for the transmission of telegraphic messages should be installed by the side of the track. By 1843 it extended from Paddington to Slough. It achieved celebrity in August 1844 when it was used to convey to London the tidings of the birth of Queen Victoria's second son, the Duke of Edinburgh, at Windsor.

Ever the businessman and always looking for new opportunities to make money, Gooch became chairman of the Great Eastern Steamship Company Ltd once the sale was completed. He had ambitious plans for the ship but first he resigned from his post of locomotive superintendent in 1864, though he continued as a member of the Great Western board. By this time the works had built a formidable reputation for the quality of its output. Gooch was appointed chairman, a position that Brunel had never managed to reach. On a salary of £2,000 a year Gooch was now head of the company he had served for so much of his life. It was one of the largest organizations in the world, carrying 19 million passengers and 8 million tons of goods during his first year as chairman, with a turnover of nearly £4 million.

In spite of this the company's financial position was precarious and Gooch's first job was to lead it out of near-bankruptcy. Economic growth in the early 1860s had stimulated another railway boom, but this came to an abrupt halt in 1866 and many railway companies went bankrupt. The industry's leaders were so concerned about the viability of the railway companies that they petitioned the government for nationalization. There was a real fear that the whole railway system would be forced to cease operations and, as chairman of the Great Western, Gooch led a railway industry delegation to meet Prime Minister Benjamin Disraeli at Downing Street. The Great Western itself had only just survived the financial crash and, despite rising passenger numbers and freight traffic, the company was struggling to pay back loans taken out at the high interest rate of 9 per cent. Gooch put forward the idea of a £1m loan, backed by the government, to rescue the Great

Western but Disraeli turned the request down, saying it was not the government's duty to interfere with the affairs of a private company. Despite Gooch's concerns, however, the railway not only survived the crisis, but started to expand again through a series of amalgamations that made it the railway with the greatest route mileage in Britain.

Gooch was now getting more involved with his new venture with the *Great Eastern* and he chartered the ship to the Telegraph Construction Company, taking $250,000 in cable stock in exchange for its use. The ship sailed from Liverpool to Sheerness, where the tanks and machinery were to be installed and the cable stowed. One of the funnels and the second-class saloon were ripped out to make way for the three huge cable tanks, each 50 foot across and 20 foot deep, and workshops, forges and machinery were installed on the main deck. Gooch had to approve all the modifications and oversee the work. He was especially concerned that the ship would be stable with all this extra weight stowed on and just underneath the main deck. The engines were overhauled and, with her cable tanks installed and Gooch on board, the *Great Eastern* set sail from Valentia in Ireland in July 1865, bound for Newfoundland. 'The work has the best wishes and prayers of all who know it,' Gooch wrote. 'Its success will open out a useful future for our noble ship, lift her out of the depression under which she has laboured from her birth and satisfy me that I have done wisely in never losing confidence in her; and the world may still feel thankful to my old friend Brunel that he designed and carried out the construction of so noble a work.'

The first attempt to lay the cable, however, ended in failure when a defect developed and, in the process of hauling the cable in from a depth of 2,000 fathoms to trace the fault, it broke. In a letter, written at 'Lat 51-40-30. Long 14-4', Gooch describes in graphic detail the vain attempts to retrieve the cable:

> We laid a little over 1200 miles of the cable when from an accident it broke and the end went down 2½ miles into the depths of the Atlantic. As before starting we believed such an event to be its death, we did not come with proper tackle to get it again and had to do the best we could

with what we had. By way of practice 3 times we hooked it and after bringing it up about a mile each time our tackle broke and let it down again. After spending 10 days in these operations & using all the rope we had it became necessary to return to England and get what is necessary and go out again. Whether we do this in October or defer it to the spring, which I think best, there is no doubt the cable will be raised, joined and completed. I can assure you it has been a very anxious time and for 12 days it was impossible to sleep. When I went to bed I only lay listening to the sound of the paddles fearing to hear them stop. After we lost the cable I got some good sound sleep – the ship has done her work splendidly and the weather has been wonderful. We have had only one heavy gale, and the Captain & all of us are quite satisfied a cable can be laid with this ship in any weather.

A year later, with her cable tanks replenished and her grappling gear improved, a second attempt was made. This time, with Gooch on board again, the mission was successful. The *Great Eastern* crossed the Atlantic from Bantry Bay in Ireland on calm seas, spinning the first cable out across the bed of the Atlantic to join the Old and New Worlds together. On 26 July 1866 the ship sailed into Heart's Content Bay, Newfoundland, and the following day the cable was taken ashore. Gooch then sent through the cable the news of their success: 'Gooch, Heart's Content to Glass, Valentia, 27 July, 6 p.m.: Our shore-end has just been laid and a most perfect cable, under God's blessing, has completed telegraphic communication between England and the Continent of America.' Ironically, after 27 years of railway innovation, this brought him greater fame in many circles than his railway designs. It also earned him a baronetcy. He had great faith in the ultimate triumph of electric power and continued his involvement with the Telegraph Construction Company, becoming chairman in 1868.

Gooch's influence on Swindon hadn't ended and in 1865, while out of the country laying the cable, he was elected Conservative MP for Cricklade, which included Swindon. He represented the constituency from 1865 until 1885, but never made a speech in the House of

Commons. He was, however, popular with his constituents – hardly surprising, though, when he declared himself in favour of abolishing income tax and leaving the liquor laws alone. Gooch's business affairs continued to prosper and he had become one of the richest men in the land. Many of his fellow engineers made large fortunes but his flair for financial matters, combined with a longer working life, a measure of luck and some shrewd investments, enabled him to accumulate even greater wealth. In 1867 he was able to lend the South Devon Railway £25,000 a year at 6 per cent interest, and in the same year production started at the Hafod Colliery at Ruabon which was owned by his company. He also managed to find the time to write his memoirs.

In personal matters, however, there was much sadness. In 1868 Margaret, his wife of thirty years, died, leaving Gooch grief-stricken. 'How much I owe to her for what has been good in my life,' he recorded in his journal. But, apart from taking family holidays with her, she seems never to have played a big part in his plans and perhaps remarks he made in his memoirs about their engagement – of being anxious and unhappy about his position, of feeling that he had been too hasty – give a truer impression of his feelings for her.

During his reign as chairman of the Great Western, Gooch's policy of rigid economies worked and dividends rose steadily. Between 1866 and 1870 annual receipts increased by 10 per cent and the number of passengers by well over a fifth. In his personal life he found happiness again when he married Emily Burder in London in September 1870. Emily was just 28, 25 years younger than Gooch, but they grew to care deeply for each other and the age difference was wiped out by her pride in his achievements and her willingness to take a full part in his busy life; something that Margaret had never done. He had been re-elected to Parliament and he was a member of the Royal Commission into Trade Unions, but it was still the Great Western that took up most of his energies.

The Swindon Works was again expanded, but Gooch had to watch the gradual collapse of Brunel's broad-gauge empire for which he had fought so hard, overseeing the conversion of the company's

Workers at the Great Western Railway works in Swindon, 1875

broad-gauge lines to the 4-foot 8½-inch gauge that now covered the rest of the country. Straight sections of the track were relatively easy, but on curved sections the rails had to be shortened. South Wales was a particularly troublesome area, with over 30 'breaks of gauge' hampering the interchange of traffic, particularly coal. The first gauge conversions had taken place in 1866 and by 1869 broad-gauge trains had ceased to run north of Oxford. Wales saw its last working in 1872, and by 1873 some 200 miles of branches south of the main line in Berkshire, Wiltshire, Hampshire and Somerset had been converted.

In spite of losing the battle of the gauges, the Great Western continued to grow rapidly in the 1870s, taking over other lines until it became the largest railway company in Britain with over 2,000 miles of track. Many of Gooch's locomotives, including most of the Iron Dukes, were still in service. Between 1873 and 1886 Gooch oversaw one of the greatest engineering feats on the entire British railway network, the 4½-mile Severn Tunnel – 'a work which,' L. T. C. Rolt says, 'in its difficulties and dangers and the determination and courage with which they were faced, is worthy to rank with the greatest achievements of the pioneers'. The need for a rail crossing of the Severn Estuary had been obvious for many years but its sheer width had always deterred the Great Western directors. Work eventually began on it in March 1873 but it took twelve and a half years to complete as the site was dogged by problems with flooding and required constant pumping operations. It was not until September 1885 that Gooch, accompanied by Lady Gooch and a party of friends, was able to travel through the tunnel in a special train, and even then the opening for regular traffic had to be delayed pending completion of a pumping station and the installation of a large ventilation fan.

Gooch's health remained good as he entered his sixties. His most important parliamentary work was for the railways and in 1881 he was made chairman of the Railway Association and chosen as one of their nominees to a select committee on passenger and freight rates. In 1885 his career in the Commons came to a close when he decided not to stand for re-election. His chairmanship of the Great Western, though, continued to dominate his life. By this time he knew that the end of the broad-gauge tracks could not be delayed for long but he did not live to see it. Final conversion of the last miles of broad gauge from London via Bristol, Exeter and Plymouth to Penzance, 177 route miles in all, did not take place until after Gooch's death at the age of 73. By this time he had become so well known in Victorian society that *The Times* issued daily bulletins on his health in the days leading up to his death at Clewer Park in 1889. Lady Gooch didn't believe in grandiose Victorian funerals and it was announced that Daniel Gooch's would take place quietly at Clewer. But in his obituaries no other British locomotive engineer received such public honour. On his death, his estate was valued at around £750,000 – almost ten times the amount left by Brunel and equivalent to about £50 million in today's terms. He had risen from a workman's wage to become one of the richest men in the land. During this time he had been locomotive superintendent of the Great Western for 27 years and had gone on to reign for another 24 as chairman. It was a lifetime of service almost unique in railway history.

Gooch was the first of the great railway company locomotive engineers. It has been said that 'while Brunel built the Great Western, Gooch made it work'. He fixed it and saved it from becoming a white elephant. There is no dispute that his locomotive designs were at the leading edge and provided the motive power that made Brunel's ever-expanding railway network function so impressively. His Swindon Works may have been built initially to serve Brunel's London to Bristol railway, but it evolved into what many regarded as the finest railway works in the world. The results achieved by Gooch with the broad-gauge locomotives he built there acted as a stimulus to technical developments on the narrower gauge. Without the broad gauge and the gauge war to which it led, locomotive design and performance would not have improved so rapidly. Gooch was certainly one of the giants of the Victorian Age, both as an engineer and as a businessman.

The 105 six-wheeled tender engines he built in the early 1840s were the first standardization on an extensive scale for any railway and with them Gooch brought mass production to the industry. The thing that made this possible, not just for products associated with railway-building but in a wide range of industries in the engineering sector including shipbuilding, machine-making and steam engine production, was the development of machine tools. And it was a workshop in Manchester where James Nasmyth set himself up that led the way.

7

James Nasmyth
1808–1890
Machine Tools and Steam Hammers

One of the things that had made the construction of large ocean-going, steam-powered, iron-hulled ships possible had been the advances that steam had brought about in the iron and steel industries. The most significant of these happened in a place called Patricroft near Manchester where a gentleman called James Nasmyth perfected the steam hammer. Until 1839, when Nasmyth invented the steam hammer, the capacity of the old water-powered hammers limited the forging of large pieces of steel. History has it that, when Brunel was planning to build SS Great Britain as a paddle ship, one of the great problems he was faced with in building paddles for a ship of this size was finding somebody who had got a big enough hammer to construct a crankshaft that would go across the whole width of the great ship. It's said that Nasmyth developed it for the Great Britain only for Brunel to then change his mind and decide on the screw or propeller rather than the paddles. So Nasmyth was left with this steam hammer – but it wasn't a failure, it enabled the men in the iron industry to make bigger ingots to be put through the rollers to make bigger plates for building bigger ships – and building bigger everything.

James Hall Nasmyth was born on 19 August 1808 in Edinburgh. During his early years he was greatly influenced by his father, Alexander, a leading artist of the day, who is regarded as the founder of the landscape painting school of Scotland. One of Alexander's hobbies was mechanics and he had a workshop where he encouraged James to work alongside him on his projects. 'When I was about four years old,' Nasmyth recalled in later life, 'I often followed my father into his workshop when he had occasion to show to his visitors some of his mechanical contrivances or artistic models. And then there were the pleasant evenings at home. When the day's work was over, friends looked in to have a fireside crack, sometimes scientific men, sometimes artists, often both.'

Before James went to school, his practical education had already started. Near his house there were many workshops where a variety of trades were carried on – coppersmiths, tinsmiths, brass-founders, goldbeaters and blacksmiths. Their workshops were all open to passers-by, who could look in to see these men at work amid the glow of fires and the beating of hammers. The young Nasmyth was fascinated by what he saw and became a great admirer of their skills. He always maintained that this row of busy workshops was his first school. At this time he was placed in the care of his eldest sister, Jane, who was 20 years older than him. She taught him to read before he was sent to a leading teacher called Knight, to further his education.

Nasmyth's father wasn't wealthy but neither was he a poor pitman like George Stephenson. He was well regarded in artistic and literary circles and had many influential friends. It provided a stimulating environment for young James as he was growing up. One day he was sitting beside his father at home making a careful drawing of a fine bronze coin, when the great novelist Sir Walter Scott came into the room to consult Nasmyth's father about some architectural plans. In the same year, 1817, James Watt, then aged 81, paid a visit to examine Alexander Nasmyth's artistic works. The young Nasmyth's interest in mechanics was ever-growing so this meeting with the 'father of the steam engine' was a particularly exciting event for him. As he got older Nasmyth began to spend more and more of his spare time in his father's workroom. When the weather was cold or wet, he always took refuge there and watched his father as he worked with his lathe and tools. Alexander took the greatest pleasure in instructing his son. Even in the most basic and humble mechanical jobs he would always direct his son's attention to the action of the tools, the construction of the work he had in hand and the manipulative processes required to carry it out. The son's keenness to help out in the workshop was well rewarded as his father instilled in him the fundamental principles of engineering.

When he was nine years old James was sent to Edinburgh's Royal High School, which he attended from 1817 to 1820. It was a distinguished school, but Nasmyth was not very impressed by it and later in his life he said he didn't learn much there, as it was merely a matter of learning by rote and cramming. 'I learnt by heart a number of Latin rules and phrases,' he said, 'but what I learnt soon slipped from my memory.' His real education continued out of school hours in his father's workshop. He started to make little toys there and he was able to earn some pocket money by selling them. Among the boys at the school there was a craze for spinning tops and Nasmyth soon became noted for the quality of the tops he made using his father's foot-lathe. His school companions all wanted to have one and they would give virtually any price for them. His craftsmanship led Nasmyth on to produce kites and tissue-paper balloons and he always had a ready market at school for anything he produced. Something else he became noted for was the manufacture of small brass cannons, all cast, bored and mounted on their appropriate gun-carriages. All through his time at the high school he carried on a trade in these and beautiful little steel models which he forged in the furnace stove in his father's workroom, which also featured a suitable anvil, hammer and tongs.

One of his schoolfriends was Jemmy Patterson, the son of one of the largest iron founders in Edinburgh. Jeremy took Nasmyth to his father's workshops, where he learned to work and turn in wood, brass, iron and steel, and saw how iron castings were made. Mill machinery and steam engines were repaired there, so he was able to observe at close quarters the way in which power was generated and transmitted. It was a perfect schooling in practical mechanics. Although he was only about 13 years old at the time, he always used to lend a hand in the workshop, where the enthusiasm he showed more than made up for his lack of strength. Later in life, when he was established as a leading engineer, he would look back on these days and say the time he had spent in the iron foundry workshops gave him the most important part of his education as a mechanical engineer. 'I did not read about such things,' he said, 'for words were of little use. But I saw and handled, and thus all the ideas in connection with them became permanently rooted in my mind.' It was the sort of practical education in mechanics that Fred admired.

Another of Nasmyth's friends when he was at school in Edinburgh was Tom Smith, whose father was a general merchant in Leith. He had an interest in practical chemistry and established a colour manufactory at Portobello where he produced white lead, red lead, and a great variety of colours used in paint. Tom Smith inherited his father's interest in chemistry and invited Nasmyth to share in his experiments. These were carried out in a chemical laboratory behind his father's house at the bottom of Leith Walk. Whenever anything was going on at the laboratory, Tom hoisted a white flag on the top of a high pole in his father's garden. As Nasmyth's house was more than a mile away, he kept a look-out in the direction of the laboratory with a telescope. When the flag was hoisted he could clearly see the invitation and was only too happy to run down the walk and join his friend in an interesting chemical experiment.

Nasmyth left the high school at the end of 1820 and continued his studies at private classes, arithmetic and geometry being his favourite subjects. At the same time his father encouraged him to practise the art of drawing and taught him to sketch with precision a whole range of different objects, both natural and man-made. This ability to reproduce accurately whatever his eye could see was to serve him in good stead. When he wasn't studying and drawing he occupied himself in his father's workshop at the lathe, the furnace and on the bench, and gradually gained experience in every type of mechanical and chemical manipulation.

By the time Nasmyth was 17, he'd acquired a considerable amount of practical knowledge in the handling of mechanical tools, and was looking for a project that would give him the chance to use his skill. He didn't have long to wait. A canal had been built to link Edinburgh with the Forth and Clyde Canal and create a direct waterway connection between Edinburgh and Glasgow. Nasmyth found out that the directors of the canal company were considering whether to substitute steam power for horsepower to move boats and barges along the canal. The scheme involved laying a chain along the bottom of the canal and passing it between three grooved and notched pulleys or rollers. These would be made to revolve by means of a small steam engine placed in a tugboat, which would tow a train of barges. Nasmyth designed a system and submitted a complete set of drawings for it to the directors of the canal company. He received a complimentary acknowledgement in writing, but some of the directors were concerned about the damage that might be caused to the canal banks by the paddle wheels so his plans were turned down.

Undeterred by this setback, he returned to his father's workshop and started to build his first steam engine. He began by making a series of sectional models of complete condensing steam engines. The first of these models was made for the Edinburgh School of Arts, where it was used to instruct mechanics in the application of steam. The second was made for Professor Leslie of Edinburgh University, for use in his lectures on natural philosophy. Nasmyth charged £10 for these models and from the profits he made he gave a third to his father to remunerate him for his keep and the use of his workshop. With the rest he purchased tickets for classes at Edinburgh University.

Each day he got up early in the morning to work at his father's lathe and sat up late at night to do the brass castings in his bedroom, which he'd converted into a brass foundry. Most of the work on the steam engine models was done in his father's workroom. The foot-lathe and stove in the workshop, together with the brass-casting arrangements in his bedroom, met all his requirements for model-making. If there was any part of a job that was beyond the capabilities of his father's lathe and his bedroom casting apparatus he went to a local smithy and foundry owned by George Douglass, who had begun business as a jobbing smith before establishing a large trade in steam engines. Here Nasmyth had the facility to take on bigger jobs. In return for the kindness Douglass showed in allowing him to use his foundry, Nasmyth decided to present him with a sample of his handiwork. He wanted this to be something special so he set out to test his mechanical skills by making a more powerful steam engine than he had ever attempted before. This would allow him to try out the large turning-lathe and the other tools and machinery in the Douglass foundry. The result of his labours was a very efficient steam engine that could drive all the lathes and mechanical tools in the workshop. In addition to the steam engine he presented to Douglass, he also received an order to make another one for a braiding manufacturer.

In 1827, when Nasmyth was 19 years old, engineers, inventors and entrepreneurs were beginning to show a lot of interest in the idea of steam carriages to run on the roads. Here was another challenge for the young engineer and he set to work on building one immediately. He had the heavy parts of the engine and carriage made at Anderson's foundry at Leith, and the whole job was completed in about four months. For the engine Nasmyth employed the waste steam to create a blast or draught by discharging it into the short chimney of the boiler at its lowest part, which he found to be very effective. At the time he cannot have been aware that George and Robert Stephenson were adopting the same method in the design and construction of *Rocket*, and it is a testimony to Nasmyth's inventiveness that he recognized the potential of using the steam blast in the chimney. When his steam carriage was completed it was exhibited before the members of the Society of Arts and successful trials were carried out on the Queensferry Road, just outside Edinburgh. The runs were generally of four or five miles, with eight passengers sitting on benches about three feet from the ground. The experiments continued for nearly three months and the members of the society were greatly impressed. But sadly it was all to no avail. The Society of Arts didn't attach any commercial value to the steam road-carriage. It was merely an experiment that they had invited Nasmyth to conduct. When it proved successful they gave him the carriage as a present but there were no contracts for the manufacture of any more. It must have been a great disappointment for the young engineer but, as he was anxious to get on with his studies for a career in practical engineering, he proceeded no further. He broke up the steam carriage and sold the two small high-pressure engines and the strong, compact boiler he'd had made for £67, a sum which more than covered all the expenses of the construction and working of the machine.

The young Nasmyth continued to conduct investigations into the powers and capabilities of the steam engine. He was fortunate that there were numerous breweries, distilleries and other establishments in and around Edinburgh where he could observe steam engines at work. All were made by different engineers, so he went round and saw as many of them as he could, and made sketches of them. It wasn't long before he became friendly with the engine tenters* at all of these establishments, who were always glad to see someone who was so interested in them and their engines.

On his visits, he began to hear of the name and fame of Henry Maudslay, and the works he had in London. Maudslay had begun his career as a blacksmith, making machinery for Joseph Bramah, who invented a burglar-proof lock that remained unpicked for 67 years. The secret of the lock was the precision with which it was made. When Henry Maudslay went on to establish his own company, his work was influenced by that same precision. In the early years of the nineteenth century most things were still made by hand. The idea of having specially built machinery to make things was still in its infancy and any machines that did exist were quite primitive. There were no standard measures and parts had to be individually engineered. This meant that nuts and bolts would be made to fit as a pair and were not interchangeable. Henry Maudslay was one of the first to recognize the importance of the standardization and interchangeability of machine parts. He was also one of the first to realize the need for a true plane surface, for obtaining precision in machine-tool production. But his major engineering contribution was his large screw-cutting lathe, which was far superior to any of its predecessors.

Nasmyth had learned that Maudslay's works were the centre for all

---

* Men who ran and maintained the steam engines in mills and factories.

that was excellent in mechanical workmanship, so he resolved to get a job there. But there was a problem. His father might have been a respected artist and well regarded in the world of art and science in Edinburgh but he wasn't a wealthy man. Nasmyth was aware that he didn't have the means to pay the large premium required to secure an apprenticeship at Maudslay's works. He'd also been informed that Maudslay was no longer taking on pupils. But Nasmyth was determined to secure a place at this great school of mechanical engineering so he decided to show Maudslay an example of his skill. He wanted to satisfy the great engineer that he was not just a student but a regular working engineer. With this in mind he set out to make a complete working model of a high-pressure engine, creating the working drawings and constructing all of the components himself.

Armed with such tangible evidence of his abilities as an engineer, he packed up the model and drawings and, on 19 May 1829, accompanied by his father, he set sail for London on the Leith smack *Edinburgh Castle*. Father and son were well received by Maudslay, but he told them frankly that his experience of pupil apprentices had been so unsatisfactory that he had decided not to take any more on, no matter how great a premium was on offer. Maudslay knew, however, that Alexander Nasmyth was interested in all matters relating to mechanical engineering, and he courteously invited him to go round the works. Nasmyth Junior, of course, accompanied them. As they toured the works Maudslay observed the earnest interest shown by both father and son. He explained the movements of the machinery to them and all the workings of the factory. When the tour was completed, James seized the opportunity to tell Maudslay that he had brought some working models of steam engines and mechanical drawings with him from Edinburgh and that he would be obliged if Mr Maudslay would allow him to show them to him. Maudslay agreed and asked him to bring them to him at twelve o'clock the following day.

Nasmyth went back to the carpenter's shop where he had left his belongings and carefully unpacked his working model of the steam engine. The next day at the appointed time he had it transported, together with his drawings, on a hand-cart to Maudslay's works, where he was instructed to leave it in a room next to the great man's office and counting house. Nasmyth waited in the library and 20 long minutes passed before Maudslay came into the room to see him. From the smile on his face, Nasmyth knew immediately that he had achieved his ambition. Maudslay complimented the young man on his practical ability as a workman, engineer and mechanical draughtsman. Then, opening the door that led from his library into his private workshop, he said, 'This is where I wish you to work, beside me, as my assistant workman. From what I have seen there is no need of an apprenticeship in your case.' It must have been a very proud moment for the young man.

After the interview Alexander Nasmyth stayed on in London for a few days and while he was out walking with his son he met an old friend, Henry Brougham. 'If I can do anything for you,' Brougham said, addressing James, 'let me know. It will afford me much pleasure to give you introductions to men of science in London.' On hearing this, James ventured to say that of all the men of science in London the one he most wished to meet was Michael Faraday. Brougham said he would arrange for this and, on returning to his lodgings with his father that evening, James found a note from Brougham enclosing letters of introduction to Faraday and other scientists. The young Nasmyth knew that he had arrived in the highest echelons of science and engineering.

On the morning of Monday, 30 May 1829, Nasmyth started work at Maudslay's workshop on a wage of ten shillings (50p) a week. Maudslay took him into his confidence immediately, treating him not as a workman but as a friend. He showed him the collection of taps and dies and screw-tackle that he had made himself for his own use and which lay in a succession of drawers near to the bench where he worked. Nasmyth noted there was a look of tidiness about the collection that seemed to be characteristic of the man. Order was one of the rules Maudslay rigidly observed, and he tried to enforce it upon all who were in his employment.

Nasmyth's first job was to assist Maudslay with some detailed modifications to a machine he had designed some years earlier for making screws. Another early job he took on was assisting him in making a small model of a pair of 200-horsepower marine steam engines. The engines were being constructed in the factory and were considered a major advance on the marine engines currently in use. Nasmyth also took an early opportunity of presenting Brougham's letter of introduction to Faraday at the Royal Institution. Faraday knew Maudslay well and promised that he would call in to see him at work. When he paid his visit, Faraday found Nasmyth working beside Maudslay in his little workshop, where a vice had been fitted up for him at the bench where Maudslay himself worked. Faraday congratulated Nasmyth on his good fortune in starting his career with the great advantage of being associated as assistant workman with one of the leading mechanical engineers of the day.

The 1820s were exciting times for a young engineer and Nasmyth was particularly interested in the descriptions he had read in the newspapers of the locomotive trials at Rainhill; he was anxious to see Stephenson's *Rocket*. Taking with him letters of introduction from Maudslay to men of influence in Liverpool, he left London for the North on 9 September 1830. After meeting Stephenson and seeing *Rocket* in action he went on foot to Manchester to have a look at some of its cotton mills. Manchester was the city that generated much of Britain's nineteenth-century wealth and pioneered many of its ground-breaking technological advances. Between 1760 and 1830 its population had multiplied tenfold as it became the world's first great industrial city and Nasmyth was fascinated by what he saw. When he arrived he would have found dozens of five- and six-storey factories, each with a towering chimney at its side billowing out black smoke. At the bottom of every chimney there was a steam engine connected to row after row of spinning machines.

The factories dominated the city, as did the ambitious and often ruthless entrepreneurs who owned them. Their workers lived in squalid conditions in the closely packed terraced houses that huddled around the factories. Many were agricultural workers who had moved from the land to meet the new factories' insatiable demand for workers, but their living conditions were grim. Alexis de Tocqueville, a

French aristocrat who visited Manchester at this time, described the scene: 'A sort of black smoke covers the city. Under the half daylight 300,000 human beings are ceaselessly at work. The homes of the poor are scattered haphazard around the factories. From this filthy sewer pure gold flows.' The source of this wealth was cotton and Manchester was 'Cottonopolis'. The town, as it then was, had been well placed to capitalize on advances made in textile manufacture as new machines were invented in the eighteenth century. It was close to Liverpool, the main port of entry for American cotton, and it had a damp climate and plentiful water. Manchester began to supply the world with cotton and the erection of mills, warehouses and housing for the growing population of workers could hardly keep up with demand.

In the mills and factories the power from a single engine or a series of engines was used to run dozens and dozens of machines. Power was transmitted by hundreds of yards of line shafts and belts. The power of the steam engine passed through horizontal shafts and toothed gearing to vertical shafts. Through yet more toothed gearing these drove horizontal shafts on each floor of the factory or works connected to individual machines by leather belts and pulleys. Horizontal line shafts were usually between 6½ feet and 16½ feet in length. They were coupled together using bearings and hangers or brackets to enable them to run the whole length of a mill or factory floor – which could be as long as 200 feet. This was the Manchester that Nasmyth came to and he was excited by what he saw, realizing that opportunities were there for somebody like himself with a mechanical bent. He might be able to improve on the complicated machinery then in use and make the manufacture of the machines cheaper.

On his return to London, Nasmyth continued to work alongside Maudslay. The work was varied and it presented him with many opportunities to come up with solutions to mechanical problems. The pupil and his eminent teacher worked together for another year but this was brought to an end suddenly when Maudslay died in 1831. Nasmyth was then taken on by Maudslay's partner, Joshua Field, as a draughtsman. The first work he did for Field was to assist him in making the working drawings for a 200-horsepower condensing steam engine, ordered by the Lambeth Waterworks Company. While he was occupied on this alongside Field he was given a lot of valuable tips regarding the design of machinery in general. One point Field often impressed on him was that it was most important to bear in mind the accessibility of parts. It was essential that, when any part of a machine had to be taken out for repair, it could be got at easily without taking the whole machine to pieces.

The working drawings for the Lambeth pumping engines occupied Nasmyth until August 1831, but by this time he was 23 years old and had no intention of carrying on much longer as an assistant or a journeyman. It was the Age of the Machine: a time when machinery was being developed to replace human effort; when modern industry was overtaking traditional crafts and agriculture. Nasmyth was aware of the opportunities and he had ambitions to set up his own business even if it meant starting in a very small way. When he informed Mr Field, he not only accepted Nasmyth's decision but allowed him to take castings of one of the best turning-lathes in the workshops. This was a very generous act, helping someone to set up who would possibly become a business rival. At the end of the month Nasmyth set sail for Leith with his stock of castings.

Back home in Edinburgh he rented a small piece of land at Old Broughton, about five minutes' walk from his father's house. Here he erected a temporary workshop, 24 feet long by 16 feet wide, and began to make machine tools. His first job was the construction of a rotary steam engine, which he completed in three months. After a few more months of labour he had everything ready to start business on his own account and he knew where that business was going to be. All the great mechanics of the day were heading for Manchester with its booming textile industry. It was already a highly mechanized trade and the servicing of the power looms and spinning machines and the development of new and improved designs called for highly skilled mechanics. It promised to be a lucrative outlet for an ambitious young engineer's expertise. When Nasmyth had visited the city on his earlier tour he had been fortunate to have introductions from Maudslay to some of the leading businessmen there. These included John Kennedy, the owner of one of the biggest cotton mills in the North of England, William Fairbairn, who after leaving Maudslay's had set up his own engineering business there, and Benjamin Hick, who had established an engineering works in Bolton. Manchester was the place to be and that was where Nasmyth headed.

On his arrival he was taken to see a place that could be used as a small workshop. It was a factory space 130 feet long by 27 feet wide at an old cotton mill on Dale Street. The rent was only £50 a year and Nasmyth thought the premises would be very suitable. He took a night to sleep on it and the following morning he was up early and immediately entered into a contract for the premises as a yearly tenant. 'Nothing could have been more happily arranged for my entering into business as a mechanical engineer and machine tool maker,' Nasmyth said of the place. 'The situation of the premises was excellent, being in the heart of Manchester. There was a powerful crab crane, or hoisting apparatus, in the upper storey, and the main chains came down in front of the wide door of my workshop, so that heavy castings or cases of machinery might be lifted up or let down with the utmost ease and convenience.'

Nasmyth soon received his first order, from Edward Tootal. It was for a new metallic piston for the small steam engine that powered his silk-winding machinery. The job had to be done overnight so that the factory could be at work as usual in the morning. Other orders came flooding in and Nasmyth's planing machine was soon fully occupied. When it was not in use on other work it was kept constantly busy planing the flat cast-iron inking tables for printing machines. In order to keep pace with the flow of work he had to take on fresh hands. He established a smithy down in the cellar of the building, so that all forge work in iron and steel could be produced promptly and economically on the premises. Week by week his order book grew. He always made sure that he carried out the work to the best possible standard and with the quality he achieved the business went from strength to strength.

When Nasmyth set up his business at the start of the 1830s Manchester was Britain's boom town, and with the opening of the Liverpool & Manchester Railway in 1830 there came a great increase in demand for machine-making tools. The success of the railway soon led to the construction of other lines, all centred on the town, and every branch of manufacture shared in the prosperity. The demand for skilled labour was greater than the supply and it was clear to Nasmyth that there was a need for machines that would automate the manu- facturing process. Most of the machine tools he was making were self-acting – planing machines, slide lathes and drilling, boring and slotting machines – so he was particularly well placed to benefit from the boom. The problem was he was outgrowing his premises. He was aware from an early stage that he would need to expand if he were to make the most of the opportunities.

Matters came to a head when he received an order for a 20-horse- power high-pressure steam engine to drive the machinery in a distillery in Londonderry. At first he was afraid that he wouldn't be able to take on the job. The size of the engine was greater than the height of his factory and it would probably occupy too much floor space in his already overcrowded workshop. At length, after giving a lot of thought to the job, he agreed to take on the order. What he decided was that, instead of constructing the engine vertically, the only way to do it was to build it lying on its side. But the combination of massive castings and a wooden floor was not an ideal one, and it led to an accident in which one end of the engine beam crashed through the floor into a glass-cutter's workshop below. There was a terrible scatter- ing of lath and plaster, dust and broken glass. The glass-cutter rushed to the landlord and asked him to come and inspect the wreckage of his workshop. The landlord looked in and saw the damage that had been done to all the glass-cutter's tumblers and decanters. Looking up he saw a gaping hole in the roof, through which the end of the engine beam was protruding. There was nothing for it, Nasmyth was told he would have to move from the premises as soon as he could, otherwise the whole building would be brought down with the weight of his machinery.

With a full order book Nasmyth had to find new premises quickly. He remembered that on the journey he had made on foot from Liverpool to Manchester in 1830, he had rested on the parapet of a

Nasmyth's slide rest lathe, one of the most important
developments in machine-tool manufacturing

bridge overlooking the Bridgewater Canal near Patricroft and gazed longingly at a plot of land by the side of the canal. He knew that it would be the perfect site for an engineering works of his own. On the same afternoon the engine beam crashed through the glass-cutter's roof, he went out again to look at that piece of land and found to his surprise that it was still unoccupied. The owner of the plot was Squire Trafford, one of the largest landowners in the area. The following morning he made his way to Trafford Hall to see him, and, much to Nasmyth's delight, the squire said he would be pleased to have him as one of his tenants. Nasmyth was offered a lease on the 6-acre plot for 999 years, at an annual rent of 1¾d (1p) per square yard. Immediately work began on the construction of a workshop that would be big enough to house the largest of the machines he was building. The premises, which he called the Bridgewater Foundry, stood adjacent to the canal and the newly opened Liverpool & Manchester Railway.

Having moved to the site promptly, in order to cope with the rapid expansion that came from increased orders Nasmyth took on a partner, Holbrook Gaskell. The articles of partnership were at once drawn up and signed, and the firm of Nasmyth, Gaskell & Company began operations. It was the start of a very successful 16-year business relationship and the company quickly gained a reputation for innovations in the design and manufacture of machine tools. In 1836 they developed an instrument for finding and marking the centres of cylindrical rods or bolts about to be turned on the lathe. In the same year a machine for planing the smaller, detailed parts of machinery was introduced and improvements were made to steam-engine pistons and to water and air-pump buckets. In 1838 self-adjusting bearings for the shafts of machinery were developed and the steam ram was invented.

By the late 1830s great progress had been achieved in making warships shot-proof by applying iron plates to their hulls. Nasmyth saw there was an opportunity here. It appeared to him that no ship would be able to stay afloat if it received a single blow on its hull from an iron-plated steam ram of 2,000 tons. 'Why,' he reasoned, 'should we continue to attempt to sink ships in battle by making small holes in the hull of the enemy when, by one single, crashing blow from a steam ram, we could crush in the side of any armour-plated ship, and let the water rush in through a hole that would be certain to send her below water in a few minutes.' This was the thinking that led to the development of the steam hammer, which became his most famous invention. It was developed very much with war in mind, but not all his inventions had such life-threatening capacity. In fact one of his best known was designed specifically to save life and limb: the screw safety ladle he invented in 1838.

The ladle came about because he had observed the great danger workmen were exposed to by the method that had been used up to then to empty molten iron into casting moulds. The white-hot fluid was run from the melting furnace into a large ladle with one or two cross-handles and levers, worked by a dozen or 15 men. The ladle held many tons of molten iron, and was transferred by a crane to the moulds. To do this required a high level of caution and steadiness. If any of the operatives stumbled and the ladle was in the slightest degree upset, hot metal splashed out on to the men, setting their clothes on fire and giving them serious burns. It was to prevent these accidents that Nasmyth invented his safety foundry ladle.

To make it he applied a screw wheel, keyed to the trunnion of the ladle. This was acted on by an endless screw attached to the sling of the ladle. This mechanization of the process meant that one man could move the largest ladle on its axis and pour out its molten contents with ease and in perfect safety. Not only was the risk of accident removed but the perfection of the casting was secured by the steady, continuous flow of the white-hot metal into the mould, and the anxiety and confusion that usually attended the pouring of the metal required for larger castings were entirely avoided. Nasmyth could have made a lot of money from patenting this invention, but recognizing that it would prevent many injuries throughout industry he preferred to make it freely available. He sent drawings and descriptions of the ladle to all the principal founders both at home and abroad and was gratified by their unanimous expression of its practical value. It was soon universally adopted.

The location of the Bridgewater Foundry proved to be a good

choice, particularly as there were large numbers of skilled workmen living in the vicinity. The nearby village of Worsley, the headquarters of the Bridgewater Canal, was particularly good for supplying the right sort of workers. They were, in the first place, labourers, and their chief employment was transporting heavy castings and machine parts from one place to another. Where they showed any mechanical aptitude, Nasmyth was able to select the most effective men to take charge of the largest and most powerful machine tools in his works, such as planing machines, lathes and boring machines.

In common with many of his illustrious contemporaries, Nasmyth had a great capacity for hard work. His dedication to building his business and his unremitting pursuit of the acquisition of a sound practical knowledge of his profession left him little time for a social life. This meant he had, in his own words, 'few opportunities of enjoying the society of young ladies'. By his thirtieth year, though, his thoughts were beginning to turn to marriage. He said that he had now 'entered upon such a course of prosperity as would justify me in taking this the most important step in my life'. In March 1838 he was travelling by coach from Sheffield to York when, as he was approaching Barnsley, he observed, 'in the remaining murky light of the evening, the blaze of some ironwork furnaces near at hand'. On enquiring whose works they were he was informed that they belonged to Earl Fitzwilliam and were managed by a Mr Hartop. 'The mention of his name,' Nasmyth said, 'brought to my recollection a kind invitation which Mr Hartop had given me while visiting my workshop in Manchester to order some machine tools, that if I ever happened to be in his neighbourhood, he would be most happy to show me anything that was interesting about the ironworks and colliery machinery under his management.' Nasmyth decided to terminate his journey and take Hartop up on his offer. He found him at home and was invited to stay the night and visit the works the next day. That evening he met Hartop's family, including his 21-year-old daughter, Anne. The following evening, after he'd been given a tour of the works, Nasmyth said, 'We resumed our "cracks" on many subjects of mutual interest. The daughter joined in our conversation with the most intelligent remarks' and he 'soon perceived in her . . . all the conditions that I could hope for and desire to meet with in the dear partner of my existence'.

Nasmyth was clearly smitten, and as he had to proceed on his journey he wasted no time in 'telling her what I felt and thought . . . and, so far as I could judge, all that I said was received in the best spirit that I could desire'. Without any delay he communicated his hopes and wishes to her parents and explained his circumstances. Although they had only just met, it was arranged that, if business continued to progress as favourably as he hoped it would, their wedding would take place in about two years. It seems incredible now that such a momentous decision could be taken in such a short time, but for Nasmyth, like many other great Victorian businessmen, work came first and the prime consideration in choosing a partner was that the woman was somebody from the right background who would fit in with his plans. He knew immediately that Anne Hartop fitted the bill. From her point of view and that of her family, Nasmyth clearly had good prospects and that was a major factor in choosing a husband. 'Everything,' Nasmyth reported, 'went on hopefully and prosperously,' and 'At length the two years came to an end. My betrothed and I continued of the same mind. The happy "chance event" of our meeting . . . culminated in our marriage at the village church of Wentworth on the 16th of June 1840 – a day of happy memory!'

Up to this time the main business of the firm of Nasmyth, Gaskell & Company had been the production of a wide range of machine tools in great quantities, but they were also beginning to receive orders for locomotives from the newly opened railways that were starting to cover the country. As the company's machine tools were particularly well suited to this sort of work, the firm began to direct more attention to this business. In the course of about ten years after the opening of the Liverpool & Manchester Railway, they fulfilled orders for the construction of locomotives for the London & Southampton, the Manchester & Leeds and the Gloucester railway companies. The Great Western also invited Nasmyth to tender for 20 of their engines and he developed special machine tools to fulfil this order. These reduced the company's reliance on mere manual strength and dexterity and at the same time increased the accuracy and precision of the work.

Nasmyth's connection with the Great Western Railway brought him into contact with Isambard Kingdom Brunel, which led to him being asked to make machine tools that were bigger and more powerful than any already in existence for the construction of the immense engines of the SS *Great Britain*. Works were erected at Bristol to accommodate the machinery and tools were made to the specification of the ship's engineer, Francis Humphreys. The machine tools were delivered and fitted to his approval and the construction of the gigantic engines was soon in full progress.

An unexpected difficulty, however, was encountered with respect to the enormous wrought-iron paddle shaft. It needed to be of a size and diameter the like of which had never previously been forged. Humphreys applied to the largest forges throughout the country for tenders for the work, but found that not one of them could undertake so large a forging. The problem they faced was that the type of forge hammer in use was the tilt hammer, which dated back to the seventeenth century. This was like a huge sledgehammer with a wooden shaft that was pivoted in such a way that its head was raised and then let fall on the anvil by a cogged wheel driven first by water power and then by steam. The strike rate of the hammer could be changed by varying the number of cogs on the driving wheel, but the stroke or length of its drop on to the anvil could not. This meant that if a very large forging was placed on the anvil, the hammer couldn't strike an effective blow. In the words of the smith, it became 'gagged'.

Faced with this dilemma Humphreys consulted Nasmyth, who thought the matter over and sketched out an idea for a steam hammer. It consisted of a massive anvil on which to rest the block of metal that was to be forged; a large block of iron for the hammer; and an inverted steam cylinder to whose piston rod the hammer block was attached. All that was then required to produce a most effective hammer was to admit steam of sufficient pressure into the cylinder, so as to act on the underside of the piston, and thus to raise the hammer block attached to the end of the piston rod. By a simple arrangement of a slide valve the steam was allowed to escape, permitting the massive block of iron to descend rapidly by its own gravity on to the work on the anvil. The long stroke that the vertical drop gave the hammer overcame the 'gagging' difficulty.

Nasmyth believed that the steam hammer he had conceived would prove successful and saw that it could be employed throughout industry for the forging of heavy masses of iron. He wrote to Humphreys at once and sent him a sketch. Humphreys was delighted with the design. He submitted it to Brunel and to Thomas Guppy, the managing director of the Great Western Steamship Company, and it was approved. Nasmyth accordingly gave the company permission to communicate his design to any forge proprietors who wanted to erect the steam hammer, on condition that it would be made in accordance with his own design. But sadly the paddle shaft of the *Great Britain* was never forged, for as we know Brunel came down in favour of the screw propeller in place of the paddle wheel.

Nasmyth's invention, however, was taken up in a new and un-expected quarter. For some years he had been supplying foreign customers with self-acting machine tools. The principals of continental manufacturing establishments made frequent visits to England to purchase machine tools and among the foreign visitors was M. Schneider, the proprietor of the great ironworks at Le Creusot, in France. Nasmyth had supplied him with various machine tools, and he was so pleased with them that the next time he came to England he visited Patricroft. Nasmyth kept his ideas for new devices, mostly in drawings, in a 'Scheme Book', which he freely showed to his foreign customers. He pointed out the drawing of his steam hammer to Schneider, who was impressed by its simplicity and practicality. A short time later, in April 1842, when Nasmyth visited France to negotiate a contract to supply machine tools to the French arsenals and dockyards, he also took the opportunity to visit the Le Creusot works. One of the things that particularly impressed him there was a large wrought-iron marine engine single crank that had been forged with a remarkable degree of precision. On enquiring how the crank had been forged, the reply was that it had been done with his steam hammer. One of

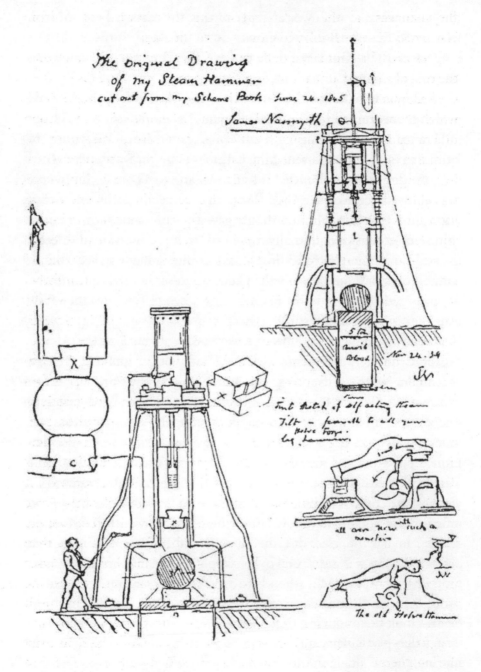

The Original Drawing
of my Steam Hammer
cut out from my Scheme Book June 24. 1845
James Nasmyth

the managers at the works had copied the drawing of it from Nasmyth's Scheme Book while on a visit to England.

Nasmyth had not taken out a patent for the steam hammer because the cost of a patent at that time was little short of £500, and his partner, Gaskell, was unwilling to lay out such a large sum on an invention for which there seemed to be so little demand. The take-up of the design in France persuaded Nasmyth otherwise and two months after his return to England he patented the hammer and began production of it in Edinburgh. He improved his steam hammer in 1843 so that steam was able to bring the hammer down with tremendous force as well as lift it up. The steam hammer made possible the forging of iron beams and steel plates larger than any that had been produced before, but it could also be controlled so that it descended so lightly that it could crack an eggshell without smashing the egg. Nasmyth set up a number of public demonstrations. At one he gave in 1845, he was loudly cheered by a group of spectators because such a saving in time by steam versus manual labour had never been witnessed before.

To demonstrate the power and capability of the hammer, he constructed a 30-cwt model with a hammer block that had a clear 4-foot range of fall. He set it to work at Patricroft where it helped greatly in the company's smithy and forge work. By using the hammer, production costs could be reduced by over 50 per cent, while at the same time improving the quality of the forgings. People travelled great distances to see it in operation and all the visitors were impressed. A key feature of the machine was that the operator controlled the force of each blow. Nasmyth enjoyed showing off how it could break an egg placed in a wine glass without breaking the glass. This was then followed by a full-force blow that shook the whole building. Once potential customers had seen it the orders started to flood in, the first from the iron-forging business of Rushton & Eckersley of Bolton. It wasn't long before Nasmyth hammers were to be found in ironworks and forges the length and breadth of Britain, enabling them to meet the engineers' demands for increasingly massive forgings. The first were of the free-fall type but they were later modified to give them power-assisted fall.

One of the most important uses of the steam hammer was for forging ships' anchors. Until its invention, large forgings like anchors had to be made by the 'bit-by-bit' process. This involved forging small pieces separately and welding them together, but the steam hammer meant they could be forged in one piece. In 1843 the Lords of the Admiralty appointed a deputation of officers to visit the foundry at Patricroft. Besides showing them his own steam hammer, Nasmyth took the deputation to the works of Rushton & Eckersley, where they saw one of his five-ton hammer-block machines in action. After witnessing the wide range of power of the steam hammer, these men from the Admiralty were satisfied of its fitness for all classes of forgings for the naval service. Within a few days Nasmyth received an official letter, with an order for a steam hammer with a 50-cwt hammer block, together with the appropriate boiler, crane and forge furnace, to equip a complete forge shop at Devonport Dockyard. This was the company's first order from the government and it was soon followed by a second, to supply all the Royal Dockyard forge departments with steam hammers complete with accessories. Nasmyth was in touch with all the leading engineers of the day, trying to sell his invention to them. One of them was Daniel Gooch. In July 1844 he wrote to Gooch reminding him that he had 'been long expecting to hear from you in reference to your having one of my patent steam hammers . . . You really ought to have one . . . we are already at No 22.'

Because he was in touch with leading engineers like Gooch and Robert Stephenson, Nasmyth was aware of what products he needed to devise to make their lives easier. One of the most successful of these was a pile-driving machine which he developed by applying the principle of his steam hammer. His first full-scale machine used a 4-ton hammer block that had a rate of 80 blows per minute. It was first demonstrated in a contest with a team using the conventional method at Devonport on 3 July 1845. Nasmyth drove a pile 70 feet long and 18 inches square in 4½ minutes, while the conventional method required 12 hours. In the next few years this success led to many orders for his pile driver for large-scale constructions all over the world. It enabled a solid foundation to be laid for the enormous structures erected over them and was used for driving the immense piles of the High Level Bridge at Newcastle, the great Border Bridge at Berwick-upon-Tweed, the docks at Tynemouth, Birkenhead and Grimsby, the new Westminster Bridge, the great bridge at Kiev in Russia and for barrages on the Nile and at Yokohama in Japan.

In the 1840s the rapid extension of railways and steam navigation, both at home and abroad, brought with it a massively increased demand for machinery of all kinds. The Bridgewater Foundry had earned itself a considerable reputation for mechanical contrivances so the workshops were always busy and the company's order book always full. But Nasmyth wouldn't rest on his laurels and he was constantly developing new machines to meet the needs of industry. The provision of high-quality, low-price iron and steel was a continuing feature of industrial expansion and in 1845 Nasmyth perfected a new method of welding iron. The mutual benefits of advances in iron and steel pro-duction and engineering are best seen in the growth of the shipbuilding industry and in 1848 Nasmyth revealed a steam-hammer form of steam engine, which was specially adapted for screw-propelled steamships. That year also saw him applying hydraulic power to the punching of large holes in iron bars and plates of great thickness.

Coal was the single most important industrial fuel and the mining industry successfully met the growth in demand as the owners opened more mines, exploited more seams and employed more men. But it was dangerous work and the frequency of disastrous explosions per-suaded Nasmyth to turn his attention to an improved method for ventilating coal mines. In 1850 he communicated the design for his Direct Action Suction Fan for the ventilation of coal mines to Earl Fitzwilliam, one of the great mine owners of the day. The earl was so impressed that he immediately placed an order for a fan of 14 feet in diameter to ventilate one of his largest pits, and more orders soon followed. Improvements like this began to make mines safer places and contributed to growth in productivity.

At the Great Exhibition of 1851 the firm contributed specimens of their best machine tools and a steam hammer with a 30-cwt hammer block. The commissioners, acting on the special recommendation of the jury, awarded Nasmyth a medal for the construction of a small portable direct-acting steam engine. A Council Medal was also awarded for the steam hammer. In the age of iron and steel, Britain was at the forefront of progress. The development of the railways and ship-building, great civil engineering projects like Robert Stephenson's bridges and the revolution in mechanical engineering where Nasmyth was leading the way were only possible because of the iron and steel industries' ability to meet demand. Bigger and more efficient furnaces were needed to produce iron in volume and in 1854 Nasmyth invented a system for puddling iron by means of steam. His friend Thomas Lever Rushton, proprietor of the Bolton Ironworks, was so impressed with the soundness of the principle, as well as with the great simplicity of turning out the invention for practical use, that he urged Nasmyth to secure the patent. Soon afterwards he gave him the opportunity to try out the process at his works. The results were encouraging. There was a great saving of labour and time compared with the old puddling process; and the malleable iron produced was found to be of the highest quality in terms of strength and purity. The process developed by Nasmyth was soon adopted by several iron manufacturers, but it wasn't long before Henry Bessemer secured his patent for the Bessemer Converter, which employed a blast of air to do the same work that Nasmyth had proposed to accomplish by means of a blast of steam forced up beneath the surface of the molten cast iron. Bessemer added some other improvements and Nasmyth's idea was completely eclipsed. Nevertheless, it demonstrated that Nasmyth was still working at the leading edge of the developments that had made Britain the workshop of the world.

The company continued to go from strength to strength. The steam hammer was particularly profitable and it became the invention for which Nasmyth is now best known. By 1856 a total of 490 had been produced. They were sold all over Europe, to Russia, India and even to Australia, and accounted for 40 per cent of James Nasmyth and Company's revenues. But in 1856, after a long and successful career, he decided to retire from the business he had built so successfully, saying, 'I have now enough of the world's goods: let younger men have their

Nasmyth with his steam hammer

chance.' He was only 48 but the constant exertion and incessant mental efforts were beginning to affect his health. He was particularly concerned about an infection of his eyes that was damaging his sight, so he retired from commercial life. He settled down near Penshurst in Kent, where he named his retirement home Hammerfield. Here he pursued various hobbies including astronomy. He built his own 20-inch reflecting telescope and with this he made detailed observations of the moon. He also co-wrote *The Moon: Considered as a Planet, a World, and a Satellite* with James Carpenter. Innovative to the end, Nasmyth mocked up an interesting series of 'lunar' photographs for the book. Because photography was not yet advanced enough to take actual pictures of the moon, he built plaster models based on his visual observations of it and then photographed the models.

Nasmyth remained happily married for fifty years until his death in 1890. When he was writing his biography in 1882 he said, 'Forty-two years of our married life finds us the same affectionate and devoted "cronies" that we were at the beginning; and there is every prospect that, under God's blessing, we shall continue to be so to the end.' And that was clearly the case. He was arguably the last of the early pioneers of the machine-tool industry, but he also appears to have been a very contented man. His inventions began at a very early age and continued for about 30 years of a busy and active life, during which he created some of our most important machine tools, including the shaper (an adaptation of the planer, which is still used in tool- and die-making) and a hydraulic press that used water pressure to force tight-fitting machine parts together. All of these machines became popular in manufacturing, and all are still in use in modified form to this day. Nasmyth was also one of the first toolmakers to offer a standardized range of machine tools. Before this, manufacturers constructed tools according to individual clients' specifications and with little regard to standardization, and this caused compatibility problems. He has perhaps not always had the recognition he deserves because very few of his inventions were patented and many of them, though widely adopted, are not acknowledged as his. Nevertheless, they brought great advances in the field of mechanical engineering. Among them were a system of transmitting rotary motion by means of a flexible shaft made of coiled wire, a machine for cutting key grooves, and self-adjusting bearings.

'Mr Nasmyth's own definition of engineering,' Fred said, 'was that it was common sense applied to the use of materials. In his case, common sense was especially applied to developing machine tools that enabled other machinery to be made. But his greatest invention and the one he is remembered for more than any other was the steam hammer.' Nasmyth was one of the first of a new breed of engineers, the entrepreneurs who built up vast business empires that became household names. While he was setting up his works at Patricroft, the seeds for a business that was to become the greatest of the Victorian engineering giants were being sown by a young lawyer from Newcastle upon Tyne, William Armstrong.

8

William Armstrong
1810–1900
Building an Industrial Empire

The inventor, engineer and gunmaker William Armstrong was one of Victorian Britain's greatest scientific geniuses and mightiest industrialists. I've seen him described as a man who stood astride the Victotrian era like a colossus and when you look at what he achieved, I think that was right. He dominated the world of engineering in the second half of Queen Victoria's reign as he built up the mighty industrial giant of W. G. Armstrong & Co. It was a time that saw the rise of the entrepreneurial engineer and the big engineering companies and the application of the technology of the Industrial Revolution to warfare. His factory at Elswick on the River Tyne manufactured cranes, large moving machinery, armaments and warships, but the interesting thing was he didn't set off on an engineering career. He started his career as a lawyer, but he was an amateur scientist who was always experimenting in his leisure time. Water power and the development of hydraulic engineering were his first and favourite areas of activity. Then developments in the generation of electricity. His house, Cragside, was one of the most remarkable of its day. By the 1880s it had hot and cold running water, telephones, a fire alarm, a hydraulic lift and, the most magnificent thing, all the electricity were generated by a hydroelectric power station. The house was the first in the world to be lit by hydroelectricity, using incandescent lamps provided by the inventor Joseph Swan. No wonder they called it the 'palace of the modern magician'.

William George Armstrong, a Tyneside industrialist, was the effective founder of the Armstrong Whitworth manufacturing empire. He was born on 26 November 1810 at 9 Pleasant Row, Shieldfield, in Newcastle upon Tyne, a terraced house with a garden at the back that ran down to Pandon Dene. It was on the edge of the city and the setting was quite rural. A stream ran through the dene and there was a farm and water-mill just behind the Armstrong house. His father, also called William, was a self-made man, who'd come to Newcastle in the 1790s from the village of Wreay, near Carlisle, to work as a clerk with a firm of corn merchants on the quayside. He was soon taken into partnership and later became the owner of the business. William Armstrong Senior played a leading part in the establishment of Newcastle Chamber of Commerce and his strong sense of public duty made him active in local politics. He was a councillor for the Jesmond ward, became a city alderman in 1839 and lord mayor in 1850. His wife, Anne, is reputed to have been a woman of culture and he had a keen interest in education. He was an early member of Newcastle Literary and Philosophical Society, and had a particular fondness for mathematics and natural history, which he passed on to his son.

The young William was a delicate boy, but his fascination with science and mechanics was apparent from an early age. He would keep himself amused with primitive pulleys made with string and weights, which he suspended from the banisters. He also had the opportunity to see men at work with machinery as his grandfather owned a joiner's shop. He was educated at private schools in Newcastle and Whickham, near Gateshead, until he was 16, when he was sent to Bishop Auckland Grammar School. While he was there, he often visited the nearby engineering works of William Ramshaw and it was during one of these visits that he met his future wife, Ramshaw's daughter Margaret, who was six years older than him. He also developed a talent for mechanics, but his father had other ideas for him. He was set on his son following a career in the law, and so he was articled to Armorer Donkin, a prosperous Newcastle solicitor who was a close friend of the family. Donkin was a bachelor and he looked upon William as an adoptive son, even making him his heir. A keen amateur scientist himself, he was to be a great influence on Armstrong's career.

In 1828 Armstrong took articles under Donkin and went to London to get a legal training with Donkin's brother-in-law, who was a special pleader at Lincoln's Inn. The trainee lawyer spent five years in London and returned to Newcastle in 1833. In 1835 he became a partner in Donkin's business and the firm became Donkin, Stable and Armstrong. The business was successful and, being securely established in what was then his chosen profession, he proposed marriage to Margaret Ramshaw. They married in 1834 and built a house in Jesmond Dene, on the eastern edge of Newcastle, where they set up home in 1836. She played a strong supporting role in all his activities, particularly in landscaping and planting Jesmond Dene and Cragside. Their marriage was childless, but it turned out to be long and stable, ending only with Margaret's death in 1893.

When Victoria came to the throne in 1837 Armstrong was still practising as a lawyer in Newcastle. But he was spending all his spare time pursuing his passion for all things mechanical and scientific and his benevolent mentor, Donkin, gave him the freedom he needed to follow his mechanical bent. Water, still the prime source of power for most of Britain's industries, was Armstrong's first area of interest and he became involved in engineering through experimentation with hydraulic machinery. 'It's amazing,' Fred said, 'when you think that this man who was to become a giant of the engineering world was completely self-taught and had no formal training in the trade.'

Armstrong was a keen angler, a hobby at which he was so adept that he was given the nickname Kingfisher. One day when he was fishing at Dentdale in the Pennines, he saw a waterwheel in action, supplying power to a marble quarry. While he was watching the idle turn of the wheel it struck him that a lot of the available power was being wasted. He calculated that only about one-twentieth of the energy in the steeply falling stream was being converted into power by the wheel and realized that the latent energy could be used more effectively if the flow was regular and concentrated in just one column. From that time on, hydraulics was his passion and he became preoccupied with the idea of obtaining the maximum power available from a descending flow, or column, of water. For the next three years, while still practising law, he spent all his spare time working on a water-powered engine. 'All the time,' Armstrong said later, 'although I had no idea of abandoning the law and regularly attended to my professional duties, I was an amateur scientist, constantly experimenting and studying in my leisure time.'

In 1838 Armstrong published a paper in the *Mechanics Magazine* entitled 'The application of water as a motive power for driving machinery'. The following year, along with Henry Watson, who was the contractor for Robert Stephenson's High Level Bridge at Newcastle, Armstrong designed and made a rotary hydraulic engine at Watson's High Bridge ironworks. The engine produced 5 horsepower from the 200-foot head of the town's water supply. The new scheme never really worked and, although the engine was acknowledged as 'a new and ingenious means of applying a neglected, cheap and almost boundless source of power', it wasn't a success. The main problem was that the water pressure was too weak and the materials available to Armstrong at the time were inadequate. The leather seals, in particular, leaked and their condition deteriorated rapidly. Little interest was shown in the engine and no one took up the invention because such a low-power engine would have only limited use in manufacturing. Undeterred by this setback, Armstrong continued his research into hydraulic power until, in 1840, he was sidetracked when he learned about a colliery engineer from Cramlington, Northumberland, who had received an electrical discharge from an emission of high-pressure steam. Armstrong was intrigued and he went to find out more. And it was from these investigations that the principle of hydroelectric energy was derived.

He wrote papers on the subject, which became known as the 'Armstrong Effect', and corresponded with Michael Faraday, who had invented the electric motor in 1821 and the dynamo ten years later. Faraday was the leading figure in the study of electricity and Armstrong gave him an account of his findings, recording experiments that he carried out with locomotive boilers. By constructing a special apparatus he was able to determine that steam was electrified as it entered the atmosphere but was not in an electrified state when it was inside the boiler. He also showed that similar effects occurred when compressed air was used instead of steam. In 1842 he made a wrought-iron boiler that was insulated by means of glass legs. He called this his 'evaporating apparatus', later renaming it his hydroelectric machine. With this he was able to produce foot-long sparks. The following year he made some bigger machines and demonstrated them in a series of lectures in Newcastle and London. Michael Faraday was so impressed with his work on this method of generating electricity that he proposed Armstrong as a Fellow of the Royal Society – no mean achievement for an amateur scientist who was still practising as a solicitor. His demonstrations were spectacular and crowds flocked to his lectures, where he would produce electric sparks to order and fire a small cannon with a spark from his finger. At one lecture public interest was so great that he was unable to enter the hall because of the crowds and he had to climb in through a window.

From this period on, water and the generation of electricity were linked in Armstrong's mind and much of his time was now spent in scientific and mechanical experimentation. In the early 1840s he turned his attention back to hydraulics. His chief interest was in the use of water as a means of distributing the power that could be produced when a head, or elevated pool, of water was made available to provide pressure. He'd already proved the viability of his ideas with his rotary hydraulic engine in 1840, but he'd not been able to establish its commercial potential. In 1845 he got his chance when the Whittle Dene Water Company was set up to improve Newcastle's inefficient and much-criticized water supply with a more powerful system fed from clean, fresh water reservoirs at Whittle Dene ten miles west of the city.

Armstrong was involved in this scheme as company secretary on an annual salary of £150, but he was less concerned with the general issues of the city's water supply than with using the higher pressure now obtainable to power machinery. The Whittle Dene reservoirs were 200 feet above sea level and Armstrong knew that this head of water would have enough power to drive hydraulic machines in the town. So he proposed to Newcastle Corporation that the excess water pressure in the lower part of town could be used to power a quayside crane specially adapted by him. Newcastle was one of the busiest ports in the country and Armstrong claimed that his hydraulic crane could unload ships faster and more cheaply than conventional cranes. The corporation agreed to his suggestion and work started on the conversion of the first crane to hydraulic power. After the indifferent reception afforded his first hydraulic machine, he decided to modify the rotary principle into that of a one-stroke piston and he adapted the design so that it could be incorporated into the mechanism of the crane. Armstrong took out a patent for 'apparatus for lifting, lowering and hauling', and in 1846 his crane conversion was successful. This first crane incorporated an important development, the hydraulic jigger. This was a combined ram and pulley device that converted linear motion to rotary motion and increased the effective stroke of the piston. In effect it used the tried and tested principle of the block and tackle to magnify the limited movements associated with hydraulic power. The experiment proved so successful that four more hydraulic cranes were built and installed on the quayside. Within a short time they came into widespread use for handling cargo in Britain's docks.

The commercial success of his hydraulic crane led Armstrong to consider setting up a business to manufacture cranes and other hydraulic equipment. By this time he'd worked for 11 years as a solicitor, but at the age of 36 he decided to give up the legal profession. Donkin, his legal colleague, supported him in his career move and provided financial backing for the new venture. He was also encouraged by James Meadows Rendel, an eminent engineer who designed and built docks, harbours and bridges. Rendel promised to put work Armstrong's way if a suitable business could be established.

W. G. Armstrong & Company was set up at the beginning of 1847 and an office was opened at Hood Street, Newcastle. It didn't take long for the success of his hydraulic cranes to become known around the country and orders began to come in. The first ones were built at Henry Watson's High Bridge works, but the firm then purchased for

£5,500 a small plot of land on the riverside at Elswick, two miles west of Newcastle, to build its own works. The land was steeply sloping but Armstrong chose this site in preference to wider, more level ground closer to the city so that he would have an independent water supply with a good head of pressure to work his machinery.

The first buildings were soon erected: a machine shop, a larger building for the boiler shop and smith's shop, an erecting shop which included the joiner's and pattern shop and a two-storey office building. With working capital of £20,000, production commenced on the site in the autumn of 1847. In the early years a wide variety of machines were manufactured. These included lathes, pumps, winding engines and steam engines but the main concern of the business was the hydraulic machinery that had so fascinated Armstrong. The first order was from the Albert Dock, Liverpool, for two hydraulic warehouse lifts at £500 each. This was soon followed by a more substantial order for four 12-ton hydraulic cranes for the Edinburgh & Northern Railway, to be used to lift carriages on and off a steam ferry across the Firth of Forth. The order book filled up rapidly and it wasn't long before an average of two cranes a week were being made. The expanding railway system and the numerous railway companies that were springing up proved to be a valuable source of business. Armstrong even adapted his system for the operation of dock gates and J. M. Rendel was as good as his word, bringing the company a contract for gates at the Great Grimsby Docks. One of the problems Armstrong faced in the early days was the fact that hydraulic machinery couldn't be operated in areas where there were no water mains or where pressure was low. In 1849, therefore, he built a 200-foot-high tower at Grimsby to overcome the problem. Water was pumped up to a tank at the top of the tower to provide a working head for the dock machinery.

Success brought diversification and soon all manner of machinery and equipment was being manufactured at the Elswick Works: a hydraulic engine for operating the presses at the *Newcastle Chronicle*; mining machinery for lead mines at Allenheads in Northumberland, and pit winding engines. The firm also began to take on a wide range of general engineering and bridge work. The Inverness Bridge, built by the company, opened in 1855 and was followed by a much bigger contract for the East India Company. Smaller products included hydraulic pumping engines for coal mines, steam engines and pumps, railway turntables and wheels for railway carriages. Work was never turned away and expansion was rapid. The extension to general engineering saw the workforce grow to hundreds within a few years. In 1849, the first of many enquiries for hydraulic swing bridges was received from Birkenhead Docks and by 1850 news of Armstrong's invention had spread round the world and the first export enquiry came in for cranes for the docks at Rio de Janeiro. By this time over 300 men were employed at the works; by 1863 this had risen to 3,800.

It was the time of the great Victorian boom. Britain was clearly reaping the rewards of industrialization as she became the most powerful economy in the world, and Armstrong's company was in the vanguard of industrial expansion. His own personal capacity for hard work was prodigious; his commitment and his stamina seemed to be inexhaustible, and nothing would ever deflect him from the job in hand. For the first 15 years of his business he never took a holiday and he would often spend the night at the factory when some urgent matter required his attention.

Armstrong also made sure that his workforce was well trained, but the biggest reason for the company's rapid growth was that Armstrong was a great innovator. One of his earliest inventions was the hydraulic accumulator, which greatly increased the efficiency of his cranes. Towers like the one he had built at Grimsby were costly and not always practical, and when supplying the Manchester, Sheffield & Lincolnshire Railway with cranes for use at New Holland on the Humber Estuary, he was unable to build one because the soil was loose and sandy. Armstrong therefore had to find an alternative means of generating the water pressure and came up with the idea for the hydraulic accumulator. The design consisted of a large cast-iron cylinder fitted with a plunger supporting a very heavy weight. The plunger was raised slowly, drawing in water as it went higher up the cylinder, until the downward push of the weight forced the water below it into pipes at great pressure. The first accumulator was capable of powering five cranes with water at a pressure of 600 pounds per square inch. Greatly increased pressures became possible, soon reaching over 1,000 pounds per square inch. In Armstrong's own words, 'The introduction of the accumulator in the year 1851 removed all obstacles to the expansion of water pressure machinery.'

The accumulator may not have been Armstrong's most spectacular invention but it was one of the most significant. It was the key to the general adoption of hydraulic systems, finding many applications in the following years and paving the way for the hydraulic supply companies of the late nineteenth century, which offered an alternative energy source in a number of major cities including London. With its invention Armstrong's business was set for a secure future and his personal fame began to spread. In many ways he was in the right place at the right time: expanding overseas trade proved very beneficial to his business and his hydraulic mechanical handling was in great demand to speed up the movement of goods from ship to railway wagons and canal barges. New overseas markets were emerging that created demand not only for the goods moved by Armstrong's machinery but also for the machinery itself.

In 1850 Armstrong received the Telford Medal, the highest prize awarded by the Institution of Civil Engineers for a paper or series of papers in the field of engineering. The following year one of his engines was chosen to provide power for the moving exhibits at the Great Exhibition. In 1854 W. G. Armstrong & Company issued their first dividend. By now the company was well established with a workforce of around 500 and full order books. The balance sheets were showing healthy profits, but these became eroded by research and development costs incurred from the failure of a project for a revolutionary new locomotive design. He produced a prototype, the *Flying Dutchman*. It was of the condensing type, where exhaust steam was fed into a condenser to obtain extra power by creating a vacuum, but, although it was technically sophisticated and quite fast, it was a design that had already been discarded by other manufacturers and it didn't generate any interest. Eventually this prototype, which had cost £2,000 to build, was broken up.

In spite of the occasional setback like the *Flying Dutchman*, Armstrong continued to push the company forward. In hydraulics in particular the company continued to go from strength to strength. In 1850 it produced 45 hydraulic cranes and two years later 75. It averaged 100 cranes per year for the rest of the century, and more than 5,000 were produced between 1847 and 1936. As his hydraulic and engineering business continued to expand, Armstrong's reputation as one of the greatest Victorian entrepreneurial engineers grew with it. In 1854 Queen Victoria went to Grimsby to see a demonstration of his hydraulic dock gates and hoists. At the same time he was appointed to a three-man team set up by the Steam Collieries Association of Newcastle to award a prize for the best method of preventing smoke in the combustion of their coal in marine boilers.

By the 1850s Armstrong's business contacts were impressive and included big names like Brunel and Robert Stephenson. He also continued to work closely with his friend the dock and bridge engineer James Meadows Rendel. When Rendel died suddenly in 1856 Armstrong supported three of the engineer's sons and took them into his firm. George Wightwick Rendel became a partner in 1858 and was for many years a designer in the armaments and shipbuilding side of the business before moving on in the 1880s to direct operations at an Italian subsidiary, the Armstrong-Pozzuoli Company near Naples. Stuart Rendel was, like Armstrong, a lawyer by training and ran the London office for many years before going into politics. Hamilton Rendel, the youngest son, spent the whole of his career working as an engineering designer at Armstrong's. In the same way, when Armstrong's associate Isambard Kingdom Brunel died, Armstrong befriended the family and took Brunel's son Henry into his works at Elswick as an apprentice. Henry Brunel remained with Armstrong's for many years. Armstrong always had a great affection for the children of family and friends and the fact that he had no children himself may well have represented a personal tragedy for him, however well he kept this hidden. The loyalty shown to Brunel's son and to the Rendel boys by the childless Armstrong may have been his way of compensating for this, echoing as it did the support he had received in his early days from the childless Armorer Donkin.

Armstrong was in many ways the archetypal Victorian paternalistic employer. His interest in the education, training and advancement of his workers stemmed from the earliest days of the business. In 1847, when he opened the Elswick Works, he instituted a selective, high-class apprenticeship scheme, taking on six young men. He believed that on-the-job training was sufficient and denounced what he called the vague cry for technical education. In 1866 a school for workers' children opened, subsidized by the firm and by a levy on the men's wages. Adult learning was catered for by Armstrong's provision of a library and the Elswick Works Literary and Mechanics' Institute. This was a Victorian phenomenon that tapped into the desire for self-improvement. Mechanics' Institutes were educational establishments set up and funded by industrialists to provide education, particularly in technical subjects, for working men. The aim wasn't merely philanthropic as the employers believed that they would benefit from having more knowledgeable and skilled employees. The institutes were used as libraries and provided lecture courses, laboratories and, in some cases, museums and were the forerunners of the public library and museum services. As well as Armstrong, Robert Stephenson, Daniel Gooch, James Nasmyth and Joseph Whitworth all set up Mechanics' Institutes. Membership of the Elswick Institute reached a peak of 33,000 before the end of the century and about 700 students attended classes each week. The library contained over 19,000 volumes and throughout the year there were literary lectures, music recitals and many other educational and cultural activities.

By the mid-1850s Armstrong's thriving export business had ensured that his products were well known throughout the industrialized world. But, successful as they were, they were about to be subordinated to what became the dominant feature of his business, the production of armaments. To protect her new colonies and trade routes Britain needed a well-equipped army and it was in the field of military technology that Armstrong achieved his greatest claim to fame.

Armstrong's first involvement with armaments came during the Crimean War between 1854 and 1856, when he was asked to produce underwater mines to blow up Russian ships that had been sunk in Sebastopol harbour. Of more lasting significance, though, was the fact that the Crimean War led Armstrong to produce his revolutionary new system of artillery. In 1854 Armstrong read about difficulties the British Army was having in manoeuvring its heavy field guns. The conservatism of the military establishment, along with financial restrictions, meant that the army had to go into the war with the same weapons it had used at Waterloo forty years earlier. Cannon was muzzle-loading and fired round projectiles in the traditional way. For 300 years the basic design of field artillery had hardly changed. Smooth-bore muzzle loaders constructed from bronze, brass or cast iron were heavy, cumbersome and slow, and so inaccurate that they could be used only at close range. They also had a lethal tendency to burst.

Armstrong felt it was time that these problems were addressed and he decided to design a lighter, more mobile field gun, with greater range and accuracy. He submitted a new design to the War Office and was given the go-ahead to manufacture a prototype. He immediately built a breech-loading gun with a strong, rifled barrel made from welded cylinders of wrought iron wrapped around a steel inner lining. The design was revolutionary, combining lightness with great tensile strength. Instead of the round cannonball that had been in use up to this time, the projectile was to be a cylindrical hollow shell containing an explosive charge designed to explode on impact. The fragmentation effect would extend the killing zone. Armstrong spent a lot of time researching the best size and shape for the projectile. His first shells weighed three pounds and had a conical base, a large cylindrical central section and a blunt, round nose. To achieve accuracy, he worked out from experiments that it would have to rotate as it flew through the air. It was a major advance on the traditional cannon. The Armstrong gun was designed to be loaded through the breech and, as the shell passed along the barrel, its relatively soft, lead outer skin bit into the rifled grooves on the inside of the barrel, causing it to spin. This extended the shell's range and accuracy. The breech-loading arrangement meant that the part of the gun that was most subject to wear, the vent, could readily be replaced because it wasn't an integral part of the barrel. It also meant that rapid fire could be achieved more easily than with muzzle loaders, which were difficult to operate because the burnt powder clogged up in the barrel. The first Elswick gun fired a three-pound shell, but this was considered too small so the calibre was enlarged to accommodate a five-pounder. In July 1855 Armstrong had a five-pounder ready for inspection by a government committee. The gun proved successful in trials, but the committee thought a higher-calibre gun was needed, so Armstrong built an 18-pounder to the same design.

The performance of Armstrong's revolutionary new artillery system appeared to make all previous guns obsolete and the army's initial demand for it was immense. However, just when it looked as if the new gun was about to become a success, a great deal of opposition arose, both inside the army and from rival arms manufacturers, particularly the Manchester-based engineer Joseph Whitworth. Whitworth had achieved distinction through his machine-tool business, through his development of extremely accurate measuring instruments and through the standardized system of screw threads he had invented, but by the 1850s he had turned his attention to developing improved ordnance and produced the Whitworth rifle, which in many ways was comparable to the Armstrong gun. In August 1858, the government set up a select committee on rifled cannon to evaluate the various designs. Seven guns were offered for examination but only those of Armstrong and Whitworth were judged to offer any serious advance on the types of guns already available. Comparative trials of the two designs were carried out and, after a three-month evaluation, the committee came out in favour of Armstrong, whose guns were more accurate and had a longer range than Whitworth's. In November 1858 the committee recommended the immediate adoption of Armstrong guns for service in the field.

Armstrong was a great patriot and he surrendered the patent for the gun to the British government rather than profit from its design. He also gave an assurance that his guns would be sold only to the home market. In recognition of his services to the nation he was awarded a knighthood and appointed chief engineer of rifled ordnance to the War Office and superintendent of the Royal Gun Factory at Woolwich. It must have been a proud and happy homecoming for Armstrong when he returned to Newcastle. A grand reception awaited him at Elswick, where his workers and their families, standing under flags and bunting, greeted him with great acclaim and congratulatory speeches. The knighthood was one of many honours he received during his life, including the Albert Medal of the Society of Arts for his inventions in hydraulic machinery, and the Bessemer gold medal of the Iron and Steel Institute for his services to the steel industry. He was created a baron in 1887, was president of the Institution of Mechanical Engineers in 1861, 1862 and 1869 and president of the Institution of Civil Engineers in 1881.

With his government contracts Armstrong was now firmly established as a leading arms manufacturer. The government knew that Elswick was the only place with the skills and resources to manufacture the Armstrong guns, but this placed Armstrong himself in the embarrassing position of being open to allegations of profiting personally from his government posts. So, in order to avoid a conflict of interests if his own company were to manufacture armaments, Armstrong created a separate company, Elswick Ordnance Company, in which he had no financial involvement. It was run under the direction of Captain Andrew Noble, a young gunnery expert whom Armstrong had met in the course of the gun trials. It proved to be one of the best appointments that Armstrong made and Noble went on to be his right-hand man in the business for the rest of his life. The new company agreed to manufacture armaments for the British government and no other. In his new position, Armstrong worked to bring the old Woolwich Arsenal up to date so that it could build guns designed at Elswick, and did this willingly in the full knowledge that the outcome would be a rival establishment to the Elswick Ordnance Company.

Between 1859 and 1863 Elswick was the monopoly supplier of heavy arms to the British government. The company manufactured 3,500 field guns for the army as well as larger guns for the Admiralty. Some of the navy's guns were still of the old muzzle-loading style, including the 110-pound cannons supplied for HMS *Warrior*, Britain's first ironclad battleship. She was the largest and fastest warship in the world and with Armstrong's firepower she was capable of destroying any other vessel afloat. For Armstrong the workload at this time was immense. He was combining intensive scientific research, which was his first love, with managing the Elswick Works and two exacting posts in London advising the government on the design and manufacture of artillery, which obliged him to open a London office in the heart of what was then the engineering district of Westminster. Throughout these years he was also chairman of the Whittle Dene Water Company.

Joseph Whitworth continued to provide formidable opposition and his dispute with Armstrong was long and acrimonious, centring on the charge that Armstrong's government contract had come about as a result of bias and undue influence. Although he had proved that his gun was the best available to the government, his rivals, led by Whitworth, continued to promote their own designs. Some of their methods were not very scrupulous and included a press campaign aimed at discrediting Armstrong. Stories were circulated that his new gun was too difficult to use, that it was too expensive, that it was dangerous and frequently needed repair. All this smacked of a concerted campaign against him and he was obliged to spend a great deal of time defending himself from erroneous and ill-informed criticism. There had been a number of accidents but all of these had been caused by incorrect closure of the breech. Many of the claims made against him stemmed purely from military conservatism. He was able to refute all of them in front of various government committees, but he was wearied and depressed by the opposition.

In 1862, following criticism of Armstrong guns in the third China War, the government announced that due to the complexity of the gun and its high costs it was to drop all its gunnery contracts with Elswick. Future orders for guns would be supplied from Woolwich, leaving Elswick without any new business. This marked the start of a period of 16 years when Elswick would not manufacture any guns for the British armed forces. The conservatism of the military establishment had won

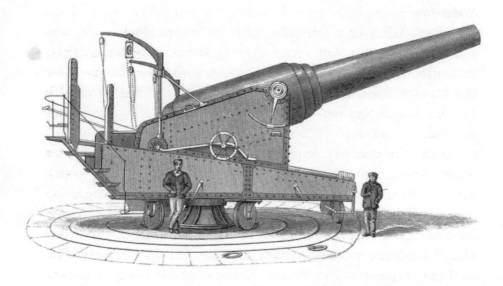

Armstrong's 100-ton gun

the day and both the army and the navy returned to the primitive and obsolete system of artillery based on muzzle-loading weapons.

Armstrong's position was becoming untenable and by February 1863 he felt it necessary to resign from his government appointment. Compensation was eventually agreed with the government for the loss of business. At first the government would not release the company from its agreement not to sell armaments abroad, so the export avenue was closed to it. Eventually the restriction was relaxed and in 1864 the two companies, W. G. Armstrong & Company and Elswick Ordnance Company, merged to form Sir W. G. Armstrong & Company. As Armstrong had resigned from his post at the War Office, there was no longer a conflict of interest. In order to survive, Armstrong was persuaded by senior staff within the company to drop his patriotic inclinations and ignore the obligation to manufacture exclusively for Her Majesty's Government. If the British Army didn't want Elswick guns any longer, they pointed out, there were plenty of foreign armies who did.

At first Armstrong appeared to be indifferent to the potential of his arms business, but he was urged, particularly by Stuart Rendel, to seek business from foreign countries. Somewhat reluctantly, Armstrong agreed to let Rendel have a go. 'If you can obtain any orders for Elswick,' he told him, 'by all means do so and to make it worth your while, we will give you 5 per cent commission on the orders you bring us.' The international arms dealer was born. It wasn't long before the first orders began to roll in. The company's first overseas orders for guns came from America, where the Civil War was in progress. Elswick supplied guns to both sides, starting a trend that became common-place in the arms trade. Other early customers included Turkey, Egypt, Italy, Denmark, Chile and Peru. Armstrong's casual agreement with Stuart Rendel was responsible for the growth of Elswick into one of the world's greatest arms manufacturers. In spite of the blow struck by the government in 1863, Elswick had recovered and was in good shape to take advantage of increasing worldwide demand for military and commercial products. Investments made in the works included more land and new workshops and machinery. Blast furnaces were built and iron ore workings at Ridsdale, 30 miles to the north, were purchased. Of the 4,000 employees, three-quarters were now in the Ordnance Department.

Seeing no reason why his design for army ordnance, which had proved so effective, should not be adapted for naval use, Armstrong began to consider a venture into this new field. Once again he met with resistance. This time it came from the naval establishment. Britain, it was argued, ruled the waves with conventional arms. The cost of replacement would be massive and, it was felt, needless. But the proven success of Armstrong's weaponry soon broke the resistance down and the Admiralty agreed to his proposals. In 1867 he signed an agreement with Charles Mitchell, a shipbuilder at Low Walker. The basis of it was that Mitchell would build ships and Elswick would arm them. George Rendel was put in charge of the operation and designed the partnership's first ships. The first order came from the Admiralty and was for a gunboat. HMS *Staunch* was launched in 1868 and over the next 15 years more ships of this type were built for the Royal Navy and for Brazil, China, Italy and Holland.

Armstrong's knowledge of hydraulics was put to good use for the control of naval guns. Up to 10-inch calibre guns could be worked by hand but for anything bigger, hydraulics was the only method. The first ship to be fitted with hydraulic machinery was the Dutch gunboat *Hydra*. The hydraulic system utilized compressed air rather than solid, heavy weights, which couldn't be accommodated on a ship. Eventually hydraulics became the standard method for supplying power to different places in naval ships, not just for the working of guns but also for ammunition hoists and rammers. By 1891 all the hydraulic systems used in the Royal Navy were manufactured at Elswick.

As the company grew bigger, Armstrong began to take more of a back seat. From 1863 onwards, although he stayed on as head of the company, he became less involved in its day-to-day running. He appointed several very able men to senior positions, who continued his work, but this layer of management also meant his relationship with the shop floor became increasingly remote. By the mid-1860s it was a very different company to the one that Armstrong had set up. A successful engineering company that had developed a sideline in guns was now on the brink of transformation into a great symbol of imperial power and might. While Armstrong presided over this new direction, the growing foreign arms trade was of little personal interest to him and he began to devote his energies to other projects like the building of Cragside, his great country house, begun in 1863.

Jesmond Dene, his house close to Newcastle, was convenient when he was a solicitor and an industrialist, but when he had more spare time he began to long for a house in the country. As a child he had often visited Rothbury and he had happy memories of the area, so in 1863, at the age of 52, he bought some land in a narrow, steep-sided valley where the Debdon Burn flowed towards the River Coquet near the market town. The land was cleared and Armstrong himself supervised the building of a house in a spectacular location on a ledge of rock above the burn. As the house was being built, he and his wife, Margaret, supervised a programme of planting trees and mosses to cover the rocky hillside.

According to his own account, his original intention was to build a small house here for occasional visits in the summer. Cragside was built between 1863 and 1866 as a weekend retreat from the pressures of his business and began as a modest two-storey lodge suitable for small shooting or fishing parties. Here Armstrong could devote himself to his real interests and he soon began to further experiment with hydraulic technology. In 1866 he dammed the Debdon Burn to store water in what became Tumbleton Lake. The 35-foot head of water created by damming the burn was used to power a hydraulic engine he installed in a small pump house in 1868. This drove two pumps that took the water from the pump house to the gardens and to a reservoir which fed a tank in one of the house's towers. The water then flowed by gravity into the house, where it was used for domestic purposes and to power labour-saving machinery.

The architect of the original house is unknown, but in 1869 Armstrong called in Norman Shaw, a celebrated architect of the day, to turn Cragside into a proper country mansion. At first he only wanted Shaw to add to the house's existing north end – not to improve or replace it – but gradually Shaw gave himself a bit more scope to bring in his own ideas. By the gradual additions that he made over the next 15 years the house came to assume the wild, picturesque outline that it has today. Even so, in all the time he worked at Cragside, Shaw was never given the free hand he really wanted. Armstrong remained in charge, supervising the whole restyling and extension of the house. Perhaps the great industrialist's independence and the fact that Shaw's brief was to extend an existing house prevented the creation of the unified architectural masterpiece that Shaw had in mind. Armstrong had a very hands-on approach and the work was done not by a building contractor but by local masons working under his direct supervision.

Over the years Armstrong continued to add to the Cragside estate and, with his team of gardeners, he landscaped and planted the whole of his land, which eventually spread over 1,729 acres (7 km²) with seven million trees. His wife Margaret was a keen botanist and she played a big part in the planting of the grounds. Not much is known about her, but she seems to have fulfilled the Victorian ideal of a kind, supportive but retiring helpmate. As the establishment of the garden progressed, work on Cragside's hydraulic system continued apace and Armstrong soon developed a further four lakes to store the water that provided the power to generate electricity and drive all the hydraulic machinery in the house. Armstrong did all he could with this machinery to lessen the burden on his domestic staff, as Fred explained:

> He had a wonderful spit over the great roasting fire in the kitchens driven by a water turbine quite a way off down in the cellar, and a passenger lift for the servants to take coal up to the open fires in the bedrooms. The lift used the same hydraulic technology that Armstrong had developed so successfully to power the cranes on the Newcastle docks, but here it was on a much smaller scale. It was controlled by a 'jigger', which was a movable ram or piston in a fixed cylinder fitted with a system of pulleys.

While Armstrong was building the house, the Elswick Works continued to prosper, and by 1870 it stretched for three-quarters of a mile along the riverside. Two key reasons for the success of the business were Armstrong's gift for bringing good scientific ideas, whether his own or other people's, to the market and the quality of the engineers and designers he employed. Prominent among these was Andrew Noble, the gunnery expert he'd taken on to run the Elswick Ordnance Works. Like Armstrong, Noble was as much a scientist as a businessman, and he became famous for his work on explosives. A key member of the management team at Elswick, he spent a huge amount of time travelling the world on company business. In 1870 the company became the British licensee for the world's first machine-gun, the American-designed Gatling gun. It provided good business and by the mid-1880s Elswick had a whole department devoted to its manufacture.

Armstrong was finding the demands of running a rapidly expanding industrial empire increasingly irksome. At heart he was always a scientist and inventor and that's what he wanted to get back to, particularly as Elswick became involved in a long-running industrial dispute. One of the turning points for him came in 1871 when over 7,000 engineering workers on the Tyne came out on strike in favour of a nine-hour working day. Armstrong, who was head of the Newcastle engineering employers' federation, took a strong stand against the strikers. His view was that the claim was simply a way of obtaining overtime payments. The dispute went on for more than four months and Armstrong came to be viewed as a cold, remote figure who had lost touch with his workers. Public opinion was on the side of the strikers and the employers had to concede to their demands. Armstrong was humiliated. The early Victorian paternalism in industrial relations that he believed in was now seen as out of date, as were the days when an individual like him could tackle anything. It was the beginning of an age of specialization in engineering; of the entrepreneurial engineer and the big engineering companies. From this point on, it becomes the story of his company rather than of Armstrong the individual.

Armstrong withdrew increasingly to country life and his

experiments with hydraulics and electricity, while retaining an honorary role within the great industrial firm he had founded. At Cragside he continued to develop the hydraulic system, making it the most extensive that had ever been put into operation on a country estate. Not only did it pump water, raise lifts and turn spits in the house, it also made silage and powered a sawmill, farm machinery and a dairy on the estate. When electric lighting became a practical possibility in the 1870s Armstrong even installed a Vortex turbine at Debdon, making it the world's first hydroelectric power station. The electricity generated there was used to light an arc lamp in Cragside's gallery, but it wasn't very satisfactory as early arc lamps were smoky, unsafe and far too bright for domestic use. Nevertheless Armstrong was the first person known to have experimented with its usage and such was his alertness to innovation in this field, he was the first to have a permanent domestic installation of the incandescent filament bulbs that had been invented almost simultaneously by Thomas Edison and by Armstrong's friend Joseph Swan. These were much more convenient to use and gave a softer light. He also continued to experiment with electrostatics and his laboratory at Cragside contained many pieces of equipment to demonstrate electrical phenomena.

These were the years when Armstrong had time to reflect on a broader picture of Britain's industrial and economic development. He was particularly concerned by the rate at which the country was using coal and challenged its use for domestic purposes. At the time, it amounted to one ton of coal a year per head of the entire population, which meant that more than 29 million tons of coal was used annually in England for this purpose alone. Armstrong believed that this was wasteful and that it could be vastly reduced by more efficient usage of stoves and grates without any loss of heat. He also believed that by using better machinery, the nation's coal mines could stay more competitive in world markets, thus guaranteeing the country prosperity. He made many predictions which in later years came true, including his view that every home would be powered by electricity and have clean running water at its disposal.

William Armstrong had been in the vanguard in establishing Britain's industrial supremacy in the nineteenth century, but he also took a pioneering interest in environmental issues and was an early advocate of the use of renewable energy. Stating that coal 'was used wastefully and extravagantly in all its applications', he predicted in 1863 that England would cease to produce coal within two centuries. In an address to the Mechanical Science section of the British Association when he was its president, he stated that 'The steam engine even in its best form remains to this day a most wasteful apparatus for converting the energy of heat into motive power.' As well as advocating the use of water power, wind power and tidal power, he also supported solar power, suggesting that the direct heating action of the sun's rays might be used in complete substitution for a steam engine. He calculated that the solar heat on one acre of the tropics would 'exert the amazing power of 4000 horses acting for nearly nine hours every day.' His ideas on the production, use and conservation of energy were a long way ahead of their time and are particularly appropriate now, in a world where demand for energy continues to rise amid concerns about the use we make of the Earth's natural resources.

For a man with such apparent green credentials, Armstrong appears to be something of a contradictory figure. By the 1870s Elswick covered some 70 acres of land and the fuel that powered the works was coal, bringing with it a huge amount of environmental pollution. But the works employed approximately 12,000 men and Armstrong took a great deal of pride in the fact that he was creating work for people, thus allowing them to live in relative comfort. The works continued to expand and, in 1876, because the eighteenth-century bridge at Newcastle restricted access to the Elswick Works for ships, Armstrong's company funded a new swing bridge, so that warships could sail up the Tyne to have their guns fitted there. The low-level swing bridge beside Stephenson's high-level bridge is still swung by its original oscillating cylinder hydraulic engine, designed to enable the centre section to swing open to allow the passage of large vessels.

With the building of the swing bridge, Elswick was opened up to

Designed and funded by Armstrong's company, the new swing
bridge over the Tyne at Newcastle enabled larger ships to move
upstream to the Elswick Works

big ships and Armstrong was able to add shipbuilding to his ever-expanding empire. It represented a major increase in the industrial potential of the business. Armstrong felt there was a need for fast ships, manoeuvrable ships with the emphasis on firepower and mobility rather than protection in the form of heavy armour plate. In 1881 and 1882 the company built a series of small cruisers for the Chinese and Chilean governments.

Armstrong was elected president of the Institution of Civil Engineers in 1881, but he was spending less and less time at the Elswick Works and more at Cragside, which now became his main home. While he was in his seventies he renewed his experiments with electricity there. The results of these experiments were published in a book, *Electric Movement in Air and Water*. In 1881 his continued interest in all matters electrical led him to go into partnership with his friend Joseph Swan in his Electric Light Company. Their Benwell factory is said to have been the first to manufacture a complete fully working electric lamp. When he demonstrated his 'Novelties in Electricity' to the Literary and Philosophical Society in Newcastle almost half a century after he had first drawn in the crowds to see them, he said, 'The hydroelectric machine was my first love, but soon after its introduction I became engaged in the hydraulic experiments which led to the establishment of Elswick.'

In 1883 Armstrong gave the Jesmond Dene Valley, together with the banqueting hall he had built, to the city of Newcastle. He retained his house next to the Dene, but from this time on all his entertaining would be at Cragside. In August 1884 the Prince and Princess of Wales and their children stayed at Cragside while they were on a tour of the North East. Armstrong continued as chairman of his company, although his role was now much more that of a figurehead than a hands-on manager of the vast business empire he had created. In this role he entertained princes and envoys who flocked to Newcastle to order arms, presiding over the birth of a trade that was to dominate the twentieth-century world economy. 'As well as using hydraulic machinery to help with the domestic chores, he also used it to impress prospective customers and visiting dignitaries,' as Fred explained:

The whole place were really a shop window for the inventions that he did. The dining room is where he entertained such guests as the King of Siam and the Shah of Persia, who came here for arms dealing, to buy guns off him, and without a doubt it must be one of the finest Victorian domestic interiors in Britain. If you look at the ceiling alone you can see there's a few good oak trees gone into it, and the fireplace is a wonderful creation. It's got to be the biggest inglenook fireplace in England. The outer arch is a great Gothic arch and it's survived very well, but I think Sir William did a bit of over-stoking because you can see there's a few nasty cracks in his mantelpiece proper.

You can imagine him sat there on a cold and frosty night, thinking of what he was going to do next with his hydraulics. But what is most interesting to me is that an industrialist like Armstrong, who was responsible for many major technological advances, chose to build his house in a traditional Old English style and then fill it with modern inventions.

By this time Armstrong's company had merged with Mitchell's to form Sir William Armstrong, Mitchell and Co. Ltd. Two million pounds were subscribed and a massive expansion took place under Andrew Noble, who had himself been knighted. The object was to boost the production of armaments and ironclads and add steel-making to the firm's capabilities. In 1884 a shipyard opened at Elswick to specialize in warship production, and Armstrong soon saw a niche in the market. Recognizing that the huge ironclads with their lack of manoeuvrability were not well suited to protecting merchant shipping during wartime, he developed the fast cruiser. The original arrangement with Mitchell's would still stand and the Low Walker yard would build merchant ships. The world's first ocean-going oil tanker would be launched there in 1885. The first vessels built at the Elswick yard were the torpedo cruisers *Panther* and *Leopard* for the Austro-Hungarian Navy.

The addition of shipbuilding represented a huge increase in the works' industrial potential and made Armstrong's into a leading international player in the armaments business, able to design, build, equip and arm from blast furnace to battleship. The first battleship built at Elswick was HMS *Victoria*, launched in 1887. The ship was originally to be named *Renown*, but the name was changed in honour of the Queen's Golden Jubilee and Armstrong himself drove the first and last rivets. The ship was a floating fortress whose awesome firepower was capable of blowing any ship in the world out of the water before its own armaments could come within range. But she wasn't invulnerable and her life was short. In 1893, while on manoeuvres, she was involved in a collision with HMS *Camperdown* and was holed below the water-line, going down with the loss of 358 men. For the last 15 years of the century Armstrong's company led the world in the manufacture of iron warships and armaments, rivalled only by the German firm of Krupps.

Unlike his father, Armstrong had little interest in politics until, in 1886, when in his mid-seventies, he was persuaded to stand as a Unionist Liberal candidate for one of the two Newcastle seats. He was, however, unsuccessful, coming third in the election. That same year he was presented with the Freedom of the City of Newcastle and in Queen Victoria's Jubilee Honours List of 1887 he was raised to the peerage with the title of Lord Armstrong, First Baron of Cragside. His last great project was the purchase and restoration of the huge Bamburgh Castle on the Northumberland coast. His aim was to restore it as a convalescent home for 'persons of superior education in reduced circumstances'. Work began on it in 1894.

In the same year Elswick built and installed the steam-driven pumping engines, hydraulic accumulators and hydraulic pumping engines to operate the counter-weighted bascules that open London's Tower Bridge. The bascules, each of which weighs 1,200 tons and carries balancing ballast of 350 tons of lead and cast iron, are lifted by huge toothed quadrants. Four coal-fired double-furnace Lancashire boilers, operating a pair at a time, supplied the steam to one of two pumping engines. They in turn pumped water into the hydraulic system at 750 pounds per square inch. The reserves of power this generated were held in six accumulators so that the system was always ready to raise the bascules on demand. Armstrong's part of the Tower

Bridge contract was worth £85,232. This included the hydraulics that worked the two passenger lifts up to the high-level walkways, which were designed to give pedestrians a way across the river at all times.

By the 1890s many people were contributing to the success of the Armstrong business, which reflected the way in which the role of the engineer was changing. Tower Bridge is one of the greatest symbols of late-Victorian engineering achievement. But who built it? By the time that it was built it was no longer possible for one man of great vision and energy to dominate a whole project. The consulting engineer for the project was John Wolfe Barry, assisted in the day-to-day running of the project by none other than Henry Brunel, who was still working for Armstrong. But the construction of Tower Bridge involved a whole committee, including Armstrong's company which supplied the hydraulic machinery that lifted the bridge. The company was involved in many of the biggest engineering projects of the day including the huge Manchester Ship Canal, built to bring ocean-going steamships to the heart of the city, 35 miles inland, and turn it into a port. When work started on building the canal, W. G. Armstrong & Co. were contracted to provide the hydraulics for all the locks and cranes along it, and for the most impressive engineering work along its length, the Barton Swing Aqueduct. It's a swing bridge that carries the Bridgewater Canal over the Manchester Ship Canal and Fred would recall how his father, who described it as the eighth wonder of the world, used to take him on a bike ride to see it.

In 1897 it must have given the 87-year-old Armstrong great satisfaction when his company took over that of his old rival, Joseph Whitworth, to become Sir W. G. Armstrong, Whitworth & Co. Ltd. Given the acrimonious history of the two companies it was a development that would have been unthinkable during the lifetime of Whitworth, but he had died ten years earlier. In the same year more shipbuilding facilities were added a mile and a half west of Elswick when the company bought the Scotswood Shipbuilding Company. Business was now booming and the 1890s marked the high-water mark of the Armstrong firm's formidable international reputation. Elswick was the only place in the world that could build a battleship and arm it completely. As well as providing ships for the Royal Navy, Elswick was building for the navies of 15 other countries. Between 1885 and 1903 a total of 92 warships were launched at the yard and the company armed many more ships that had been built elsewhere. The Japanese Navy was one of Armstrong's biggest customers and by the time of the Russo-Japanese war at the beginning of the twentieth century, Elswick-built ships made up almost half of the Japanese fleet. It was even claimed that every Japanese gun used in the battle of Tsushima in 1905 was provided by Elswick. Most of the Russian fleet had been built further down the Tyne at Hawthorn Leslie's and Swan Hunter's yards. 'So,' Fred commented, 'the rivalry in Newcastle's pubs between the workers from the yards as the ships they'd built blew each other out of the water must have been interesting.'

By the 1890s the manufacture of arms and warships had become one of Britain's biggest industries and Armstrong had turned a brilliantly successful engineering firm into a symbol of imperial might, with his Elswick and Scotswood factories employing 30,000 men. By the end of the nineteenth century, gas, electricity and hydraulic power were beginning to do many of the things that steam engines had done. Armstrong was at the forefront of many of these developments because, as well as his entrepreneurial ability and capacity for hard work, he had those other great qualities admired by the Victorians – innovation and inventiveness. To the people of Elswick the works he had created was more than just a firm; it had become an institution that gave its workers a sense of identity and belonging. For many of them, to be an Armstrong man was a source of pride. Within the course of 60 years what had been a green-field site when Armstrong opened his factory had become a smoky sprawl of blast furnaces, foundries, machine shops and dockyard. For mass production on this scale, the great advances made by men like Nasmyth in the development of machines and tools were vital. One of the most important of these was the hydraulic riveter and the Elswick Works would have echoed to the sound of it.

Many of the wealthy industrialists who made their fortunes from the Industrial Revolution became benefactors to the cities that had helped them to create their wealth. Armstrong was no exception and he began to devote his managerial and legal skills to the wise public use of the vast fortune he had built up. Much of his immense wealth was devoted to gifts to Newcastle. He had donated the long wooded gorge of Jesmond Dene to the people of the city in 1883, as well as Armstrong Bridge and Armstrong Park nearby. He made many gifts to the Royal Victoria Infirmary, which was rebuilt following a donation in his memory, and gave large sums to the city's museum and university, which he had originally founded in 1871 as the College of Physical Science. It was renamed Armstrong College in 1904. Above all, he helped to turn Newcastle into one of the most prosperous cities in Britain.

In the last years of his life the restoration of Bamburgh became Armstrong's main concern, but he would not live to see its completion. His health had started to fail when he was in his eighty-seventh year and a sudden chill in the autumn of 1900 led to his final decline. Just before Christmas he was forced to take to his bed and he died at Cragside on 27 December 1900, aged 90. Unlike the grand funerals of some of the great engineers and industrialists, Armstrong's was a simple, unpretentious affair. The hearse was drawn by two farm horses and led by estate servants. It was followed by a procession of workers from the estate and mourners brought from Newcastle by special train. He was buried in Rothbury churchyard alongside his wife, Margaret, who had died in 1893. Her death had been a great loss. The couple had always been very close and the support and advice Armstrong received from her throughout his career had been invaluable, as had been the sheer hard work she put into the creation of their homes at Jesmond Dene and Cragside. As the couple had no children, Armstrong's heir was his great-nephew William Watson-Armstrong. He was succecded as chairman of the company by his one-time protégé, Andrew Noble.

William George Armstrong has been described as a man who 'stood astride the Victorian era like a colossus'. Certainly in terms of his achievements he was, but for such a philanthropist it is perhaps unfortunate that Armstrong's name and that of his company is first and foremost associated with the manufacture of weapons of war. But there is no evidence that Armstrong had any qualms about his decision to go into armament production. He once said: 'If I thought that war would be fomented, or the interests of humanity suffer, by what I have done, I would greatly regret it. I have no such apprehension.' He went on to say: 'It is our province, as engineers, to make the forces of matter obedient to the will of man; those who use the means we supply must be responsible for their legitimate application.' His thinking was full of contradictions, especially his somewhat dubious assertion that it was less barbarous to engage an enemy at long range than to fight him in close combat. Whatever his justification, the company he founded was in at the beginning of the international arms trade, and through its activities and those of his great Manchester-based rival Joseph Whitworth, Britain achieved a position of world dominance.

9

Joseph Whitworth
1803–1887
The Nuts and Bolts of the Economy

It's no use having great engineering ideas if you've not got the right tools to do the job, and that's where Joseph Whitworth comes in. He was the first man to come up with tools that would make very accurate machinery and he invented a machine that standardized screw sizes, so everybody could make nuts and bolts that were all practically the same. From the beginning of the Industrial Revolution, each workshop had its own system and nuts and bolts were all individually made, with many different screw threads. I've actually worked on machinery where each nut was made to fit the bolt, and when you screwed them on they waggled about as they went down, until they actually landed on the face they were meant to go on. But Whitworth realized that if nuts and bolts were standardized and if you could measure things accurately it would make life easier for everyone. His micrometer was capable of measuring to an accuracy of one hundred-thousandth of an inch. He also introduced something that was essential for good-quality, precise engineering work – a standard for the flatness of plane surfaces.

Whitworth was without any shadow of a doubt one of the great Victorian mechanical engineers, and I'd put him up there by the side of men like George Stephenson and Isambard Kingdom Brunel. Like them he was a determined man who by sheer force of character was used to getting his own way. It has been said that he could be a difficult man to deal with, a perfectionist who was intolerant of imperfection in other people's work. He was a harsh taskmaster and he was never afraid to speak his mind. I've read a description of him that said, 'He has a face not unlike that of a baboon; speaks the broadest Lancashire; could not invent an epigram to save his life; but has nevertheless "a talent that might drive a genii to despair" and when one talks to him, one feels to be talking with a real live man.'

Joseph Whitworth is best known for his development of a rationalized system of screw threads that bears his name – British Standard Whitworth (BSW) – and for his introduction of precise standards of accuracy in manufacturing. He was one of the first generation of manufacturers to pioneer machine-tool building as a distinct profession.

Whitworth was born in Stockport, Cheshire, on 21 December 1803. His father, Charles Whitworth, had a variety of jobs. At one time he was a loom maker in the textile industry but he was also a schoolmaster and he later became a Congregationalist minister. Joseph was taught by his father until he was 12 years old. He then went on to William Vint's Academy at Idle, near Leeds, for 18 months. It was run by Dissenters, members of a religious body who separated from the established church because they disagreed on matters of belief, and used new teaching methods of a practical nature. This Dissenter education also questioned accepted ideas, something which perhaps contributed to Whitworth's later achievements.

When he was 14 Whitworth was indentured as an apprentice at his uncle's cotton-spinning mill at Darley Dale in Derbyshire. The plan was that he would become a partner in the business. Right from the start he was fascinated by the machinery and it didn't take him long to master the techniques of the spinning industry, but, even at this young age, he noticed the rough standards of accuracy and was critical of the machinery. It was this that led to his ambition to make much more precise machines. So great was this ambition that in 1821, when he was still only 17 years of age, he went against the wishes of his family and left the mill to join Crighton and Co., a leading manufacturer of mill pumps and textile machinery in Manchester. In those days, the working mechanic had no machinery; the hammer, the chisel, the file and the primitive lathe were the only tools he had at his disposal. Whitworth went on to work in several other engineering firms in Manchester as a mechanic, working at a bench, until he obtained a position as a skilled millwright at Houldsworth & Co., a big cotton mill in Lever Street. Later he said that the happiest days of his life were when he was a journeyman there, but Whitworth was ambitious and he decided to seek employment in London in order to further his career.

He left Manchester on his twenty-first birthday in December 1824, heading for London via canal. He travelled by barge and slept wherever he could. On the way he met a 24-year-old bargeman's daughter from Tarvin, Cheshire. Her name was Frances Ankers and it was love at first sight. Within a week the couple eloped, making their way towards Nottingham. On 25 February 1825 they stopped at Ilkeston in Derbyshire, where a priest married them. As she was not able to read or write Frances marked the register with a cross. At the time neither her father nor her sisters thought the marriage would survive, but the couple stayed together for 30 years.

When they eventually reached London, Whitworth, like James Nasmyth later, found employment at Henry Maudslay's Machine Tool Engineering Works on Westminster Bridge Road. He was one of 120 employees there and he worked in the relatively humble position of bench fitter because, he said, 'he wanted to attain perfection' and Maudslay's tools were then as close to perfection as an aspiring young engineer could hope to get. Many other great engineers, such as Richard Roberts, the inventor of the planing machine, Joseph Clement, the inventor of the water tap, and Nasmyth, chose the same employer. It has been said that 'Maudslay's works became the breeding ground for men whose fame as engineers would equal his own.' It was in this school of inventors that Whitworth gained the practical knowledge and mechanical skill that enabled him to go on to make a major contribution to the world of engineering. While he was there he saw a bench micrometer in use for the first time. This was a tool used for work in which accuracy of measurement was essential. Maudslay claimed that it gave him absolute truth and humorously called it his 'Lord Chancellor'.

Under Maudslay's tuition, Whitworth developed great skill as a mechanic, and among the many skilled workmen employed there he came to be regarded as the best. He developed a method of creating truly flat surfaces and pioneered machine tools for milling, turning, slotting, shaping, gear cutting and drilling, all to a high degree of accuracy. Whitworth learned to build top-quality machinery using the very latest ideas and began to create precision machine tools – machines made for the purpose of producing other machinery. Before he was 30 he succeeded in producing plane surfaces with a degree of precision hitherto unknown and this formed the basis for nearly all his other machines. He also introduced a box-casting scheme for the iron frames of machine tools that simultaneously increased their rigidity and reduced their weight.

Whitworth stayed at Maudslay's for three and a half years, impressing everybody there with his engineering skills, before moving to Holtzapffel and Company in 1828 and Joseph Clement in 1830 to add to his experience. It was the perfect grounding for him. Within the space of five years, Whitworth had worked for all the leading machine-makers in London. Clement especially was far ahead of his commercial rivals and his work on constructing Charles Babbage's 'Difference Engine', or mechanical calculator, was the most intricate and difficult commission that had ever been undertaken. With it, Babbage was the first man to envisage the idea of a computer, but engineering methods and tolerances were insufficiently developed to manufacture the machine successfully. That, together with the fact that it was so far ahead of its time, meant that the project was doomed. Whitworth worked on components for this far-sighted project and it must have given an aspiring engineer profound insights into the levels of precision that it was possible to attain. But Whitworth wanted to go into business on his own account and could see the potential of mass production, especially in the North of England. The time he spent in London had been invaluable. He had made the best possible use of London libraries and learned societies and he was now eager to put his knowledge to the test. The time to make the move came in 1833, when government funding for Babbage's Difference Engine dried up. Whitworth lost his job and at the age of 29 he returned to Manchester.

In the early 1830s the cotton industry was booming. At the heart of it, Manchester was fast growing into the engineering capital of the world. As well as mill machinery and engines, the city was becoming a locomotive-building centre of importance and for a short period it equalled the North East in terms of production. These were 'glorious times for the engineers'. In the spinning and weaving factories there was a growing demand for mechanical work of a high quality to improve the complicated machinery and to make the manufacture of the machines cheaper. Whitworth could see that producing more efficient and precise machines would bring great advantages and he began searching for suitable premises for a small workshop. He had little money and wanted a place with one or two simple machines. He found what he was looking for in Port Street, took over the premises and proudly screwed his name above the door: Joseph Whitworth, Toolmaker from London. At first he couldn't get the business off the ground even though he worked from dawn to dusk. He felt it was because his workshop was so small and insignificant that nobody could find it, so he moved on after only six months. When he found larger premises at 44 Chorlton Street the work started to come in. Initially it was just minor repairs and other small jobs such as making taps and dies. His first major order was for a machine to flute textile machine rollers and he then began to manufacture lathes and other machine tools, which were renowned for their high standard of workmanship. But he hated requests for credit, either for his own purchases or when selling machinery he had made. He never allowed machinery to leave the premises unless it was paid for in full, and this slowed down his early progress.

Whitworth's education had given him a good understanding of business affairs and the company prospered. It had started off as a one-man operation, but once it got off the ground it quickly grew to a substantial size. His first wage bill in May 1833 was a mere £2 10s, but this had increased to almost £50 by April 1834. One way of charting

Whitworth's progress is to look at the various patents he took out at this time. Obtaining a patent involved a complicated application process and a lot of expense, and Whitworth could only have done this if he had great faith in his products and sufficient financial backing to pay for the patent and to sue anyone who tried to infringe it. He took out a surprising number of patents in the early years, which suggests that he already had some ambitious schemes and that he'd found the time to cultivate some wealthy contacts to invest in his company.

His first independent patent was lodged in 1834 – a machine for turning and screw-cutting studs and hexagonal bolts, which did away with the inaccurate and relatively expensive procedure of threading nuts and bolts by hand. This patent set the pattern for a whole series of inventions and improvements to tools and machinery that would revolutionize the manufacturing process. He was aware of the growing demand for machine tools in the 1830s, and of the rapid progress being made in mechanization. The problem was that different manufacturers used nuts, bolts, screws and other components for their machines that were all of different shapes and sizes. Whitworth knew that this problem had to be addressed and he talked all the time of the need to standardize precise measurement, but inevitably there was resistance to his ideas. Many people said that new machinery, improved skills and higher wages would be needed, and it was generally thought that a lot of small engineering shops would go bankrupt if they went down this road. These were valid concerns at the time, but Whitworth was convinced that this was the only way forward.

His work in this field built on that of Maudslay, but introduced far more fundamental thinking into the problem of producing accurate machinery. A good example was his work in making a true surface by scraping and comparing three matching planes. From these apparently simple ideas came the accuracy and method for which Whitworth became famous.

What he was doing was revolutionary. Previously, a manufacturer who wanted a piece of machinery would have had it custom-made. If it was large, it would usually have been made on site, and built into the walls of the building to give it stiffness and solidity. Before 1800 it would have been built mainly of wood, with just a few metal parts. Then in the early part of the nineteenth century, this changed as iron castings became more widely available. Industry soon realized iron's potential and manufacturers began to appreciate that, although building a machine of iron took a lot more time and trouble, the finished product would be much more durable and allow more precise movement than a machine constructed of wood. Machine-tool builders started setting up their own businesses and instead of responding to commissions, they produced standard machines and then went out and sold them. Whitworth was one of the first to do this, and his business soon became one of the biggest.

Between 1834 and 1849 Whitworth took out a total of 15 different patents and it was during this period that most of his important machine tools were brought to perfection. In 1840 he developed a measuring technique called 'end measurements' that used a precision flat plane and measuring screw, both of his own invention. In the same year he published his first paper, 'Plane Metallic Surfaces or True Planes'. At this time true planes were still being produced by grinding the surfaces of plates alternately with emery powder and water and he pointed out that this was as imperfect as it was laborious. Grinding, according to Whitworth, was objectionable because it was unreliable. If one plane was true and the other was not, grinding would give part of the error to both, instead of imparting the true plane to each. Whitworth stressed that 'all excellence in workmanship depended on the use of true plane surfaces', but a true surface, instead of being in common use, was virtually unknown. The valves of steam engines, the tables of printing presses, surface plates and slides of all kinds required a high degree of precision, but there were no tools capable of achieving this.

After repeated efforts involving a lot of labour and ingenuity, Whitworth succeeded in originating the first true planes ever made. The work of producing copies of them sufficiently accurate for workshop purposes then became comparatively easy. One of his most successful machines for this work was his edge planing machine, which could be made to almost any size. He had one made in his own works that was capable of making a cut 40 feet in length. The bed of the machine was 50 feet long and its grooves were considered the longest true planes that had ever been made. The economy of this invention was just as impressive as its mechanical precision. The previous cost of planing surfaces done by hand was twelve shillings (60p) a foot. Now with this machine it could be done for a penny a foot. From his primary inventions a whole range of tools, gauges and machines were produced for drilling, shaping, slotting and many other purposes, and as a result of these improvements the manufacture of machinery increased at a great rate. Because of the exactness and uniformity of manufacture that had been made possible by his inventions, manufacturers could now supply the component parts of a machine in any number, all perfectly interchangeable. Another of his inventions, the Whitworth Quick Return Mechanism, was developed to drive the cutting tool on shaping machines. The device speeded up the return of the tool to the beginning of the cutting stroke and so saved time.

Whitworth's reputation and that of his machines was growing. They were well designed; they were built to a high level of accuracy and they were tough and practical. The machine tools that he was now manufacturing were far in advance of anything else on the market at the time. He had been one of the first men to realize that a machine must be made to a very high standard if it was to produce parts of an equal standard. He built his business on accurate measurement and the standardization of his company's output. By his multiform applications of the true plane, the slide and the screw he enabled mechanics to work with a speed, precision and cheapness hitherto unknown. All this meant that there was a great demand for these new machine tools and the growth of the business was rapid. Towards the end of 1842 Whitworth was producing 50 tons of machinery a week. Then between 1848 and 1851 the number of his employees increased from 277 to 636 and output increased to over 200 tons a week.

Whitworth's machine tools brought a revolution in the manufacture of engines and other machinery, but it was the improvement he made to the screw that was his greatest contribution to engineering.

For many years he had observed that mechanics suffered great inconvenience owing to the variety of threads adopted by different manufacturers for the screws and bolts they used in steam engines and other machines. It meant that the work of repairing them was expensive and imperfect. Whitworth saw that this could be remedied very easily by the adoption of a uniform system in which the threads would always be the same for a given diameter. In 1841 he produced a paper on a universal system of screw threads and presented his ideas to the Institution of Civil Engineers. His basic idea was that standard gauges, graduated to a fixed scale, should be used as a constant measure of size. This would enable any manufacturer to mass-produce interchangeable machine parts at a low cost. At his works he made an extensive collection of screws and bolts from all the major workshops throughout Britain and worked out the average thread for different diameters. Using these averages, he produced dies for a series of screws and manufactured them to these set sizes. The result was the 'Whitworth thread' with a depth and pitch of constant proportion, giving the 'V' thread an angle of 55 degrees. He also drew up specifications for the number of threads per inch for various diameters. The thread was first introduced in his own workshop and by 1858 it had become the first nationally standardized system. It was its adoption by the railway companies, who until then had all used different screw threads, that led to its widespread acceptance so quickly.

Whitworth also produced a few unusual items such as the besom cart, a horse-drawn street-sweeping machine, which he patented in 1842, and a knitting machine which was patented in 1846. Ironically, the besom cart did more to bring his name to the notice of the general public than all his machine tools put together. It consisted of a series of brooms suspended from a wrought-iron frame that was hung from the end of a cart. Whitworth took out a patent for the design, established a company to operate the carts and along with a few friends in local government made substantial profits from the scheme. After it had been in operation in Manchester for ten months, it was reported to have changed that town from one of the dirtiest into one of the cleanest of large British towns. A contemporary account said

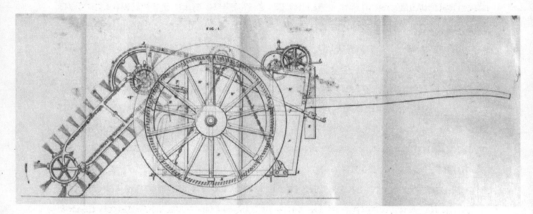

Whitworth's besom cart, complete with rotating brooms to the rear

the power of the machine was extraordinary, being equal to 30 men.

The volume of tools he produced over the first 15 years of business is not known, but by the time of the Great Exhibition in 1851 Whitworth was able to put on a huge display. It was bigger both in its size and in its range than anyone else's there. The display was greeted with great enthusiasm and the reports of the juries on the machinery departments were full of compliments. Over 20 of his machines were judged to be 'of first rate excellence' and it was clear that he was the foremost mechanical engineer of his day when his machines won more awards than those of any other exhibitor. These included medals for his engineers' machine tools, measuring machine and knitting machine. His success came from the fact that his ideas were very advanced for the time and his tools of exceptional quality. He was also very good at marketing them vigorously; he was extremely ambitious and unashamedly self-promoting. By the time of the Great Exhibition he had firmly established his business as the leader in the machine-tool trade not just in Britain but throughout the world. In 1857 Prince Albert made a point of visiting the Whitworth works several times, and consulted Whitworth on a wide range of manufacturing issues. Another result of his success at the Great Exhibition was that the British government consulted him on means of improving army weaponry.

Among the other displays that impressed the public at the Great Exhibition were the American exhibits of rifles and handguns. The military too made note of them, realizing that American manufacturers were much more advanced than the British at making this sort of small arms. The Americans staged a Great Exhibition of their own in New York in 1853, which effectively set British industrial techniques against those of the United States. A delegation, made up of George Wallis, principal of the Birmingham School of Art, which included the only school of rifle design in Britain, Professor John Wilson and Whitworth, was asked to attend the American exhibition and report back to England. The three commissioners left the Thames on 10 May 1853 on the steam sloop *Basilisk* and landed at New York two days late after a bad crossing. While they were there Whitworth and Wallis visited a number of factories in Philadelphia and Baltimore, and observed that while technology and ideas in repetitive production were far in advance of those in England, England's tool-making was superior to that of the United States. As early as 1835 Whitworth had been exporting lathes and other machines to Francis Lowell, the largest textile manufacturer in the United States. Whitworth had also sold machines to companies in Massachusetts and Connecticut. The machines that Whitworth saw in common use in the factories he visited with Wallis were the offspring of his own quick-return lathes and other machines. Whitworth had every confidence in his own engineering skills but he wondered just how long it would take America to overhaul the lead he had given England in the field of machine tools.

He was full of praise for American management for running the industry as it should be run and was so impressed by their working practices and their willingness to use labour-saving machinery that on his return he joined forces with George Wallis and wrote 'The Industry of the United States in Machinery, Manufacturers and Useful and Ornamental Arts'. The following year he introduced some of the ideas from the American system, now called mass production, to his works, which were extended and laid out in such a way that it was easy to bring in new machinery that would save time and labour. This sort of mechanization and mass production was completely dependent on the engineering principles being put forward by Whitworth and on the machines that he and others were making, and it has been said that he was the founding father of modern production engineering. As Fred put it:

He's not as well known as Stephenson or Brunel, but he's one of the most important men in the whole history of engineering because he realized that if it were possible for all engineers to use the same system, machined parts would be made much better, and mass production would be possible. In 1830 they reckoned a good workman could achieve an accuracy of one sixteenth of an inch but by 1850 Whitworth's tools were measuring to one ten-thousandth of an inch.

He didn't take on big projects like railways and steamships, but he produced the machine tools that made these things possible. The work he did had such a big impact that his contribution to mechanical engineering is as important today as it were in his own lifetime.

All Whitworth's work related to the need for absolute accuracy to achieve high standards in engineering. At a meeting of the Institution of Mechanical Engineers in Glasgow in 1856 he read a paper on the essential importance of possessing a true plane as a standard of reference in mechanical constructions. 'All excellence of workmanship depends on it,' he said. 'Next in importance to the true plane is the power of measurement.' He went on to describe elaborately the method for securing a true plane; namely, by scraping, instead of by the ordinary process of grinding. At the same meeting he exhibited a machine he had invented by which a difference of a millionth part of an inch in length could be detected in an instant. As an illustration of the minute quantity represented by a millionth part of an inch, he said it was only necessary to rub a piece of soft steel a few times to diminish its thickness by a millionth of an inch. He also put forward repeatedly his favourite idea of uniformity and proper gradations of size of parts in all branches of mechanical engineering. This, he said, was the chief means of achieving economy of production and he always emphasized too the need for proper lubrication.

When the Crimean War broke out in 1853, despite claiming to be a pacifist, Whitworth turned his attention to the production of armaments. During the course of the war, British Army guns proved to be very outdated. The favourite weapon at the time was the Enfield rifle, but it was made by hand and when it became necessary to obtain rifles in large quantities it was found that the private makers in Birmingham were unable to cope with the demand. The Army Board of Ordnance decided to open their own small-arms factory and approached Whitworth in 1854, asking him to design and build machine tools for the mass production of their standard issue Enfield rifle. From 1854 Whitworth conducted a series of experiments to determine the best form of weapons and ammunition. He became a member of the Small Arms Commission and insisted on including in its report a proviso that all government contract work should be checked against templates and gauges, and that each gauge should be numbered on each drawing. Whitworth lived in a large house called The Firs that had been built for him in Fallowfield, South Manchester, and on part of this estate he had a shooting gallery built for his experiments. Using this range, which was nearly half a mile long, he carried out exhaustive tests and 20 patents relating to arms production were issued to him between 1854 and 1878. He wasn't satisfied with the performance of the Enfield rifle, so he designed his own Whitworth rifle. This had a smaller bore of 0.45 inch which was hexagonal.

Whitworth had always had a reputation for belligerence and he was now becoming increasingly quarrelsome. He complained that he was not well and doctors advised him to rest more, but he took no notice. His wife, Fanny, seems to have borne the brunt of his complaints. They had been married for over 30 years but for the last ten her husband had spent most of his time at work or travelling. The pair grew more and more estranged. Regular invitations to functions arrived addressed to 'Mr & Mrs Whitworth' but more and more often Whitworth went on his own. Prince Albert himself sent an invitation for the couple to join him and the Queen at Osborne House on the Isle of Wight, in December 1856. The prince wanted to try out Whitworth's rifle and Whitworth attended on his own. By this time, after two years' experimenting, Whitworth was producing rifles that easily outperformed the rest and yet the British Army were still using the French-designed Enfield-Minié rifle. A select committee was set up to examine why the British Army had not been supplied with a more efficient weapon than the Enfield. Mr Hussey Vivian, Member of Parliament for Glamorgan, asked why the French-designed rifle was being used in preference to the superior Whitworth rifle and declared, 'Mr Whitworth's rifle beat the best rifles in the French army by two and three to one.' Mr James Turner MP said that Joseph Whitworth 'ended by producing the very best weapons ever invented'.

In the meantime, still in 1856, Britain imported American personnel and tools, to re-equip the Royal Small Arms Factory at

Enfield, north-east of London. Whitworth must have hoped to win the commission to make all the machinery for the gun factory himself, but, in spite of the fact that he appeared to be so well placed, he failed to get the contract. This may in part have been due to his belligerent nature and what was regarded as a certain uncouthness in his manners. Worse was to follow when in 1859, despite its apparent superiority, the Whitworth rifle was rejected by the Board of Ordnance because they claimed the new bore design was too small and had been found to be prone to fouling. A committee of officers gave conflicting accounts of the rifle but on the whole they reported that it was unsuitable for the British Army. Individual members of the committee, however, came out emphatically in its favour. One of them, General Hay, who was then considered among the greatest authorities on the subject, reported that the Whitworth rifle, as compared with the Enfield, possessed great increase in precision and range, great increase of strength and durability, and great increase of penetration. And this wasn't the only evidence in its support. In 1860 the National Rifle Association put out an advertisement calling for the most perfect rifle that could be invented. The competition was open to arms manufacturers from all over the world and at the trials the Whitworth was not only declared the best rifle but was adopted immediately by them. Queen Victoria inaugurated the first prize meeting of the association at Wimbledon in 1860 by firing the first shot with a Whitworth Sharpshooter rifle. The Queen scored a bull's eye with the rifle at a range of 400 yards. It was mounted on a mechanical rest, which depended for its exactness on the use of one of Whitworth's true planes.

Whitworth continued with his arms experiments and demonstrated the shape of projectile best adapted for flight and penetration. Up to this point bullets and shot had been spherical but he showed that the head should be shaped to the curve of least resistance and that the rear should be tapered off. He also demonstrated that the form of the rear was particularly important to achieve long ranges. After determining the principles that should regulate the construction of guns and the projectiles fired from them, Whitworth next sought to improve the material from which they were made. In the earlier years of his artillery experiments all guns were made from iron, but one of the greatest difficulties he encountered in achieving the degree of accuracy he required arose from defects in the iron. He was now finding that the weapons he was creating needed a better metal for their construction. The obvious answer was steel, but many people believed that this was an unsafe material to use for ordnance. It was a view that changed after 1856, when Henry Bessemer worked out how to make cheap, high-quality steel in volume.

Bessemer's father was an engineer who set up a business to make the metal type that was used in the printing industry. As a young man Bessemer learned metallurgy here and made numerous inventions, such as a typesetting machine, and found new ways of making gold paint and lead pencils. He also began to experiment with metals and became interested in steel-making when he was trying to find ways to produce better guns. Steel had been around since 1740 when Benjamin Huntsman introduced the process of making crucible steel from bar or blister steel. A resident of Sheffield who worked as a clockmaker in Doncaster, Huntsman developed the relatively simple method of purifying blister steel by melting it in crucibles and skimming off the impurities that floated to the surface. The liquid steel was then poured into a mould and left to solidify. This produced an ingot of cast or crucible steel that had a uniformly high degree of purity. High-quality steel like this had never been produced before and so, with both his technique and his product, Huntsman laid the foundations for the steel industry. That the industry didn't take off immediately was largely due to the fact that crucible steel could not be produced cheaply in bulk. It wasn't until 1856 that this difficulty was overcome when Bessemer patented a process by which molten pig iron could be turned directly into steel by blasting air through it in a converter. This cut out the wrought-iron stage, dramatically reduced the cost of producing steel and made it possible to manufacture large amounts of good-quality metal. It was lighter in weight than iron and also stronger, making it ideal for everything from ships and railway locomotives to cutlery and guns.

Whitworth showed his interest in improving the quality of the material used for guns about a month after Bessemer's public announcement of his great invention, in his address after being elected president of the Institution of Mechanical Engineers:

> With regard to the manufacture of malleable iron and steel, it was with great gratification that I read the account of the Bessemer process, so beautiful and simple as apparently to leave nothing further to be desired ... I may mention that in making rifle barrels for the experiments I have undertaken for the Government, one of the greatest difficulties I encounter in attaining the degree of accuracy I require arises from defects in the iron. What we want is iron of great strength, free from seams, flaws and hard places. Inferior iron, with the use of other defective and improper materials, is perhaps the main cause of one of the greatest errors committed in the construction of whatever in mechanism has to be kept in motion.

The material that Whitworth was looking for was steel and, after the Bessemer process became a success, he turned his attention to the adaptability of steel for making guns. But, believing that its qualities would have to be improved before the prejudices of the military establishment could be overcome, he decided to find a way of improving steel even further. Bessemer steel was hard enough, but it didn't have the required ductility. Ductility was essential, but it couldn't be obtained without forming air cells, which made the steel unsound. As far as he knew, the only method in use for working steel to make it close, strong and ductile was to compress it when it was in a solid state with expensive machinery. Convinced that this process could be improved upon, he began to experiment. Between 1863 and 1865 he laboured constantly at this work, finally attaining his aim after around 2,500 experiments. The process that he developed consisted simply of subjecting the steel in its fluid state to such a high pressure that the air or gas bubbles were pressed out of it. He found that a pressure of not less than six tons to the square inch was required, and that under that pressure, a column of steel was compressed in five minutes to the extent of one and a half inches per foot. He also found that the larger the mass of steel, the more effective the hydraulic pressure was.

The trouble was that this process was difficult and dangerous, and at first he experienced many failures. One of the major difficulties was making materials and machinery that were capable of resisting the enormous pressure he had to use. Whitworth started by making small presses for compressing the steel and gradually increased the size of his apparatus until he found that it could be used safely in the production of artefacts of any required size, such as propeller shafts and cylinder linings for the largest marine engines, torpedo chambers and large-calibre guns. At last he made an 8,000-ton press and installed it in his works, where his workmen were so afraid of the consequences that might result from the application of so much pressure to fluid steel that they always ran away when the pressure was put on.

When the steel that was produced was tested along with the best metals that had been made previously, Whitworth's was found to be superior to them all in strength and ductility. His field guns could now be forged solid and then bored and rifled. It was a major step forward not just in the strength but also in the efficiency and accuracy of ordnance. Sir E. J. Reed, chief constructor for the Admiralty, expressed his view that 'No one who has considered the process of Sir Joseph Whitworth and has examined the steel produced by it can, I think, doubt for a moment that it is a more close, more compact and a more perfect material than any other description of steel in existence.'

Through the screw threads that bear his name and the Whitworth rifle, Joseph Whitworth's name will be forever associated with engineering and with guns, but to the people of Manchester it has other associations. The Whitworth is the city's main art gallery and one of the main buildings on the Manchester University campus is the Whitworth Building. It is recognition of the fact that as well as being a great engineer Whitworth also took a strong interest in education, art and culture. He was a member of the General Council for the Exhibition of Art Treasures of the United Kingdom and over the summer of 1857 an iron and glass pavilion was built in Manchester Botanical Gardens at Old Trafford to house the exhibition. In the same year he was elected a Fellow of the Royal Society. Both honours reflected how widely respected and influential he had become, and he lost no time in promoting engineering standards within the institution.

Whitworth was one of the first people to point out the advantages of decimalization and the fact that the common fractional system was impossible for precision work. Although decimalization was not to be introduced in Britain for over a century it is yet another example of how forward-looking Whitworth was. But in the 1860s it was the development of armaments that occupied a lot of his time. During this period, he constructed many field guns with steel barrels designed to work as both muzzle-loading and breech-loading. All were high-quality weapons suitable for the army or the navy. Although negotiable, the prices were higher than those of his biggest competitor, William Armstrong. A 4.5-bore 32-pound gun cost £400, a 5.5-bore 70-pound gun was £700 and his new 7-inch 120-pound gun with a hexagonal barrel cost £1,350. But they were good.

The fame of the Whitworth rifle soon spread abroad and large orders were received from the French government. Napoleon III also sent an officer to Whitworth's testing range at Southport to see some of his large guns tested and indicated that he was prepared to negotiate the purchase of the patent for the rifle for France. In 1862 a committee appointed by the British government reported that makers of small-bore rifles having any pretence to special accuracy had copied to the letter the three main elements of Whitworth's design, namely the diameter of bore, degree of spiral and large proportion of rifling surface. But it was not until 1874 that the government adopted his principles and even then it wasn't done under his name. The Board of Ordnance accepted the Martini-Henry rifle, which had used Whitworth's basic principles, and concluded that the smaller bore size was in fact suitable for a military weapon.

As well as rifles Whitworth developed a powerful cannon and another dispute began with the Board of Ordnance in 1862, when this was rejected because it was not of the traditional design. The ethos of the age may have been progressive, but the military bigwigs were

Whitworth (third from right) at trials for one
of his guns on Southport Sands, 1860

clearly stuck in the past. The cannon was, however, supplied to France, New Zealand and other foreign governments. During the American Civil War the *Times* correspondent with the Confederate army stated that it was impossible to praise too highly the performance as a field piece of the 20-pounder Whitworth. 'There is no other gun on the Continent,' he reported, 'which can compare with it in lightness, precision and length of range. Again and again one single Whitworth gun has forced Federal batteries to change their position, and eventually to fall back.' The renown of these guns became so universal that Whitworth received enquiries for them from almost every government in Europe. In spite of this the British Army, conservative as ever, remained unimpressed. Then, in 1864, the British government arranged for another series of trials to take place at Shoeburyness to test the relative qualities of the Whitworth guns and those produced by his great rival William Armstrong. After the firing of more than 2,500 rounds of shot and shell and a great deal of deliberation, the committee of artillerists reported that they could not determine which was the superior gun. Whitworth's ordnance failed once again to be adopted by the British government, even though his guns continued to be exported to other countries in large numbers.

Further trials were held and, on 23 April 1867, *The Times* reported that the Enfield rifle had been completely beaten by the Whitworth, in accuracy of fire, penetration and range. Using only half a charge (35 grams of powder) its lead alloy bullet penetrated through seven inches of elm at a reduced distance of 20 yards. A steel bullet went through a wrought-iron plate 0.6 inches thick. The War Office representatives were amazed; it was the first time that a rifle bullet had gone through an iron plate. Whitworth astonished the world yet again when in 1868 he produced a field gun that could fire projectiles further than they had ever been fired before. Its range was 11,243 yards with a 250-pound projectile and 11,127 yards with a 310-pound projectile. In other words a mass of 2¼ cwt could be fired a distance of nearly six and a half miles.

Along with other arms manufacturers of the time like Armstrong in Britain and Krupp in Germany, Whitworth was changing the face of warfare, increasing massively the destructive power of the weaponry that a nation and its armies had at their disposal. There can be no doubt that the weapons being developed at this time were largely responsible for the carnage that was to come less than 50 years later, in the trenches of the First World War. Whitworth's position on this and his moral stance appear to be somewhat ambivalent. As a man who continued to describe himself as a pacifist, Whitworth came out with an interesting justification for the company's arms-manufacturing activities. 'Were it not,' he said, 'that the increased destructiveness of war must tend to shorten its duration and diminish its frequency – thus saving human life – the invention of my projectiles could hardly be justified; but believing in the really pacific influence of the most powerful means of defence, these long projectiles I call the "anti-war" shell.'

Whitworth's reputation and that of his company were spreading and beginning to be recognized on the international stage. In September 1868, after witnessing the performance of one of the Whitworth field guns at Châlons, Napoleon III made him a member of the Légion d'Honneur, and about the same time Whitworth received the Albert Medal of the Society of Arts for his instruments of measurement and uniform standards. Under Whitworth's leadership, membership of the Institution of Mechanical Engineers rose rapidly and he was elected for a second term of office in 1866, the only individual to have served two terms as president. He was also a pioneer in making the prosperity of his business a source of benefit to his workforce. Shares of £25 were offered to the foremen, draughtsmen, clerks and workmen, and Whitworth and his workers held between them 92 per cent of the shares – thus they had practical control of the company. But the importance of his contribution to engineering was still not recognized by everybody. An article published in the *Manchester City News* commented that 'Mr Whitworth's foot rule, on which he had the thirty-second parts of an inch marked, was regarded as a curiosity, and many did not hesitate to affirm that to work to such a standard was an unnecessary refinement.' Undeterred by his critics, he continued to press forward on all fronts. Although the Whitworth

Whitworth (second from left) with other members of the Institution of Mechanical Engineers, including William Fairbarn (far right), shortly after being elected president for a second term in 1866

process for casting steel under pressure, 'fluid compressed steel', had been patented in 1865 and he built a new steelworks near Manchester, it was not until 1869 that the apparatus was completed and in a position to manufacture 'Whitworth steel' in quantities fit for use in his works.

Whitworth was now completely estranged from his wife Fanny but he made sure she never experienced any financial problems. He bought her a house and supported her with an adequate income until her death in 1870. This was hardly a problem for Whitworth because he had become incredibly wealthy. He was still living at The Firs, which was convenient for his factory, but like many of his contemporaries who had amassed fortunes from their industrial empires, he had higher aspirations. He used some of his money to purchase a substantial country estate in Darley Dale, Derbyshire, including a large residence called Stancliffe Hall. The year after Fanny's death he married Mary Louisa Hurst, the daughter of Daniel Broad Hurst, one-time Manchester city treasurer. His second wife was 25 years younger than him and after their wedding in London the couple moved into Stancliffe Hall. At first, Stancliffe stood on a bare hillside but Whitworth transformed it into one of the most beautiful landscaped garden estates in England. He brought in the celebrated gardener Edward Milner, and the architect T. Roger Smith to rebuild the house between 1871 and 1872.

The Hall dated from around 1670 and had been in the hands of several different owners but Whitworth wanted to extend it and have it decorated in a style that suited him. Royal decorators G. J. Grace of London were employed for much of the internal work, which included designs by Augustus Pugin. A noted feature of the gardens was the rockery that Whitworth had constructed out of a sandstone quarry. Once he moved in he appeared to relax more and enjoy Stancliffe, showing a particular interest in his stud farm and trotting ponies. He also collected paintings, mainly watercolours.

Whitworth and his new wife shared a common interest in educational issues. Not surprisingly, the great engineer himself took a particular interest in engineering education, and in 1868 he

announced his intention to give £100,000 to found a series of scholarships for the encouragement of young men in scientific and technical
education, and the advancement of mechanical engineering. He wrote
to the prime minister, Benjamin Disraeli, about the scholarships, saying that they were intended to 'encourage students to combine practice
with theory, and artisans to combine theory with perfection in workmanship'. At that time the leading men in educational and scientific
matters were deploring England's deficiency in technical education, so
examinations in practical workmanship were held in his workshops in
Manchester. These were always open to students who wanted to
practise the working details of mechanical engineering. As a strong
believer in the value of technical education, Whitworth insisted that
boys should learn the correct use of tools from the very beginning of
their schooling.

He also backed the new Mechanics' Institute in Manchester, which
went on to become the University of Manchester Institute of Science
and Technology, and he helped to found the Manchester School of
Design. In recognition of his services to education and the donations
he made to educational foundations, Whitworth was created a baronet
in 1869 at the age of 66.

Throughout his career, Whitworth continued to receive awards. In
1867 at the Paris Exhibition he won three bronze medals for his
machine tools and one of only five Grand Prix awards won by British
engineers. At the London International Exhibition he won a silver
medal in 1873 and a bronze in 1874. In 1872 he was made a
commander of the Brazilian Imperial Order of the Rose and in 1874 he
was awarded a Royal Medal by Carlos VII, King of Spain. These were
great honours and by this time Whitworth had established himself as
one of the greatest engineers of the Victorian Age. In presenting the
Freedom of the Turners' Company to him in 1875, its warden Sir C. H.
Gregory said:

Well has he merited fortune, fame and honour. Raised by his Sovereign
to rank and title, he has been honoured by other men of science with
the distinctions of F.R.S. He has devoted a noble share of his well-

289

earned fortune in munificent endowments for the higher education of mechanical engineers. When he is taken from us, he will leave his monuments in the workshops of the world; and as monks of old sang requiems over the graves of departed heroes, so young mechanics trained by his liberality, will keep the name of Sir Joseph Whitworth green in their grateful memory for all time.

As he approached the end of his career, Whitworth's attention was largely absorbed in experiments connected with the improvement of small arms and artillery, and in trying to persuade the government to accept his schemes. The machine-tool business became neglected and was allowed to 'run on its reputation'. By this time the compressed steel he had developed was in general usage. In 1876 the two screw-propeller shafts of the naval vessel *Inflexible* were made of steel compressed by this process. The shafts were 283 feet long and weighed 63 tons. If they had been made of wrought iron they would have weighed 97 tons. The *City of Rome*, launched in 1881 and described as a floating palace, had a crankshaft made of Whitworth compressed steel. There were many uses for the material and Whitworth himself proposed to reduce the weight of railway carriages by using it instead of wrought iron. This would bring significant savings in the cost of running a railway, and steel did start to replace iron as the preferred material for railway carriages.

Whitworth's interest in ordnance continued with demonstrations of artillery capable of piercing armour plate more than four inches thick and shells with fuseless detonation. With the increase in the efficiency of weapons of destruction, fears began to surface that it might be impossible to make materials capable of resisting their power. So, no sooner had Whitworth provided efficient ordnance than he began to study the construction of armour, and in 1877 he produced his 'impregnable armour plating'. This was formed from his fluid com-pressed steel built up in hexagonal sections, each of which was composed of a series of concentric rings around a circular disc. These concentric rings prevented any crack in the steel from passing beyond the limits of the one in which it occurred.

A trial of this sort of plate in Manchester in 1878 yielded some remarkable results. A shell weighing 250 pounds was fired from a 9-inch gun at a section of armour plate nine inches thick, supported by a wooden backing set against a sandbank. The force of the impact was so great that the target was driven back 18 inches into the sand, but the target itself was left undamaged. Experts in the field declared that this new plating would create not only a material that was invulnerable to any missile employed in warfare, but a lighter armour than any in use for large ironclads. Whitworth had invented remarkable guns and armour plate but the conservatism of the military establishment and its resistance to change meant that the Board of Ordnance persisted with the manufacture of guns of inferior materials and continued to ignore the principles of gunnery that Whitworth advocated. It was not until 1881 that steel was introduced for the manufacture of ordnance at the Royal Gun Factories in the Royal Arsenal at Woolwich. The conservatism wasn't just restricted to the military establishment. Although his system of screw threads had been universally accepted in Britain by the 1860s, it was not until 1880, when his standard gauges and screw threads were in common use, that they were officially adopted by the Board of Trade.

By the 1880s the company Whitworth had founded had grown at an astonishing rate. In 1834 his workforce had totalled 15, by 1854 this had increased to 368 and in 1874, when his works were made into a limited company, he was employing approximately 750 workers. This had risen to over 1,000 in 1880 when the company moved to a new works at Openshaw, Manchester.

In his later years Whitworth and his wife spent their days seeing to the affairs of the estate at Stancliffe and his original house in Fallowfield as well as travelling abroad a great deal. He also found enjoyment in walking, riding and billiards, but his health was deteriorating. Realizing that the heart palpitations he was experiencing were a warning, he started to attend the church of St Helen, in Darley Dale. Unfortunately, however, he stopped going after he had a disagreement with the vicar about village education. He retired to Monte Carlo in the hope that the climate would improve his health, but it was here at the English Hotel that he died on the evening of 22 January 1887. His trustees were directed to spend the fortune he had amassed on philanthropic projects and this they still do to this day.

In terms of inventions and innovations his career had been prolific. Although he didn't create great railways or bridges or steamships, Joseph Whitworth invented the machine tools that made them possible. Before his innovations all the parts were made individually for each job and not with any real accuracy. But his precision tools meant that parts could be made exactly the same over and over again and the same tools could be used for a lot of different projects. He did not, as Maudslay had done, train many people who would go on to become high-class mechanics themselves. His influence was in the way in which his designs were widely studied and imitated. The work he did from the 1830s through to the 1850s was at the forefront of technological innovation, but later, displaying some of the conservatism he had encountered in government departments, he refused to innovate and ignored what his competitors were doing. Charles Porter, who was one of his American associates in the 1860s, reported that Whitworth 'divided all other toolmakers into two classes, one class who copied him without giving him any credit, and the other class who had the presumption to imagine that they could improve on him'. Porter concluded: 'His feelings toward both these classes evidently did not tend to make him happy.' By the end of his career it is clear that he had been overtaken by other manufacturers, who continued to push the boundaries of technology. The machines that his firm produced were still very good, but that was no longer enough as they were now old-fashioned and could not compete with some of the more technically advanced machines on the market.

Whitworth's work in the field of armaments had brought him into bitter conflict with his rival, William Armstrong. Their animosity was not resolved during Whitworth's lifetime and, if he had lived, he would probably have had very mixed feelings when his company merged with Armstrong's in 1893 to form the massive Armstrong Whitworth Company. The merged company had factories at Elswick, near Newcastle, on the north bank of the River Tyne, and at Openshaw in

Manchester. The contribution that the company went on to make during the 1914–18 War was massive, supplying 13,000 pieces of artillery, 100 tanks, 47 warships, 240 converted merchant ships, 1,000 planes and 3 airships as well as 14.5 million shells, 18.5 million fuses and 21 million cartridges.

His most notable invention, without any doubt, was the Whitworth thread with its standardized thread pitch for various sizes of nuts and bolts. This invention led the way to production-line manufacturing, as the uniform system that he developed came to be adopted throughout the world.

The world's first production line was at Richard Garrett's works at Leiston in Suffolk. Garrett's was one of Britain's pioneering heavy engineering companies. They started off as manufacturers of agricultural tools and equipment, but when the steam locomotive was developed the company saw there was a market for a similar but lighter machine for use on farms. They began to manufacture what they called a small portable steam engine and when they exhibited it at the Great Exhibition they took so many orders that their existing facilities were totally inadequate. To meet the huge increase in demand they had a building designed and constructed specifically for mass production of these engines on an assembly line. In 1853 the Long Shop, as it became known, was completed, one of the first flow-line production assembly halls in the world.

With the coming of steam to the farm, the agricultural landscape changed dramatically. Steam engines began to replace the horse as manufacturers like Garrett's, John Fowler of Leeds and Fred's favourite, Aveling & Porter of Rochester, rose to the challenge of mechanizing the farm.

Aveling & Porter's 'Liverpool Roller'

10

Thomas Aveling
1824–1882
Steaming Down the Road

Thomas Aveling, a farmer from Kent, was a pioneer in the application of steam power to ploughing, road haulage and driving agricultural machinery. The traction engine that he developed is basically a mobile steam engine that evolved from the crude stationary engines of the eighteenth century. A traction engine is a strange sort of machine that has gone out of fashion now. It was developed from a lot of other engines and it all started off not in urban industrial areas, but on the land, in the country of all places, where all the effort was put in either by animals or the human frame. By the 1840s the locomotive boiler had been developed up to almost the standard it is today. Basically, there was a boiler barrel, a firebox and a lot of pipes through the middle. There was, of course, water in the boiler, fire in the firebox, hence its name, and the products of combustion went through the tubes and up through the chimney. This formed the basis of the traction engine. To begin with, the earliest traction engines were all adapted portable engines, with the cylinders over the firebox and chain drive. At first the steering was done by horses, later by a steersman on the front of the engine and then to the system we know today. Different makers had different ideas as to which side the steering should be situated, right or left.

Of all the leading manufacturers, Fred had a particularly high regard for Aveling. His famous steamroller *Betsy* and the convertible compound steam tractor that he spent so many years restoring were both Aveling & Porter engines. 'Through his ingenious technical innovations to steam engines and road rollers,' Fred said,

> Thomas Aveling made a massive contribution to the development of mechanical road transport and progressive farming machinery. He first introduced simple chain drives in 1860 and his inventions took the traction engine to new levels of speed and sophistication. This created the prototype for the engine that was to stay in commercial use for almost a century. It earned Thomas Aveling the recognition of 'father of the traction engine'. It was Aveling who made most of the technical innovations that are incorporated in every 'modern' traction engine and steamroller.
>
> Aveling & Porter, the company he set up with Richard Porter, was an agricultural engine and steamroller manufacturer. The two men entered into partnership in 1862, developed a steam engine three years later, and produced more of them than all the other British manufacturers put together. His early life did nothing to indicate the brilliance that would emerge; in fact many considered him slow and dim-witted.

Thomas Aveling was born at Elm, Cambridgeshire, on 11 September 1824, the eldest son in a family of three boys. His father died when he was still young and his mother went to live in Rochester, Kent, where she married a clergyman, the Revd John D'Urban of Hoo, who ruled Thomas and his brothers with a rod of iron. Aveling retreated into himself and it was only when he left home that his true character and abilities began to shine through. His first employment was as an apprentice to a farmer, Edward Lake of Hoo. This gave him the opportunity to familiarize himself with the new steam-powered farm machinery and it wasn't long before he started to demonstrate his bent for mechanics and engineering. He began by doing repairs for neighbours but was soon looking for ways to make improvements to their machines.

While working for Edward Lake, Aveling married his employer's niece Sarah, the daughter of Robert Lake of Milton Chapel near Canterbury, and in 1850 he acquired his own farm, Court Lodge, at

The Amalgamated Society of Engineers, Machinists, Millwrights, Smiths, and Pattern Makers was the result of a successful attempt to form a national trade union in 1851. In just ten years, membership swelled to over 33,000.

THE GREAT EASTERN ON THE STOCKS,
AS SEEN FROM THE RIVER.

The construction of Brunel's SS *Great Eastern* at Millwall. John Scott-Russell, eminent shipbuilder (*top, second from right in top hat*), went into partnership with Brunel to build the enormous ship, though the two men were permanently at loggerheads as costs and schedules spiralled out of control.

By far the largest ship in the world at the time, Brunel's SS *Great Britain* was first launched in Bristol on 19 July 1843 in the presence of Prince Albert. Fred himself paid a visit to the restored ship while filming *Victorian Heroes*.

Above: Aveling & Porter's road roller was trialled with great success in Hyde Park, London in 1866. The arrival of the rollers to smooth the city's roads was heralded by the *Illustrated London News* as 'one of the most desirable metropolitan improvements'.

Right: With great pride, Fred drives his 1912 Aveling & Porter convertible compound steam tractor out of his shed after completing its restoration in 2004.

Above: James Nasmyth's steam hammer in his foundry at Patricroft near Manchester. He enjoyed showing off how it was capable of cracking the shell of an egg placed in a wine glass, without breaking the glass.

Left above: Machine tools for planing, drilling, slotting and boring on display at Joseph Whitworth's stand at the Great Exhibition, 1851.

Left below: An Armstrong Gun at Fort Fisher, North Carolina during the American Civil War. When Fort Fisher fell to Union forces on 15 January 1865, the gun was seized as a war trophy and transported to the United States Military Academy at West Point, New York, where it remains today.

A conference of engineers for Robert Stephenson's Britannia Bridge, including Stephenson (*seated left*), Joseph Locke (*seated, second from right*) and Isambard Kingdom Brunel (*seated right*).

The increasing popularity of rail travel necessitated the construction of the Britannia Bridge to carry the Chester and Holyhead Railway over the Menai Straits and provide a direct rail link between London and Holyhead.

Fred and the author during an attempt to recreate a demonstration of the cantilever principle (**bottom**), which underpins the construction of the Forth Bridge. The human cantilever shows how the men's arms and the anchorage ropes come into tension when a load is put on the central girder and its weight passes through the men's bodies and down into the ground.

Above: A recreation of the famous moment in 1897 when Parsons's *Turbinia* sped through the fleet during the Naval Review at Spithead in the presence of Queen Victoria.

Left: *Turbinia* on her sea trial off the north-east coast. Her captain and lookout, Christopher Leyland, stands on top of the conning tower.

Left middle and bottom: Parsons's early sketch of the steam turbine blades used in the radial flow turbine engine.

Ruckinge on Romney Marsh. In the census of 1851 he was described as a farmer and grazier employing 16 men and 6 boys. He must have been quite successful but his main interest lay in making improvements to farm machinery rather than raising animals and crops. He was particularly interested in the power of steam and he could see that there were tremendous possibilities if the mechanical power of the steam engine could be applied to farming.

During the 1840s British agricultural engineers were manufacturing iron-framed ploughs, cultivators, harrows, seed drills, threshing machines and grinding mills. But none of them had attempted to apply steam power to the farm. Barn machinery was driven by horse engines. For steam power to be applied successfully to agriculture it was essential that the power source should be transportable, so the first agricultural engines consisted of a locomotive-type boiler on four wheels. They were manufactured by Clayton & Shuttleworth of Lincoln and became known as portable engines or simply 'portables'. 'This,' said Fred,

was basically a very simple machine. They were not self-propelled and needed to be pulled by horses. The men in the country, the blacksmiths and village mechanics, decided that they would get a small locomotive boiler and place it on four wooden wheels with a pair of horse shafts at the front for moving from place to place. On top of it they put a crankshaft and a cylinder with a flywheel, which enabled it to drive a wide variety of machinery by an endless belt. In the early days of portable threshing these engines accompanied most of the machines that were sold, with these engines as the power unit. On farms, portables could be used to drive an infinite variety of machines. As well as ploughs and threshing machines, early milking machines, big saws and crop driers took their power from portables, as did a variety of crushers, cutters and pulpers, and they were still in use well into the twentieth century.

In Victorian and Edwardian times the portable engine became the universal provider of mobile power. It was used on construction sites for driving pumps, mortar mills and mixers; in quarries for working

An early example of a portable engine powering a threshing machine

crushers; in sawmills for powering saws and planers; in brickyards for turning pugmills; and in joineries and other workshops for driving overhead line shafting. In fact there can have been few types of medium-sized machines capable of operation by an endless belt that were not, at some time or other, paired up with portables. This went on for some time until production ceased in the late 1930s with the development of the petrol paraffin tractor, which was less costly to operate, but they were still in use into the 1950s. Companies like Marshall's of Gainsborough were making portables right up till the 1940s for export to South America for sugar beet works.

Agricultural general-purpose engines were the most common types to be seen around the countryside. They were basically used as a mobile power plant for threshing, tree pulling and general farm duties. All early threshers were stationary engines very much like the engines used in a mill or a mine, but the first portable thresher appeared in the 1840s, and from then on this type rapidly replaced the fixed type. They were not generally owned by the farmers themselves, but were operated by contractors touring from farm to farm.

With the introduction of mechanization to farming, the mid-nineteenth century was a time of great opportunity for an ambitious agricultural engineer. Aveling recognized this and in 1851 his interest in engineering led him to set up a business in partnership with his father-in-law, producing and repairing agricultural machinery. Many local farmers had bought the portables that had been developed by Clayton & Shuttleworth and Aveling became a sales agent for the company. By 1856 Clayton & Shuttleworth had built over 2,000 of these machines and other agricultural engineers started to manufacture them on a commercial scale. Aveling could see that there was great potential here, particularly if he could develop a machine for threshing that could get around a farm under its own steam. When the threshing machine had first appeared in portable form it was on a wheeled frame, which enabled corn to be threshed straight from the rick rather than having to be carried to the barn. The problem for the average farmer was that this combination of steam engine and threshing machine involved costs that only the biggest could afford. This led to the arrival of the threshing contractor who had to keep large teams of horses to move the engine and the threshing machine around the farmers' lands. Fred commented:

> Aveling was not happy with them because of the hassle involved in moving them around. He said it was an insult to mechanical science to see half a dozen horses drag along a steam engine and compared it to six sailing vessels towing a steamer. I always felt a bit sorry for the horse in front of the traction engine. The only way of steering the thing was still a pair of horse shafts at the front with obviously a carthorse in between the shafts. And if the guy with the regulator, that's the tap that makes the steam work the engine, got a bit out of hand, accidents could happen. No one ever actually recorded if there were any terrible disasters like running over the horse or the horse losing its feet or anything like that, but there must have been a few unfortunate old Dobbins who met a fairly violent death.

The logical development of the horse-drawn portable engine was the traction engine, which could not only drive machinery but could also get around the farm under its own steam and haul other pieces of machinery around. It was Aveling's ambition to achieve just this; he wanted to make the engines self-moving. With this in mind, in 1858 he acquired premises at 24 High Street, Rochester, with workshops nearby at 27 Edwards Yard and set himself up in business as an iron founder and agricultural engineer. Among other things, his catalogue showed that he was an agent for steam plough sets, portable steam engines and agricultural machinery including threshing sets, reaping and mowing sets, circular saw benches and portable grinding mills. But Aveling wanted to manufacture his own machines and he set to work on what has come to be regarded as the first traction engine.

His idea was to use the same power unit as the portable to provide traction and put front wheels on to replace the horse. The engineer would drive the machine to where it was needed for threshing corn, sawing timber, pulling down trees, pile-driving, direct haulage of ploughing tackle and lifting huge blocks of stone for harbour works. In 1859 Aveling took out a patent for a 'self-propelled road locomotive with devices for giving more or less tension to the driving chain and also for disengaging the drive so that a traction locomotive can be used as a stationary portable engine at will'. Although he had his own small foundry in Strood on the site of what was later to become Aveling & Porter's Invicta Works, Aveling's premises were not big enough for him to construct his own locomotives when he came up with the design, so he had one built by Clayton & Shuttleworth.

With this design he succeeded in making a self-moving machine by fitting a long drive chain between the crankshaft and rear axle of what was a standard Clayton & Shuttleworth portable, effectively creating the first traction engine, Aveling's Patent Locomotive Steam Thrashing Train. 'The whole thing looks a bit ancient compared with the modern combine harvesters,' Fred said,

> but it was an ingenious use of steam for agricultural purposes. The steam engine powered the threshing machine by a belt connected from the flywheel. Wheat or oats were shovelled into the thresher at one end and went through rising and falling shafts, which separated the grain and discharged the straw at the other end. The grains passed through a number of sieves for grading and were finally discharged through three different holes where they were collected and sorted. The flywheel and belt also powered a spiked ramp, which carried the straw up to the top of the rick.

The traction engine had arrived. A heavy engine could now be moved around a farm much more easily. The characteristic engine of the early years was eight horsepower, single or double cylindered. Aveling first introduced simple chain drives in 1860 and his inventions took the traction engine to new levels of speed and sophistication. The engine still had to have shafts attached to the swivelling fore carriage at the front, but now only a single horse was necessary to steer it. Aveling was not content with this. He wanted to be able to dispense with the horse altogether.

In 1861 Aveling went on to establish his main works on the site of the foundry at Strood, where he had the capacity to build 34 of the 7½-ton engines in his first year. One of the first things he applied himself to in his new works was getting rid of the horse. He decided to put a dog clutch on the end of the crankshaft and a big sprocket on the back axle. A lever was operated by a steersman who sat at the front of the engine, a system that became known as Aveling's 'pilot steerage'. This was the prototype for the traction engine that was to stay in commercial use for almost a century.

Now that he had developed the agricultural steam engine to this level, Aveling and other manufacturers were soon put under pressure by farmers and contractors to make an engine that would be capable not just of moving itself but also of towing the threshing machine from farm to farm. Bigger engines were developed, two-speed gearing was introduced and gear drive took the place of chains. In the mid-nineteenth century, general-purpose engines, as they became known, were the most numerous types of traction engines. They were used mainly by threshing contractors who went round the farms. As well as the engine, the threshing outfit consisted of a drum, a straw elevator and sometimes a chaff cutter. It was driven by a long belt from the fly-wheel of the engine. The contractor provided the outfit, the driver and a man to feed the threshing drum, while the farmer supplied the coal, the water and the unskilled labour. During the months when the engines were not engaged on threshing work, they were used on saw benches and sometimes drove water pumps.

Aveling continued to develop his engine and in 1861 he took out a patent for the steam-jacketed cylinder. Fred explained how it worked: 'The steam leaving the boiler comes up through the bottom of the cylinder block and then goes right round the outer circumference of the cylinder into the stop valve chest, which is the valve that controlled the steam entering the valve chest proper. This kept the steam really hot and stopped it from condensing, which is bad news in a steam engine as it washes all the cylinder oil away and the lubrication.' In 1862 Aveling's engine was awarded a medal at the International Exhibition at South Kensington and everybody who saw it was impressed.

Soon after he established his works it became apparent that Aveling needed more capital to expand the business, so in 1862 he went into partnership with Richard Thomas Porter. Porter, the son of a grocer, was born in 1834 in Sheffield. Not a wealthy man, he married Marian Atkins in 1861, and it is thought that she may have been from a wealthy family. As well as bringing money into the company, Porter began to look after the commercial side of the business and a London office was opened in 1863 at 72 Cannon Street. This left Aveling free to concentrate on the engineering. Trading as Aveling & Porter, the company sold engines they described as a 'patent Agricultural Locomotive Engine for Threshing, Ploughing and General Traction Purposes'. The company displayed the famous rampant horse and Invicta inscription on its products from 1864, and this is still seen today on numerous preserved Aveling engines like Fred's steamroller *Betsy* and his convertible compound steam tractor.

The company's main customers were the contractors and it didn't take them long to realize that, in addition to their agricultural duties, engines could also be used to haul trailer loads of manure, bricks, stone, coal or timber over long distances. Aveling too was quick to appreciate these possibilities and it was from early applications like this that faster and heavier road locomotives were developed. 'Road locomotives,' Fred said, 'were designed for heavy haulage on the public highways. They were usually larger than the normal traction engine and were fitted with three-speed gearing as opposed to two in most traction engines. They were also sprung on both front and rear axles. An extra water tank was fitted under the boiler so that greater distances could be travelled between water stops. These were very powerful traction engines capable of pulling loads of up to 120 tons.'

A contemporary report described road trials for one of the first Aveling engines to be used for this purpose.

A trial of one of Aveling's patent road locomotive engines was made in Rochester in the presence of several foreigners of distinction. The engine manufactured by Messrs Aveling and Porter was one of 10 horsepower and had behind it a load of 21 tons on five carriages, which it took up Star Hill, along the new Road to the Station, returning through the narrow streets of Chatham with the greatest facility. We understood that the visitors were astonished at the rate with which the heavy mass moved up and down the hill and the manner in which the long train turned the sharp corners of the streets. They appeared to be well pleased and altogether favourably impressed with the application of steam to common roads.

Soon after the portable steam engine first appeared on the farm, farmers and engineers wanted to find a way for the power of steam to be applied in the fields for the actual process of cultivation. Coming from a farming background himself, Aveling was convinced that steam ploughing would have great advantages over horses, particularly on heavy clay lands. But it was clear to him and to other pioneers that the traction engine itself was too heavy for direct ploughing and another method was needed. Aveling gave it a lot of thought and in 1856 he produced the first steam plough. It was so successful that Kent farmers presented him with an award of 300 guineas (£315). 'He turned out to be a born engineer,' Fred said, 'with all the skills of a natural mechanic. Like any good mechanic he'd got that ability to work out how things worked just by looking at them.' But it was a competitive field and it was another of the great traction-engine pioneers, John Fowler, who became the most successful exponent of steam cultivation. Fred explained:

> Another gentleman called John Fowler, who founded his famous firm in Leeds, had grand ideas of ploughing by steam. He was one of the first to see the potential of developing a small portable steam engine for use in agriculture and he manufactured some of the first steam-powered ploughs and threshing machines. During a period of more than 30 years he made the construction and use of traction engines his special study, carrying out the most extensive and exhaustive experiments regardless of expense.

Fowler was born in Wiltshire in 1826, the third son of a wealthy

Quaker merchant. When he was young he gained valuable experience in farming methods that was particularly useful later on in his life when he became a pioneer of mechanized agriculture. He joined a firm of general engineers in Middlesbrough, where his thoughts first turned to the mechanization of agriculture after he saw the terrible consequences of famine in Ireland after two years of failed potato crops. He believed that conditions might be improved by better land drainage and gave up his job, determined to mechanize drainage by the use of steam. The result was his Mole Drainage Plough, shown at the Great Exhibition of 1851 and built for him by another of the great agricultural engineering companies, J. R. & A. Ransome of Ipswich, pioneers in the field of traction-engine development. This 'mole drainer' was a great shell-shaped piece of iron with a knife on it. The knife was stuck down into the ground and dragged through the clay by brute force. It cut a slot in the clay and left a round hole in it down below. This created drains under heavily clayed land.

The principle was sound but dragging it directly through the ground was heavy work for a team of horses, so another means of traction needed to be found. What Fowler came up with was a double winch, each half of which could be powered by a portable engine. The rope from one winch barrel was led, via an anchored pulley, to the front of the plough, while the rope from the other passed round a pulley anchored at the opposite end of the field. This second rope only served to return the plough to its starting point before making another working pull. Fowler realized that this power could be applied to more general ploughing for cultivation, but there were snags. First, it was a very cumbersome apparatus and, although this was acceptable for the one-off operation of land drainage, it was too slow for routine cultivation. Secondly, it was going to be necessary to develop some form of two-way plough to get round the problem of the time-and-energy wasting return pull. Fowler's solution was what became known as the balanced plough, which consisted of a see-saw frame with a central two-wheeled axle as its pivot. On this frame he mounted two sets of ploughs. They could be brought into action alternately by tilting the frame, thus eliminating the need to turn a single plough at the end of each furrow.

A portable steam engine, being used with ploughing
tackle to draw a plough, *c.* 1860

In 1858 Fowler was awarded the £500 prize offered by the Royal Agricultural Society of England for his balance plough. He was said to have spent ten times the amount of the prize money on his experiments to produce it. His first successful ploughing engine was built for him by Clayton & Shuttleworth. After this, however, sets of ploughing tackle were built for him by several different contractors until he set up on his own in Leeds in the 1860s. Fowler continued with his double-barrelled winch and anchor pulley system for several years, mainly because he was anxious to evolve a system of cultivation that could be powered by an ordinary portable farm engine and so brought within the financial reach of the average farmer. Eventually, however, he had to give up this idea and he mounted his double winch beneath the boiler barrel of the engine, which drove it through gears and a vertical shaft. But this engine still required the use of an anchor pulley so Fowler abandoned the system in favour of two engines. Fred explained how the system worked:

Fowler was highly successful in introducing pairs of traction engines standing one on each side of a field. The earliest ploughing engines were weird things – basically a portable engine with a great winding drum under the boiler. They were driven by gearing from the crankshaft and an endless wire rope going all the way round a field, supported by anchors which had big bobbins for the rope to go round. Each one was equipped below the belly of the machine with a huge revolving drum, which could take up to 800 yards of metal rope. Each engine pulled in turn to draw a simple plough across the field. At the end of each line the plough was lifted out of the soil and a second one put in before that was dragged back across the field in the opposite direction. It must've taken a long time to set one of these things up and it needed a lot of men.

The Fowler system made it possible to plough more deeply than they had been able to do before without compressing the soil with heavy wheels. The trouble was that the engines were expensive to buy and fuel costs were high, but the results were impressive. The early ploughing engines had no steering gear. Instead a pair of shafts was fixed to the front of the engine, and the machine was guided by good old-fashioned horsepower. But farmers soon demanded a change to the nuisance of using a horse when they had paid a lot of money for the new steam technology, so the ploughing engine was given its own steering. Steam ploughing was a revolution. It was reckoned that a man and two horses working a 54-hour week would plough an acre a day. But with steam power, using two engines, five men and a water-cart boy plus a horse for pulling the water cart, the average was 15 acres a day.

Steam ploughing had great advantages over horses, particularly on heavy clay lands, because there was enough power to break up the soil thoroughly, making for easier harrowing and drilling. It also helped with drainage if horses did not walk in the furrows and compact the soil. While Fowler was working on his system, Aveling continued to develop plough tackle and advertised single-engine plough sets, consisting of one locomotive, a balance plough or cultivator and a detached winding windlass with 1,600 yards of steel cable. But he soon realized that Fowler's double-engine system was superior and he adopted that. The only difference was that the Aveling & Porter engines were generally smaller than Fowler's. There were only a handful of competitors, including Fowler, Charles Burrell, J. & H. Maclaren of Leeds and John Allen & Sons of Oxford. Fowler's engines came to dominate the field, but Aveling's plough tackle was successful in the late 1860s and 1870s and success in ploughing trials at Beauvais in France led to orders from Napoleon III. The two-engine ploughing set was far too expensive for all but the biggest farmers so steam ploughing, like threshing, became a job for the contractor. Fred explained:

> The look of the landscape began to change, with smoke rising from the green fields. Generally the ploughing and threshing was done by teams of enginemen brought in seasonally by agricultural contractors. Steam began to be applied to other uses on the land: drying grain, cooking animal food and above all drainage. When you go to places like Lincolnshire have you ever wondered about the size of all those monster fields and all dead flat? I think most of that really, apart from God's

efforts in making it reasonably flat, is ploughing up and cultivating. That was nearly all done by big companies that owned as many as 20 sets of ploughing engines. Forty engines must've been a lot of expense when you first bought them.

Aveling's biggest seller was his 'general-purpose engine'. These were the most common types of engines to be seen in the countryside. They were basically used as a mobile power plant for threshing, tree-pulling and general farm duties. As in so many other areas of engineering, in the middle of the nineteenth century Britain led the world and orders began to flood in to Aveling & Porter, not just from Britain but from Prussia and Australia. 'What a time it must have been,' Fred always used to say, 'when Britain's engineers and mechanics were all looked up to. I think I'd like to have lived then, you know, when we made all these beautiful engines and sold them all over the world. Can you imagine going to work every morning and making these things? It would have been quite a pleasurable do.'

Engines built by Aveling's for Australia, capable of hauling six wagons of five or six tons each, cost £530 but they reduced the costs of transportation dramatically. From the copper mines to the port, the use of the Aveling & Porter engines brought the cost down from £10 to £2 per ton. In 1864 one of their road engines, *El Buey*, which was made for the Traction Engine Company of Buenos Aires, hauled a load of 28 tons up Star Hill in Rochester – 305 yards long, with an incline of 1 in 12. Early Aveling & Porter traction engines were 'chain engines', which used chains to drive the wheels rather than gears. The same basic design was used in road rollers and in chain-drive tram locomotives built during the 1860s.

According to one story, Aveling got the idea for traction-engine-type tramway locomotives from Charles Beadle, an Erith coal merchant. Beadle had been supplying coal to a paper mill at St Mary Cray, hauling it in trailers from the quayside at Erith with an Aveling road locomotive. When he acquired his own wagons on the railway that ran from Erith to St Mary Cray, he had no further use for the road locomotive so he claimed to have fitted flanged wheels to it and used it for shunting on his sidings. This was the sort of mechanical ingenuity and inventiveness that appealed so much to Fred.

Aveling heard about Beadle's adaptation of his engine and proceeded to produce his own tramway locomotive. The first, No. 132, was supplied to John Tilden and Company of Lambs Walk Chalkworks, Greenhithe, in December 1864. Another was ordered the following year and several were supplied to the Admiralty for work at Chatham Dockyard. The engine weighed nine tons and had a single cylinder on top of the boiler. This was surrounded by a steam jacket, as in Aveling's other engines. It had a piston diameter of 10 inches and a stroke of 12 inches and it was fitted with link-motion reverse gearing. The carrying wheels were four feet in diameter and the leading axle passed under the barrel of the boiler, with the trailing one placed behind the firebox casing. They were made of cast iron with steel tyres. The boiler was an ordinary locomotive boiler, containing 60 tubes. Fuel was carried in a coal bunker on the footplate behind the firebox and the engine carried 350 gallons of water in two tanks. It was basically a traction engine placed upon railway wheels so that it could run along a track.

Aveling's tram locomotives could be made to almost any gauge, which greatly increased their market potential. One for a 3-foot-gauge tramway went to Brisbane and one for a 5-foot 6-inch gauge tramway was made for India. In reality the locomotives were little more than traction engines with buffers front and back. They had an advantage over conventional railway locomotives in that they had flywheels that could be used to drive all sorts of machinery, including stone crushers and grinding mills, when they were not in use as locomotives. As a result they found employment in quarries and brickworks. At Gray's Chalk Quarry four engines were capable of taking 20 loaded wagons up the bank. Two of the engines replaced two earlier locomotives and the resultant saving was substantial. They could also be used as ordinary portable engines for working pumps. A contemporary description of an Aveling tram engine stated:

This locomotive, which weighs 12 tons, has wrought steel brackets flanged upwards and outwards above the firebox thus giving ample room for the gear, which is all within the brackets, the eccentrics being next to them, and the valve facings of the castings contain the high and low pressure cylinder. The engine has a short wheelbase, all four wheels couple-driven by a large steel idle wheel on the off side. She is capable of a speed of 16 mph and ascends a gradient of 1 in 15 with a load of 30 tons with ease, passing also with smoothness the sharpest of curves . . . The cost is only two thirds that of the ordinary contractor's engine, whilst there is the advantage not possessed by the ordinary locomotive of an engine with accessible crankshaft and flywheel for belt driving of pumps, stonebreakers, circular saws and other fixed equipment.

The engines were particularly well adapted for use in quarries and similar places where heavy loads had to be moved at slow speeds, and in such situations they did the work at about half the cost of horse-power. In spite of this the design was quickly abandoned as technology advanced, but several hundred were built and sent all over the world. Out of all these, only one is known to exist today. It is Aveling's 0-4-0 tram engine built in 1872, which can now be seen at the London Transport Museum in Covent Garden. This is the world's oldest surviving traction engine. The features you see on it were standard for the next 60 years. Gear drive was now the rule rather than the exception, steering was by chain and bobbin, water tanks were an integral part of the engine and coal was carried in a bunker behind the driver.

Transport by rail had been revolutionized by the invention of the railway locomotive and it seemed logical that steam power should be used for transport on the roads. Although there had been experiments with steam carriages and steam buses as far back as Richard Trevithick's *Puffing Devil* in 1801, the agricultural traction engine was the first type of mechanically propelled vehicle to appear on British roads in any numbers. In 1865 Aveling & Porter produced more of the machines than all the other British manufacturers combined, but opposition to steam road locomotives was still strong.

Great pre-Victorian engineers like Thomas Telford had given Britain a network of metalled roads and a huge and flourishing coaching industry had developed to carry passengers and mail along these roads. With the development of the traction engine, the powerful vested interests of coach proprietors and horse dealers played upon the conservatism of public opinion by exaggerating the dangers of steam vehicles on the roads. Pedestrians would, they claimed, be mangled under the wheels of the fiery monsters, crops growing in the fields by the roadside would be burnt by flying cinders or they would wither and die, and animals would be frightened. Opposition also came from many of the Turnpike Trusts, bodies that had been set up by Act of Parliament to collect tolls for maintaining the roads, who claimed that road locomotives would damage road surfaces.

The notorious Locomotive Acts of 1865 imposed a speed limit of 2 mph in town and 4 mph in the country. Another clause required the locomotive to consume its own smoke. They also insisted on three men to work an engine, one driving, one steering and the third walking in front with a red flag. The Red Flag Act, as it became known, also laid down that any damage done to the roads by a traction engine had to be paid for by the engine's owner – whereas if damage was done by horses pulling an engine no one was liable. Aveling spent a lot of time in court, helping to defend cases against locomotive owners and opposing turnpike trusts and highway boards who were attempting to ban road locomotives. In spite of the opposition there was no stopping the traction engine and they continued to sell, mainly because their cost for the transportation of heavy loads was equivalent to half that of horse-drawn wagons.

By the late 1860s the military establishment was becoming increasingly interested in the possibilities presented by the traction engine for hauling artillery. Under the headline 'Aveling Traction Engines haul artillery into position', the *Illustrated London News* reported that

> during the Easter Volunteer Review, a combined assault by land and sea was made on Dover Castle. An outstanding event of the review was the operation which was performed on the Saturday, of drawing a battery of guns from the railway station up Castle Hill by means of two of the patent traction engines of Messrs Aveling & Porter, Rochester, who were able to

send them over to France in the way of business, and having them ready at Dover, lent them for this purpose as a trial of their powers.

Soon after this, a government committee was set up to consider military applications of the traction engine and Aveling & Porter were commissioned to construct an engine suitable for hauling siege guns into position. The company produced the first 'Steam Sapper' in 1870, but it was too heavy. In 1871 a lighter engine, 'Sapper No. 2', was constructed. At 6 hp it was the lightest engine of its power that had ever been built and at its trials it pulled a 15½-ton load up Star Hill, Rochester. After this the army bought many 'Sappers' for haulage purposes. One of these was a convertible that could be converted from a road to a tramway locomotive. 'Sappers' were also used at camps for pumping water and a number saw service in the Boer War.

Possibly the best known of all steam engines built for the road is the steamroller, and it was Aveling who designed and built the first roller to be used in Britain in 1865. He could see that the existing roads needed better surfaces for the wheeled vehicles of the time which were constantly increasing in weight to haul ever-heavier loads. It is believed that he turned his attention to road rollers because of the poor condition of the roads in Kent, on which he had to transport his engines and farm products. Although he was responsible for many developments on the General Purpose Traction Engine, Aveling & Porter are best known for their production of steamrollers. It became Aveling's most famous product and no fewer than 8,600 were built, around two-thirds of the total number of engines constructed by the company. They were really an adaptation of the traction engine, with many common components, and in the last years of manufacture convertible engines were built that could be used as traction engines or steamrollers. Its design, however, had one important variation in that it used a very heavy flywheel that was quite different to anything used in chain-drive traction engines.

The idea for a steam-propelled road roller had already been tried out in France and India. Two French firms built rollers that were tested in the Bois de Boulogne, Paris, in 1860 and 1861. The first steamroller to be built in Britain was a huge machine weighing around 30 tons and designed by W. Clark, chief engineer of the Municipality of Calcutta, and the inventor William Batho of Birmingham. It was shipped to India in 1863, where it worked successfully. Aveling's early rollers were built in collaboration with Batho and are usually known as Batho rollers. Basically they took a traction engine and put two conical-shaped rollers with a central pivot on it instead of front wheels. The trouble was that the conical-shaped rollers had a nasty sliding effect. So they then developed a pair of front forks and two rollers. Steering was by means of a ship's wheel operating a chain to the steering roll.

The best-known Batho roller is Aveling & Porter No. 1, the famous 'Liverpool Roller', the first production road roller in the world, built in 1867. It weighed 30 tons and had a 500-gallon water tank. The order came from the Corporation of Liverpool, where the borough engineer said it led to a great improvement in the management of the streets. Aveling & Porter's first rollers were tested in Hyde Park, London, and in Rochester and Chatham. The Hyde Park trials were recorded in the *Illustrated London News*:

> The use of steam rollers for the purpose of crushing stones and smoothing the surface of our macadamized roads has long been advocated one of the most desirable metropolitan improvements. Though we must wait a little longer before we see these effective and economical machines employed in the streets of London, it is satisfactory to observe that the First Commission of Her Majesty's Works has resolved to give them a trial in the parks and one has been doing good service in Hyde Park during the last two or three weeks, to the admiration of numerous spectators.

Enquiries for a further 20 of these machines led to the setting-up of a production line and by the end of 1869 ten of these machines had been exported to the USA, France and India. The first engine exported to America went to Central Park, New York, where the park commissioners reported that the machine had given great satisfaction in rolling macadamized roads and had been very economical, rolling in one day at a cost of 10 dollars as much as was accomplished in two days by a seven-ton roller pulled by eight horses at 20 dollars per day. But the 30-ton roller soon proved to be too heavy so Aveling turned his attention to developing one which was lighter and more manoeuvrable. His patent roller No. 509 of 1871 featured chain-operated front-roll steering. The front rolls were conical in shape and provision was made for them to be able to adjust to the contours of the road. This roller won for Aveling the Order of Franz Joseph at the Vienna Universal Exhibition of 1873.

While he was developing the steamroller the ever-inventive Aveling produced another variant on the traction engine. This was a small engine fitted with a crane and it was named 'Little Tom'. He did further work on the design and by 1874 he had developed an improved version capable of lifting up to two tons. It had wrought-iron wheels with compensating motion for turning sharp bends without disconnecting either wheel. This meant that both could be kept in gear at the same time, which helped to prevent any slipping. The engine could be driven and steered and the crane could be operated from the footplate by one person. It was another winner for Aveling when it was awarded a special gold medal by the Royal Agricultural Society in 1876 and a gold medal at the Paris Universal Exhibition in 1878. The company now devoted itself almost exclusively to the manufacture of traction engines, ploughing engines and steam road rollers and was granted numerous patents.

As the traction engine developed, further improvements were made. The portable engine had the cylinder block over the top of the firebox, which is the hottest part of the engine, and the crankshaft supported on two brackets just behind the funnel at the front end. But there was a problem with this as the thrust of the connecting rods on the crankshaft, which was doing the driving, wrenched away at the studs that held the brackets to the boiler barrel at the coldest end of the boiler. This would often cause horrible leaks. 'So Aveling,' Fred explained,

invented things called horn plates. He riveted two extra plates to each side of the firebox and formed a sort of a box above it that contained all the castings with the bearings in and the actual crank and some of the gearing that then went down to the back axle. This arrangement avoided the stress previously applied to the boiler plates and the leakages and corrosion around the bolt holes that resulted from this. It also made the whole rear end of a traction engine very strong and enabled them to put a lot of nuts and bolts through the boiler to hold the cylinder block on, which meant that because there was a horizontal push it didn't spring as many leaks at the front end.

The first locomotive to carry this invention was exhibited at the Royal Show, Oxford, in 1870. As well as the horn plates, it also incorporated a geared rather than a chain drive and had conventional front-wheel steering. In the same year a simplified link-motion reversing gear was introduced.

Aveling's achievements were further recognized at the Royal Agricultural Society show at Wolverhampton in 1871, when he won the £50 prize for the best Agricultural Locomotive Engine with a 10-horsepower model, and a silver medal for a 6-horsepower engine. Away from the works he began to take a leading role in local politics and was active in promoting the Liberal cause. He represented the Strood and Frindsbury Ward on Rochester Council and was mayor in 1869–70. One of his greatest concerns was to make improvements to the embankment of the River Medway on the Strood side, and he had a hand in laying out the Rochester Castle Gardens. He also had a great interest in education and sat for several years on the Rochester School Board. He was a supporter of the 1870 Education Act and a keen advocate of children being taught practical skills that would be of use to them if they followed their fathers into manual work. He was also anxious that the provision of education shouldn't be too heavy a burden on the poorer classes. As an employer he was a hard taskmaster, always expecting high standards and keeping only the best men. In common with a lot of paternalistic Victorian employers he provided them with facilities, particularly for improving recreational activities. He was particularly keen on keeping them out of public houses and with this object he opened a lecture room for his workers where talks were given on educational, social and political subjects. Aveling himself took the chair at these gatherings and his workers were encouraged to take part in the discussions. At the works he built a large mess room that was fitted with cooking stoves for men to use during their breaks.

Throughout his life Aveling continued to improve the design and performance of the traction engine. In 1878 he took out another patent for an arrangement of gearing that involved all gears being placed between the bearings rather than being overhung as they had been previously. This made the engine stronger, narrower and more compact. The company made other essential equipment including water carts and the travelling living vans that traction enginemen slept in by the side of the road when they were on a long journey. Aveling's standard timber-built living van could accommodate six men. It had a day compartment with a cooking stove, cupboards for food and crockery, a table and seating. A partition opened up a sleeping compartment that held six bunks. The firm also manufactured wagons that carried four or six tons. The wheels were made of cast iron and wood and it was possible to drop the sides and the tail. Aveling also tried to develop a steam reaping machine that was propelled and carried by one of his crane engines. A model was tested in 1871, but it does not appear to have been a commercial success. Another example of Aveling & Porter's engineering skills can be seen in the massive covered slips at Chatham Dockyard. These Leviathans of steel were built before the great London train sheds and are understood to be the oldest and largest steel-framed structures still in existence.

Aveling also continued to make improvements to the steamroller and in 1880 he designed an improved front-roll assembly that became universally adopted. He made the front rolls parallel rather than conical by mounting a vertical pivot pin to carry a steering fork which spanned the rollers. This in turn provided a mounting for the axles and steering chains. Single-cylindered engines consumed a lot of coal and water and it was Aveling, virtually simultaneously with John Fowler, who first introduced the compounding system. This used the steam twice, first in a small cylinder at high pressure and then in a large cylinder at a lower pressure. It was then expelled up the chimney, pulling the draught through the fire to make it burn well. This development was introduced on both traction engines and steamrollers in 1881 by both Aveling and Fowler.

Aveling was elected to the Council of the Royal Agricultural Society of England in 1875 and served on its Implement, Chemical, Education and Showyard Contracts Committees. His major contribution to the society involved pushing through and overseeing the building of a chemical laboratory. He was also chairman of the mid-Kent branch of the Farmers' Alliance and a member of the Institution of Civil Engineers. Yachting was his favourite relaxation and he was active in the management of the Royal Victoria, Royal Cinque Ports and other yacht clubs. But it was an interest that was to cost him his life. He died on 7 March 1882 at the age of 58, after contracting a chill that turned into pneumonia aboard his new 28-ton yacht, *Sally*. His place as head of the firm was taken by his son Thomas Lake Aveling and under his management the firm continued to expand.

The company had employed about 400 men in 1872 but by 1895 this had grown to 750. Traction and other engines took second place to steamrollers and Aveling & Porter carried on manufacturing rollers until after the Second World War. Many remained in service well into the 1960s and today outnumber all other kinds of preserved steam engines. All surviving traction engines, road locomotives and steamrollers are more or less based on the Aveling patents. It was Aveling's designs that made mechanical road transport possible and created the modern highways that we take for granted today. 'Without the steamroller,' Fred said, 'roads could never have been made suitable for high-speed mechanically propelled vehicles. Every nation seemed to buy one of ours and if you look at pictures of foreign road rollers they have all got Fowler or Aveling similarities. It is as though they bought an Aveling, pulled it to pieces and then used all the bits to create a similar sort of style.'

Despite all the advances that had been made, however, the railways overshadowed road transport for the rest of the nineteenth century. Steam locomotives for use on roads continued to be developed but they couldn't compete with the railways. One of the reasons was that road owners charged heavy tolls for a road locomotive to use the turn-pikes. These could be up to 15 times the toll for a horse-drawn vehicle. But this wasn't the only reason. The main one was that these vehicles were simply not good enough to compete with the railways. Rails could bear much heavier weights than the roads and steam locomotives on rails could pull far more carriages and wagons than a road locomotive could. In the later part of the nineteenth century the railway network continued to grow and this began to pose even greater challenges for the railway engineers. Bridge-building in particular became more daring and dramatic, leading to the greatest disaster in the history of British civil engineering and the greatest triumph of Victorian engineering – the construction of the iconic Forth Railway Bridge by the Scottish engineer William Arrol.

11

William Arrol
1839–1913
The Pinnacle of Victorian Engineering

William Arrol was a great Scottish civil engineer and bridge builder, and the man responsible for some of the most advanced bridges and cranes in the UK and around the world. He revolutionized the art of bridge-building with his great innovation, which involved building the structure on land then rolling it out, span by span, to the place to be bridged. The Forth Railway Bridge, Tay Bridge and Tower Bridge in London are among his most famous constructions. Machinery was his bent and wherever possible machinery took the place of hand labour because it was much more accurate and it made it a lot faster to get a job done. He was also very inventive and he designed the riveting machines that were used to build the Forth Bridge. When this monumental feat of structural engineering opened in 1890 it must have seemed like one of the great wonders of the world.

William Arrol was born in Houston, Renfrewshire, in 1839. His father was a cotton spinner who later became a manager at J. & P. Coats, the thread manufacturers in Paisley. It was a good job that provided a reasonable living for his family but they were not well off and from the age of nine William had to combine working as a piecer in a bobbin mill in Johnstone with his schooling. But William didn't like factory work and when he was 14 he started a four-year apprenticeship as a blacksmith with Reid's of Paisley, studying mechanics and hydraulics at night school at the same time. He was keen to get as much experience as he could, so, once he finished his apprenticeship, he decided to ply his trade as a journeyman blacksmith in different towns throughout Scotland and England for a further six years.

At the age of 24, Arrol returned to Glasgow where he was appointed foreman in the bridge and boiler departments in the Bridgeton works of Laidlaw and Sons on the eastern edge of the city. Three years later, in 1866, while he was at Laidlaw's, he was handed responsibility for the construction of the West Pier at Brighton, but Arrol had greater ambitions and, not content with his rapid rise in his chosen trade, he set up in business for himself in 1868 on his life savings of £85. He started out on a small site in Bridgeton, not far from Laidlaw's, and here he took on general blacksmithing work, repairing machinery and boiler-making. He never turned down a job and his philosophy was simple: 'I look for work because I want to do it,' he once said. 'I stick to it because I like it; and I always do it as well and as quickly as I can.' With this philosophy it wasn't long before his order book was so full that he needed larger premises and he began constructing the wide-span, steel and glass workshops of the Dalmarnock Ironworks in the east end of Glasgow in 1871. His design for the works gave it the height and strength he needed for the sort of large-scale engineering contracts he had set his sights on and for the machinery he would need to fulfil them.

In 1875 he undertook his first major construction, when he won the contract to build a bridge over the River Clyde at Bothwell for the North British Railway. He had never built a bridge before, but this did not deter him. In the late 1870s he founded William Arrol & Co. and secured a second bridge contract, this one for another crossing over the Clyde leading to Glasgow Central Station for the Caledonian Railway. Arrol was a great innovator and he demonstrated his inventiveness in the way he tackled these first two bridges. Until this time all bridges had been constructed on site but his iron bridge at Bothwell was built on land before it was rolled into place as a complete structure.

His Caledonian Railway Bridge at Glasgow Central was a major engineering project, with cylinders made of some of the largest castings that had ever been seen. During its construction Arrol invented a mechanical driller and a hydraulic riveter, which proved successful and brought great savings in time and money on the project. The Caledonian Railway's constructing engineer, Benjamin Blyth, was impressed, and he drew particular attention to Arrol's inventiveness. When the bridge opened, the railway's chairman expressed the hope that Arrol might establish his reputation with the success of this 'great engineering undertaking'. The chairman's hope was soon to be realized and the 1880s saw Arrol embark on the construction of three iconic bridges that established his reputation as one of Britain's greatest engineering contractors.

During the Victorian era, engineers and their locomotives were virtually unstoppable; when faced with any obstacle they would construct a bridge or tunnel or cut an embankment. As a result, as the nineteenth century progressed, bridge-building became ever more daring and dramatic. The North British Railway controlled the route from Carlisle to Edinburgh but to reach Dundee and Aberdeen it had to cross the two great estuaries of the Forth and Tay. Plans were drawn up for bridges by the eminent engineer Thomas Bouch, whose ambition was to build the world's two biggest railway bridges. He undoubtedly saw himself in the role of the heroic engineer. His Tay Bridge was to be a long, narrow single track made up of 89 girders of varying lengths sitting on piers and running 100 feet above the high-water mark. For the crossing of the Forth, Bouch proposed two suspension bridges linked together on an island in the centre of the estuary. Although it was shorter, the Forth Bridge's dimensions dwarfed those of the Tay. The widest span on the Tay Bridge was 240 feet while each Forth Bridge span would be 1,500 feet and the Forth's height was five times greater. The Tay, thanks to the efforts of Dundonian merchants, was the first to be built and Bouch's 'Beautiful Railway Bridge of the Silvery Tay' was opened in 1878. With a length of over two miles the Tay Bridge was the longest railway bridge in the world, but it was soon to earn a place of notoriety in the history of British civil engineering.

In 1879 Bouch's plans and specifications for his bridge over the Forth were completed and, fresh from his triumph on the Caledonian Bridge, Arrol secured the contract to construct the bridge foundations and superstructure. The foundation stone was laid on 30 September and construction work began immediately at Queensferry, on the south bank of the Forth. Bouch was now at the pinnacle of his career. His Tay Bridge, the longest railway bridge in the world, had been open for a year and his plans for the Forth Bridge, the largest in the world, were hailed by members of the engineering profession for their innovation and daring. *The Times* called the bridge 'the most remarkable application of the suspension principle in the world'. Bouch's place in the hall of fame of heroic Victorian engineers looked assured – but then disaster struck. On a stormy night in December 1879 the unthinkable happened and the Tay Bridge collapsed as a train was going across. The engine and its carriages plummeted into the river below and all 75 people on board lost their lives. The disaster shocked the nation. It was one of the worst in British railway history and an inquiry concluded that it was caused by faults in the design, construction and maintenance of the bridge.

The disaster and resulting loss of confidence in Bouch's plans put paid to any ideas he had for constructing the Forth Bridge. His plans were scrapped. Although it wasn't his fault, it was a financial catastrophe for Arrol as his sub-contractors had to be paid for supplying and fabricating parts for him. Substantial sums were needed. Eventually it was agreed that the bridge company would pay for all the materials on site and award him £27,500 in compensation for breach of contract. Forty per cent of this was to be treated as payment on account if he was awarded the contract for a new bridge over the Tay, and a further 35 per cent if he was awarded the contract for a newly designed Forth Bridge within five years.

Soon afterwards the works at Queensferry were suspended and the Forth Bridge workmen were dismissed. Bouch died in 1880 at the age of 58. It has been suggested that he may have had a heart condition, and overwork and stress certainly contributed to his early death. One of Bouch's designs had been for an iron viaduct near Montrose. The

South.Esk Bridge was built at the same time as the Tay Bridge. At the time of the disaster it hadn't been given its passenger certificate. When it was inspected it was found that the bridge deviated from the approved plans so much that it had to be taken down and rebuilt. The reconstruction of the bridge was put out to tender and Arrol won the contract. It was here, in the strong currents of the South Esk, that he pioneered a method of construction using a four-legged pontoon or construction platform which he had designed. It was the prototype for the platforms he was to use when he secured the contract to rebuild the Tay Bridge, which was now under the direction of William Barlow as consultant engineer.

The future of the east coast route, however, looked uncertain. The Tay Bridge disaster appeared to have confirmed nature's supremacy over the engineers but the east coast railway barons were determined to have their line. The Tay Bridge, they decided, would be reconstructed with William Arrol as contractor, and later he would take on the colossal bridge over the Forth, whose design was being thoroughly reappraised by the Forth Bridge Railway Company in the light of the tragedy on the Tay. Arrol put in a tender to construct the new bridge over the Tay and this was accepted in October 1881. He was to say later that securing this contract was the proudest moment of his life, but in the months between the Tay Bridge contract being signed and the Board of Trade permitting work to be started, there was a dispute about the removal of the old bridge. Arrol made good use of the time, drawing up detailed plans for the job, calculating all the components that would be needed and identifying what machinery he would require. There was little evidence of this preparatory work in Dundee, however, and rumours began to circulate that the bridge project had been cancelled. When Arrol was informed of this, he replied that his men were working day and night preparing the appliances necessary to carry out the work. About a dozen steam cranes were being built, he said, 'so that when the works are commenced, they will be carried out at all possible speed'.

Arrol now began to plan the layout of four acres of land on the north bank of the Tay Estuary between the arches of the viaduct that the railway ran on as it approached the bridge. Here he built a railway line and siding so that he could bring materials as close to the construction site as possible. He also erected a large workshop here and converted the arches of the viaduct into others. On the south side he built an enormous jetty out into the river and erected a cement store. To finance this he requested and received a cash advance. A completion date for the new bridge was now agreed for the end of 1885.

Construction work on the Tay Bridge began with a blast of rock for the foundations on 30 June 1882. When work on the bridge itself started, the first job was to sink the caisson foundations.* These would take up the greatest amount of time and effort and the major share of the finance. There were 86 pairs of caissons altogether and Arrol's plan was to sink pairs of caissons in three different places simultaneously. To get the machinery he needed to do this out into the river, he built floating construction platforms. Each of these platforms or pontoons was made up of five waterproof flotation tanks with four wrought-iron tubular legs, 60 feet long. When it had been floated into position the legs of the pontoon were extended hydraulically down to the river bed. The pontoon was more than just a platform; it was a mid-river construction site manned by 20 men, divided into day and night shifts. On it there were three steam cranes, a concrete-mixing machine, steam engines to power the excavating machines and a bothy where the men could shelter and take their meal breaks. Two large holes 25 feet square at the centre of each pontoon were designed to carry a pair of caissons. These were assembled on the shore, lifted into place in the holes and suspended there while the pontoon was towed to its mid-river site.

Once they were in the right place, the insides of the wrought-iron caissons were lined with brick. This was done a section at a time and as each stage was completed, the caisson was lowered hydraulically through the hole in the base of the pontoon. Then another stage of iron and brick was added on top,† and the process would be repeated until the caissons touched the bottom. Once they were on the river

---

* A caisson is a retaining, watertight structure used to work on the foundations of a bridge.
† Fred used much the same technique when he dug his mineshaft in his back garden.

bed, enough silt was extracted through the bottom of the caisson for it to sink down two feet.

The need for a bridge over the Forth as well as one over the Tay was quite simple. The North British Railway Company, whose main line between Edinburgh and Dundee was cut by the firths of Forth and Tay, was under pressure to bridge the gaps. Rail links across both of the estuaries had been seen as inevitable for a generation; the only things needed to make it happen were the technology and the materials. The technology was acquired painfully with the disaster on the Tay and the material, steel, had become available in quantity thanks to Bessemer's recently developed process. Stringent requirements were set for the new bridge design and the bridge that resulted was the greatest engineering wonder of the Victorian Age, incorporating two major innovations, the use of steel and the cantilever principle. It was to become the largest railway bridge ever built.

On 21 December 1882, soon after work on the Tay Bridge had started and almost three years to the day since the disaster, Arrol was awarded the contract for the Forth Bridge as part of a single project consortium with other contractors, after the directors of the newly formed Forth Bridge Company had invited the three lowest tenderers to consider whether they might be prepared to combine to build the bridge. When they agreed, the consortium they set up took the name Tancred Arrol and offered to build the bridge in a single contract for £1.6 million. The board accepted and an agreement was signed that the bridge would be built according to the design of John Fowler, the chief engineer. It was to be completed five years from the day of the contract – 21 December 1887.

Fowler was one of the best engineers of his time. He had started a railway construction business in 1841, building many of the small rail systems that were later combined into the Manchester, Sheffield & Lincolnshire Railway, and in 1861 he entered a long association with Benjamin Baker as consulting engineer. Together they designed the London Metropolitan Railway and Victoria Station; they oversaw pioneering work on the development of the London Underground and they built many bridges, including the Pimlico bridge that carried the first railway across the Thames in 1860. Their expertise took them all over the world. Fowler was general engineering adviser to the viceroy of Egypt and Baker was consulting engineer for the Hudson River Tunnel in New York and the Aswan Dam in Egypt. He also worked on St Enoch's Station in Glasgow and, on the death of Brunel, he became consulting engineer to the Great Western Railway.

Although Fowler was the chief engineer, the Forth Bridge was largely the work of his junior partner, Benjamin Baker. Baker had a flair for engineering design and an understanding of materials that he'd picked up when serving an apprenticeship at the South Wales Ironworks at Neath Abbey. He combined a reputation for sound theory with great practicality and he and Arrol enjoyed a particularly good rapport. They were about the same age and both had done metalwork apprenticeships. But then, while Arrol was building up his fabrication business, Baker was gaining an international reputation for research into the properties of materials on long-span bridges and on the strength of beams, columns, arches and brickwork.

Fowler and Baker's plan was to build the biggest railway bridge in the world – not with iron, but with the relatively new material of steel. The Forth Bridge was the first to use the new steel produced by the Siemens open-hearth process and it was designed using the most thorough structural analysis possible. The bridge is an enormous cantilever construction with 1,700-foot main spans – a world record for many years. It consists of three double cantilevers known as the Queensferry, Inchgarvie and Fife cantilevers. This steel colossus, the like of which had never been seen before, rose above the waters of the Firth of Forth between 1883 and 1890.

'The engineers with their gigantic works sweep everything before them in this Victorian era,' Benjamin Baker declared. But in Fred's opinion the Tay Bridge disaster was the reason why the Forth Bridge was so grossly over-engineered. The builders of the Forth Bridge certainly took extraordinary precautions to allay the public anxiety that lingered for a long time after the collapse of the Tay Bridge. Stringent safety margins incorporated into the design were tested on models under different conditions, including the extreme of simulated hurricanes in a wind tunnel. Since the fatal failure of the Tay Bridge had been its inability to withstand excessive wind pressure, the tests on the Forth Bridge models were calculated to allow for maximum rigidity of the bridge structure under the vertical stress of a fully loaded moving trainload and under the horizontal stress of wind pressure up to hurricane force.

Great effort was also put into ensuring that at all stages of construction the unfinished structure would be as invincible to the elements as the completed structure. Every stage of the work was to provide a secure base from which the next stage could proceed.

The construction of the Forth Bridge fell into two parts. The years 1883 to 1885 were devoted to sinking the caissons and building the piers that would support the superstructure. Then between 1886 and 1890 the superstructure itself was constructed. Soon after contracts were signed, a start was made on work at both North and South Queensferry. Arrol spent the first six months on preparatory work, erecting temporary site buildings and inventing machinery. The riveting machines used on the Forth Bridge were of his own design, developed specifically to overcome the unique problems of building this huge structure.

Developing new tools and machinery was something he appears to have found very satisfying and he invented multiple drilling machines. His ingenuity was astonishing. To make the site operational, he had to demolish and relocate the coastguard station at North Queensferry in order to construct an enormous pier. He also built timber huts for the workmen, a canteen, stores, dining rooms and reading rooms. Further accommodation was added later as the workforce grew. On the South Queensferry shore he built a work yard with offices, workshops, furnaces, steam engines and cement stores as well as a sawmill, an accumulator for providing hydraulic power, an assembly plant, housing for the workers and their families and numerous huts and store rooms.

South Queensferry's sloping shore was terraced to provide land for what was known as the drilling yards. The steel plates used in the construction of the bridge were 16 feet long and 6 feet wide. These were delivered by train to the sidings at South Queensferry, where cranes would unload them and stack them beside the workshops for heating and pressing. They were lifted red hot from the furnaces and pressed into the right shape on hydraulic presses. When they had cooled down they were moved to the drill road for assembly into the tubes that made up the superstructure of the bridge. All the rivet holes were drilled here before the tube was disassembled ready for transport to site and re-assembly on the superstructure. It was like a giant Meccano set. To service the three principal workstations at North and South Queensferry and on the island of Inchgarvie, jetties were built for loading and unloading cranes and construction materials, and for mooring barges which were used to convey briggers* from the company's paddle steamer.

At the end of 1883 workmen's cottages on both sides of the Forth were filled to overflowing and work was well under way on the construction of the north and south masonry piers, which would support the approach viaducts, and on building the coffer dams and caissons. For all the innovations in its design, the superstructure of the bridge would only be as stable as the groups of four platforms on which the cantilevers would stand. Half of these were on dry land but the other six had to be built in caissons that were floated out to the site of the cantilever towers. These 400-ton, 70-foot diameter wrought-iron cylinders would provide a watertight box for underwater construction work.

The caissons for Inchgarvie and North Queensferry were already under construction on the beach at Queensferry. Only 18 months after the contract had been signed, the South West Queensferry caisson was launched on 26 May 1884 by the Countess of Aberdeen. The other five underwater caissons were soon floated out to the site of the future cantilever towers. Concrete was then poured into them until they sank to the bed of the estuary. A temporary coffer dam was built around the top of each caisson to enable work to be done there and down on the river bed a steel cutting edge around the inside of the circumference extended seven feet below the concrete floor. The water that

---

* The name given to the thousands of men who built the Forth Bridge.

was contained within this cutting edge between the concrete and the river bed was pumped out and replaced with compressed air to ensure that the pressure at that depth didn't allow the water to re-enter. Shafts, each with an airlock, led down through the concrete to what was now a working chamber, 70 feet wide and 7 feet high, where the diggers excavated the soil from the river bed. The workmen descended through the airlock on an iron ladder to excavate the base for each caisson. Once the mud and clay had been dug out, the giant under-water metal cylinder was lined with blue Staffordshire brick and filled with concrete. Then the cutting edge was driven further down into the river bed.

As the work in the caissons progressed, impromptu inventions had to be made to deal with problems as they arose. On one occasion the boulder clay on the bed was much harder than had been anticipated so Arrol invented a hydraulic spade that was capable of breaking it up, which none of the existing tools could do. It was operated by three men; two of them lifted it while the third fixed the head and turned the cock that admitted the water pressure. It was extremely unpleasant and arduous work in the compressed air of the seven-foot-high chamber on the river bed.

Arrol was well aware of the danger to men working in compressed air below sea level. He knew of the accidents during the construction of New York's Brooklyn Bridge and St Louis's Eads Bridge, where 16 men employed in the caisson foundation work died and another two were permanently crippled due to working in the dangerous atmos-phere created by the compressed air. Arrol organized his workforce so that men worked in shifts and the deeper the caisson, the shorter the shift. The shifts of the 27 men working in the South Queensferry caisson were limited to 6 hours and to 4 hours in the deeper, higher-pressure caisson off Inchgarvie, followed by 8 hours off. Working conditions were terrible and many of the diggers suffered acute pains in their arms and legs, accompanied in the worst cases by a kind of paralytic stroke once they had emerged from the airlock. Long exposure to these high pressures could sometimes lead to paralysis of nerves, causing workmen to walk awkwardly with a slight stoop and suffer violent cramps. Almost all the workers suffered from acute ear-ache and the deeper the caisson was sunk, the worse it got. Arrol himself suffered permanent partial deafness because he disregarded the time limit for staying down below.

Two men died during the caisson work on the Forth Bridge, but given the dangers of the job this relatively small number was a remark-able achievement, particularly as the men were literally digging away at the foundations on which they stood. If the caisson had sunk too quickly they would have been squashed between the river bed below and the thousands of tons of concrete above them. Arrol had every reason to be apprehensive because he knew the fate of the diggers in the caissons below the River Neva in St Petersburg, where one of the caissons suddenly sank 18 inches. Of the 28 men who were working in the chamber at the time, 9 were imprisoned and of these only 2 were taken out alive. The rest were smothered in mud.

In late 1884 the Forth Bridge contractors had to go to the bridge company to ask for extra capital to buy more machinery because expenditure so far had been in excess of what had been anticipated. When Fowler and Baker were sent to investigate, they found that the three contracting firms had not merged effectively into a single firm as they had agreed. Instead there were muddled lines of responsibility and Arrol's method of delegation that he had employed successfully on the Tay Bridge wasn't working across three firms with inevitable divided loyalties. Fowler and Baker laid down stringent conditions if they were to support the request for more money. The main one was that divided responsibility had to come to an end and Arrol was given control over the entire project. He had to appoint a general super-intendent of works who would oversee foremen, each of whom would have responsibility for particular parts of the construction. The inten-tion was to make a single efficient firm out of the three separate contracting companies.

The responsibility for the entire Scottish east coast line, through the simultaneous construction of the longest and the largest railway bridges in the world, was now in the hands of Arrol. On Fowler and Baker's recommendation, the bridge company agreed to provide a further £80,000 to Tancred Arrol for the purchase of plant, subject to audit of the contractor's accounts and the plant becoming the property of the railway company at the end of the project. The company then offered a bonus of £350,000 if the bridge opened to passenger traffic by October 1889. The contract required the contractor to take every care of the workers, containing a proviso that compensation for any accidents had to be deducted from his terminal bonus. So Arrol had a financial imperative to ensure the highest possible safety standards.

Risks were inevitable in constructing two bridges of this scale over water but Arrol was a paternalistic employer and he did all he could to minimize them. Many of his lesser-known inventions, such as riveters' cages, mobile furnaces to heat the rivets and movable working platforms, were devised to make conditions easier, more convenient and less dangerous for his workmen. During the five-year construction of the Tay Bridge there were only 14 deaths, mostly from drowning. On the Forth Bridge lighters were always on hand to rescue workers if they fell in the water and the company had its own doctors on site and ambulances to transport the men to hospital if their injuries were more serious. In 1876 Arrol had set up the Dalmarnock Accident Fund, to which the company contributed 11s 3d (56p) for each £100 of wages. The purpose of the fund was to cover doctors' fees, compensation, accident insurance and any other costs arising from an accident.

In 1884 Arrol established an annual Festival and Assembly of the Employees of Wm Arrol & Co. (Tay Bridge Works). This took place in the Thistle Hall, Dundee, and the workers and their families enjoyed a musical evening of singers, instrumentalists and a comic. He also organized twice-yearly regattas for the workers. Crews were made up either by the jobs they did, like riveters versus painters, or by the place on the bridge they worked, like pontoon men versus girder men. He clearly had a high regard for the men who took the risks and did all the hard work. When he received the Freedom of Dundee after the Tay Bridge had been completed he said of his workers:

When a skirmish takes place with a few half-starved Arabs, and the report of the engagement comes home, a great deal is said about the commanders and their conspicuous gallantry is painfully elaborated; but very little is said of poor Tommy Atkins except the list at the end of the story which gives the number of privates who have been killed or wounded. Now our working privates, like the other fighting privates, were the men upon whom it fell to do the business. They carried their lives in their hands for the better part of eight or nine years, and I think they are not to be passed over at the end of the battle as so many unimportant items in the camp of the commander.

With the two biggest projects in the history of British civil engineering up to that time, Arrol had given himself a massive workload. In the mid-1880s, when he was acting as contractor on the new Tay Bridge as well as the Forth, he rose at five o'clock each Monday morning at his Glasgow home to be at his nearby works at six to check on progress. He would then board the train for Edinburgh and the Forth Bridge, where he would work for the rest of Monday and Tuesday. On Tuesday evening he would catch the last train to Dundee to arrive there at 11 p.m. ready for work on the Tay Bridge at six the following morning. The Tay Bridge team met at dawn on the Wednesday and Arrol would spend the rest of the day inspecting the construction work. He would return to Glasgow late at night to be at his Dalmarnock works first thing the following morning. Then he would be off again to the Forth and the Tay before catching the North British sleeper from Edinburgh to London on Friday night for meetings with Fowler and Baker at their London offices on Saturday. This sort of work schedule would have been impossible for anybody who had a family life, but this wasn't the case with Arrol. His wife had become deranged soon after he married. There were no children so he was able to devote all his time to bridge-building.

While he was working on the Forth and Tay bridges he also won the contract for the construction of London's Tower Bridge, so he had to fit in a site meeting there first thing on Saturday morning. His work was now taking him much further afield and around the same time he secured a contract for a viaduct over the Hawkesbury River in New South Wales. With so many contracts, the Dalmarnock Ironworks was working at full capacity and Arrol left the daily running of it in the hands of his brother, James, assisted by a large staff of carefully selected foremen. Arrol's time had become very stretched but he was an excellent organizer and very good at delegating. With so little time to spend on each of his major construction projects, he organized his site staff on what he described as his one-man principle. This involved giving a particular man the responsibility for the success of the part of the work under his control.

By the beginning of 1886 the caisson work on the Forth Bridge had been completed and a large amount of material for the superstructure had been prepared. But, further north, progress on the Tay Bridge was slow. In the first six months Arrol's men managed to lay only seven caissons and foundations were not completely laid until the autumn of 1886. This delayed the bridge's completion until 18 months later than had originally been scheduled, even though Arrol had 700 men working on it day and night. Once each pair of caissons was in place, concrete was poured into them to make them solid so that brick columns could be built on top of them. Before these were begun, however, temporary girders were laid across them and loaded with cast-iron blocks to test their strength and stability. All this was done under the watchful eye of the Board of Trade. No chances were being taken with the foundations and none was being taken with the steelwork. Each section was temporarily erected at Dalmarnock, partially riveted together, then disassembled and transported by train to the bridge. The legs of the superstructure were bolted to their brick and concrete bases by eight 20-foot-long bolts. Then the final sections of the superstructure were lifted from barges into place on the piers by a five-ton steam crane.

Work was completed on the Tay Bridge in 1887. On Friday 10 June, the directors of the North British Railway, accompanied by engineers, officials and guests, travelled in a special train made up of two saloons first to inspect the partially completed Forth Bridge, then to go on through Fife to make the first crossing of the new Tay Bridge. The bridge opened for goods traffic the following Monday and was tested for passenger traffic later that week. Trains ran across at 40 mph and

Arrol walked slowly over the bridge inspecting the track. The bridge formally opened for passengers on Monday 20 June to coincide with the fiftieth anniversary of Queen Victoria's accession, and walking across the bridge was advertised as a Dundee tourist attraction.

Work continued on the Forth Bridge, where four columns of concrete faced with Aberdeen granite rose up from the waters where the caissons had been sunk for each of the towers. These were capped by the enormous steel base plates of the superstructure, held down by foundation bolts which went down to a depth of 26 feet within the foundation piers. The skewback, which was a multiple joint where ten separate structural members of the bridge were buckled together, was then fixed to the base plate on each of the piers to hold together the five separate tubes and five box girders that made up the cantilever. These were the most complicated part of the whole bridge structure.

The next stage was to erect the three great steel towers on top of them. Inside each 12-foot-diameter tube there was a hydraulic lifting press, whose function was to raise the erection platforms, staging and decks that would be constructed around the tubes. On the deck of the erection platforms there were cranes and rivet furnaces with a lower deck reached by a ladder that had shelters for the briggers. The work was done in stages and, when all the components had been assembled into a tube or girder and riveted, the platform would be raised up to the next stage until the towers stood at their full height of 343 feet. Each riveting gang, which was made up of two riveters and a rivet boy, was paid on piece work. The boy would heat the rivets in an Arrol-designed, oil-heated portable furnace and throw them red hot to his riveters, who would catch them with a special tool. With the towers in place, the erection of the cantilevers or girders could begin. Crowds watched from the shore as the girder arms were built out from the towers by men and machines suspended between sea and sky.

The whole of the superstructure was built in large sections in the works on the South Queensferry shore and the rivet fixtures were all tried before being disassembled and taken out to the piers by works vessels, then placed in situ by cranes, hoists and men with riveting machines. In effect, the bridge was built twice, such was the obsessive attention to detail and safety. Since freestanding scaffolding couldn't be erected over the water for work on the cantilevers, the bridge itself acted as scaffolding for its own construction. Thus the steel cantilever arms were built out from the cantilever towers. Each had to be built out on either side of the tower at the same rate to keep the whole structure in equilibrium. At the ends of the cantilevers were large platforms or cages above and below, on which the men worked, replacing the temporary bolts that had been put in on the shore with rivets.

As soon as a fresh lot of steel plates was added to the tubes or an additional girder section was riveted to the top arms, the erection platform that hung from the structure was slid out and a new section of work was begun. When this was completed it gave the necessary support for a further extension. As the cantilever arms extended further from the towers, a report in *The Builder* likened the three cantilever towers to three enormous ships with the tubes projecting like gigantic bowsprits over the water and everything hanging out in the air unsupported. The cranes that had started from the top of the Inchgarvie island tower moved slowly towards the south and the north to meet the two others that had come from the tops of the Queensferry and Fife towers.

At the height of construction, 4,600 men from Scotland, England, Ireland, France, Germany, Italy and Sweden were working round the clock on the bridge. The foreign workers who had appeared in great numbers to lay the caisson foundations stayed on to construct the final stages, which included laying the asphalt pavement for the permanent way across the bridge. By mid-1887 the highest work was taking place and 15 men were killed in a six-month period. Arrol was sensitive to the accident figures and the Board of Trade inspectors were keeping a close eye on them. But they reported that no reasonable precautions for the men's safety had been omitted. Arrol himself was sufficiently sure of his safety precautions to let the many visitors to the bridge go as high as they wanted. From the first summer Arrol's organization of welfare for his employees was impressive. When work started on the bridge the Forth Bridge Sickness and Accident Fund was set up with compulsory membership at eight pence for every person engaged by Tancred Arrol, which contributed 22 shillings (£1.10) a year.

In 1887, the year of Queen Victoria's Golden Jubilee, the three cantilever columns finally reached their full height. On Jubilee night bonfires were lit on the surrounding hills and the central towers of the bridge were illuminated with hundreds of electric arc lights. Crowds gathered on both shores to celebrate. With the completion of the three cantilever columns the engineer's vision was approaching reality and from this point onwards progress was rapid. By July 1889 all the cantilever arms had been completed and all that was left was to fill the two central gaps of 350 feet each between the giant projecting steel tubes. These were joined together by laying continuous girders between them, each about 350 feet long, 40 feet high at the ends and 50 in the centre.

The central girder on the southern span was ready to be put in place by early autumn and the briggers began its construction. It was built from the two ends of each cantilever in a precise and highly organized operation, until the two ends met in the middle, joining the Inchgarvie cantilever to the South Queensferry cantilever. On 15 October the workmen cheered Forth Bridge Company directors as they walked across the bridge. Only a 60-foot gap remained between the Inchgarvie and Fife cantilevers, and this was bridged by a temporary gangway lifted up from a barge by cranes on each end of the uncompleted central girder. Early in November the final girder was ready to be connected and this was done on the morning of 14 November.

The completed bridge was subjected to stringent tests before its opening. In January 1890 two trains were taken on to it made up of 100 coal wagons and 6 locomotives. The gross weight was 1,800 tons. The trains were driven slowly abreast and brought to a halt on the central girder connecting the Queensferry and Inchgarvie cantilevers. Board of Trade inspectors reported that 'this great undertaking, every part of which we have seen at different stages of its construction, is a wonderful example of thoroughly good workmanship with excellent materials, and both in its conception and execution is a credit to all who have been connected with it.'

But engineering on this scale didn't come without its price and 57 lives were lost during the construction of the bridge. A total of 518 men were taken to hospital, while the fate of 461 injured men is not recorded. However, this toll could easily have been much greater, given the dangers of working below sea level and at great heights. Wire ropes saved many lives. Accidents could have been doubled without them. The lack of accidents during the caisson operations was also a remarkable achievement. There were a few incidents, including one where the North West Queensferry caisson ruptured while being pumped out, the sea rushed in and two men were killed. On another occasion a few men were buried up to their chins in the mud and on another, a caisson suddenly dropped seven feet while men were working underneath.

The bridge, which cost the colossal sum of £3.5 million to build, was a triumph of engineering skill and hailed at the time as the eighth wonder of the world. It would, it was predicted, lead to a revolution in the art of constructing bridges of this kind. The grand opening of this monumental piece of structural engineering was on 4 March 1890, when the Prince of Wales, with the assistance of Arrol, drove in the last rivet. The engineers' model loft at Queensferry was transformed into a banqueting hall for the lunch that followed and in his speech the prince said, 'It is highly to the credit of everyone engaged in the operation that a structure so stupendous and so exceptional in its character should have been completed within seven years.' Arrol's achievement in building this and the new Tay Bridge were described by the prince as 'monuments of his skill, resources and energy' and he announced that Queen Victoria intended to make William Arrol a knight. The Victorian public finally had what they wanted – safety, reassurance, stability and strength – and the achievement put Scotland in the forefront of civil engineering expertise. The Tay and Forth bridges were notable not just for their size but also for their many engineering innovations, particularly the use of steel and the riveting method developed by Arrol to attach the girders to one another. Both bridges

Edward Prince of Wales drives in the last rivet before
the opening of the Forth Bridge, 1890

are still known for their high safety factors, a natural result of the under-design of the first Tay Bridge by Bouch.

The building of the Forth Bridge was one of the great highlights of the heroic age of engineering. It was the largest bridge that had ever been built and the first with a steel superstructure. The bridge's great length, including the approach viaduct, is 2,765 yards or just over one and a half miles. The length of the cantilever portion in the middle is one mile and 20 yards. In its construction over 50,000 tons of steel were used and the height of the steel structure above the water level is over 370 feet, while the rail level above high water is 156 feet. About 8 million rivets were used in the bridge and 42 miles of bent plates were used in the tubes. This was the largest civil engineering structure built during the nineteenth century and when it was completed it was the largest span bridge in the world.

In 2000, when a major refurbishment was under way, Fred had an opportunity to climb all over it and have a good look at everything:

> It's amazing when you think how the great cantilevers are not really mechanically connected at all. In order to allow for contraction and expansion they are just linked up together like a chain. It is because of this, of course, that when you stand on the very top of it, 350 feet up in the sky, where we were, and a locomotive comes on to the bridge under the cantilevers, you can feel the whole thing rock. Quite a fantastic feeling and a credit to the men who built it. And all based on the cantilever principle. I would love to have seen it when steam trains used to come thundering across and to have been able to get up there on the girders with one of the painting gangs. Today the bridge is still very busy. It carries 150 trains a day, but most of them are small diesels.

In spite of his great achievements in Scotland, for many people Arrol's most famous feat was the building of London's internationally recognized landmark, Tower Bridge. The great Gothic-towered, hydraulically operated road bridge has been a symbol of London ever since it was completed in 1894. But despite its outward appearance Tower Bridge is actually a steel bridge. Inside its castle-like exterior there is an enormous steel frame that was built by Sir William Arrol & Co. Construction started in 1886 and took eight years with four other major contractors involved, including William Armstrong, whose company was responsible for the hydraulics that operated the lifting gear. Two massive piers, containing over 70,000 tons of concrete, were sunk into the river bed to support the construction, but the biggest single item in the budget was Arrol's steelwork: his share in the Tower Bridge contract was a massive £337,113. Over 11,000 tons of steel provided the framework for the towers and walkways. Oiled canvas was wrapped around the steel framework, which was then washed with a solution of cement to prevent rusting. On the completion of the steelwork the bridge was clad in Cornish granite and Portland stone. This was done not just to make it blend in with the Tower of London next to it, but to protect the steelwork against the weather. 'When you come into one of the towers,' Fred said, 'you can see it's a great steel skeleton that's all riveted together. Beautiful riveting it is as well. The whole thing would stand up really without all the fancy stonework and beautification on the outside. It's a wonderful bit of ironwork.'

In the last years of Queen Victoria's reign Arrol was involved with many of the greatest civil engineering projects of the day: he built the Nile Bridge in Egypt, the Hawkesbury Bridge in Australia, the Keadby Bridge in Lincolnshire and the Warrington Transporter Bridge. In 1908 his company was also contracted by Harland and Wolff Shipyard, Belfast, to build a large gantry (known as the Arrol Gantry) for the construction of three new super-liners, one of which was *Titanic*. Like the ships themselves, the gantry crane was one of the largest built at the time, comparing with transporter bridges in length, height and lifting power.

However, no project was bigger than the construction of the Manchester Ship Canal. Arrol was responsible for building most of the bridges along the 35-mile canal, using Siemens-Martin open-hearth steel for the girder work in conjunction with wrought-iron floor plates to resist corrosion. The swing bridge linking Manchester with the new docks at Salford was the heaviest in the country at the

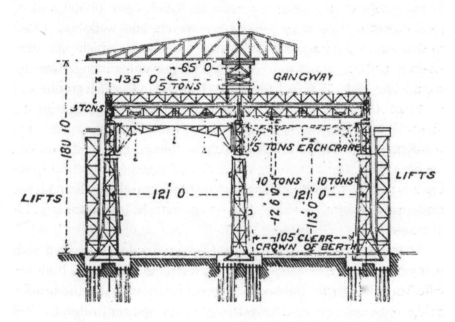

Section through the Arrol Gantry built at Harland and Wolff's shipyard in Belfast for the construction of ships such as *Titanic*

time of its construction. The great contracting engineer was a man after Fred's own heart. One of Arrol's guiding principles was his belief that practical experience was an essential for success and he was contemptuous of the armchair engineer who wouldn't get his hands dirty. These were Fred's sentiments too. When granted the Freedom of the town of Ayr in 1890, Arrol said:

> My character is representative of the working classes of Scotland. As one of those who has been able to raise themselves by their own energy and industry I hold it altogether wrong that so many young men are not learning trades. Give them, certainly, the best education you can, but at the same time, give them a trade along with their education. Our trade has got into the hands of a few, and you cannot get so many decent tradesmen. If you advertise for a tradesman you will perhaps get a single application. Whereas if you advertise for a clerk you will get 400 or 500.

In 1895 Arrol was elected MP for South Ayrshire as a Liberal Unionist and served for ten years. He also served as president of the Institution of Engineers and Shipbuilders in Scotland from 1895 to 1897. He spent the later years of his life on his estate at Sealfield near Ayr where he died in 1913, leaving £317,749 in his will, and he was buried in Woodside Cemetery, Paisley. On his death he was hailed as having revolutionized the science of bridge-building and his Dalmarnock Ironworks had become Britain's biggest girder construction works, occupying around 20 acres and employing nearly 5,000 men. His company, Sir William Arrol & Co. continued in business until 1969, when it was acquired by Clarke, Chapman.

A self-made engineering genius behind some of Britain's most iconic structures, he is rarely given the credit his achievements merit. Hard-working and innovative, William Arrol exemplified the heroic engineer. He was the self-made Victorian technocrat who took great pride in his rise to fame and fortune from humble origins. He was the very embodiment of the Victorian dream, but he was also a twentieth-century figure as the scale of his engineering triumphs took the railways into a new era. It was a time when the modern world was being created and nobody played a more significant part in this process than one of Arrol's contemporaries, Charles Parsons – the man who revolutionized electricity generation and marine transport with the invention of the steam turbine and ensured that steam would continue to be used in the age of electricity.

12

Charles Parsons
1854–1931
Steaming into the Twentieth Century

William Armstrong was perhaps the greatest innovator of the Victorian Age and nothing he attempted was a failure. But he didn't seem to have quite the same bravado as Brunel. That was to be found in a man who served his engineering apprenticeship with Armstrong and worked with him on pioneering forms of electricity generation before leaving to set up his own firm. There he developed a steam turbine for the purpose of directly driving dynamos, which had been powered by piston engines and transmission belts until then. Charles Parsons is acclaimed as one of the greatest engineers this country has ever produced. He was a remarkable man and brilliant engineer who built the first turbine-powered boat and demonstrated it by literally running rings around the Royal Navy's finest ships. But his greatest contribution to the modern world was the development of the turbine for power stations to bring electricity into every home and factory and to supply power to trams and railways. I suppose you could say that Charles Parsons and his steam turbine is to the twentieth century what James Watt and his engine were to the nineteenth century. Everybody has heard of James Watt but not many people have heard of Charles Parsons.

Charles Algernon Parsons, the youngest of six sons of the Third Earl and Countess of Rosse, was born into one of the most outstanding scientific families of his day. His father was a leading astronomer and president of the Royal Society, well known for his construction of a large reflector telescope at the family seat, Birr Castle in Ireland. Parsons was born at 13 Connaught Place, Hyde Park, London, on 13 June 1854 but brought up at Birr Castle. Charles and his brothers enjoyed a privileged life. The months of May and June were always spent in London and July and August with their grandmother in Brighton, before they returned to Ireland in the autumn.

Birr Castle was a rendezvous for the leading scientific men of the day, so that as a boy Parsons was nurtured in a stimulating intellectual atmosphere. The technical and scientific household encouraged the strong interest the young Parsons showed from an early age in mechanics and engineering, and it was the perfect setting for an aspiring inventor. A fire had destroyed the central part of Birr Castle, but after restoration it retained its thick walls and old moat where a forge and workshop were constructed. A furnace was added to melt brass and lathes were installed for wood and ironwork. Another addition was an engine house with machinery for polishing specula (metallic mirrors) for telescopes. From an early age water and boats played an important part in Charles's life. One of his favourite pastimes was rowing and he and his brothers, who were also keen sailors, went on voyages around the British coast in the family yachts. Charles received his early education at home, where his father engaged a private tutor for his sons, the astronomer Sir Robert Ball. Sir Robert encouraged his pupil to spend time experimenting in the castle's work-shops and one of his earliest inventions was a depth-sounding machine that was put to good use in one of his father's yachts. The depth of the water was determined by measuring pressure, which was recorded in a barometric tube. Charles also constructed a steam engine that was used to provide power for grinding the reflector of a telescope.

In 1871, at the age of 17, Parsons left home for Trinity College, Dublin, where his father had been chancellor. He did very well there and won prizes for mathematics and German. After two years in Dublin he went on to St John's College, Cambridge, but there was no engineering school so he was unable to take a degree in the subject that interested him most. Instead he took the Mathematical Tripos. Occasionally there would be lectures in mechanics which he would always attend, eager to learn as much as he could about the subject. He also found time to pursue his interest in water and boats, joining the university rowing club. He was a strong oarsman and proved a useful member of the Cambridge crew. But his studies were not neglected and he graduated with first-class honours in mathematics.

In the 1870s, when Parsons was at university, the Industrial Revolution was in full flow. Great reciprocating steam engines of one form or another mainly powered it but problems were arising, as Fred explained:

> A lot of machinery was driven by bevelled cogwheels and shafting and the noise was horrific. It got so bad a generating station in Manchester actually closed down because of complaints about the racket. The steam engines were connected to machines by line shafting – which is a complex system of belts and pulleys that transmits power from one engine to many machines – and would usually be in a separate engine house next door.
>
> Now that these things are all gone it's hard for people to imagine how noisy they were but I had a friend who was the chief mechanical engineer for a textile firm and he had to go round repairing steam engines. On one occasion it was the middle of the night and they thought they'd ironed out the problem with the engine, which had a great deal of bevel gearing in its transmission to different parts of the works. They decided they would give it a trial run. The next thing they knew, outside the mill gates were about 20 people who had been woken up from the noise of the gearing and thought it was 7 o'clock and time to go to work!

All the noise made by steam engines in mills and factories led to a quest to find something that didn't create such a din. The answer was electricity. Throughout the second half of the nineteenth century, electrical generators and motors started to be built, and electricity began to be used to drive factory machinery instead of steam. It changed the whole concept of powering all kinds of equipment. Up to this time the belts, pulleys and gears were the only way to take energy from the point of generation and deliver it to the point of use some distance away. Sooner or later, energy would be delivered to a motor over electric conductors and would substantially change the way work was done.

The beginnings of the age of electricity were back in the 1830s, when the railway pioneers like George and Robert Stephenson were transforming the face of the country. And the development of electricity as our major source of power is inextricably linked with steam power. Michael Faraday, born in 1791, was a pioneer of scientific discovery. He knew from earlier experiments that electricity could produce magnetism, so why, he asked, couldn't magnetism produce electricity? In 1831 he came up with the solution. Electricity could be produced through magnetism by motion. He discovered that when a magnet was moved inside a coil of copper wire, a tiny electric current flowed through the wire. Thus the basic principle of the dynamo was established – a machine that would convert mechanical energy into electrical energy by means of electromagnetic induction. Faraday's first electric dynamo or electrical generator was crude and provided only a small electric current, but the principle was established that if some sort of revolving engine could be devised, electricity could be generated. After reading about his work, a young Frenchman called Hippolyte Pixii constructed an electrical generator that utilized the rotary motion between magnet and coil rather than Faraday's to-and-fro motion in a straight line. All the generators in power stations today are direct descendants of the machine developed by Pixii from Faraday's first principles.

The first public supply of electricity was produced in 1881, for street lighting at Godalming in Surrey. The town council considered electricity as an alternative to gas when their contract for gas lighting expired. What probably swayed them was that the electric bid was £195, £15 less than the gas bid. The source of power for the generator was one of the waterwheels at a local leather-dressing mill, half a mile from the town centre. The following year, 1882, saw the birth of purpose-built power stations. On 12 January Thomas Edison opened the Edison Electric Light Station at No. 57 Holborn Viaduct. Soon after, on 27 February, the Hammond Electric Light Company opened the Brighton power station, which claims to be the first permanent and viable public power supply. By 1892 it was realized that electricity could also be used for heating and two years later it was possible to 'cook electric'. In 1918 electric washing machines became available and the next year the first refrigerator appeared. By this time electricity had been accepted as the energy of the future and the word was getting around: everyone wanted electricity.

But the mass supply of electricity was made possible through steam. Parsons, among others, realized that a rotating machine or turbine powered by steam would be able to provide the right sort of power for a dynamo. But nobody had been able to devise an efficient turbine. 'The first turbine of which there is any record,' Parsons said, 'was made by Hero of Alexandria, 2,000 years ago, and it is probably obvious to most persons that some power can be obtained from a jet of steam either by the reaction of the jet itself, like a rocket, or by its impact on some kind of paddle wheel.'

Throughout the nineteenth century the development of the machine had occupied the minds of engineers and inventors. Trevithick had devised a whirling engine that was a version of the steam turbine four years before Watt's death. But Watt was as sceptical about it as he was about the development of high-pressure steam. Then in America around 1837, William Avery invented what he called the traction steam wheel. This was used for driving circular saws and cotton gins. The steam was introduced into a rotor through a hollow shaft and through the force of the jets on the blades he obtained rotation. The rotor was 5 feet across and the speed of the jets was 880 feet per second. But the device was not very efficient so a better and more economical engine was needed. Throughout the nineteenth century more experiments were carried out, but no great headway was made until Parsons started to study the problem. As Fred explained:

In Britain there were no less than 200 patents taken out for gas and steam turbines between 1784 and 1884, which was the year Parsons

351

C. A. PARSONS.
ROTARY MOTOR.

No. 328,710.

Patented Oct. 20, 1885.

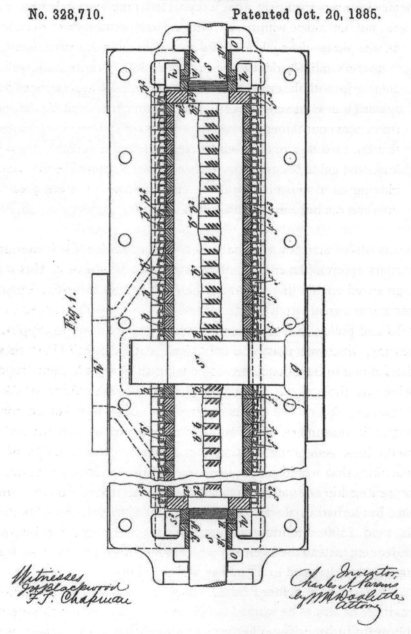

Witnesses
J. Blackwood
F. S. Chapman

Inventor,
Charles A. Parsons
by M. M. Doolittle
Attorney

Patent for Parsons's rotary motor

patented his design for a steam turbine – the first successful one. Before this progress had been very slow in the field of turbines. Number one, they were very inefficient. They wasted a lot of energy and they revved too fast. Of course with the centrifugal forces created, some of them blew to pieces sending debris flying at half the speed of a rifle bullet.

It wasn't until Charles Parsons made his turbine that someone really got to grips with the design. The modern steam turbine as perfected by Parsons is in some ways merely a development of the windmill. Jets of steam come out through guided blades and hit another set of blades that are fixed to a rotor, making it revolve. The steam expands as it leaves the guide blades and makes the rotor turn, just like the wind blowing on a windmill. But a turbine is encased, so much greater pressures can be generated than with a windmill.

It was while Parsons was still a student at Cambridge that he designed a rotary epicycloidal engine and constructed a model of it. This was a high-speed engine that used a circular movement to drive a dynamo and it was a great step forward because it did away with the need to use belts and pulleys, which were cumbersome and subject to slipping or gearing, which was noisy and inefficient. After university Parsons was determined to be an engineer, so he went to Newcastle upon Tyne to serve his time as an apprentice at the Elswick Works of W. G. Armstrong & Co. The company may have been best known for its hydraulic machinery, ships and armaments but it also worked on methods of generating electricity, particularly on the design of the machines that would be required to provide the rotary motion. An apprenticeship was rather unusual for a young man of Parsons's social class but he had what was called a 'premium' apprenticeship, for which he paid £500. Premium apprenticeships were not for ordinary craftsmen; instead the intention was that they would provide the training for men destined to fill managerial positions.

It wasn't long before Parsons began to show what an outstanding engineer he was as he worked with Armstrong on the development of the steam turbine. The objective he set himself was to produce power by utilizing the velocity of a jet of steam, instead of using the pressure of the steam to drive a piston as in the ordinary reciprocating engine. It was evident that a jet of steam could be made to turn a wheel by acting on blades set around its circumference, or alternatively it could be used to develop power by its own reaction when escaping from an orifice in a rotating wheel or arm. Both approaches had already been tried by innumerable inventors, but the hitherto insuperable difficulty in constructing a practical turbine lay in harnessing the velocity of the steam. Even steam at a comparatively low pressure escaping into the atmosphere may easily be travelling at more than 2,500 feet per second, or over 1,700 miles an hour.

Parsons, therefore, went back to basics. He started by looking at the simple water turbine but soon realized that there was no exact parallel between a rotor powered by water and one driven by the kinetic energy of steam, and that however fast the rotor was made to revolve, it could only absorb a fraction of that energy. But he worked out that if a number of turbines were arranged in a series on a common shaft and the steam went from one to another, it would utilize the energy of the steam more fully. Used in association with a condenser, a device for reducing the heat of the steam and turning it back into water, a multiple-stage turbine like this could harness the entire pressure of the steam from high pressure at the inlet to zero at the outlet.

Parsons produced his first steam turbine while he was still an apprentice and Armstrong allowed him to link it with a dynamo for an arc lamp at the Elswick quayside, but the company didn't adopt the scheme for mass production. Parsons wasn't to be put off and he took his idea to a number of other companies including Kitson's, a Leeds engineering firm known principally for building railway locomotives. They manufactured the engine, producing 40 of them to power dynamos. The association Parsons formed with the company led him to move to Leeds when he completed his four-year apprenticeship at Elswick in 1881.

With the opening of the first power stations the need for an efficient steam turbine to turn the generators was pressing, and the potential market for anybody who could develop such a machine was huge. Parsons was well aware of this but he had to earn a living and while he was at Kitson's his attention was diverted as he spent two years on experimental work involving rocket-propelled torpedoes. The experiments proved unsuccessful, but while he was in Leeds he met Katherine Bethell and married her on 10 January 1883 at the Church of All Saints in Bramham. Even during his honeymoon, Parsons was so taken up with his work on torpedoes that he took his new bride, along with a mechanic, to the local engine trials every morning. They arrived every day at 7 a.m. in a bitterly cold winter, so it was hardly surprising that Katherine caught rheumatic fever – not an ideal start to married life. Fortunately, by the spring Katherine had fully recovered and they were able to resume their honeymoon, this time in warmer climes. They spent five months away and they visited America, mainly New Mexico and California. On their return to England they set up their first home in lodgings in Leeds, where Katherine taught Parsons needlework. It is said he became a skilled embroiderer.

The following year Parsons moved back to Tyneside with his bride, where he became a junior partner with ship equipment manufacturers Clarke, Chapman & Co. of Gateshead to head their electrical department. This position gave Parsons the opportunity to return to his major interest. While he was there he perfected his first multi-stage, blade-reaction turbine. The idea was a relatively simple one but its realization in practical form was not, for it involved the solution of mechanical engineering problems that stretched contemporary technical know-how to the limits. The improvement and application of the turbine was to be Parsons's chief occupation for the rest of his life. It was a job for which he was particularly well suited for he had a practical type of mind allied to great mechanical aptitude. This combination of skills enabled him to surmount the formidable technical problems that barred the way to the manufacture of a successful steam turbine. He patented his turbine engine on 23 April 1884 and devised a generator to go with it.

His turbine was an immense technological leap forward but his intention from the outset had been that it should be used for generating electricity, directly coupled to a generator. However, for him to develop the turbine for the new power stations that were beginning to appear, he would have to address a number of issues. He realized that the problem with most early turbines was that the steam expanded in one go, which was inefficient. The solution Parsons came up with depended on theory rather than the old experimental methods of Newcomen and Watt. Early turbines with single blades turned too fast and sometimes self-destructed, so he decided to use a series of blades to let the steam come in at a very high pressure and then expand as the blades got bigger. This made the turbine more economical and is basically how a modern turbine works. In his own words, Parsons

> dealt with the turbine problem in a very different way. It seemed to me that moderate surface velocities and speeds of rotation were essential if the turbine motor was to receive general acceptance as a prime mover. I therefore decided to split up the fall in pressure of the steam into small fractional expansions over a large number of turbines in series, so that the velocity of the steam nowhere should be great. Consequently . . . a moderate speed of turbine suffices for the highest economy.

Parsons knew that if the turbine was to be accepted the speed would need to be moderated. The turbine that he developed had 15 stages of expansion; in other words, there were 15 sets of blades. This effect of slowing down the velocity of the steam is called compounding. It was a brilliant move and the moderate-speed turbine that resulted could be put to much more practical use. The blades had to be made to a specific shape and finished to a high degree of accuracy. There could be no contact between the moving parts and the fixed ones that surrounded them so there was always the problem of steam leaking, but this was gradually reduced. 'It is said,' Fred remarked, 'that Charles Parsons sketched the original drawing for the reaction blades in his turbine on the back of an envelope. It was so successful it took £100,000 of research to improve it by only 2 per cent, which in my opinion is testimony to the instinctive knowledge and genius of Mr Parsons.'

In order to use the turbine for the generation of electricity, Parsons designed an integrated high-speed dynamo directly driven from the turbine. In a generator, the shaft and armature spin round, and Parsons's steam turbine provided the power for this. The armature is made of a large coil of copper wire which moves around past magnets and that creates an electric current. The speed required for the generators in use at the time was 1,200 rpm, but Parsons's first steam turbines revolved at 18,000 rpm so he had to design a generator to utilize the high speed of his turbine. In doing so, the turbine generator was created and it became the world's most important means of producing bulk electric power. Combined steam turbine and turbo-electric generator sets became a practical working proposition and Parsons gave an early description of his breakthroughs in the *Proceedings of the Institution of Mechanical Engineers*. It was a major technological leap forward and Parsons was on the threshold of revolutionizing power generation using steam. His work was to be key to many twentieth-century accomplishments. Fred explained its significance:

> Almost all the electricity we use in the UK today comes from generators driven by steam turbines. The steam is obtained by burning fuels such as coal, oil and gas or from nuclear reactions. The heat is used to turn water into steam and it is the power of the steam which makes a turbine spin. The idea of using the expansion of steam to make a machine turn is hundreds of years old. Everybody had a go at it. But really the deep knowledge and the understanding of steam and its expansion and the materials needed to build a practical steam turbine were all put together and developed by Charles Parsons and this revolutionized electricity generation.

Parsons's turbine proved a complete success and the company began to manufacture steam turbo-generators to provide electric lighting for ships. Everything was working out well for Parsons at work and at home. His daughter, Rachel Mary, was born on 25 January 1885, followed by a son, Algernon George, born on 19 October the following year – both at home at Elvaston Hall in County Durham. The young family lived here for ten years. Parsons was a great family man and these were happy times. In his home workshop, with Rachel and Algernon by his side, he found the time to apply his inventive mind to building all kinds of toys for them. There was the 'spider', a small spirit-fuelled three-wheeled engine that travelled around the garden, and a steam pram for carrying the children. There was even a small flying machine, which was also fuelled by spirit.

Parsons was a hard worker who was dedicated to his business but he always had the capacity to get away from it and relax. One of his favourite leisure-time pursuits was fishing, particularly trout fishing. He always said that his best catch was at Lord Armstrong's home, Cragside. Armstrong, also a keen fisherman, was out with him one day. Their catch was good but they had forgotten that it was the first day of September and a water bailiff came and confiscated their fish and their rods, telling them that they were fishing illegally. In the meantime Lady Armstrong had been waiting to cook the trout but it never arrived.

With a happy and settled home life, Parsons's career continued to forge ahead. By 1884 his first steam turbine was running successfully at Gateshead and during 1884–5 two small portable turbine sets were completed there. In 1887 he became known as the 'Designer of Plant for the Generation of Electricity'. In that year, ten of his turbo-generators, with power ranging from 15 to 32 kilowatts each, supplied most of the lighting for the Newcastle Exhibition by means of in-candescent lamps. Around the same time the Chilean battleship *Blanco Encalada* arrived at Armstrong's Elswick Works for new boilers and armaments and while she was there she became the first warship to be fitted with a Parsons turbine and dynamo set for electric lighting. By the time Parsons was 30 he was well on his way to a successful engineering career. In May 1887 he was making 4-kilowatt generator sets for the Suez Canal and completing similar contracts for the Italian, Spanish and Chilean navies. His turbines were rapidly being improved and particular attention was paid to the relationship of the velocity of the steam to the velocity of the blades.

The success of Parsons's designs led him to dissolve the Clarke, Chapman partnership and together with friends he started his own firm, C. A. Parsons & Company, in 1889. The firm set up a manufacturing plant at Heaton Works near Newcastle to make steam turbines and high-speed electrical machinery suitable for coupling straight to turbines. The factory covered two acres and it had its own blacksmith's shop as well as testing rooms and offices. The total staff numbered 48. Parsons and his partners continued to see the potential for steam turbines to drive electrical generators, but the risks involved in developing them were formidable. Turbines required exacting tolerances on their dimensions even by modern standards. Added to this, the vane profiles in the turbines were completely new and were very complex shapes to manufacture. If this wasn't enough, the company had all the problems of finance associated with a new start-up, and one particularly serious problem that Parsons hadn't anticipated. One of the conditions of his partnership with Clarke, Chapman was that the patents of anything he developed while he was with them would belong to them even if he left. This meant that in the early days at Heaton he wasn't able to use his preferred turbo design, the parallel or axial flow type, but had to settle for what he regarded as a less efficient model in which the flow of the steam was radial.

It wouldn't be long before Parsons's turbo-generators were supplied to power stations but it took a great deal of persistence on his part before he could get them there. By 1888, although about 200 of his turbo-generators were in service, they were employed almost exclusively for ship-lighting duties, and no electric light company had yet taken any interest in them. Parsons therefore decided that he would himself have to effect the introduction of the turbine into the industry that it was destined to dominate. So, aided by friends, he founded the Newcastle & District Electric Lighting Co., which began operations in January 1890 with a station at Forth Banks equipped with a pair of 75-kw turbo-alternators. It was the first public power station to be powered by a steam turbine. But even this demonstration of its suitability for power-station service failed to arouse any general interest, and Parsons had to accept the financial risk of investing in companies formed to supply electricity to Cambridge in 1892 and to Scarborough in 1893 in order to give them sufficient confidence to install turbine machinery.

Sets of increasing power and efficiency now began to be made at his Heaton Works and by 1892 the power of Parsons's turbines had increased from the first prototype of 4kw in 1885 to 100kw. His timing was perfect and a market began to emerge as people realized that electricity could also be used in heating and cooking. The big break-through came in 1894 when Parsons managed to recover his parallel flow patents from Clarke, Chapman and the company was able to manufacture more efficient turbines and achieve great success in the field of turbo-generators for the power industry. Turbines were much cheaper to build than the more cumbersome reciprocating steam engines and they easily reached the speeds needed for generating electric power. Three 4-ton 100kw radial flow generators were installed in Cambridge Power Station in 1895, and used to power the first electric street-lighting scheme in the city. Parsons not only provided it with the turbo-generators, but led the way for more than a generation in every important development of power-station machinery.

The modern turbine as developed by Parsons at this time has three stages – the high-pressure, intermediate-pressure and low-pressure sections. Fred described how it worked:

Because the incoming steam has very high energy – about 2,500 pounds per square inch at 1,000 degrees Fahrenheit – the high-pressure section has small blades. Then, as some heat is lost, the steam is sent back to the boiler to be reheated up to 1,000 degrees. The next section is the intermediate-pressure section and in here the blades are bigger. After passing through this the steam then goes to the low-pressure section. By the time it gets here a lot of the energy has already been removed from the steam so the blades here are the largest in the turbine. The steam leaves through the bottom of the turbine, is condensed back into water and is then sent back to the boiler to be made into steam again. And so it goes on.

From an early stage Parsons had realized that the steam turbine could also be used for many other things, particularly marine pro-pulsion. This, like electrical generation, required high efficiency and steady loads. Marine propulsion had the additional requirement of smooth operation and a high power density engine. Parsons knew that his turbine could provide this. In 1893 he began work on adapting his turbine engine to propel ships. Parsons's original 1884 patents had made reference to the potential for using turbines in marine propulsion, and when he recovered his patents from Clarke, Chapman he became free to explore this. He decided to build a small boat to show the world what the steam turbine in marine form was capable of doing. He drew up plans and in 1894, with a group of five friends, he formed the Marine Steam Turbine Company. The prospectus stated: 'The objective of this company is to provide the necessary capital for efficiently and thoroughly testing the application of Mr. Parsons's well known steam turbine to the propulsion of vessels. If successful, it is believed that the new system will revolutionize the present method of utilizing steam as a motive power, and also that it will enable much higher rate of speed to be attained than has hitherto been possible with the fastest vessel.' Other advantages proclaimed by the new company included a reduction in vibration of the propeller and the fact that the turbine would take up less space than the older reciprocating engines and use fuel more efficiently.

The first boat constructed was a demonstration vessel. The 100-foot, 44-ton-displacement steam yacht *Turbinia* was built in 1894 and designed by Parsons himself. He wasn't a naval architect by training so he started by making models to find out what the most suitable shape would be for the hull and what power would be needed for it. His first model was only two feet long and he towed it on a pond at Ryton on Tyne, close to where he lived, with a fishing rod and line. He also carried out tests on a pond at his Heaton Works. Later he scaled his two-foot model up to one of six foot, driven with a twisted rubber band. During these tests Parsons paid particularly close attention to the waves formed by the models. He knew already that the vessel he was planning would have a very low freeboard (the distance between the waterline and the open deck), so the size of the waves would be critical.

In early 1894 work began on building the hull of the full-size *Turbinia*. It is thought that workers from the Tyne's shipyards were brought in to help with the construction of the revolutionary new vessel. Parsons's Heaton Works were over a mile from the Tyne and his workforce were engineers, not metal workers, and didn't have the skills needed to build a steel ship, so construction of the hull was contracted out to the sheet-metal-working firm of Brown & Hood at Wallsend-on-Tyne. They were not shipbuilders, but they were experienced in working with the thin steel that was to be used to keep the weight of the vessel down. The steel itself was made on the other side of the river in Jarrow. The engine and all the machinery were manufactured at the Heaton Works. Initially a single radial-flow turbine engine drove one propeller shaft, which at 2,400 rpm developed 960 horsepower. It had a series of fixed and rotating discs, each carrying rings of blades. The steam flowed outwards between a pair of discs, passing alternately between fixed and moving blades. It then passed inwards behind a moving disc to flow outwards between the next pair of discs. The blades increased in height from disc to disc to allow for the expansion of the steam and the steam passed across inner portions of the discs through holes near the shaft. The expansion of the steam as it left the guide blades provided the rotative force.

Designed purely for speed, *Turbinia* was extremely long and narrow, 104 feet long but with a beam of only 9 feet. She was fitted with a double-ended water tube boiler working at 210 psi. She was launched on 2 August 1894, but the results of early trials were a great disappointment to Parsons. The top speed reached by the boat was less than 20 knots, falling well short of what he had anticipated. Tests revealed that the fault lay with the propeller. A phenomenon called cavitation occurred when a propeller was rotated above certain speeds, which paradoxically caused a great loss of power. This was because the propellers were spinning so fast that the water pressure decreased, forming a cavity full of bubbles. The result was that the power was going into making the bubbles rather than moving the boat forward.

The turbine design was pushing at many technological constraints simultaneously and this was just another of the problems that Parsons had to remedy. To do so he constructed a test tank in which the action of propellers of different shapes and sizes could be studied. From the calculations he made from these observations he concluded that the remedy for the cavitation problem was to operate at lower rpm with multiple turbines and propellers. He made several propellers varying in diameter and pitch until he found the one that would give him the best results. He also replaced the single radial-flow turbine with three of the more efficient parallel-flow engines linked to three propeller shafts. On each shaft he put three small propellers to give the vessel nine in total. These three shafts were driven by high-, intermediate- and low-pressure turbines which together developed 2,000 horsepower. Never before had it been possible to pack so much power into one small hull. A fourth turbine was coupled to a central shaft for reversing.

With these changes *Turbinia*'s performance improved dramatically. Parsons himself sailed in her, braving with the rest of the crew the soakings they got at high speeds as great waves crashed on to the deck. To avoid the rough seas *Turbinia* did some of her trial runs along a straight stretch of the River Tyne known as the Northumberland Dock Mile, but the river was busy and before she could make a run her lookout had to ensure the stretch was clear. *Turbinia*'s captain was Christopher Leyland, a director of the company and a former naval officer. He acted as lookout while Parsons took charge of the controls in the engine room, accompanied by two engineers. Down in the vessel's two stokeholds it was very cramped and there was only room for one man at a time to swing his short-handled shovel. On returning from a trial run, one of the stoker's jobs was to repaint *Turbinia*'s broad yellow funnel because the fire that came from it licked the paint off when she was driven fast.

The results of the trials were spectacular. *Turbinia* regularly clocked up speeds of over 30 knots and eventually reached a maximum of 34.5 knots, equivalent to nearly 40 mph on land. The boat was capable of speeds higher than the fastest destroyers afloat, but nobody was taking any notice. The investment up to this date had also been huge: 'The practical development of this engine,' Parsons said, 'was commenced chiefly on the basis of the data of physicists, and as giving some idea of the work involved in the investigation of the problem of marine propulsion by turbines, I may say that about £24,000 was spent before an order was received. Had the system been a failure or unsatisfactory, nearly the whole of this sum would have been lost.'

Parsons decided it was time to persuade the Admiralty to place an order for a turbine-driven ship. To make them aware of the advantages of his engine he came up with a daring and dramatic publicity stunt. As Fred tell us:

> The story of *Turbinia* is one of the truly great engineering tales. In 1897, as part of her Diamond Jubilee, Queen Victoria was reviewing her great naval fleet at Spithead on the Solent. It was the largest collection of warships ever to have been gathered together at anchorage, with 5 columns of ships 6 miles long including 50 battleships. There were 165 ships flying the White Ensign, including battleships of the Majestic and Royal Sovereign Class, cruisers, old ironclads, gunboats, destroyers and at one end of the line 6 sailing brigs, the last remnants of the age of masts and yards. The entire fleet was manned by over 38,000 officers and men.
>
> What a sight it must have been – all of them shining with gleaming brass and draped in patriotic bunting. It was the time when Britain ruled the waves and the Spithead review gave a chance to show the world that it was Britain's might at sea which had won her an empire. Along with the Queen and the Prince of Wales many of the crowned heads of Europe were there to marvel at the power of the British fleet. Then into the middle of it all an uninvited guest came speeding through – the fastest thing anybody had ever seen on water. It was the little 44-ton experimental steam turbine vessel that had been built by Parsons.

Parsons had turned up at Spithead uninvited to make the point, not only to the Admiralty but also to the foreign naval representatives, that his boat was faster by far than any other vessel there. Travelling at up to 34 knots, *Turbinia* sped past all the conventional vessels.

As *Turbinia* raced through the lines of warships the authorities became alarmed and sent out a patrol boat to try to stop her. The navy began to chase the tiny vessel, but was left hopelessly behind. There was no boat in the Royal Navy capable of catching her; the fastest destroyers of the day could do only 27 knots. The wash *Turbinia* created nearly sank the pursuing naval vessel, but before any disciplinary action could be taken Prince Henry of Prussia sent Parsons his congratulations and requested another run. *Turbinia* had triumphed. It was a magnificent spectacle and a convincing demonstration of a major breakthrough in naval construction and engineering.

Parsons's vessel astonished all those who witnessed the event but initially the establishment was not amused. *The Times* reported:

> At the cost of a deliberate disregard of authority, she [*Turbinia*] contrived to give herself an effective advertisement by steaming at astonishing speed between the lines A and B shortly after the Royal Procession had passed. The patrol boats which attempted to check her adventurous and lawless proceeding were distanced in a twinkling . . . Her speed was simply astonishing, but its manifestation was accompanied by a mighty rushing sound and by a stream of flame from her funnel at least as long as the funnel itself. Unless these commonplace but very serious defects can be corrected, it is manifest that the system of propulsion devised by Mr Parsons cannot be applied to torpedo boats, for whose operations silence, secrecy and invisibility are indispensable.

Despite the disapproving tone of the *Times* report, Parsons had attracted the attention of the people who mattered and his audacious demonstration was to have a lasting effect on marine propulsion. With the exception of the brigs, every vessel at anchor that day was fitted with reciprocating engines, but when, just 17 years later, in July 1914 the last fleet review before the First World War was held, all the most important ships present were driven by steam turbines.

Spithead marked a turning point in the fortunes of the marine steam engine and the steam turbine could no longer be ignored. The Royal Navy soon realized the great advantages of steam turbines and they began to send high-ranking engineering officers on *Turbinia*'s trials in the North Sea. Crew members would row the guests out to the vessel. Once they were on board they would be given a short tour of the boat and the crew would extol the virtues of the turbine. They would be told that the propellers turned at around 2,500 revolutions a minute with very little vibration. For their trip out to the open sea they were issued with oilskins, but they were allowed to stand in the little wheelhouse if they wanted to take shelter from the waves that swept over the deck when the boat was travelling at speed. The noise of the engines and the roar of the sea as it crashed against the bows would have been deafening. But the men from the navy were impressed.

The French government also showed great interest in Parsons's revolutionary new design and after his publicity stunt at Spithead he sailed across the Channel in *Turbinia* for the Paris Exhibition, where she was to give another demonstration of her capabilities. An international meeting of naval architects was taking place and it was a perfect opportunity for further promotion of the marine turbine. She staged a spectacular series of speed runs along a stretch of the River Seine and the visit was a great success. The French navy minister was there and small steamers from Rouen formed a lane for *Turbinia* to speed through as crowds lining the river bank cheered loudly. Later she proceeded to Le Havre, where, in the distance, the Newhaven–Dieppe steamer was travelling towards England. *Turbinia* easily caught up with her and sped round her in circles, before breaking off to make for Grimsby and the Tyne.

The success of *Turbinia* really amounted to two innovations – the steam turbine for ship propulsion and the slenderness of the hull. The turbine permitted vessels to be driven at speeds that had previously been impossible, and enabled those speeds to be maintained in the roughest of seas. It was soon adopted for all new navy ships as well as for great ocean-going liners. Parsons Marine Steam Turbine Co. Ltd set up new offices and workshops at Wallsend, which became known as the Turbinia Works. In 1898 the Royal Navy placed an order with Parsons for a turbine-driven torpedo-boat destroyer. The boat was named HMS *Viper* and it was built by Hawthorn Leslie of Hebburn-on-Tyne with Parsons's company supplying the engines. Parsons's investment of £24,000 in the development of the marine steam turbine was now paying off. The navy were so pleased with *Viper* that they ordered another turbine destroyer, which they called *Cobra*. This was built by Armstrong Whitworth at their Elswick yard. Both boats were launched in 1899 and both easily passed their sea trials, almost matching *Turbinia*'s speed.

But in 1901 disaster struck when *Viper* went on the rocks off the Channel Islands and broke in two. No lives were lost but with *Cobra* it was a different story. Seventy-seven men drowned when the ship broke in two and sank off the Lincolnshire coast on its delivery voyage from the Tyne. 'I rather think,' said Fred, 'that the stresses and strains of the turbine were too much for the slender construction of the hull. There were a lot of men who worked for Charles Parsons on board the ship on that maiden voyage tinkering with the machinery and he never really got over the fact that some of his own men were drowned.' Initially Parsons and his associates thought this double disaster would affect the marine turbine programme but their fears proved to be unfounded. Thankfully, the Admiralty didn't lose confidence in Parsons. A special investigation found that no blame could be attached to the turbine engines of the vessels and the navy went on to show its confidence in the invention by ordering more turbine-powered warships.

In 1902 a third turbine-driven destroyer, HMS *Velox*, entered service followed by the destroyer HMS *Eden* and the cruiser HMS *Amethyst*. All three ships performed well and in 1905 Admiralty designers recommended that all new Royal Navy vessels should be equipped with the steam turbine engine. In 1906 the first of a new class of big gun battleships, HMS *Dreadnought*, was launched at Portsmouth and she was powered by turbines.

The adoption of the steam turbine wasn't confined to naval vessels and within ten years of the launch of *Turbinia* several turbine vessels were in service crossing the Atlantic. By this time the steam turbine had almost replaced the reciprocating steam engine on the oceans. The first passenger ship to be driven by turbines was the Firth of Clyde pleasure steamer *King Edward*, built in 1901. It was the first commercial steam-turbine-driven ship in the world and was built on the Clyde for

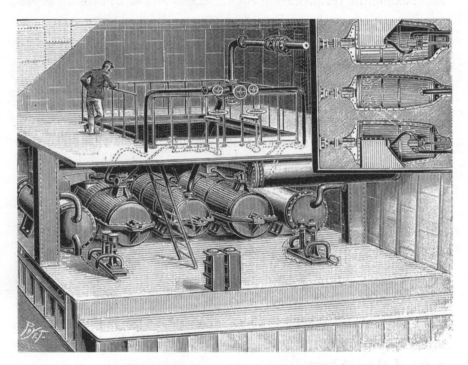

Parsons's steam turbines installed *in situ*, 1904

a consortium including the shipbuilder William Denny of Dumbarton, Charles Parsons, and John Williamson who operated the ship. The turbine was then successfully used in big, fast ships like *Victorian* and *Virginian*, which, in 1905, became the first passenger liners powered by turbines to cross the Atlantic. Twenty-six ships were now powered by Parsons's direct-drive steam turbines. Their introduction was the climax of the development of the steamship, superseding the reciprocating engine at sea. The reciprocating engine was not entirely replaced, however, as there was a problem in that the turbine was initially only suitable for speeds over 16 knots. In order to adapt it to slower vessels, the combination system was introduced. This involved a reciprocating engine taking the first part of the expansion of steam, and the turbine taking the last part. The reciprocating engine expands the steam to around atmospheric pressure and the turbine continues to expand the steam until it is down to the pressure in the condenser.

One of Parsons's greatest successes came in 1907 when the 31,000-ton Cunard liners *Mauretania* and *Lusitania* went into service between Liverpool and New York. Both were fitted with turbine engines of such power that they were capable of speeds of around 25 knots. The contract to build them was the result of an agreement in 1903 between Cunard and Parliament that two large passenger ships should be built to re-establish British supremacy in the Atlantic. There were stipulations that the vessels had to be made available to the Admiralty in time of war and that each vessel was to be capable of maintaining a speed of 24 to 25 knots.

Lusitania was the first to enter service. She was built on the Clyde by John Brown and when she was launched in 1907 she was the largest ship in the world at 787 feet long and 31,550 tons. A month after her maiden voyage she captured the Blue Riband for the fastest crossing of the Atlantic but her career was short-lived. With the outbreak of the First World War in 1914, *Lusitania* and other transatlantic liners were at risk from German U-boats. On 16 January 1915 in choppy seas on the way to Queenstown, Ireland, the ship was running from possible German subs. To try to keep his vessel safe the captain raised the

American flag because America was still neutral. His action became world news, but it failed to protect his ship. On 17 April, about 20 miles off the Old Head of Kinsale, the ship was torpedoed by a U-boat. There was a second internal explosion and the ship sank, taking 1,198 people with her. It was this that brought the United States into the First World War.

Mauretania was built at Swan Hunter and Wigham Richardson's Wallsend yard on the Tyne. Her engines were built by the Wallsend Slipway & Engineering Company to Parsons's design. They drove the ship's quadruple-screw propellers, generating 73,000 horsepower. *Mauretania* was launched for sea trials on the River Tyne in September 1906 amid scenes of great jubilation among the Tyneside craftsmen. *Turbinia* steamed alongside the 790-foot ship at Swan Hunter's yard shortly before she left. After flawless trials she left Liverpool on 16 November 1907 bound for New York. There were more than 50,000 cheering spectators. The crossing took 5 days, 18 hours and 17 minutes at an average speed of 21 to 22 knots. In September 1909 *Mauretania* claimed the record for the fastest westbound crossing and her speed and reliability became legendary, earning her a reputation she would keep until the end of her career. She held the Blue Riband longer than any other liner – 20 years on the westbound passage and 20 on the eastbound.

Not only was it a tribute to her as an engineering feat but also to Parsons's unquestionable engineering courage. A man who would take responsibility for the 70,000-horsepower turbines of the *Lusitania* and *Mauretania* when the most powerful turbines afloat did not exceed 14,000 horsepower and who would construct a 25,000-kw turbo-alternator for a foreign power station when his previous largest unit had a capacity of no more than 6,000 kw was certainly not lacking in boldness. Queen Victoria had died in 1901 but the heroic age of engineering lived on in him into the twentieth century. There was, however, nothing reckless in his nature. His courage was tempered with prudence and he would never allow himself to be persuaded into any undertaking that he felt instinctively to be unsound.

Mauretania and *Lusitania* were great engineering triumphs for

Parsons but he wasn't prepared to rest on his laurels. All the ships that had been fitted with Parsons's turbines so far had direct drive from the turbines to multiple propellers, as on *Turbinia*. This system was fine for passenger ships, where speed of turnaround was essential, but it was unsuitable for the general run of merchant shipping, where speed was less important than operating economy. The next step, therefore, was to test-develop turbines that had speed reduction gearing that would enable big ships to cut down on fuel consumption. Parsons devised a geared turbine engine in which twin turbine units were linked by reduction gears to a single propeller shaft and in 1909 he successfully refitted the cargo steamer *Vespasian* with these engines. The new machinery was 15 per cent more efficient than the reciprocating engine, and an alteration to the propeller increased this to 22 per cent. The new machinery, which was much lighter than the old, had a high-pressure and a low-pressure turbine, each driving a pinion at 1,400 revolutions; this connected to a spur wheel on the screw making 70 revolutions per minute.

Again the investment had been huge. 'In order to prove the advantage of mechanical gearing of turbines in mercantile and war vessels,' Parsons said, 'about £20,000 has been recently expended, and considerable financial risks have been undertaken in relation to the first contracts.' But again it proved to be a wise investment. Gearing promised to play a particularly important part in war vessels by being more economical at low speeds. Parsons's Turbinia Company went on to build two 30-knot destroyers of 15,000 horsepower with this arrangement. The geared turbine came to be adopted on a wide range of vessels from cargo ships to fast passenger liners and warships. It superseded the direct-drive engine that had pioneered the way so that nearly all of the great ocean-going liners on the Atlantic run – such as the *Queen Mary* launched in 1934, *Queen Elizabeth* in 1938 and the *United States* in 1951 – were propelled by geared turbines.

Turbinia herself met an unfortunate fate. In 1907, she was moored alongside the company works at Wallsend. Across the river Robert Stephenson & Co. had a boat-building yard and when they launched one of their boats it came straight across the river and chopped the little *Turbinia* in half. 'There are famous pictures of it,' Fred remembered, 'on the quayside all bent in two – a bit of a sad end to such a famous and pioneering ship. But she survived the mishap and was repaired. Later on somebody decided to saw it in two and sent the important bit, the turbine and the boiler, down to London and stuck it in a museum where it reigned for many years. Now the whole thing has been reunited and they've got it all fixed back together at the Discovery Museum in Newcastle upon Tyne.'

As well as being used for the generation of electricity and for marine propulsion, Parsons's turbines were installed to work blast furnace blowers and centrifugal pumps. They were cleaner and more efficient than reciprocating engines and, as the turbines used the exhaust steam from other engines, there were less clouds of steam blowing off to waste. The first turbine to be used in a rolling mill was a 750-horsepower exhaust turbine in Scotland, which revolved at 2,000 revolutions per minute. With a double reduction of helical gears it drove the mill at 70 revolutions. A flywheel also helped to equalize the speed. Parsons predicted that from this moment the use of land and marine turbines would steadily increase and improvements would continue to make turbines more and more efficient. Fred explained the way that his invention revolutionized industry:

The introduction of electricity into industry enabled engineers to do away with hundreds of miles of line shafting and belts and all the unnecessary friction that this developed from the main source of power. As early as the 1900s in America they were critical of the business of using a single steam engine to drive a whole lot of machines. Factories became filled with individually driven machines, like a lathe with an electric motor stuck on the end of it or an electric motor on the end of a shaft. The beauty of all this is the fact that you're not wasting any energy. Before the turbine, if you had a great line shaft that was being turned by a steam engine, it was on the go all the time. Of course the fires were burning, the steam was being generated and the wheels were all going round for nothing until you moved the belt shifter and got the lathe going. With a steam turbine, when you press the button the machine starts and when you depress the button the machine stops. It is as simple and as efficient as that.

Turbines were Charles Parsons's passion, but he still found time to develop other interests. In 1906, two trumpet-shaped objects were to be seen near the front of the Queen's Hall in London. They had been developed by Parsons to increase the volume and richness of tone of the instruments in the orchestras that played there. Parsons had taken out patents in various recorders, gramophones and sound systems and it was one of these, which he called the Auxetophone, that was on trial here. It was a device for the amplification of musical and vocal sounds without any of the tone distortion that came from reproduction by means of a mechanical diaphragm. The principle of the instrument was the production of the sound by controlling the flow of compressed air through a valve, in imitation of the action of the vocal cords in the human throat. The valve could be operated by a needle travelling over a gramophone record. Auxetophones were used successfully to re-inforce the sounds of the violins, cellos and double basses of Sir Henry Wood's orchestra in the symphony concerts at the Queen's Hall in 1906, and met with the enthusiastic approval of the great conductor. The musicians, however, objected to the reduction in the number of performers that resulted from this and the experiment had to be abandoned. The Auxetophone was as remarkable for its mechanical perfection as for the volume and purity of the sound it produced, but its usefulness came to an end with the invention of the amplification of sound by electrical means.

Charles Parsons took out over 300 different patents for his in-ventions. As a family man, some of his inventions were used to entertain his children. His wife, Katherine, was also a keen engineer who became an honorary Fellow of the North East Coast Institution of Engineers and Shipbuilders and a founder member of the Women's Engineering Society. Unlike many of the wives of the great Victorian engineers, Katherine was a modern woman who took a keen interest in her husband's affairs including the running of his works. She was said by the *Heaton Works Journal* to have 'played an effectual part in promoting friendly relations between capital and labour'. But there was tragedy in their lives when their son, Algernon, was killed in action during the First World War. Their daughter, Rachel, however, followed in her parents' footsteps by becoming an engineer. This was a very unusual profession for a woman in the Edwardian era. During the First World War she was a director of Heaton Works and later became one of the few women members of the Institution of Naval Architects. Parsons himself received many awards for his work. On 6 November 1902 he received from Sir Michael Foster, the secretary of the Royal Society, the Rumford Medal for his invention of the turbine and its extension into navigation. On 5 March 1910, when he was living at Holeyn Hall, Wylam on Tyne, he was appointed sheriff of the County of Northumberland. On 10 June 1911 he was appointed a Knight Commander of the Bath, made a Freeman of the City of Newcastle in 1914 and in 1927 he was given the supreme distinction of the Order of Merit, the first engineer ever to receive this honour.

One of the most remarkable features of his character was his extraordinary modesty. He had a shy and retiring nature and was never one to boast about his achievements. Even when at the height of his fame he never took any great credit for his achievements or acknowledged that his ability was anything out of the ordinary. This natural humility led him to expect other people to possess an insight equal to his own, and he was always ready to listen to any reasonable argument and to discuss it on terms of equality. His manner was always kindly, courteous and considerate, though he did have a temper which was inclined to flare up occasionally when he thought people were being careless or idle or when he was faced with stupidity of thought or action. He gave freely and generously of his knowledge to the proceedings of scientific and technical societies, and many of them conferred on him their highest distinctions in return. The leading European and American technical institutions also showed their appreciation of his merits by electing him to honorary membership, while nine universities awarded him honorary degrees. His love of ships and the sea continued to the end of his life and in retirement he and his wife went on voyages to Africa, South America, the West Indies and Canada.

Parsons also continued his family's association with optical matters. As early as 1899 searchlight reflectors were produced at Heaton and from 1921 Parsons began to purchase glass and optical instrument companies. His aim, he said, was to transform the British optical industry. In 1925 he purchased Sir Howard Grubb & Sons and renamed it Grubb, Parsons & Company. This allowed Parsons to produce large telescopes for the world's great observatories. A 74-inch reflector made for an observatory in Toronto was at the time of its construction the largest instrument of its kind made in Europe, just surpassing his father's 72-inch telescope at Birr Castle. But Parsons did not live to see the triumph. In January 1931 he and Lady Parsons travelled to the West Indies on board the *Duchess of Richmond* and then on to Venezuela, going by car to Caracas where he fell ill. It was thought that the climate did not agree with him. He returned to the ship and spent the following day in his bunk thinking that all he had was a chill, but there was a problem with his circulation. It was thought that it would improve with rest, but in Kingston Harbour on 11 February 1931, as the sun was setting, he passed away. He was 76 years old.

Charles Parsons was undoubtedly one of Britain's greatest engineers, whose most important legacies were the cheap and efficient generation of electricity and the revolution he brought to marine propulsion. His invention of the steam turbine transformed electricity generation, with the method he introduced still basically the way that it is done today, and he had the satisfaction of seeing it adopted for all major power stations throughout the world. Few inventors ever lived to see their projects come to fruition like this. His work in power generation alone transformed society with his earliest 7.5-kw generator leading to sets of 200,000-kw output within his own lifetime. He was able to see the way that the cheap electricity made possible by his turbine radically improved people's lives. Street lighting became universal in cities and major towns. This led to a cut in crime and it also meant people could work through the night. It brought along with it electric trains and electric tramcars and all manner of electrically driven apparatus – even early vacuum cleaners by the 1900s. Trams and trains enabled the population of big cities to move out into what we refer to now as suburbia. With little commuter trains into the city for work, they could also enjoy escaping to the countryside or the seaside at weekends. Parsons and his companies had effectively switched on the lights of the twentieth century.

Fred summarized the enormous impact his work had and the place he holds in the pantheon of great engineers and inventors:

Charles Parsons revolutionized marine propulsion with his invention of the world's first steam turbine vessel. It was this sort of confidence and bravado that typified the engineers of the Victorian Age and helped them to capture the public imagination. But his work was to have an even greater impact on the provision of power for transport, industry, home and office, which we still rely on today. Although steam engines of all types remained in use until the 1960s, from the late 1880s onwards the reciprocating steam engine began to give way to the steam turbine, with Charles Parsons following in the footsteps of Newcomen, Watt and Trevithick as one of the great figures in the history of steam power. The long-term social effect of the steam turbine was as great as that of Watt's steam engine and with it Parsons made sure that steam would continue to be used in an age of electricity.

As for himself, Fred would often say how much he would have liked to have been around in Victorian times:

If I had been I think I would have done all right then in my little workshop because it was a time when the skills of making things like my engines were highly valued. I think somehow or other that's something we've lost now. We were the workshop of the world when we used to make all that big heavy stuff, but we're not now. Us English now are not best prepared to get our hands dirty like we used to do in them days and other nations have taken that over. It's all very sad really.

Chronology

1819   Birth of Queen Victoria.

Cotton Mills and Factory Act limits working time for children between the ages of nine and sixteen to twelve hours per day.

Peterloo Massacre, Manchester. Parliamentary reform meeting attacked by troops.

The steamship *Savannah* becomes the first steamship to cross the Atlantic.

1821   Michael Faraday publishes work on electromagnetic rotation.

1823   Opening of Robert Stephenson & Co.'s Forth Street Locomotive Works, Newcastle.

Charles Babbage begins work on his calculating machine.

1825   Opening of the Stockton & Darlington Railway.

Work begins on the Thames Tunnel with Marc Brunel in charge.

1827   German physicist Georg Ohm introduces law concerning the flow of electric current.

1829   The Rainhill Trials.

First police force established by Robert Peel.

1830   Opening of the Liverpool & Manchester Railway.

The Baltimore & Ohio Railroad opens in the US.

Lord Dundas, William Fairbairn's first iron ship, built in Manchester.

James Nasmyth sets up the Bridgewater Foundry.

Brunel commissioned to build Clifton Suspension Bridge.

1832   The Great Reform Act is passed.

Joseph Whitworth works with Charles Babbage on his Difference Engine, the first calculating machine and forerunner of the modern computer.

1833 Brunel appointed chief engineer for the Great Western Railway.
Joseph Locke appointed resident engineer for the northern section of the Grand Junction Railway.
New laws passed to prevent the exploitation of children in textile factories.
US inventor Samuel Colt develops his revolver.
Abolition of slavery throughout the British Empire.

1834 New Poor Law establishes workhouses.

1835 William Fairbairn opens his shipyard at Millwall on the River Thames.
First steam railway on mainland Europe opens between Brussels and Malines.

1837 Queen Victoria comes to the throne.
Opening of Grand Junction Railway.
Daniel Gooch appointed locomotive superintendent of the Great Western Railway.

1838 Coronation of Queen Victoria.
Completion of the London to Birmingham Railway.
Opening of the Great Western Railway between Paddington and Maidenhead.
Launch of Brunel's *Great Western* steamship.
William Armstrong develops his first rotary hydraulic engine.

1839 Electric telegraph installed on a section of the Great Western.
James Nasmyth perfects the steam hammer.

1840 Daniel Gooch's first *Firefly* delivered to the Great Western.
Marriage of Queen Victoria to Prince Albert of Saxe-Coburg and Gotha.
Postal system introduced: one penny per letter to anywhere in Britain.

1841 Opening of Box Tunnel and completion of Great Western Railway from London to Bristol.
Development of 'long-boilered' locomotive by Robert Stephenson.
Joseph Whitworth produces his paper on a universal system for screw threads.
Thomas Cook runs the first excursion train.
Thomas Brassey takes an army of navvies to France to embark on the construction of the French railway system.

1842 Daniel Gooch drives first Royal Train.
Nasmyth demonstrates the first pile driving machine.
Mines Act passed prohibiting the underground employment of women and children.

1843 Opening of Swindon Works.
      Thames Tunnel opened and SS *Great Britain* launched.
1844 William Fairbairn develops the Lancashire boiler.
      Samuel Morse sends the first telegraph message between Washington and Baltimore.
1845 First Sikh War. Britain embarks on the conquest of Kashmir and Punjab.
1846 'Railway mania' year. Two hundred and seventy-two Acts of Parliament are passed for new lines.
      First successful hydraulic crane developed by William Armstrong.
1847 Foundation of W. G. Armstrong & Co. and opening of Elswick Works.
1848 Caledonian Railway opened from Carlisle to Glasgow and Edinburgh.
      Brunel's atmospheric railway scrapped.
      The Year of Revolutions in France, Germany, Austria-Hungary and Italy.
      California Gold Rush starts.
1849 High Level Bridge, Newcastle, opened by Queen Victoria.
1850 Opening of Britannia Bridge.
1851 Great Exhibition of Industry at Crystal Palace.
      Armstrong invents the accumulator.
1852 Fairbairn contracted to work on the establishment of the Small Arms Factory at Enfield.
      Frenchman Henri Giffard makes the first flight in a steam-driven balloon.
1853 India's first railway opens between Bombay and Thane.
1854 Start of the Crimean War. Charge of the Light Brigade.
      Work begins on the development of the Whitworth rifle.
1855 Development of the Armstrong gun.
1856 Treaty of Paris ends the Crimean War.
      Bessemer invents process for mass production of steel.
      First railway in Africa between Cairo and Alexandria.
1857 Indian Mutiny attempts to oust Britain from India.
      First passenger lift invented by Elisha Otis and installed in New York department store.
1858 Queen Victoria proclaimed ruler of India.
      Launch of SS *Great Eastern*.
      First transatlantic cable running from Ireland to the US via Newfoundland is laid.

1859   Thomas Aveling takes out a patent for a self-propelled road locomotive.

Publication of Charles Darwin's *On the Origin of Species*.

First oil well drilled in Pennsylvania.

Work begins on the construction of the Suez Canal.

Opening of Brunel's Royal Albert Bridge.

1860   Construction of the London Underground begins.

1861   Start of the American Civil War.

Abraham Lincoln elected president of the US.

1865   End of American Civil War. Slavery abolished.

President Lincoln assassinated.

The Red Flag Act imposes a speed limit of 2 mph in towns and 4 mph in the country on road locomotives.

1867   Canada becomes a British dominion.

1868   Launch of Armstrong's first gunboat, HMS *Staunch*.

1869   Opening of the Suez Canal.

Transcontinental Union Pacific Railway completed in the US.

Last convict ship to Australia.

1871   London connected with Shanghai by underwater electric cable.

US reporter Henry Morton Stanley tracks down British explorer David Livingstone in Central Africa.

1874   Factory Act limits working week to 56.5 hours.

1875   France adopts a republican constitution.

H. M. Stanley confirms the source of the Nile.

1876   Queen Victoria proclaimed Empress of India.

Internal combustion engine invented by Nikolaus Otto.

Alexander Graham Bell patents the telephone.

1877   Joseph Whitworth produces his 'impregnable armour plating'.

Thomas Alva Edison invents the first phonograph.

1878   Salvation Army founded by William Booth.

1879   The Tay Bridge Disaster.

1880   Joseph Whitworth's standard gauges and screw threads (BSW) officially adopted by the Board of Trade.

Boers declare war on the British and drive them out of Transvaal.

1881   First public supply of electricity to Godalming, Surrey.

First electric tramway opens in Berlin.

1882   Contract for the construction of the Forth Bridge awarded to Tancred Arrol.

First purpose-built power station; the Edison Electric Light Station opens at Holborn Viaduct.

1884 Armstrong opens shipyard at Elswick to build warships.

Charles Parsons patents his design for a steam turbine and devises a generator to go with it.

Sir Hiram Maxim invents the machine-gun.

1885 Development of first automobile by Gottlieb Daimler and Karl Benz.

Completion of Canadian transcontinental railway.

1886 Karl Benz patents the first automobile.

Completion of the Severn Tunnel.

1888 George Eastman develops the first Kodak camera.

1889 C. A. Parsons & Co. set up to make steam turbines and high-speed electrical machinery.

Completion of the Eiffel Tower.

1890 Opening of the Forth Bridge.

1893 The independent Labour Party holds its first meeting.

New Zealand becomes the first country in the world to give women the vote.

1894 Charles Parsons sets up the Marine Steam Turbine Company and builds *Turbinia*.

Opening of the Manchester Ship Canal.

Opening of Tower Bridge.

1895 Invention of wireless telegraphy (radio) by Guglielmo Marconi.

The Lumière brothers invent the cinematograph.

1896 First modern Olympic Games held in Athens.

1897 Queen Victoria's Diamond Jubilee.

Charles Parsons demonstrates *Turbinia* at the Spithead Review.

Merger of Armstrong, Mitchell & Co. with Joseph Whitworth & Co. to form the engineering giant Armstrong Whitworth.

1898 Royal Navy places an order with Charles Parsons for *Viper*, a turbine-driven, torpedo-boat destroyer.

Marie and Pierre Curie discover radium.

Kitchener leads the British to victory against the Sudanese and takes Khartoum.

1899 Start of the Boer War.

1901 Commonwealth of Australia proclaimed.

Queen Victoria dies and is succeeded by her son Edward VII.

Acknowledgements and Sources

I am enormously indebted to Fred for introducing me to the subject of Victorian engineering and for ensuring that so much of his enthusiasm for all things Victorian rubbed off on me, and also to the BBC for giving me the opportunity to make so many programmes with him. My thanks go to Doug Young at Transworld for allowing me to continue with the work that Fred was so keen on, and to my editor Rebecca Jones in particular for making sure that I made the explanations of the engineering as clear as possible, brought the characters to life, and made some reference to the general social and historical context.

Most of the content of the book has been based on research that was done for programmes that I made or would have liked to have made with Fred over the years. For that I would like to thank the researchers who worked with me, particularly Helen Barry, Kathryn Hall, Natalie Konopinski, Bob Sandy, Nick Watson and Clare White. In addition to my research notes for the programmes I have also consulted the following sources:

Bibliography
Briggs, Asa, *Victorian Things*, Batsford Ltd, 1988
Burton, Anthony, *On the Rails: Two Centuries of Railways*, Aurum Press, 2004
Chapple, Phil, *The Industrialisation of Britain: 1780–1914*, Hodder & Stoughton, 1999
Cole, Grenville S., *Arms and the Man: W. G. Armstrong, First Baron of Cragside*, Lady Armstrong, 1996
Devey, Joseph, *The Life of Joseph Locke*, Richard Bentley, 1862
Dougan, David, *The Great Gun-maker: The Life of Lord Armstrong*, Sandhill Press, 1992

Gooch, Daniel, *Diaries of Sir Daniel Gooch, Baronet*, Kegan, Paul, Trench and Trubner, 1892

Jeans, William T., *The Creators of the Age of Steel*, Chapman & Hall, 1884

Jones, Robin, *Isambard Kingdom Brunel*, Mortons Media Group, 2006

McKean, Charles, *Battle for the North*, Granta Books, 2006

McKenzie, Peter, *W. G. Armstrong: The Life and Times of Sir William George Armstrong*, Longhirst Press, 1983

MacKay, Sheila, *The Forth Bridge: A Picture History*, Moubray House Publishing, 1990

Nasmyth, James, *James Nasmyth, Engineer: An Autobiography*, John Murray, 1897

Newsome, David, *The Victorian World Picture*, John Murray, 1997

Parsons, Sir Charles, *The Steam Turbine: The Rede Lecture, 1911*, Cambridge University Press, 1911

Platt, Alan, *The Life and Times of Daniel Gooch*, Alan Sutton Publishing, 1987

Pole, William, *The Life of Sir William Fairbairn*, Longman Green, 1878

Preston, J. M., *Aveling & Porter Ltd.*, North Kent Books, 1987

Rolt, L. T. C., *Isambard Kingdom Brunel*, Longman Green, 1957

Rolt, L. T. C., *Victorian Engineering*, Penguin, 1970

Saint, Andrew, *Cragside*, The National Trust, 1992

Smiles, Samuel, *The Life of George Stephenson and his Son Robert Stephenson*, Harper and Brothers, 1868

Smith, Ken, *Stephenson Power: The Story of George and Robert Stephenson*, Tyne Bridge Publishing, 2003

Smith, Ken, *Turbinia: The Story of Charles Parsons and His Ocean Greyhound*, Newcastle Libraries & Information Service and Tyne & Wear Museums, 1996

Whitworth, Joseph, *Miscellaneous Papers on Mechanical Subjects*, Longman, Brown, Green, Longmans and Roberts, 1858

Woolmar, Christian, *Fire & Steam: How the Railways Transformed Britain*, Atlantic Books, 2007

Webography

http://heritage.imeche.org/Home

www.spartacus.schoolnet.co.uk

Isambard Kingdom Brunel:

http://www.bbc.co.uk/history/british/victorians/brunel_isambard_01.shtml

Daniel Gooch:

www.swindonweb.com/?m=8&s=9&ss=272&c=1108&t=Sir%20Daniel%20Gooch

Charles Parsons:

www-g.eng.cam.ac.uk/125/1875-1900/parsons.html

Joseph Whitworth:

www.whitworthsociety.org

Picture Acknowledgements

Endpapers (hardback edition only): SSPL/Getty Images

Page 30: Mary Evans Picture Library/Alamy; 44, 151, 232, 287, 306, 320, 340: Getty Images; 54 bottom, 66, 114, 198, 217, 256, 294, 346, 368: SSPL via Getty Images; 78: © The Royal Society; 100: © Vintage Power and Transport/Mark Sykes/Alamy; 105, 134: © Illustrated London News Ltd/Mary Evans; 138: Popperfoto/Getty Images; 144: Institution of Civil Engineers; 202: Mary Evans Picture Library; 229, 284: Greater Manchester County Record Office (with Manchester Archives); 248: 19th era 2/Alamy; 274: by courtesy of the Mitchell Library, Glasgow City Council.

First colour section
Images listed clockwise from top left. Page 1: Fred and the *Rocket*: courtesy The View From The North. Pages 2–3: scale drawing of the Killingworth locomotive, *c.* 1815, probably by George Stephenson: SSPL via Getty Images; George and Robert Stephenson by John Lucas, 1851: Institution of Civil Engineers; 'The pleasures of the rail-road', 1831, engraving by Henry Heath: © The Trustees of the British Museum [1994,0515.17]; 'Great Western Railway train emerging from a tunnel', frontispiece by John Cooke Bourne to his book *The History and Description of the Great Western Railway*, 1846: SSPL via Getty Images; engineering drawing by J. Farley of Robert Stephenson's long boiler locomotive, 1841: SSPL via Getty Images. Pages 4–5: Brunel's Thames Tunnel, 1827: SSPL via Getty Images. Pages 6–7: 'Opening of the First Public Railway', 1825, colour print after John Dobbin: SSPL via Getty Images; 'Tring cutting, 17 June 1837', from John Bourne's *Drawings of the London Railway*, 1839: © World History Archive/Alamy; 'Train Crossing Chat Moss Bog', from T. T. Bury's *Coloured Views on the Liverpool and Manchester Railway*, 1831: Getty Images; Edge Hill tunnel: courtesy The View From The North. Page 8: Cragside: courtesy The View From The North; staircase at Cragside: © NTPL/Andreas von Einsiedel; Armstrong's hydroelectric machine: Science Photo Library.

Second colour section
Images listed clockwise from top left. Page 1: trade union scroll of the Amalgamated Society of Engineers, Machinists, Millwrights, Smiths and Pattern-makers: ARPL/HIP/TopFoto/TopFoto.co.uk. Pages 2–3: view of the *Great Eastern*, 1851: Getty Images; ' Launch of the steamship the *Great Britain* in the presence of H.R.H. Prince Albert, July 1843', lithograph: © Bristol City Museum and Art Gallery/The Bridgeman Art Gallery; Fred and the *Great Britain*: courtesy The View From The North; 'The *Great Eastern* on the stocks', *c.* 1855: SSPL via Getty Images. Pages 4–5: Aveling & Porter steam roller, Hyde Park, 1866: Mary Evans Picture Library; painting by James Nasmyth of his steam hammer, 1832: Getty Images; Whitworth's stand at the Great Exhibition, 1851: SSPL via Getty Images; an Armstrong gun, Fort Fisher, North Carolina, *c.* 1863: Getty Images; Fred driving an Aveling steam engine: courtesy The View From The North. Pages 6–7: detail of *Conference of Engineers* by John Lucas, 1851–3, left to right seated: Robert Stephenson, Charles H. Wild (secretary), Joseph Locke, I. K. Brunel: Mary Evans Picture Library/Institute of Civil Engineers; view of the Forth Bridge: courtesy The View From The North; a demonstration of the cantilever process published in the *Graphic*, 1890: Getty Images; Fred and David Hall doing the same demonstration: courtesy The View From The North; Britannia Tubular Bridge during construction, lithograph by George Hawkins, 1849; SSPL via Getty Images. Page 8: *The Naval Review at Spithead* by Eduardo de Martino, 1898: The Royal Collection © 2011 Her Majesty Queen Elizabeth II; *Turbinia*: Science Photo Library; steam turbine blades, sketch by Charles Parsons, 1897: Institution of Mechanical Engineers/ Mary Evans Picture Library; radial flow engines originally fitted to the *Turbinia*: SSPL via Getty Images.

Index

Page numbers in *italics* denotes an illustration